PREFACE TO THE JOURNEY OF THE SONGHAI PEOPLE

THE WORLD-CLASS LITERACY AND SCIENCE OF THE SONGHAI PEOPLE, THE ANCESTORS OF AFRICAN AMERICANS.

It was the year 1584, during the rule of Emperor Askia Muhammad The Third, emperor of the Songhai Empire. The news had come from Songhai agents in Europe and in Algeria, that the Christian Europeans and the Muslim Arabs were planning an invasion of Songhai. The emperor's advisors told him that as strong as their forces were, they could not withstand the combined assault of the Europeans and Arabs., even though the Songhai Empire was larger than the continent of Europe.

The emperor was also advised that the Europeans had been waging war on nations of Africa to the east and south of Songhai and those prisoners-of-war were being sent in chains to the new world across the Atlantic Ocean to be worked to death in the fields and mines of those countries. They advised him that Charles I of Spain had been granting permission to international merchants since 1516, to ship the captives of those weaker African nations to Spanish colonies.

But there was something of even greater disturbance to the emperor. He learned that the European conquerors had been spreading the lie that their captives were illiterate. And the way that they were able to perpetuate that lie was to take the babies out of the arms of their parents as soon as the prisoner-of-war ships arrived in America. Those babies would grow up, separated from the knowledge of their ancestry and never know the truth of the world-class literacy of their parents. They would believe only the lies of their white conquerors.

What was Songhai to do?

After numerous conferences, the heads of the various provinces and the heads of the universities hit upon a plan. The plan was to bury their scientific manuscripts, their medical and legal treatises and other evidences of their world-class brilliance. The plan was built on the hope that one day their descendants would dig up the thousands of trunks and learn first-hand of the world-class literacy and scientific knowledge of their Songhai ancestors. They buried their priceless manuscripts in the sands of Timbuktu in the country of Mali.

The trunks lay buried for nearly four hundred years. Tens of thousands of manuscripts were hidden in musty storage rooms, and stashed in mountain caves to protect them from conquerors and colonizers, most recently the French, who left in 1960. Even though millions of manuscripts have been brought to light, archeologists feel that millions of books remain buried..

The campaign to rescue Mali's manuscripts began in 1964, four years after Mali won its independence. That year, UNESCO representatives met in Timbuktu to create a master plan to preserve the region's hidden writings. Mali opened the Centre Ahmed Baba, named after Muslim-kidnapped last president of Sankore University.

With funding from the United Nations and supported by South Africa, the center sent staff members into the countryside to locate lost manuscripts. One such collector, Abdel Kader Haidara, began searching for funding on his own. In 1997, he met Dr. Henry Louis Gates Jr. of Harvard University who was making a television series abut Africa.

Haidara showed his manuscripts to Gates, who broke down and cried like a baby.

"Why are you crying?" asked Haidara.

"Because", replied Gates, "I have been believing and teaching that the ancestors of African Americans had no literacy, and relied on griots for our history. I just found irrefutable proof that that has been a gross lie. Our ancestors had world-class literacy. I will help you get your money."

Dr. Gates procured for Haidara a grant from the Andrew Mellon Foundation which allowed him money to continue searching and in addition allowed him to construct a library which now has 9,000 volumes.

The Mellon grant led to other large grants for those with access to family collections. So the millions of manuscripts being preserved are increasing daily. Hundreds of thousands of manuscripts at Timbuktu are in the Songhai language, not Arabic, and in the hands of families who refuse to turn them over to the Europeans or "Europeanized" Black people.

Now we have definite proof that the European Christians and the Arab Muslims fabricated the whole myth of African American ancestral ignorance and illiteracy to justify their inhuman and cruel treatment of their Songhai captives. NOW WE KNOW that America's refusal to incorporate the true Songhai history of grandeur and beauty into the textbooks, magazines, television and motion pictures is the shame of being caught red-handed in that monstrous lie.

What is of inestimable importance is that a cursory reading of some of the manuscripts reveals the sophistication, scholarship and morality of the Songhai African ancestors of African Americans.

The manuscripts paint a portrait of Timbuktu as the Cambridge or Oxford of its day, where from the 1300's to the late 1500's students came from as far away as the Arabian Peninsula to learn at the feet of Songhai masters of law, literature and the sciences. Songhai astronomers charted the movement of the stars, Songhai physicians provided instruction on nutrition, the therapeutic properties of desert plants, the art of surgery including removal of eye cataracts, and the science of transplanting human limbs.

"The collectors tell us that our Songhai ancestors buried the books deep in the ground. But thanks to them, the desert has at last begun to surrender its secrets." Hiadara told Dr. Gates.

By Edward W. Robinson, Jr., J.D., LL.D.   July 2 , 2009

DOCUMENTATION
Smithsonian Magazine, December 2006
www.smithsonian.com

Intellectual Legacy of Africa
www.muslimmuseum.or/TimbuktuManuscripts.aspx

The Hidden Treasures of Timbuktu (Fall 2008 Books) **By John O. Hunwick and Alida Jay Boye**
www.thamesandhudsonusa.com/new/fall08/551421.htm

National Geographic—blog my wonderful world.org

The Treasures of Timbuktu
UMMAH FORUM
WWW.UMMAH.COM/FORUM/SHOWTHREAD.PP?T=72768

Timbuktu—Wikipedia
www.en.wikipedia.org/wiki/Timbuktu

www.---youtube.com

THE JOURNEY OF THE SONGHAI PEOPLE

LIFT EVERY VOICE AND SING

LIFT EVERY VOICE AND SING TILL EARTH AND HEAVEN RING
RING WITH THE HARMONIES OF LIBERTY
LET OUR REJOICING RISE HIGH AS THE LISTENING SKIES
LET IT RESOUND LOUD AS THE ROLLING SEA;
SING A SONG FULL OF THE FAITH THAT THE DARK PAST HAS
   TAUGHT US,
SING A SONG FULL OF THE HOPE THAT THE PRESENT HAS
   BROUGHT US,
FACING THE RISING SUN OF OUR NEW DAY BEGUN
LET US MARCH ON TILL VICTORY IS WON.

STONY THE ROAD WE TROD, BITTER THE CHASTENING ROD
FELT IN THE DAYS WHEN HOPE UNBORN HAD DIED
YET WITH A STEADY BEAT, HAVE NOT OUR WEARY FEET
COME TO THE PLACE FOR WHICH OUR FATHERS SIGHED?
WE HAVE COME OVER A WAY THAT WITH TEARS HAS BEEN
   WATERED
WE HAVE COME, TREADING OUR PATH THROUGH THE BLOOD
   OF THE SLAUGHTERED,
OUT FROM THE GLOOMY PAST TILL NOW WE STAND AT LAST
WHERE THE WHITE GLEAM OF OUR BRIGHT STAR IS CAST.

GOD OF OUR WEARY YEARS GOD OF OUR SILENT TEARS
THOU WHO HAS BROUGHT US THUS FAR ON THE WAY
THOU WHO HAS BY THY MIGHT LED US INTO THE LIGHT
KEEP US FOREVER IN THE PATH WE PRAY.
LEST OUR FEET STRAY FROM THE PLACES OUR GOD, WHERE
   WE MET THEE
LEST OUR HEARTS DRUNK WITH THE WINE OF THE WORLD
   WE FORGET THEE
SHADOWED BENEATH THY HAND, MAY WE FOREVER STAND
TRUE TO OUR GOD, TRUE TO OUR NATIVE LAND.

by James Weldon Johnson

THE JOURNEY OF THE SONGHAI PEOPLE

Second Edition
Fifth Printing
Copyright © 1987 by Clavin R. Robinson, Redman Battle and
Edward W. Robinson, Jr.
through The Pan African Federation Organization
All Rights Reserved Worldwide.
No material in this book can be copied except for reference footnotes up to six hundred worlds.
Written permission must be obtained for more than 2,000 sequential words.

Printed in United States of America

ISBN 1-880205-29-7

Library of Congress Catalog Card No. 92-056144

Special thanks to
Deborah Fox, Terry Heard and Paul Elias, Artists/Illustrators
Krystal G. Jackson, Typist
Education Heritage — African inc., PO Box 18828, Phila., PA 19119
C. Robinson —113 E. Mayland St., Phila., PA 19144
R. Battle — 1835 W. Diamond St., Phila., PA 19121

RESTORING THE TAPESTRY OF WORLD CULTURE

The story of man's sojourn on earth has been long, painful, and glorious. World culture can be likened to a great tapestry woven with black, white, yellow, and brown threads. For four hundred years, the contributions of Africans and African-Americans who, for millenniums wove their black threads into the tapestry, have been torn from cultural memory—the black threads of the tapestry ripped out to justify the genocide against a whole people and the rape of a whole continent.

It is the hope of the many persons who contributed to the writing of this source book that we shall one day have a corrected history that includes the contributions to world culture of all ethnic groups.

Until the day this happens, we offer this work in the hope that the information contained therein will be woven into the context of currently-taught history.

Dr. Edward W. Robinson, Jr.

THIS DIGEST WE HAVE WRITTEN WAS A SUPREME TEST TO PRESENT THE TRUTH AS WE HAVE RESEARCHED AND STUDIED. SOMETIMES TRUTH MAY BE CONTROVERSIAL. TO THIS WE QUOTE ISAIAH 1:18 "COME LET US REASON TOGETHER SAITH THE LORD, THOUGH YOUR SINS BE AS SCARLET..."

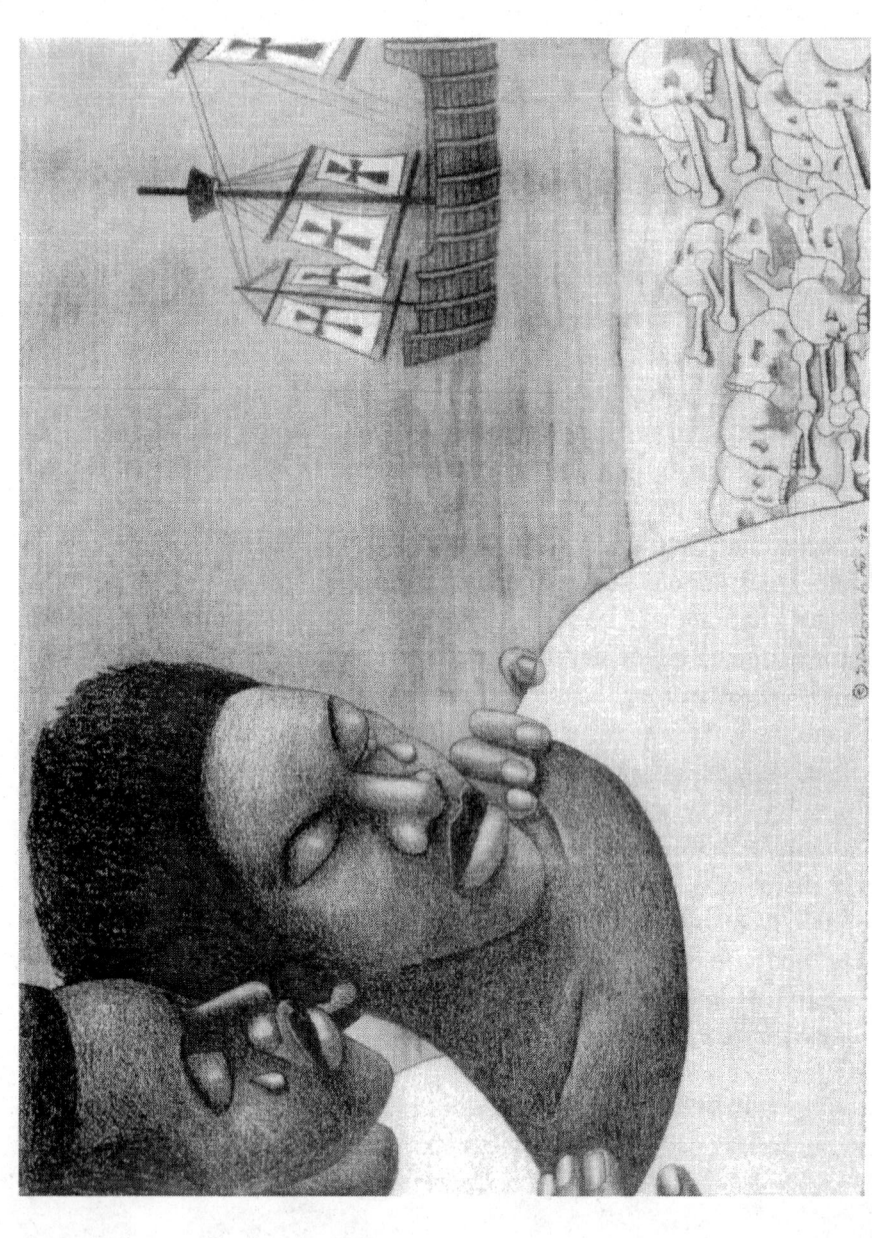

We have come, over a way that with tears has been watered. We have come, treading our path through the blood of the slaughtered.

DEDICATION

This book is dedicated to the Battle, Robinson, Russell, Thomas and the Richardson families, their African forebearers and their descendants.

It was because of the love and the strength in our genes that was passed down, making possible our survival along with God's help of course.

Furthermore, we want to project this writing as a reminder of the unvarnished truth about how, when, where, what and why this terrible scourge happened to Africans at home and here in the Americas.

We want our posterity to know all of the whys and wherefores about the greatness of the African people, and also the course we must take to regain our former dignity, glory and world respect.

If we do this, then our children will walk tall, they will eventually shed the present mind negatives they now have. They will not want to fall into the devil's dope dungeons, his alcohol taverns and other western world vices.

Their parents will begin to fulfill their true sense of obligation. On that point, we shall not err again. The fundamental error we made in the past was to judge mistakenly. We judged other races as having the same humanity and compassion with which we are naturally endowed.

Last but not least, this book is dedicated to all the women of African descent. Wherever they are.

They stuck by us when there was no might in our hand to protect her or ourselves. Many, many times she saved the lives of her son, husband, brothers and father with her body, during that terrible period of our captivity.

Black men owe a debt of not only gratitude but love and loyalty, because she was on our side when we were losing. We haven't quite stopped losing yet.

Therefore, PAFO sees the Black Woman as the most beautiful and the most understanding. We think this poem says it best of all.

THE BLACK WOMAN

Black queen of beauty, thou has given colour to the world!
Among other women thou art royal and the fairest!
Like the brightest of jewels in the regal diadem,
Shinest thou, Goddess of Africa. Nature's purest emblem!

Black men worship at thy virginal shrine of truest love.
Because in thine eyes are virtue's steady and holy mark.
As we see in no other, clothes in silk of fine linen.
From ancient Venus, the Goddess, to mythical Helen.
When Africa stood at the head of the elder nations.
The Gods used to travel from foreign lands to look at thee:
On couch of costly Eastern materials, all perfumed,
Reclined thee as in thy path flow'rs were strewn
   —sweetest that bloomed.

Thy transcendent marvelous beauty made the whole world mad.
Bringing Solomon to tears as he viewed thy comeliness;
Antony and the elder Caesars wept at thy royal feet,
Preferring death than to leave thy presence, their foes to meet.
You, in all ages, have attracted the adoring world.
And caused many banners to be unfurled;
You have sat upon exalted and lofty eminence,
To see a world fight in your ancient African defense.
Today you have been dethroned,
   through the weakness of your men,
While, in frenzy, those who craved your smiles
   and your hand,
Those who were all monsters and could not with love
   approach you—
Have insulted your pride and now attach your good virtue.

Because of disunion you became mother of the world,
Giving tinge of robust colour to five continents,
Making a great world of millions of colour races,
Whose claim to beauty is reflected through our black faces.

From the handsome Indian to the European brunette.
There is a claim for that credit of their sunny beauty
That no one can e'er take from thee, O Queen of all women.
Who have borne trials and troubles of racial burden.

Once more we shall, in Africa, fight and conquer for you.
Restoring the pearly crown that proud Queen Sheba did wear;
Yes, it may mean blood, it may mean death;
    but still we shall fight,
Bearing our banners to Victory, men of Africa's might.
Superior Angels look like you in Heaven above.
For thou art fairest, queen of the reasons, queen of our love.
No condition shall make us ever in life desert thee,
Sweet Goddess of the ever green land and placid blue sea.

Written by Marcus Garvey

VITA OF CALVIN RUSSELL ROBINSON

Calvin R. Robinson attended Philadelphia's public schools. Several years later he went back to school to obtain a degree in business administration from the Wharton School of finance, but unforeseen circumstances curtailed his studies. Later, he enrolled in classes of Hebrew and Hebrew Science; which flowed right in line with his theology courses at The Twentieth Century School of Bible Research, which he had taken previously.

He was one of the original founders of the Pan African Federation Organization and became chief coordinator of its activities and head of the History Department. He along with Redman Battle and Dr. Edward W. Robinson, Jr., formulated the PAFO structured history course.

He was the co-author of a book, "Marks Of a Lost Race." He also co-authored the book "Cultural Genesis."

Mr. Robinson was employed with the Black-owned Provident Home Life Insurance Company for thirty-six years as an Agent and Staff Manager. His expertise, as a salesman and his relationship with people, lead him to receive honors and awards many times during his tenure as Top Agent of the Year and Staff Manager of the Year. He is presently employed at Crisis Intervention Network.

He has been a member of the African Methodist Episcopal Church since birth. He has been a member of the Senior Choir, the Usher Board, and active in many other organizations. He presently sings with the Concert Cathedral Chorale.

He is a dedicated and strong family man. He and his wife Marian, are blessed with six daughters; Valerie, Rita, Ethel, Patricia, Selena and Diane. He has one granddaughter, Tishema, and four grandsons, Christopher, Earl, Malik and Julius.

Mr. Robinson is the current President of the Pan African Federation Organization, and remains dedicated to freeing the minds of Americans from ethnic contempt.

VITA OF REDMAN BATTLE

Redman Battle was born in Sharpburg, North Carolina. He was educated in the Detroit, Michigan and Philadelphia, Pennsylvania school systems.

He attended the Twentieth Century School of Bible Research and Theology and he graduated with high honors.

He took courses in World History, African History and African American History.

In 1971, he was co-founder of the Pan African Federation Organization and helped to develop Black history classes. He became director of its research and review department. He developed the concept of the Profiles of African and African American History, which is a two-act play. He is the current first vice-president of PAFO. He is the co-author of a book "Cultural Genesis."

Mr. Battle is also a world traveler. He has been to Egypt and other African countries. He studied the Egyptian Mysterie System and other sciences. His resolve is to be a humanist and a true Pan-Africanist.

VITA OF DR. EDWARD W. ROBINSON, JR.

Dr. Edward W. Robinson, Jr. attended Philadelphia's public schools. He received his Baccalaureate in Business Administration from Virginia State University, his graduate credits from the University of Pennsylvania and a Juris Doctorate degree from Temple University School of Law.

Dr. Robinson headed the Philadelphia School District Committee on African and African American studies for four years, co-authored the guidebook, "The World of Africans and Afro-Americans," copyrighted by the Philadelphia School District. He headed a faculty that taught corrective history to hundreds of teachers in ten-week courses. Dr. Robinson co-produced three educational historical films and established the Department of Afro-American Studies in the School District of Philadelphia.

He produced the best-selling historical album, "Black Rhapsody" and is author of an unpublished novel on African history, "Songhai." He is producing a series of films, the first of which is *The Songhai Princess*. He has lectured extensively for the past several decades.

Dr. Robinson was affiliated with the Provident Home Life Insurance Company, ending thirty-five years as president. He holds the position of vice president of North Carolina Mutual Life Insurance Company, the largest Black-owned business in the world. He is presently in retirement.

He has been a member of the African Methodist Episcopal Union Church since birth. He currently sings with the Concert Cathedral Chorale, and serves as an officer on the Trustee Board.

He served as Executive Deputy Secretary for the Commonwealth of Pennsylvania and as Deputy Secretary for the Pennsylvania Utilities Commission. He was formerly assistant managing director for the City of Philadelphia and an executive with the Philadelphia Housing Authority.

He is involved in numerous civic and social organizations.

Dr. Robinson and his wife, the former Harriette Cox, are co-authors of several books, the parents of two children, Pamela and Michelle, the proud grandparents of eight and they have two adorable great-grandchildren.

VITA OF HARRIETTE COX ROBINSON

Mrs. Robinson received her baccalaureate degree in Elementary Education from Cheyney University and her graduate credits from Temple University.

She has been a member of Janes Memorial United Methodist Church for more than thirty years, serving as President of the Senior Choir and as member of various commissions and organizations.

Mrs. Robinson sings with the Concert Cathedral Chorale of A.M.E. Union Church of Philadelphia.

For thirty-five years she taught in the Philadelphia Public Schools and was awarded a Certificate of Merit for Outstanding Performance and was nominated as "Teacher of the Year." Among her many other awards and commendations, she received an award from the Chapel of the Four Chaplains.

Mrs. Robinson is actively involved with the National Association of University Women, the National sorority of Phi Delta Kappa (Director of Public Relations), member of Opera Ebony, the Afro-American Museum of Philadelphia, the Pennsylvania Coalition of Black Women and the Association of Black Storytellers.

She has co-authored a booklet "Twas the Night Before Kwanzaa" and co-produced the musical "Black Rhapsody."

VITA OF ELAINE ANNA ROBINSON RICHARDSON

Elaine A.R. Richardson was born in Philadelphia, Pennsylvania and educated in the Philadelphia public schools. After graduating from the Philadelphia High School for Girls, she pursued further courses, and worked as a proof reader and typesetter for a well-known printing firm.

She married David P. Richardson, and was blessed with two lovely children, one of whom Elaine Jr., met her demise at an early and tender age. Their other child became a well known State Representative, David P. Richardson, Jr.

After raising her family, she went back to school to complete her education. She graduated cum laude from Temple University, with a B.S. in Education. She also did her graduate studies at Temple. For thirty-four years, she worked closely with the school system as a volunteer, president of Home & School Associations, teacher's aide, and is presently a teacher in the public schools of Philadelphia.

Mrs. Richardson has been a member of the African Methodist Episcopal Union Church of Philadelphia since birth. She has been a member of the Senior Choir, Usher Board, and other organizations. She currently sings with the concert Cathedral Chorale of the church, a member of the lay Organization, and President of the Stewardess Board No. 2.

She has been a surrogate mother to many young people in need throughout the years. She was blessed to have four lovely grandchildren and a lovely great-grandchild.

Her concern for her people came from a long background of deep family ties with her parents. Her parents, Edward and Ethel Robinson, and grandparents, Alfred and Mary Anna Thomas Russell, taught her to love her race, her family, and herself; and to be a credit to each, by trying to help others. To this end she studied World History, African and African American History. She became a consultant for the Pan African Federation Organization as well as one of its qualified teachers.

TABLE OF CONTENTS

BRIEF OUTLINE OF THE HIGHLIGHTS xxvi

INTRODUCTION xxix

PRELUDE OF A JOURNEY xxxii
The Major Impacts of the Problem on African Americans xxxii
Manifestations and Definition of a Problem xxxii
Cause, Manifestations and Definitions of a Problem xxxiv

SESSION I
A LITTLE ABOUT THE PHILOSOPHY
AND HISTORY OF PAFO 1
Sociological Equation...8
Orientation 9

SESSION II
OUR RAISON D'ÊTRE...13
Our Purposes and Goals...19
Looking Forward 23
The Value of History 24
An Enriched African History 26
Cultural Glue 27
History and Its Value Continues 29
Definition of Civilization From a Historical Perspective 31

SESSION III
WHITE RACISM—ANTHROPOLOGICAL DEVELOPMENT
AND ITS EFFECT ON PEOPLE OF COLOR 37
The Chellean Axe Science 38
The Effects of the Glaciers 39

Mutation and Natural Selection in Europe 40
Mutation and Natural Selection in Africa 41
Hair 41
Protection Against Head Lice 43
A Reason for Evolved Hair 43
Background of the Brainwash Against African Peoples 44
Social Darwinism and Why The Inhumaneness of Whites 46
The Single Bone Theory 48
The Cress Theory 49
The Genetic Theory of The Dawn Man Syndrome 50
The Pre-frontal Cortex Theory 50
Recapitulation Science 53
Hair and Skin Colors 55
Why the Brain Is So Well Protected 56
Hair Glossiness 57
Skin Color 58
Melanin 59
ADVANTAGES OF MELANIN 61
Protection against Aging 61
Protection Against Harmful Radiation 62
Protection Against Air-Borne Abrasives 63
Protection Against Harmful Effects of Cold Air 63
Protection Against Long Immersion in Water 63
Speedier Muscular Response 64
Melanin Produces Better Sight 64
Melanin Provided Information to the Brain 65
Features and Other Structural Characteristics 65
The Nose 65
The Gluteus Maximus Buttock Muscles and the Lips 66
Lips 66
Is Evolution Still Going On? 67
The Blood 68
Rh Factor 68

SESSION IV
AFRICAN CONTRIBUTIONS AND THE
EXISTING SOCIETIES—B.C. 71
The Great Contributions of African Women In Developing
Civilization 73
The Cartesian Theory 81
Origin of African Democracy 82

SESSION V
THE DEVELOPMENT OF THE WESTERN SUDAN 89
Pre-Ghana 89
Ghana (300 A.D. - 1100 A.D.) 89
Mali's Rise 91

SESSION VI
SAGA OF THE MANSAS AND THE FAMOUS HAJJ 93
Sakura 93
The Blacks of Darien 94
Mansa Musa's Famous Hajj 95

SESSION VII
SONGHAI'S BEGINNING 99
Sulayman Nar and Ali Kolon 99

SESSION VIII
SONGHAI'S EXPANSION 103
Part I 103
Sunni Ali Ber Marched Into Timbuktu Without Opposition 103

SESSION IX
THE BEAUTIFUL CITY OF JENNÉ 107
Jenné Was Founded in the Thirteenth Century 111
Nursing and Care of the Sick 111
Personification of Black Respect of Acquisition of Jenné And
Songhai's Expansion 113
Acquisition of Jenné 115

SESSION X
THE SHORT REIGN OF SUNNI ALI BER'S SON 117
The Reason the Arabic Language Was Accepted......................117
The News of Sudanese Gold...121
The Original Moors 121
African Origin of So-Called Arabic Numbers........................122
The Conspiracy..125
Why Didn't Africans Invent the Gun?..............................126
Ahmad Babo 126

SESSION XI
THE INCURSIONS OF AFRICA AND ITS EFFECTS ON
AFRICA'S "RACE FIRST" TRADITION 129
How the Matrilineal System was Used Against Us
After the Hordes of Asians Invaded Africa 132
Summary of the Two-Cradle Theory..................................132

SESSION XII
WESTERN AND CENTRAL SUDAN
SOUTHWEST AFRICA-(ANGOLA) & QUEEN NZINGA........135
THE FALL OF THE SONGHAI EMPIRE.............................135
QUEEN NZINGA OF ANGOLA 136
SLAVE CHILDREN OF THE ARABS 141
THE MIDDLE PASSAGE 143

SESSION XIII
BRIEFS ON THE MIDDLE PASSAGE AND
THE TRIANGULAR TRADE 145
THE POWER BEHIND THE WORLD SLAVE TRADE
WERE THE ROYAL FAMILIES 145
THE MIDDLE PASSAGE WAS THE CROSSROADS
AND MARKETPLACES OF DISEASES 146

SESSION XIV
BREAKING IN THE CAPTIVES FOR
PLANTATION WORK IN THE NEW WORLD 149
THE REPORT OF SIR HANDS SLOAN.............................149
WHEN THE OVERSEER WAS IN CHARGE 150

SESSION XV
OUR FATHERS AND MOTHERS IN REVOLT AGAINST
THEIR CAPTORS (ALSO THE MAROONS) 153

SESSION XVI
THE LIFE STYLE OF BLACKS, AND UNMITIGATED
PRESSURES TO DESTROY BLACK FAMILY DURING
BONDAGE 169
THE "WHITE IS RIGHT" CONCEPT 171
CAPTIVITY ON MAINLAND UNITED STATES (1638-1862) 174

SESSION XVII
THE CIVIL WAR 177
AMENDMENT TO THE CONSTITUTION WHICH WILL
FOREVER DENY CONGRESS THE RIGHT TO
ABOLISH SLAVERY IN THE STATES 178
HOW BLACK SOLDIERS WON THE CIVIL WAR 180
THE BATTLE OF NEW MARKET HEIGHTS, VIRGINIA 187
BLACK SOLDIERS CAPTURE NEW MARKET HEIGHTS 189

SESSION XVIII
THE PERIOD OF THE BLACK RECONSTRUCTION 199
BLACKS MAINLY REWROTE THE CONSTITUTIONS
OF THE SOUTHERN STATES 200
NIGHT QUICKLY RETURNETH 204

SESSION XIX
THE CONTROLLING MACHINES 207
THE VARIOUS METHODS OF SUPPRESSION AND
OPPRESSION WERE INSTITUTED 207
HOW THE ENGLISH LANGUAGE WAS USED TO HURT
BLACK PEOPLE 209
A SAD COMMENTARY 214

SESSION XX
THE POST-RECONSTRUCTION FREEDOM-
FIGHTING ORGANIZATIONS AND INDIVIDUALS 219

SESSION XXI
FROM MARCUS GARVEY TO MALCOLM X AND
DR. MARTIN LUTHER KING TO JESSE JACKSON 229
Part II 234
THE COMPARISON YEARS, THE 1800'S v. 1900'S 237
THE PROPHETIC CRYSTAL BALL 239

SESSION XXII
THE ECONOMIC EFFECTS OF RACISM RE:
PEOPLE OF COLOR 243
RACISM—IS IT PROFITABLE TODAY? 244
CONTINUING MANIFESTATIONS OF
RACISM AND BLACKS COUNTERING IT 248

SESSION XXIII
THE SPIRIT OF NATIONALISM 251
EVALUATION ANALYSIS AND SURVIVAL OVERVIEW ... 251
METHODS TO ACHIEVE SOLIDARITY 253
SETTING PERSONAL EXAMPLES 254
TRULY UNDERSTANDING BRAINWASH 255
OUR TOTAL FOCUS 260

SESSION XXIV
LET THE HEALING BEGIN 265

EPILOGUE 269
THE IMPORTANCE OF KINSHIP TIES 271

SELECTED BIBLIOGRAPHY 272

SOMETHING TO PONDER 281
Material From A Workshop 281
Questions Asked By
Dr. Frances Cress Welsing: 282
Frightening Statistics 284

THE AFRICAN CONTINENT 285
Size, Shape, and Geological Composition of the Continent 285
Climates and Vegetation 287

Resources 287
Diseases 288

BRIEF HISTORY
Of the Universal Negro Improvement Association
and African Communities League 289
What is U.N.I.A. 291

A MESSAGE FROM THE PRESIDENT OF PAFO 293
Current Active Members 293

PAN AFRICAN FEDERATION ORGANIZATION
RECOMMENDS THE FOLLOWING BOOKS 296

ADDENDUM
Chronology of the Push for Rights of African Americans 298

THE WILLIAM LEO HANSBERRY NOTEBOOK 320

THE ICING
Black Peoples' Contributions to Ungrateful America
The Spirit of 1776 342
Implications of the War 344
The War of 1812 and how the
Black Man Figured in its Execution 344
Reasons for the 1812 War 346
Our Indian Brother 347
Native Americans and Blacks: A Proud Legacy 349
First Black Renaissance in America 350
Black Renaissance—Phase II 353
The Buffalo Soldiers 356

DO YOU KNOW THESE BLACK MEN
AND THEIR INVENTIONS? 359
List of a Few Significant Inventions 369

BRIEF OUTLINE OF THE HIGHLIGHTS; BY SESSION

Session I: Page 1
A little about the philosophy and history of PAFO

Session II: Page 13
Our Reason for Existence that is essentially the value of history. "Blacks are really apes who can speak"—mental violence. Anthropological (our looks) and cultural (what happened) history. African history is the cake and African American history is the icing.

Session III: Page 37
Proconsul; Chellean Axe Science; Glaciers; Why the Caucasian did not develop evolutionarily much past Australopithecus; Benefit of African characteristics; Four theories of why Europeans killed 96 million out of 126 millions. The Recapitulation Science; Not racism but TRUTH.

Session IV: Page 71
Early civilizations; Early African democracy; Elimination of African civilization by Europeans; Enumerated African contributions to culture of the world.

Session V: Page 89
The history of Ghana and Mali.

Session VI: Page 93
Sakura and his trip to Central America before Columbus

Session VII: Page 99
The beginning of Songhai; Ali Kolon—escape from Mali.

Session VIII: Page 107
The story of Sunni Ali Ber

Session IX: Page 107
The acquisition of Jenné; The death of Sunni Ali Ber.
Session X: Page 117

Spread of Islam; Takeover of Askia; Moors and their history; Why we didn't invent the gun (page 1); Quote of es Sadi, "I saw the ruin of learning and its utter collapse...." He was an eyewitness to the invasion of Songhai.

Session XI: Page 129
Invasion of Africa; Impact on various mixed races.

Session XII: Page 135
Invasion of Songhai; Queen Nzinga (1620-1683); Arabs are "white"; Profits of the captivity-of-Africans' trade; Our suicides.

Session XIII: Page 145
The horror of the Middle Passage; the horror of the instruments of torture.

Session XIV: Page 149
Breaking-in the captives; "Only the strong survived...and we are their children."

Session XV: Page 153
Revolts; The Maroons-Cudgo of Jamaica; Gabriel Prosser's revolt of 1800; Denmark Vesey—1821; Harriet Tubman.

Session XVI: Page 169
P.O.W. living conditions—it's a wonder that we survived; Ma'at; Political power of the South; The beginning of the Civil War.

Session XVII: Page 177
The Civil War; Amendment prohibiting abolition of "Slavery" endorsed by Lincoln; 36,847 casualties and 31,000 maimed. Statue of Liberty, first model of an African woman (page 193).

Session XVIII: Page 199
Black Congressmen; Lieutenant Governors of Mississippi, Louisiana, South Carolina; First Senator—Bruce; Reconstruction—ten years; Rise of the Ku Klux Klan.

Session XIX: Page 207

Mechanisms of control; Psychological warfare against African Americans; the English language trauma; Story of Sarraounia; Stories of resistance to white oppression.

Session XX: Page 219
Booker T. Washington; Ida B. Wells Barnett—a founder of NAACP; 1913 statistics owned 550,000 homes; operated 937,000 farms; 40,000 businesses; 700 million dollars accumulated. We have made no progress. "Progress" an inaccurate and self-defeating term applied to us. The accurate explanation is "Our three-century struggles against white tyranny has produced a reprieve in a few areas." The goal is "Presumption of adequacy."

Session XXI: Page 229
Lynchings during World War I; Envy towards returning soldiers who had "killed white men (Germans);" Lynchings protested during Harlem Renaissance; Claude McKay; The duty to tear up the pictures of the white Christ and Madonna; Marcus Garvey; THE PROPHECY OF 1989 THROUGH THE 1990'S BY ANALYZING THE LAST HALF OF THE 1800'S; This prophecy is valid IF we continue to leave out the de-programming of America.

Session XXII: Page 243
THE PROBLEM; Economic effects of white racist society; Vietnam statistics (page 1); Struggles against manifestations only, are fruitless; Profits for whites of racism.

Session XXIII: Page 251
Background of THE PROBLEM; Statement of THE PROBLEM; THE SOLUTION (page 1) REPROGRAMMING THE TOTAL SOCIETY." Manifestations or symptoms incorrectly labeled "Problems."

Session XXIV: Page 265
Let the healing begin; The effects of the "Healing Balm."

Epilogue: Page 269
Our 250 year holocaust and fifty million murdered compared to Jewish holocaust.

INTRODUCTION TO THE JOURNEY OF THE SONGHAI PEOPLE

BY MARK HYMAN - AUTHOR, HISTORIAN

The Pan African Federation Organization (PAFO) is a dynamic group of dedicated people who built PAFO from a germ of a Pan-African idea to the present. The founding families of PAFO comprise the superstructure of a monumental heritage and tradition of selfless contributions.

This book, The Journey of the Songhai People, is a masterpiece of Afrocentrism. It emphatically points to the African American psyche; the Black man's acquisition of his stolen manhood and his ownership of it. The book directs events when Africans in Africa and in the diaspora look to their splendid heritage. Heroes in the book profile the past and portend the future.

PAFO, in presenting this book in its own name has offered to readers vital facts for survival—mainly the history needs to nurture the necessary mental well-being, in science, in mind control, in sterling pride, in identifying the problem and its solution. It expounds on the survivalist techniques for every day life.

In this book, PAFO points to great African kings like Mansa Musa; in the cultural freedom denied to Marcus Garvey in the twentieth century; to Garvey who was denied the right to build for his people. No period in African American history goes untouched, whether the period of the Black pharaohs (Piankhy, Tirharka, So. Ahmes, Tutankhamen and others), or down to Black Reconstruction Congressmen in Southern America after the Civil War (Rainey, Lanier, Hyman, White, Lynch and others). Document after document will enrich as well as guide.

The book cries out to the myriad manifestations of the basic problem. It identifies the basic problem of programmed contempt against African Americans' physical and cultural African genesis.

The Journey of the Songhai People is an extremely useful book that is tremendously enlightening to the reader. At the same time, it reaches out to have him/her aid in the solution of deprogramming the entire American psyche.

It is an eternal book, full of ageless and priceless information. It is a strong, powerful document composed by the energies of many people and many professionals led by PAFO's President, Calvin R. Robinson. This book should find a home in libraries across the world and in the most modest of homes. Few books fall into all of these categories.

Mark Hyman, Ph. D.
Author, Historian
Philadelphia, PA
October 28, 1987

THE BLACK FAMILY PLEDGE

A Restatement of Dr. Maya Angelou

Because the memory of our illustrious African ancestors was forcibly wrenched from our minds, our children no longer give us honor.

Because we have strayed from the path our ancestors cleared for us, our children cannot find their way.

Because the mental violence has been so harsh and cruel, we have forgotten the God of our ancestors and misled by the teaching of our oppressors.

Because the media has caused us to sink deeply into the swamp of self-hate, our children engage in daily bloodbaths.

Therefore, we pledge to bind ourselves to the task of reprogramming ourselves and those who loathe us, about the beauty, grandeur and sophistication of our African past.

In honor of our ancestors who led the world in science and humaneness,

We make this pledge.

Redman Battle, Edward and Calvin Robinson

PRELUDE OF A JOURNEY

THE MAJOR IMPACTS OF THE PROBLEM ON AFRICAN AMERICANS

MANIFESTATIONS AND DEFINITION OF A PROBLEM

A problem is when a condition has evolved to such proportions that it inhibits one or more persons, including a nation, to successfully neutralize or solve the condition. The condition or problem may be inadvertently instigated by oneself or by an outside force, mankind or by nature.

Manifestations of a problem can be likened to one having a fever. The fever is not the problem; it was caused by something else. What the fever simply does is try to condition the body's defenses to fight the body's problem. In the case of African people, the manifestations are like the fever. We become sick, nauseous. We fail to identify the problem because we are so busy with the symptom.

I. Statement of The Problem:

The Problem is that the entire American society, inclusive of African Americans has long been and is being continuously programmed by the media of communication to believe that the African genesis (beginnings) of African Americans is savage, bestial, bereft of intelligence, sub-human and primitive.

II. Some inner impacts of The Problem:

A. An aspect of an inner (within the African American community) impact is the INTRA impact, i.e. on the individual himself:

    1. One of the major results of the INTRA impact is the diversion of the creative energy of the pre-frontal cortex from its abstract reasoning ability to the non-productive creation of defense mechanisms that are subconsciously used to protect the ego in an environment hostile to its development. Low achievement in mathematics is an example.

    2. Another result of the INTRA impact is abnormal fear of rejection or failure. This is especially measurable in the area of product selling.

B. Another aspect of an inner impact is the INTER impact.

1. One of the major results of the INTER impact is commonly referred to as "Black-on-Black crime." The national fratricide rate is by far the highest of any group in the world.

2. Another result of the INTER impact (i.e. the impact manifesting itself between and among African-Americans with each other) is non-support of Black businesses by Blacks. The shameful lack of support sports the dubious honor of being the most successful boycott in the world.

3. To the above we can add the high divorce rate, political factionalism and other "crab-in-the-barrel" activities. In short we can say that the INTER impact manifests itself as lack of "cultural glue."

III. Some outer impacts of The Problem: (i.e. impacts from outside the African American community bludgeoning African Americans literally and figuratively).

A. The most destructive of outside forces is PSYCHIC TRAUMA. This results from being hated by everyone, especially the dominant society. In any setting, from the home, to the classroom to the campus, to the workplace, to the institutions of this society, to the communications media, contempt and loathing directly or indirectly, blatantly or subtly, day after day, year in and year out cause serious psychic harm to all African Americans. The bean experiment showed that the beans that were merely ignored failed to blossom as did the beans that had pleasant thoughts beamed at them by the dominant person.

B. Other manifestations of outer impact are discrimination in delivery of goods and services, segregation and job discrimination.

C. By far the most blatant of outer impact are acts of violence by the dominant group by individuals, unorganized groups and through their organizations of Skinheads, White Aryan Brotherhood and the Ku Klux Klan groups.

Note: All of the above was written in February 1991. Since then, the Los Angeles police beat an African American unmercifully. It was broadcasted nationwide on all major networks, showing very graphically what we are saying in "C" above. That beating was not an isolated case. Beatings and killings of African Americans by police go on continually all over America. The intensity and frequency are increasing. They will continue to increase, directly connected to the increase in the impact of television and motion pictures. The only difference between the Los Angeles case and the scores of other unmerciful beatings and killings that go on continually is that the Los Angeles' case was televised.

It is, therefore, clear that the answer is the creation of a flood of television and motion picture dramas portraying the beauty and grandeur of Songhai.

CAUSE, MANIFESTATIONS AND DEFINITIONS OF A PROBLEM

There were once two men arguing. They were standing on top of a mountain with steep sides. Finally, one punched the other in the jaw with such force that he began falling head over heels down the steep slope getting broken, bruised and bloody in his fall. He began screaming in anguish.

A magician in his little helicopter flew up beside the falling man, stopped him momentarily from falling by waving his magic wand and asked him why he was screaming. The man replied, "I am screaming because I have a problem." The magician asked him what his problem was. The man replied, "My problem is that man on top of the mountain. He struck me. He's my problem." The magician told him, "I will solve your problem."

The magician released his magic wand. The man started falling again, head over heels, and began screaming loudly again. The magician flew to the top of the mountain, and killed the man who had struck the falling man.

The magician, hearing the man screaming again, flew down, waved his magic wand, stopped the man in his fall and asked, "Why are you still screaming? You said that your problem was the man on top of the mountain. I have eliminated him. Therefore, your problem should be solved."

The pained man replied, "Evidently, he is not my problem. He was the cause of my problem. My problem must be the broken bones, the bruised and bloody body and the terrible headache I am suffering."

The magician sprang right to work—splinted his broken bones, applied coagulants for his bleeding, put balm on his bruises and administered aspirins for his headache. The magician then waved his magic wand—the man began tumbling down the side of the mountain the third time and resumed his screaming again.

Again, the magician flew down—waved his magic wand, stopping the man in his fall and exasperatedly asked again, "Why are you screaming? You said that your problem is that you got broken, bruised and bloody and a headache. I fixed you up. Therefore, your problem is eliminated."

"Again, evidently," whined the man, "that wasn't my problem. The broken bones, the bruised and bloody body and the headache were the RESULTS, THE MANIFESTATIONS, THE SYMPTOMS of my problem."

"So," asked the magician, "if the man on top of the mountain was the cause of the problem, your broken bones, your bruised and bloody body and the headache, the symptoms of your problem, then what is your problem?

"My problem," said the now wiser man, "is, I CAN'T KEEP FROM FALLING."

"Then why didn't you say that in the first place?" asked the magician as he PULLED THE MAN INTO HIS HELICOPTER AND THUS SOLVED THE MAN'S PROBLEM.

And so it is in the African Americans' futile and frustrating pursuit of freedom in America. We, of the Pan African Federation Organization understand that elimination of the white man will not solve our problem. The present-day Caucasians' ancestors were the cause of the problem.

We understand that our disproportionately large ills in the areas of discrimination, Black on Black crime, drugs, lack of physical, mental, and spiritual health and our disproportionately huge deficit in education, unemployment, poverty, etc., are merely symptoms, or manifestations of a problem. The fruitless pursuit of these SYMPTOMS will not and cannot improve the quality of life of African Americans. The monumental studies of The Kerner Commission, the Urban League and the NAACP attesting to the retrogression of the quality of life for African Americans bear irrefutable proof of the foolhardiness of trying to solve a problem by attacking its symptoms.

"Then," like the magician asked, "what is the Problem?"

PAFO replies, "THE PROBLEM IS THAT THE ENTIRE SOCIETY, INCLUSIVE OF AFRICAN AMERICANS, IS BEING, AND HAS CONTINUOUSLY BEEN PROGRAMMED TO BELIEVE THAT THE WEST AFRICAN GENESIS OF AFRICAN AMERICANS WAS STEEPED IN BESTIALITY, SAVAGERY, PRIMITIVENESS, ABYSMAL IGNORANCE AND SUB-HUMANNESS."

PAFO further elaborates, "The programming is and has been projected by the media of communication. The problem is deepening because of the increasing effectiveness of projection and the intensity of the viewing of television of Americans.

"The solution lies with the de-programming of America concerning the truth of the West African genesis. The subliminal programming must be effected with literally hundreds of dramatic episodes based in fourteenth, fifteenth, sixteenth and seventeenth Century West Africa."

We, therefore, call for dramatic scripts for animated cartoons, dramatic scripts for feature films, dramatic scripts for stage plays and musicals, dramatic scripts for operas. Manuscripts for children's, young adults' and adults' books are also a "must."

We shall continue to fight for the freedom for which our forefathers strove, that is, FREEDOM FROM HATRED OF OUR PHYSICAL AND CULTURAL AFRICANNESS BY THE ENTIRE SOCIETY INCLUSIVE OF AFRICAN AMERICANS. The revolutionary army that will achieve that freedom will be armed to the teeth, not with swords, but with pens. We, the undersigned know what history will say of us who clearly see the solution to THE PROBLEM.

We have a clear vision of what our illustrious ancestors are saying to us, "Well done, our children."

SESSION I

A LITTLE ABOUT THE PHILOSOPHY AND HISTORY OF PAFO

Hearing such statements today as "rub him out," and many other homicidal terms, makes us wonder when did Black people get this kind of mentality and by whose teachings. Blacks of the older generation remember a better period in time when our relationship with each other was much more brotherly and sisterly. A time when individualism had no abode in the fabric of our being, and when Blacks felt safe in their neighborhoods, but fearful in white communities. It was a time of few jobs, little money, but plenty of self and racial pride, love and fun with the help of such greats as Joe Louis, Nat King Cole, Jesse Owens, Ink Spots, Sugar Ray Robinson, Marian Anderson, George W. Carver, Ella Fitzgerald, Louis Armstrong—to mention a mere few. Some of PAFO also remembers when we began to change, and more importantly "Why?"

It began when Adolph Hitler and Germany wanted their African colonies back from the Allied powers, thus starting World War II. We started making big money too fast, (this was only the tip of the iceberg). It was like moving from a hot room of 98° to a cold room of only 20°. We didn't properly make the transition. That cold room representing cold cash, the hard cold facts of business, where sentimentality had hardly any place. It was a time of neglecting the children for the war effort, for big money, big cars, moving into big houses, etc....A time of ultra materialism and not enough time for personal affection. Thus setting into a motion a vicious circle of events that germinated the gang problem, adult homicidal mentality, robberies, dope, all forms of sex degeneration—all of which are increasing at an alarming rate.

With our help, PAFO aims to change this trend and we can—together! Knowing one's history and achievements in part—accounts for family stabilization. PAFO believes that Blacks must search for and dig out the hidden facts of our great past and structure it for teaching in an alternative set-up. We must build a bridge to the time and place when we were a nation and not imitators. We are teaching our young males their future duties for achieving manhood. Black females suffer because of a lack of a positive projected Black manhood. We advocate the development of mind power, as in the words of one of our fathers. The Honorable Marcus Garvey—"Not by power, nor by might, but by my spirit." When we develop this kind of attitude, we can then be truly Black in deed—for we will not provide strong drinks and dope for our children....We will tolerate each other more....We will support bona fide Black business....We will not exploit each other. Yes, our aims are high and noble. We will do the seemingly impossible, and that's why in February, 1971, PAN AFRICAN FEDERATION ORGANIZATION was born. It was founded by Calvin Robinson, Redman Battle, and William Mikell, also known as Abdull Ahi-Suleiman.

Our first support pillars were Diadra Watson, Virginia Treherne, Lorraine Laney, Pauline Pitts, Elaine Richardson, C.T. Simpson, Ronald Coleman, Katherine Hall, and Cynthia Vasser. In those early days, with the severe gang problem going on, our function primarily was dealing with helping to save the lives of our youth. We did this by working with some of the established organizations and leaders at that time. They were Father Paul Washington, David P. Richardson, Jr., Walter Palmer, Clarence Harris, William Meeks, Edward W. Robinson, Jr., and Lee Montgomery. These brothers were members of the Black Peoples' Unity Movement (BPUM), to mention a few. Other organizations included Crisis in Education, Freedom Library (John Churchville), City Wide Black Community Council, the Universal Negro Improvement Association (UNIA).

We were involved in many marches for Civil Rights of Blacks even locally on such issues as Blacks not allowed in Girard College, Strawberry Mansion High School with the incomparable Cecil Moore of Philadelphia, Pennsylvania.

We gave various types of affairs to raise money to help fight those issues at that time. We helped people, on an individual basis, with some needed finance. We gave a play on Profiles of African American and African History, and gave the proceeds to the UNIA, Marcus Garvey Shule and other organizations.

We also gave award certificates to people whom we felt were deserving at that time. Some of them at that time were Hardy Williams[1] (father of the independent Black political movement), the North Carolina Mutual Insurance Company, Supreme Life Insurance and the Provident Home Industrial Mutual Life Insurance Company. Also included in those awards were some radio personalities of Philadelphia's station WDAS. This is basically what PAFO was doing; trying to help our people out of our dilemma and showing appreciation.

It was not until September 1973 that we added another dimension to our endeavors. Redman Battle, Calvin Robinson and Dr. Edward Robinson wrote a text book called *The Journey Of The Songhai People*. It is a historical documentary on the people of the Western Sudan in Africa where the overwhelming majority of our people here in America come from. Elaine Anna Richardson and Harriette C. Robinson were our chief consultants for putting this digest together.

It was from that point in time that PAFO began to slacken up in the area of the Civil Rights marches, etc. This is not to say that we were not supportive of those who were. As a matter of fact, we were very much financially involved for the cause. However, we felt there was an area that needed more attention as a key to the door to our freedom. We began teaching and lecturing throughout the Black community at-large to all those who had an ear to hear.

We believed that learning our history such as the great contributions Blacks made world-wide was the key to freedom...not only in development but all that which is called civilization. However, there is something missing because we are still killing each other at an alarming rate. We soon began to realize that negative movies and television were making more of an impact than all of our teaching. This text will deal with some of the aspects of this dilemma.

There is another piece to this puzzle that we did not fully recognize until 1981. We, the authors of this text, met with our consultants to brainstorm. We were trying to *identify* the problem as opposed to worrying about the manifestations of the problem. With Dr. Edward W.

---

[1]Senator of Pennsylvania

Robinson spearheading the probe to identify the problem, he called a meeting in February, 1982, to present his findings to the rest of us. We concluded that he was correct when he asserted that the problem was rooted and grounded in the programmed loathing of our anthropological features and the disdainment of Africa, our ancestral home. Later sessions will have more detail on this most important doctrine.

PAFO's role in this ongoing saga is not only to instruct you in the history of our people, but equally important to help guide our philosophical resolve towards greater ethnic cohesion.

PAFO cannot emphasize enough for people in general and African Americans in particular to express their feeling of gratitude and love for those who gave and are yet giving so much to the cause of our people. Early on in this portion, we mentioned a few who are and did give so much. However, we would be remiss if we did not pour libations of spiritual waters for Dr. Martin Luther King, Malcolm X and Elijah Muhammad, Dr. J.S. Croom, Louis Farrakhan, Dr. Ben Jochannan, Dr. Chancellor Williams, Lerone Bennet, Dr. John Jackson, Carter G. Woodson, Tony Brown, Ivan Van Sertima, Prophet Noble Drew Ali, Mrs. Mattie Humphrey, Cecil B. Moore, Jesse Jackson, Drucella Houston and last but not least, the honorable Marcus Garvey. This does not count the unsung heroes whose names have been erased with time, and yet without them most of our known heroes might not have been heard of. We remember Goldie Watson and the Civil Rights Congress, Wilson Long, Samuel Evans[2], Walter and Yvonne Hutchins and their "Black House"[3], Dr. John H. Clark, also Jim Lester.

Pan African Federation Organization says to all of those concerned about Black unity, advancement, love and respect "Thanks." For they will live forever in our memories.

We feel that an explanation about the function of the mind is very important in understanding the importance of this text.

Basic to the highest development of mankind was the brain, which is the vehicle of the mind. Because it is truly the least understood in the whole universe is why we feebly attempt to unravel its mystery. One of the most frustrating things plaguing the human family is trying to understand why a person does or does not do a certain thing. People immediately say, he or she is crazy for not doing or doing the opposite

---

[2] American Foundation for Negro Affairs. (AFNA)
[3] A neighborhood learning center. A beacon of light and truth. It was the quintessence of black intellectualism.

of what people expect someone to do or not do.[4]

Many negative things are said about Africans and African Americans in their behavior patterns towards white people. People of the world in general whisper about Blacks as we continue to acquiesce to whites in the face of all kinds of insults and personal indignities.

According to Webster, the word *psyche* means the mind, especially as an organic system serving to ADJUST THE TOTAL ORGANISM TO THE ENVIRONMENT.

There are many statements and books written about the mind, and yet it is the least understood.

James Allen, in his book, *As a Man Thinketh,* says, "Mind is the Master Power, it moulds and it makes; man is mind, and forever more, he takes the tool of *thought* and he fashioneth what he wills. He can bring forth a thousand joys or a thousand ills. He thinks in secret and it comes to pass; his environment is nothing but a looking glass."

PAFO adds another dimension to that scenario of *As a Man Thinketh*— "As mankind is *taught* so are his thoughts and as a man thinketh in his heart, so is he."

We will be dealing with the many paradoxes that the mind produces especially when negative or positive conditions prevail on that mind.

Herein, we are dealing with the African, and in particular, the African living in the Americas. We are confronted with two types or two phases of mind confrontation with the reality of almost complete white domination in standards of what is called beautiful or ugly. What is called good or bad, what defines manhood and womanhood, what is success or failure in this American society or even what is right or wrong. American literature in particular and world literature in general is replete with satirical platitudes about African Americans and Africans. We will address some of those platitudes.

First let us consider mind confrontations with the reality of white domination.

Since Black people are the victims of a programmed brainwashing, it is hardly conceivable that the overwhelming majority are not subdued by it. This is evident by our behavior patterns when we still think that white is right and Black is wrong in so many phases of our journey through life. Mind you, that many Black people are not ever aware of the brainwash and many more who think they are aware but know not

---

[4]especially love affairs, for example, etc.

how to calculate the extent of the brainwash because most of it comes through subliminal seduction.

For a moment or two, let's focus on manhood. If you don't have a job and you don't make above the poverty line or don't drive certain types of cars, you will be dubbed as a failure, even with a willingness to work. Black men as a whole are stereotyped as lazy, shiftless; and only interested in sex, alcohol and illegal drugs.

Manhood must always be defined for the setting in which it occurs. A man in Siberia may be different from a man in Chicago. Yet biologically they share the same drives and limitations, but *their societies may decree totally different roles*. For the Black man in this country, it is not so much a matter of acquiring manhood, as it is a struggle to *feel it's his own*. Whereas the white man regards his manhood as an ordained right; and the Black man is engaged in a never ending battle for its possession. Stereotyping of Blacks, has a long long history, and we will attempt to give a background of the whys and wherefores of this poison. Before we project these scenarios, we must tell more about the behavior of African Americans.

There are a host of Black people that defend white people's injustices against Black people. Here are some of the paradoxes of the mind that are produced because of the dominate society's obsession for complete control over non-white persons.

Let's look at various talk shows throughout the nation as well as newspapers editorials. The talk shows and the Black newspapers seem to have more than enough Black people defending white aggression against Blacks. Some of the rhetoric that Black defenders of whites goes like this. "Black on Black Crime is something we do against each other, so you can't blame white people. Black people not supporting Black bona fide businesses is not the Asian or White man's fault. We hear Black people saying that Blacks are racists, and that racism is not associated with power. We hear Black people on radio and television shows and writers saying that Blacks make too many excuses."

On that last statement, that is truly the opposite of what is factual. Black people generally agree that Black people are their own worst enemy, and they do not see the white man as the enemy especially on those aforementioned issues.

Why do we, Black people, in general think like this, about an enemy that has and is yet doing so much against us? Why do we continually excuse him? The answer is, we are programmed into an almost irreversible brainwashing. Too many Black people believe that brainwashing isn't that powerful to cause us to be like we are as a people. They think, that's just the way we are.

If programming (brainwashing) wasn't that potent, then explain to us how little tiny England was able to keep hundreds of millions of East Indians divided for so long or millions of Africans in Africa divided against themselves that it took long numbers of years to overthrow their colonial control.

If we could just stop blaming ourselves for a moment, we could, maybe, begin to really understand the power of mind control and how it works. Then very objectively we must begin to deal analytically in trying to solve the problem.

In not fully understanding the intricacies of the working of the mind, (*we* more often than not) make the wrong conclusion in our judgment of people in general, but especially about the Black race as a whole. Then what we're talking about is Black People's almost vehement castigation of each other in almost every facet of our endeavors to do things.

Let us look at these castigations that so many of us heap on our brothers and sisters. We call each other ugly without let-up. We give up very, very easily on ourselves, and then say, "I have to get Whitey to do it" (Whatever it may be). Products sold by white people are better than products sold by Blacks, even though both may be purchased from the same distributors. It's the case where we say "the white man's coal burns hotter and his ice is much colder." It's the case that white women understand and are more tender than Black women and likewise white men not only provide better but are more sensitive to a Black woman's needs than Black men.

In analysis, maybe an aspect or so may be true in the above statements. Yet, in reality, ninety percent of this pro-white feeling is only in our minds. This is again because of the deep-seated negative mind set or programming against anything that's not white.

We will excuse whites almost no matter what they do against us. Yet, we are the ones whose land was invaded and our people kidnapped. In that process, Africa lost one hundred million people and only two million made it here to these shores. Even though we heard of the Stockholm Syndrome, the kidnapping of Patty Hurst and the fifty-four hostages held by Iran when Jimmy Carter was president of the United States, we may not have properly evaluated it in relation to Africans being kidnapped and brought here.

In the Stockholm Case of the bank robbers holding the bank employees as hostages, it was the hostages that started identifying with the so-called cause of the robbers and expressed desire to marry several of them.

Patty Hurst, millionairess, did the same thing. Likewise, the United States hostages in Iran began to sympathize with *their* captors.

Even though being held captive and working from sun-up to sun-down without a payday for more than two hundred and forty-six years, we, Africans, here in America, began identifying and fighting for the white cause. The rationale subconsciously since they did feed us, even though it was very poor and they didn't kill *us all*. The Stockholm and Patricia Hurst cases which were later probed, came up with the same general rationale of why the victim sides with the oppressor. In the case of the Black Americans kidnapped from Africa, the scale was grandiose.

SOCIOLOGICAL EQUATION*

$$CULTURE + ENVIRONMENT = FRAME\ of\ REFERENCE \pm OPPRESSOR'S\ REACTION \pm OTHER\ PEOPLE'S\ REACTION = BEHAVIOR$$

*Thanks to James Bowles, MS.

We think this equation may sum up what we attempted to explain in the above.

Why the mind works like that is not totally clear, although there are some logical concepts or ideas that have been advanced. Some sociologists say the prefrontal cortex has two functions, but only can do one very well at a time.

In short or long periods of extreme hostility, it persuades the rest of the mind and body to accept certain indignities for the survival of the body adjusting to the environment. Yet not *always* does this occur in all people at the same time. If it did, then there would be no heroes.

One last aspect of this psychic puzzle, as we see it, is the subconscious adherence to the power call. There is material law that attracts people towards a power beyond the reach of the less powerful. In that context, so goes the theoretical consensus that the more powerful are adored, admired, loved, respected and envied. They (the powerful) set standards of beauty, styles, fashions and codes of "ethics" in the main. In the area of race dominance where the downtrodden race is faced with all kinds of indignities, to say the least, this negative behavior of the powerful is more than generally accepted. Therefore, the mystery continues.

So we say to Science Officer Spock and Captain Kirk, that space is not the final frontier, but rather the unchartered voyages into the depth of the *mind*; in that unstructured universe where some of us half heartedly seek-out-of-body experiences for super knowledge but are afraid when after we are about to let go, quickly say, "Scotty, beam me aboard."

ORIENTATION

Because of their plot to condemn Black-skinned African people to unending slavery, economic or otherwise, the Europeans, Arabs especially, and even some Asians schemed up to blot out all records of the great African past. Therefore, we are now going to learn the name of the oppressor's game.

Let us say here and now that the upper echelon of the white race knows our history better than most Black people. These white scholars in the educational system control the education of Blacks, not only in the United States, but throughout the world. Therefore, they see no need, even now, to take a new look at the history of Blacks from its beginnings, and start the work of restoring the pages they deleted or ignored.

Actually, they are doing the opposite. Their histories and other "scientific" studies of Blacks are presented just as they have been for three hundred years. With the rise and spread of independent African states and the Black Revolution in America, these scholarly representatives of White supremacy quickly reformed their techniques of mind control. They set up, in Europe and the United States, highly financed African Studies Associations, societies, institutions, history journals, and "African Periodicals" of various kinds—*all* under complete white control and direction. Their African studies programs were pushed in the colleges and universities, far ahead of the general demand by Black youths for Black studies. As a matter of fact, a recent survey shows a great decline by Blacks for Black history. As the latter demand developed, Black youths discovered that white professors not only had the field occupied, but were still teaching their traditional viewpoint on "race" and we must change this.

In the continuing crusade to control minds of the Blacks through the nature of their education, which also includes religious education, the Bible and the Koran notwithstanding, American and British scholars led. They are as ruthless and aggressive in their scholarly pursuits on races as their co-partners are in seizing and controlling the wealth and people of other lands. Having established strong national and international "African Associations" and journals, they even attempted to control research activities in Africa. They proceeded to flood the world with hastily thrown together African "histories," pamphlets, and publications on just about every subject that could stand a Black tide.

From their all-powerful position of strength, they continue to arrange and re-arrange the world as it pleases them, naming and classifying people, places, time and things. For the sake of general confusion, they used the birth of Jesus as a focal point of history, the A.D. and B.C. doctrine. Another point on furthering the general confusion is found in the following doctrine:

In the United States, whites known to have any amount of Black blood, no matter how small, are classified as Blacks. In Africa, and North Africa in particular, they do the very opposite for different reasons. Blacks with any amount of Caucasian blood are classified as whites. (BECAUSE IN AFRICA, WHITES ARE SO OUTNUMBERED, WHILE IN AMERICA, BLACKS ARE SO OUTNUMBERED). This scheme was rigorously applied in the history of Egypt, for example, where even unmixed Black Pharaohs became white, and the original Black population was never referred to as Egyptian at all. Black kings founded and ruled from the first dynasty. Blotting Blacks out of history included such tactics as replacing African names of persons, places and things with Arabic and European names. One wave of the master's magic wand, and Black Hamites, and even Cushites, like their earlier Egyptian brothers, are no longer African. Their periodicals of African history are carefully arranged in such a way that African history becomes the history of Arabs and Europeans in Africa, and not the history of Africans.

END OF SESSION I

PAUL ROBESON, a great world-wide singer, actor, linguist, scholar and political activist. He denounced racism and injustice, and the State Department revoked his passport.

SESSION II

OUR RAISON D'ETRE

This is the story about Black people, now living in America and known by many different names, such as Negro, Colored, Tan Yanks, Afro-Americans, Coons, Niggers, Spooks, shine, and many more unsavory ones.

The United States Census Bureau has a 1990 projected African American population of thirty-six million representing 11.8% of the total population.

To get a *point* of understanding over, Blacks in America, for the most part, are going in almost as many directions as there are Black people in the United States of America. This is due in part to the drug culture spin-off, brainwashing, and "the way out" music, with it's sordid sexual overtones, and with words so suggestive, so as to make children confused, hindering the proper building of their moral fiber and spiritual direction. These conditions exist in part because of the massive influx of dope *purposely* pushed into Black neighborhoods to help create these chaotic conditions.

We have joined every religious cult in the world and are not even mindful of our Traditional African religious concepts.

In politics, we are Democrats, Republicans, Socialists, Communists, or whatever. We are Elks, Odd Fellows, several types of Masons, and we belong to all kinds of Greek fraternities and sororities. We are all kinds of colors in physical and political complexions, trying to get to this or that place, and really not going anywhere.

Yes, some Blacks in sports say they have made it, some professions think they have made it, the very deeply religious think nothing else is worthwhile. All of these different "minds" which Black people possess are a major factor in our being so fragmented, and as a result, Blacks are on the bottom rung of the social, financial, educational, and ethnic cohesive ladder. This book is dedicated to the Black men and women in hopes that, as they read the amazing accounts of their journey in time, piecing together the tapestry of their glorious past, as well as the innumerable setbacks perpetrated by the Asian-Euro-Arab enemies, that they will experience a new birth.

Deep in the recesses of the Black peoples' mind, there resides a force that has persisted throughout these long years of degradation. In PAFO, we have a saying, "In the spirit of our Fathers and Mothers, protected by their blood, we shall give tongue to each of their wounds." This force and spirit, truly has been the mystery of our ability to survive, in spite of many forces arrayed against us: the forces of negative religion, color racism, politics, negative education, physical brutality and psychological warfare against our minds, the destruction of our civilization through the medium of false history and re-classification of the history periods.

Sociologists, psychiatrists, and psychologists have all agreed that no other ethnic group has had to endure what the African has endured. In control groups, where tests have been made for comparatively short durations, white subjects went almost completely insane when they were subjected to a *fraction* of the horrors that Blacks are subjected to, and have been subjected to for more than three centuries. (Read *Mark of Oppression* by Kardiner and Ovessey, also *Black Rage* by Grier and Cobbs.) The so-called experts cannot figure out what keeps us going. This mystery is also what keeps the white power structure upset and geared up to cut down even the *possibility* of us being able to survive above his most stringent limitations on us.

As you proceed into this history, you will see that all nationalities were and are the recipients of the great and good things that Africans so heavily contributed to the world civilization. The Africans were the first in just about everything concerning civilization advancement (Ref. *Cultural Genesis*) (PAFO).

We ask you to read and study this book with an open mind, and allow the spirit of our fathers and mothers to guide you to the truth of your past, which is the beginning of your future.

Before we begin this journey from Africa, we, the Pan African Federation Organization, through its history department, would like to set the tone for this important history documentary you are about to read, *The Journey of The Songhai People*.

We will mainly be writing about the people of Western Africa, but by no means will we be ignoring any of the other sections of Africa.

Many excuses for not wanting to learn about Black history have been invented by Black people; such as being too busy, don't want to be bothered with anything Black and many other frivolous reasons. Of course we realize that brainwashing plays a major role in this negative attitude toward ourselves, and is reinforced by whites by denouncing Black groups that teach the real truth of our history. Reasoning should tell us that they must fear the possibility of our learning the truth, otherwise they wouldn't go all out to either water down or to make an outright mockery of this precious truth.

Black groups that teach Black history are branded as hate groups, and as usual, many Black people fall for this kind of brainwashing. If we analyze the so-called hate situation between white and Black people, you will find that what is taken for hatred, when applied to Blacks is their reaction against being hated, rejected and oppressed. The thinking elite "whites" know this very well because they wrote the educational program in the first place. When they cry "racism in reverse" or "reverse discrimination" and "reverse segregation," they are saying in effect, that "Only we whites may be racists! Only we whites may discriminate or segregate, but not you Blacks." All white organizations that exclude Blacks everywhere are normal and proper from the white perspective, but an all Black organization excluding whites? Perish the thought. Whites fleeing en mass from cities throughout the nation to avoid integrated schools and fair housing laws. *These* are the real separatists, not the Blacks who never fled from the whites at all, except to possibly avoid being lynched.

Yet those Blacks who said, "Let them go! Let us not pursue them! Let us stay where we are, stand on our own feet as men and women and begin to build and improve our schools and communities"—these, not the whites, are denounced as separatists or Black Nationalists. Even with the loss of tens of millions of Black people during the so-called "slave trade," which was our physical POW period, the partitioning of Africa by the whites, stealing the cultural treasures and wealth. Yet Blacks do not hate the whites as a whole.

We (PAFO) say that this does not seem quite normal even though we know that we are the most spiritual people in the world. The spiritual name of Africa is called Alkebu-lan, which means the "land of the Spirit People."

Taking the critical analysis of this Black dilemma, we found it necessary to go to the root cause.

Some psychologists and sociologists say that the root cause of *Blacks not hating whites is the white God doctrine and brainwash.* The doctrine is steadily being projected in the Black Mind by the major religious sects. All the religious material of ninety-nine and eight-ninths percent of the churches produce white pictures of angels, the Madonna and Christ, the prophets and the apostles. Also, with the revising of the meaning of certain words in the dictionary, to make Black wrong, despicable, offensive, illegal, etc: while making "white" good, honorable, clean and God like, etc. Therefore, if God, Jesus, the prophets, apostles and the angels were white, then the white people on earth must be the earthly representatives of God. It has been said that this really has changed the psyche of Black people, causing them not to be aware of the damage being done to the mind.

In our search for the truth, it was revealed to us by the spirit of our ancient forefathers and mothers that the True creator would enlighten us if we would seek diligently for the truth. We found, that it was at Nice-Rome in 325 A.D. when Constantine the Great started the great switch from the Black Christ and the Black Madonna worship to white. At that time, the religions of the world were projecting their concepts from Black Egypt, where the Black Madonna and her child were known as Isis and Horus. When Constantine did what he did, there was a big dispute. He had to use his influence as Emperor to call a meeting of the Ecumenical Council. The final result was that a majority voted to change the color of the Mother and Child to white. This took years and years to do because even though Rome had power, the Blacks did not accept it. Theodosius I continued to suppress the truth and did so with much physical violence against Blacks. In the white hierarchy, they knew that if they were going to be the masters of the world, that they would have to make the earthly image of God look like them. Some originals did escape the change.

Incidentally, **Pope John Paul II** said, that when he goes to Poland, he visits his church, with its **original Black Madonna** and **Christ child**.

The white savior perception, was not only true in Christendom, but also in the Moslem Religion. Mohammed is depicted as a white Arab in most Moslem countries, paralleling him with Jesus. One has just to observe and to be convinced that this was a master stroke to set the stage for complete subjugation of Black people the world over. This, along with the general brainwashing is a big factor contributing to our disunity. Yet, thinking whites know about our great past, and fear our "innate" potential. Perhaps you may not have noticed or understood the signals from the white world—signals that tell how tremendously important the whites regard *any* movement toward *unity* among Blacks. This was very noticeable, when in the 1968 Olympic Meet, Blacks who were victorious gave the Black Power clenched fist salute. Well, you would have thought that Marcus Garvey, Denmark Vesey and Nat Turner had returned from the grave to lead an army against the white world; the way in which the newspapers had projected such a negative verbal venom. You would have thought that they were gangsters instead of mere athletes.

When Stokely Carmichael popularized the term "Black Power," the white press went crazy trying to convey to Blacks that the kind of power to get should be green power, Bible power, job power, you name it, just anything but Black people having power. Unity among the Blacks has been prevented for so many centuries that the various mechanisms to keep Blacks disorganized have been perfected in the Western system of race control. Newspaper articles in Philadelphia, Pennsylvania, tell of the methods used by the F.B.I. to cause suspicion and distrust between the S.C.L.C. and local Philadelphia organizations. Investigation shows that this was also true throughout the country up to and including the present.

We hope that as you read and study this text, that in spite of all the tactical maneuvers projected by the white power structure against Black people's thrust for self determination, manhood and dignity, that somehow we shall overcome it.

In the classifactory system of kinship, we Africans reckoned relationship between the group first, and the individual second. This system tended to put the love for ethnic consciousness on an extremely high level. As you can see we have lost this because of this white environment that projects the individualistic and materialistic side of people. Not knowing our all-important history that promotes love and ethnic consciousness, this negative white environment tears us apart worse than other nationalities. The lack of the knowledge of our great past provided no psychological cushion to neutralize these negative forces produced by the anti-Black environment. There was much more loyalty in Black people's ranks during the days of our forced captivity than now. Several reasons for this loyalty were that then we were not as far removed mentally from our origin. We could still remember the names of our heroes, the universities we had built, our beautiful stone houses and our inside plumbing fixtures. We related and identified with power and greatness. After all, we were only prisoners-of-war here. Another reason for this loyalty, centered around the raw, harsh treatment inflicted by the oppressors, and sometimes this alone stimulated enough loyalty with the desire to fight and die for the freedom we wanted so badly. In those days, we really knew that freedom meant control of our ethnic destiny, like the white Jews or other nationalities; but today our *concept* of freedom really means freedom from society's programmed contempt of African looks and African history.

By being denied our history, we are forced to identify with the enemy, (in our minds). Yet, he (the enemy) denies us full citizenship while at the same time they projected Africa as an undesirable through the Tarzan-like pictures. This is why most of us, especially in times past, didn't want anything to do with African history. And, that's why we have been a race in name, rather than in fact, in terms of sentiment rather than a full consciousness, and we have only had problems in common, rather than enjoying a beautiful and good experience together since our captivity.

However, while all of the foregoing has contributed to anti-Black sentiment, they are but manifestations of the one basic problem. That one basic problem is that the total society, inclusive of us African Americans, has been fed a two-century continuous diet of lies about West African cultural and anthropological history. One of the greatest documented sources for this truth is found on page 145 of Kenneth Stampp's book called *The Peculiar Institution*. We have been made to believe as well as whites that our "...African ancestry tainted (us) and that (our) color was a badge of degradation."

This universal hatred of our African blood by *everybody including us* explains unequivocally why whites discriminate against us and move away from us AND Blacks discriminate against us and move away from "us." It explains why whites maim and kill us AND Blacks maim and kill us. Blacks kill each other at such an alarming rate that I, as a Black have an 1800% times greater probability of being murdered by another Black than a white person has by another white person.

Hatred and loathing of African blood is the reason why no laws will work—neither fair housing, nor equal employment opportunity, nor human relations laws, nor affirmative action—none. Hatred finds a way around the law.

It is why, as Alvin Poussaint, a noted psychologist says, "When a Black is about to deal the death blow to one of the almost 14,000 Black victims in 1987, he always utters a curse of anti-Black contempt, 'Here, you big-lipped m...f...' or 'Take this you Black b...' or 'you nappy-head b...'" PAFO asks rhetorically, "Is there no balm in Gilead? Is there no physician there?" We are trying hard to heal with the truth.

We have to undo these lies about the history of Africa and our African blood. PAFO is dedicated to undo those lies.

The beauty and grandeur and sophistication of our West African culture is laid out for you in the following pages. Included, also is the truth of the how and why of our color and physical features so that you will, at last, realize that they are *not* badges of degradation but tributes of advanced evolution.

Let us now proceed into these pages of truth and with this good frame of reference.

OUR PURPOSES AND GOALS

To recreate
in the minds of our people the glory, the pomp, the splendor and the honor that was ours in a land far away from where the kidnappers carried us.

To bring
about that feeling of nostalgia that most ethnic groups feel when reminiscing. We have just as much a right to that feeling as any other nationality.

In order to do this, PAFO must build a bridge to the time and place when we were not imitators of the Europeans or other ethnic groups. We must teach our male children their future duties for achieving manhood. We must teach respect and understanding that will grow into a love that was once our before the implanting of ultra-materialism into the fabric of our being.

To develop
an intertwining philosophy based on the culture of the Songhai Empire, and out of the experiences of the degradation suffered on this American soil. We, in this country, having been subjected to the greatest trauma in the history of mankind was yet able to develop some of the world's greatest talented people; such as statesmen, poets, doctors, scientists, philosophers, inventors, lawyers, and many other people of renown.

As Harriet Beecher Stowe, said..."The Black people in this country while being held in involuntary servitude led the way for the fight for freedom. It was the Black man who fought in every war here for the acquisition and the preservation of white freedom." "Bravery," she said, "under such circumstances has a peculiar beauty and merit." For those who don't know, she was a white woman.

We, therefore, must advocate the ideology of how much the individual can contribute to the whole society and to vigorously pursue the extended family concept, thus making the acquiring of material wealth only a means to an end and not the end itself.

This concept that was an African initiative, acted as a safeguard for the preservation of the society. This concept evolved because our environment was essential to the spirituality that Africans became noted for. Therefore, it should not be mystifying that our children were the best behaved in the world. The African societies did not need jails, halfway houses, and youth detention centers. This naturally included adults as well as children, but this was not the case in societies dominated by Europeans.

If you check back in the history of the Grecians and the Roman Empires and read about the social decorum, it would probably shock you. The youth, as well as the older people were involved in sex orgies on the street and in the public squares. People bet money on those who were so engaged in those activities. Promiscuity almost totally unchecked, graffiti marking on houses, government and public buildings that later writers of history called it a disgrace. (*Greek and Roman Mythology* by W.S. Fox)

Here in America, because of the clash of African ideals and how African society translated their value system into meaningful relationships, they automatically became the values of African Americans. Not immediately, of course, but as our stay in America became more extended, great dissent occurred within the African American family. African Americans began to change their ideas about such things as God and discipline of their children which was the beginning of acceptance of European standards. African Americans started saying "I'm not going to raise my children like I was raised" and mind you this was in the light that we were taught to "Honor your father and mother." We started accepting the material of books written by Dr. Benjamin Spock on how we should rear our children in the middle 1940's. We and others without question started letting school counselors make contracts between ourselves and our children involving the do's and the don'ts of child behavior in and out of school. Then the television and movies started negatively training our children and other children too. Various child psychologists, sociologists and others said that corporal punishment was wrong for children. Let them rebel unrestrained these so-called experts said. They are only acting out their frustrations. After that, children got away with calling adults by their first name. They started answering with a "huh," a "what," a "yeah," a "no." No more "yes ma'am" or "no ma'am" or "yes sir" or "no sir" even though in the military you have to answer yes or no sir or ma'am. In other words, adults and parents put the military above their own worth. This breakdown in parental respect has far-reaching repercussions. Some of the manifestations of these repercussions occurs in physical attacks against the parents by their own children. Also, there was a very significant increase of attacks on senior citizens; mainly women and very old men. There was a general increase of robbery of all forms and younger and younger children being involved in crime. The whole idea of this society, in general, allowing their children to intimidate them is preposterous. One thing is clear, we allowed it to get out of hand, and if it is to be righted, we (collectively) will have to do it. This is and was not an African way of life. Negative imagery of Blacks on television and movies only reinforces racists propaganda against Blacks and all of this is connected—hurting Black people more so because of cultural deprivation.

We hope that these history sessions will awaken a deep desire in you to contribute toward helping Black people find their real selves. Last, but not least, we propose to suggest to you what being Black really means. Let us first say, that it *doesn't* mean how well pigmented one is. It *doesn't* mean how much of a beard one has grown or how large their Afro-bush may be. It *doesn't* necessarily mean whether or not you are using an African name or even having visited Africa. To PAFO, *being Black means* to *aid* Black people to avoid dope. It means to give respect to the female and the female, in return, giving respect to the Black male. It means not to buy strong drinks for minor children. It means to love each other more than ever *before*. It means *going out of your way for each other*. It means not to exploit each other in any way; to support Black bona fide businesses, to *develop more faith* in each other. *Above all* it means to stick by the code, once you *commit* yourself to it and it seems as though you are the only one sticking by it.

On the love portion of the above, we want to impact on what the beauty of love was and how it existed on the highest obtainable level in our home continent Africa (Alkebu-lan).

As you will see, in the forthcoming sessions, all of mankind travels the road of physical and mental development and had at one time gone through the stage of total beastliness. Blacks have traveled farthest away from the instincts of the beast, towards the lines of love and understanding more than any other ethnic group.

Eleven and a quarter generations, which is about three hundred and ninety-one years of an anti-Black environment have produced about twenty-five thousand Black homicides a year and going up steadily. Based on this information, PAFO proposes certain steps to help release us from this particular bondage that is eroding our great moral fiber.

We are attacking the problem with the sword of truth and the shield of *love*. In the realm of *ethnic love*, love of the total race, for survival from the African concept of things has always been *race first*. That means considerations of marriage, and other individual wants and desires generally conformed to the interest of the total society. The rationale being that the society produced the individual, not the individual who produced the society. Yet, there was room for flexibility under various circumstances. Since love is a many-splendored thing, description of it can be difficult. For instance, it can be tender. Yet, to a child on punishment for its own good, it is taken in the negative realm. We yet have not really defined it, but we can safely say that we have felt or seen its manifestations. PAFO attempts to teach how to portray love, and how necessary it is in the understanding of Black or corrective history.

We must first start with love of our race, then love of the family. This automatically transfers to ourselves. How do we answer each other? Do we ask or answer sweetly with love, or do we take love for weakness as the dominate society does? Do we greet each other in the true spirit of Blackness? Are we sincere with one another in every facet of our daily dealings with each other? Can we have a simple disagreement on a point of view without being *disagreeable?* Do we view each other in the light of realizing that our *actual future* existence, individually and particularly as a race or a nation depends on how and what we think of each other, and not on the so-called mercy of another race of people who are programmed against a Black skin. If we do not understand this love concept, in relation to our beautiful history, then we will have missed the *reason* for history. *Only if we* implement this great African concept and truly believe in it, will we begin to generate a power to free us from all negative forces that tend to bind us. Power is *organized energy or effort*. Success is the development of that power with which to get what is rightfully ours.

The words of one of our fathers, Frederick Douglas were to the effect that, "If any people wants freedom and refuses to fight for it, he is like the man who wants crops and refuses to plow the ground. He might want rain, but fears the clouds and thunder. The only language that the enemy knows is power." Douglas also said, *"Power only concedes to power, it always did and it always will."*

Mental power is the greatest personal achievement to attain. Learning the knowledge and truth about our fathers and mothers, leads to the development of mind and spirit, and this is the key needed to accomplish our purposes and goals. The honorable Marcus Garvey gave us a hint when he said, "Not by power nor by might, but by my spirit saith the Lord of Hosts."

LOOKING FORWARD

In this approximately 155,000 word digest, we are merely trying to present the essence of our Black past, Western African, in the main, and so should just serve as a beginning for you to be about seeking more abundant information. Upon perusal, it should accelerate your desire to delve completely into authentic writing and find all of the available answers to make you well-rounded in this subject.

This information is designed to perpetuate amongst Black people in this country, a new kind of awareness....For too long, Black people living in America have known only of the Black American Experience, but even this has been in the negative, because of the truth being hidden by the oppressor.

The American school system systematically excluded the contributions that Africans living in America had made during both the chattel period and the post chattel period. By and large, Africans in this country don't even know who Dr. Charles Drew was or Louis Latimer, Granville T. Woods, Jan Matzelleger, E.J. Robinson, or others. The exclusion of this knowledge about Black people was and is not mere coincidence, but a deliberate and diabolical plan to forever erase the ethnic consciousness of a once mighty people, and to prevent recognition and respect of us by whites.

Then, to add insult to injury, the oppressors, with malice aforethought, resolutely brainwashed Blacks of the ensuing generations (whites as well) into believing that Africa was a backward continent and its inhabitants should not be accorded the dignity of men. The motion picture and television industry always portrayed Africa in the negative. *All of the history books were rewritten to exclude Black accomplishment, and to correspond with the brainwash.* We almost had no choice but to swallow it.

PAFO is attempting to show that the Africans in our West African homeland had a great and beautiful civilization. Had this civilization not been interrupted by a calculated sneak invasion—with the aid of mercenaries, there is no telling how far world civilization might be advanced today.

While Europeans were still running around naked, drinking blood out of the skulls of their conquered dead and painting their bodies blue, Africa was experiencing the beauty of architectural phenomena, swinging gardens suspended in mid-air, and vast medical achievements.

The time is now out...for Truth to be forever on the scaffold, and Wrong forever on the throne; because that scaffold sways the future and behind the dim unknown stands God amidst the shadow keeping watch o'er his own.

THE VALUE OF HISTORY

Knowledge of race history, is to that race, exactly as an individual's memory is to that individual.

Without memory, an individual lives in an eternity of unconnected moments, totally dysfunctional and unlearned. He cannot do even the simplest task, for every task requires some memory. He is a full amnesiac.

Partial amnesiacs have no memory prior to a certain point in time. They do have limited function. They are physically sick, have low energy levels and are uncreative. These individuals can never reach the peak of their innate capacities because of the fear and uncertainty of that closed chapter in their lives.

The masses of African Americans suffer from partial cultural amnesia because of a certain deliberate program that wiped the slates of our memories clean of true African events prior to the cotton fields of America.

However, the monsters who perpetrated this cultural genocide were not satisfied. After wiping the memory slates clean, they wrote upon those slates a series of vicious lies. They wrote on the slates, on the minds of all, Black and white alike, that the African is really an ape that can speak. They wrote on the slates, of the minds of all, that the African evolved in the heartland of the jungles of Africa where not even the faintest glimmer of the light of science and learning could penetrate. They wrote on those slates no ability to behave properly. They programmed all of this upon the minds of all, Black and white alike.

Fortunately, medical history abounds with recitals of cures of individual amnesia.

Similarly, the Pan African Federation Organization has records of marvelously progressing recoveries from cultural amnesia.

We hasten to add that total erasures of the lies and the rewriting of Truth has not entirely taken place, hence we say "marvelously progressing recoveries."

The values of the knowledge of racial history are vividly delineated in the case histories of PAFO.

One such PAFO case history took place, some years ago, when Dr. Edward W. Robinson, Jr., challenged the school system of Philadelphia, Pennsylvania with the statement that he could bring Black youths suffering under the inability to perform mathematical functions to the ability required by their school grade. He kept fifty-seven of them a week. He gave them massive doses of African history for nearly three days. The next two days, with love and respect he imparted to them the mathematics sent down from our fathers. They quickly learned.

Why? Because of three reasons:

One—Because, he as a teacher had been deprogrammed from being contemptuous of African people and re-programmed to love and respect African people as a group, as a race. In other words, he had high teacher expectancy of them *because* they had African heredity.

AND

Two—Because his knowledge of African history produced loving and kind thoughts toward them, the children, this produced a positive aura or psychic field conducive to high productivity in them. This is a newly discovered phenomenon first observed by horticulturists. When a dominant personage (the horticulturist) beams loving and kind thoughts toward flowers, they bloom directly in proportion to the intensity of the psychic field produced by the dominant personage. The same is true on the human level.

AND

Three—Because, he injected massive doses of VITAMIN I (Identity) in the form of enriched African history—this released the full mental energy of the pre-frontal cortex to concentrate upon the abstractions contained in mathematical computation. The pre-frontal cortex, according to the Institutes of Mental Health is that part of the brain that does at least two things:

1. Its energy, which is limited and measurable, solves abstract problems of which mathematics is its highest form or

2. Its energy continuously creates defense mechanisms to defend the ego in a society that is hostile to that ego.

It can't do both well, simultaneously.

The children's brains injected continuously with history, taught in an exciting and creative way wrested from the pre-frontal cortex the necessity for creation of defense mechanisms. Hence, the bulk of the energy flowed uninterruptedly toward the solution of the mathematical problems.

Thus, from this and many other case histories of PAFO we can begin to list the benefits of the knowledge of an enriched African history.

AN ENRICHED AFRICAN HISTORY

One may ask, "What is *enriched* African history?"

We answer, "Cultural *and* anthropological history." Cultural history of Africa is wise, necessary and good. But, anthropology is an absolute necessity. African anthropology scientifically explains our physical characteristics in such a dynamic way that the learner will view, in the end that instead of being badges of degradation, our hair, facial features, skin color and bodily build are characteristics of advanced evolution.

One may ask, "Why Africa—we're here in America?"

We answer, "The cotton fields are that point in time, before which we have "cultural amnesia." That amnesia must be cured. It is about Africa that the myths have been fabricated. It is no myth about Booker T. or Carver. White America reluctantly allows African American history to come through. They will even sweeten it. But, our trauma results from myths about Africa, both culturally and anthropologically. Therefore, we must correct the current myths.

African history is the cake and African American history is the icing. No matter how sweet the icing, if the cake is made by our detractors from decayed ingredients, the whole cake is defiled and will be thrown away. Thus, we must make the cake ourselves from the pure ingredients of Truth.

The values flowing from knowledge of enriched African history are:

1. Unbelievable heightening of our and our children's abstract and mathematical intelligence.

2. Limitless increase of our creativity in all areas as well as in the areas of science, literature and music.

3. Tremendous increase of our joy of living, our physical energies, our mental health.

4. Abounding love of African adults and children not only individually but collectively.

5. Loss of hatred of those who ravaged our homeland, raped our mothers, murdered our fathers, and defiled our racial honor. Hatred condemns and cripples the hater. The loss of this hatred redeems. We will learn that he is forced by his evolution under Europe's harsh glaciers to behave as he does.

6. Production of a society-wide aura of positive psychic energy that will foster Black intellectual and spiritual flowering that will bring America and the world ever nearer to becoming truly civilized.

Therefore, by re-programming ourselves and America, we can walk out of the four hundred years of white mental bondage, out of our slum ghetto of physical and mental prisons, free at last.

CULTURAL GLUE

Equally important in readying for this continual battle against a hostile environment is cultural "glue." Let us explain what it is.

Cultural "glue" is a binding force produced by an ethnic, racial, religious or cultural group for the physical and cultural preservation and enhancement of that group. It serves both as a sword and shield. It serves as a sword in making sure that the group achieves its rightful share of goods and services and as a shield against attacks, physical, mental and political.

Cultural "glue" (CG) consists of numerous ingredients.

The most important of these ingredients are:

1. The knowledge of a common ancestral homeland.

2. The appreciation and honor of that homeland.

3. The appreciation and honor of heroes and heroines of that homeland.

4. The carrying on of traditions relating to deepening of appreciation of the homeland.

5. Appreciation of the language of that homeland.
6. Appreciation of the music of that homeland.
7. The belief in a mystique concerning the people of that homeland.
8. Continual exposure to drama portraying the beauty, grandeur and sophistication of the homeland culture.

Cultural glue, when it exists within an ethnic, religious or cultural group, "binds" the members of that group together, for achieving, among other things, group protection, group dignity and honor, group material enrichment, group political power, group financial power, group physical and mental health, positive group recognition and group educational achievement.

Cultural "glue" (CG) exists within the overwhelming majority of racial, ethnic and religious groups of the world. And within those groups, CG has existed from time immemorial.

Without CG, a group is like a person with AIDS (Acquired Immune Deficiency). It is vulnerable to every illness of society. It suffers disproportionately physical, mental, emotional and financial ills. Suffering from those ills over a long period of time saps the group's strength as does the sufferings of a person with AIDS.

The group is too weak to fight back. Too weak to even be aware that it is dying. Some of the pronounced indications of its illnesses are:

1. Its reluctance to diagnose its own illnesses.
2. Its tendency to blame the members of the group for the illnesses.
3. Its hatred of its image—physical characteristics.
4. The physical murders of members by members of the group.
5. The political assassination of members of the group by members of the group.

Cultural "glue" was deliberately and artfully destroyed in the main by the American captors of Africans over a two-century period. The main neutralizing ingredient of the "glue" is described vividly by Dr. Kenneth Stampp in his monumental work, *The Peculiar Institution*, where he documents on page 145 that the African was made to feel that his physical characteristics were badges of degradation and his land of origin a "taint." Melville Herskovits, in his *The Myth of the African Past*, also describes in vivid and documented detail how the captive African was made to feel that he was a subhuman creature with no history in the land of his origin.

It is now "put-back" time. It is now re-creation of cultural "glue" (CG) time.

We have studied long and carefully the three-century road over which the destruction of the African American CG took place. We have studied those devices and techniques used by other groups to maintain, enrich and strengthen their CG. We have come to the conclusion that it is possible to gradually infuse within the African American community the all-important cultural "glue." It is possible to accomplish this within the next decade. By the year 2000 an appreciable amount may be created.

The creation of cultural "glue" (CG) can be achieved when over a period or time a relatively small group of us do the following:

1. Create drama for stage and screen (and television) showing the beauty, grandeur and sophistication of Songhai, West Africa.

2. Dramatize on stage and screen (and television) the greatness of African heroes.

3. Extend and strengthen the celebration of Kwanzaa—basically an African-set celebration.

4. Push for a form of meaningful reparations translating the funds therefrom into stage and screen (and television) dramatization.

5. Attack those dramatizations on stage, screen and television that tend to destroy the honoring of African ancestry, and which reinforce our illnesses and stereotypes.

The reason for the honoring of our African ancestry along with its rich history *in dramatic form is that it was precisely this route that our detractors took when destroying our cultural "glue." We must take the same route going the opposite way—the way of TRUTH.*

HISTORY AND ITS VALUE CONTINUES

"Why study modern history or any history at all?" Such a question is quite natural and right, on the part of the boy or girl who is confronted with an 800 page history book. It is a question that should be answered at the very outset, because no one can study any subject with much interest, or benefit unless he understands clearly just what it is that makes the subject worth studying.

Two of the greatest benefits that can be derived from the knowledge of history is not only the receiving of a better understanding of the present, but more importantly, that knowledge of history will provide the information with which to shape the *future.*

Place yourself in the position of a successful business man who, as a result of an accident, has a sudden loss of your memory. You would not know where your office is, nor how to get there. You would not know what successes you had achieved, what you are supposed to do today, nor how to plan for future successes. For all of your knowledge and experience would be entirely lost. You would have to start all over. You would not know the reasons for your present situation. You could not call on experience and knowledge to plan for a successful future. If your business rivals stole your records, they could tell you all kinds of falsehoods. This could reduce you to an impoverished, blubbering idiot. That condition is called amnesia. Amnesia is not just limited to individuals. A whole race can have amnesia. It is a truism that "History is to the human race, what memory is to the individual."

Let us elucidate a bit on the realm of *memory*.

There is a direct correlation between the knowledge of history of mankind and the memory of individuals. In February 1983, Newsweek Magazine published an article concerning the human brain. One of its main points was in the area of memory.

"Memory," the article said, "underlies the highest function of the brain, from multiplying two numbers to developing a sense of 'Self.' It lifts humans out of an eternity of unconnected moments to create a sense of continuity and unity with their past."

Memory of an individual explains what he is doing and why. The collective memory of a group of individuals explains what *they* are doing and why.

For example, we, African Americans kill each other daily over trivia at a rate so horrendous that it defies imagination—more than 1800 percent greater than any other race in America. Only knowledge of history can explain why we are immersed in this fraternal blood bath, and only knowledge of history can provide us with the means to stop the killings.

We must turn to corrective history for answers. Perhaps the following illustration will make this point clearer. If you were trying to invent a better type of motor car you would first of all want to know for what purpose each part of the mechanism had been designed; whether it worked well or badly and whether there were any parts that had once been useful, but were no longer needed. Similarly, we would be most unwise to question the present social and political institutions ignorantly and blindly. We would have to begin to turn back into the past, because the past has made the present what it is.

The Black man in America ridicules the time way back there by saying: "How much 'bread' does that get me or what has that got to do with now?"

Well, it is an undisputed fact that you must understand that the past is the present—that without that was, nothing is, that of the infinite dead, the living are but unimportant bits. Therefore, by arming ourselves with the heritage of some of the world's greatest thoughts of the past—that is, our past, the Black man can walk out of the four hundred years of white mental bondage, free at last. Free in mind, they can walk out of their slum ghetto of physical and mental prisons, free at last. Yes, ours is a noble history of people who built and led some of the world's highest civilizations, a people that brought to those civilizations a wisdom, a sense of justice and warm humanity that other races have often lacked.

DEFINITION OF CIVILIZATION FROM A HISTORICAL PERSPECTIVE

We feel that the African, himself, must define that which he was actually responsible for—that was civilization itself. This is most important because the powers of western civilization have proclaimed themselves as the forebearers of that institution called civilization. In so doing have convinced most of today's world that the African has virtually made little or no significant contributions.

The search of any large library will reveal ponderous tomes in treating the history of civilization, but strange enough, the authors of these voluminous works never tell us just what they mean by the word civilization.

We can always consult a dictionary where we are informed that civilization is a state of being civilized and/or organized and this is no doubt true, but it is not particularly enlightening. Therefore, we shall attempt to formulate a scientifically accurate definition of civilization.

We may begin by saying that civilization is a form of culture so it is first necessary to define culture. Speaking precisely, culture may be described as a patterned behavior. In other words, culture may be described as a patterned behavior in which the individual learns either through instruction or imitation, from other members of his social group. Culture consists of all forms of human behavior except those found among the apes. Among the forms of behavior common to men and ape are the following:

1. Impulses towards mating and parenthood (Refer to Session IV, Prefrontal Cortex Theory).

2. The impulses to play, hunt and explore.

3. Tendency to imitate and show off, to attack when angry and to take flight when frightened.

4. Desire for companionship.

The above are classified properly as noncultural activities. The forms of behavior specifically restricted to man are truly cultural activities and they are listed below.

1. Growing of crops.
2. Domestication of other animals.
3. Cooking
4. Weaving of clothes
5. Use of language, which may be defined as the expression of definite ideas by means of the larynx, lips, and tongue.

Now we are in a position to give an adequate definition of civilization for civilization is nothing more or less than literate culture, a bare definition will not help much, but the brief but brilliant explanation of the meaning of civilization from the pen of a distinguished social anthropologist is most illuminating:

"A society is civilized only if it contains scholars and scientists. The scholar consolidates and clarifies the knowledge which has already been acquired and hands it to the scientist who seeks to increase the knowledge."

The Belgium anthropologist, Emil Torday, in Volume 54 of *The Journal of the Royal Anthropological Institute* has noted that a piece of iron, possibly a tool, was found wedged in the masonry of the Great Pyramid of Egypt. Of this fact, we feel quite certain. J.A. Rogers, a member of the Paris Anthropological Society, when visiting Egypt some years ago climbed to the top of the Great Pyramid and he observed this fragment of iron lodged between two stone blocks of this great ancient structure. Iron tools were used by the ancient Egyptians in building the great Pyramid is stated as a fact by Herodotus. It may be to cite an English scholar "*as some indeed suspect that the science we see at the dawn of recorded history was not science at its dawn, but represents the remnants of the science of some great and yet some untraced civilization, until now. Where, however, is the seat of science to be located?*"[1]

---

1 Lord Raglan, *How Came Civilization*, p. 3-4.

History is a restorer of the truth. Like the roots of the tree, it must feed that tree with the waters of knowledge. PAFO's Chapter Four will give more in-depth information on the seat of civilization and will reveal the truth of the African woman and how it was she that laid the foundation of civilization.

Arthur Schomburg[2], the Sherlock Holmes of Black history, as he was called, said: "History must restore what our captivity took away, for it is the social damage of our captivity that the present generation must repair, and offset."

Let us, for a moment, impact on our being in captivity and what it took away from us as a people so that you may see the damage inflicted on us.

It was not just the restriction of our physical movements such as having to have permission to even see about a sick family member. (Very much like it is in the Republic of South Africa today.) We had to do each and every bidding of the captor such as to renounce indignation, love, anger, hate, sorrow over the death of loved ones that might have been beaten to death. They imposed on us the denunciation of our beautiful homeland and the concept of ourselves as human beings. We were made to automatically smile at all the tragedies that they inflicted on us. Swift and immediate brutal punishment was meted out to us if immediate obedience was not adhered to. This was done to instill fear in the other captives and to heighten respect for white authority. By forbidding us to mention anything about our homeland and glorious past, *the curtain of our past began to descend, especially as the newborn generation replaced the first captives. The mental violence in deed and in fact did irreparable damage to the psyche of so many of our people. Mental violence was so harsh and cruel that it wrenched the mind out of its cerebral sockets crushing the bones of beliefs and altering ethnic behavior patterns.*

In Kenneth Stampp's monumentally documented work on our captivity in his book *"The Peculiar Institution"* (page 145), he points out why the system of our captivity went to such extremes to blot from the memory of man our glorious past. There was a strong economically-based reason. Our fathers had revolted hundreds of times. They were fighting, "troublesome property."

We were on our way to fighting out of captivity by 1800. But the cap-

---

2 He was of Puerto Rican stock.

tors discovered to their joy that if they kept the children from knowing of our glorious African past they would cripple their minds with amnesia. The Bourbon South and their Northern industrial henchmen added the final crippling blow. They brainwashed the children into believing that their physical characteristics (our beautiful coloration, our full features, our hair; the only human hair on this planet) were badges of degradation."

Those children, brainwashed, grew up. They were docile, anti-African and pro-white. Gone was the family stability. Gone was the fuel for revolts. Gone was our love of Africa. Gone was our neurological stability.

The system in 1805 was saved temporarily in its physically and psychologically degrading form. Our fathers however, recovered somewhat fifty-eight years later and turned the tide of battle in the Civil War, winning the war for the North.

However, the psychological damage persists to this day, perhaps in a more deadly form.

To save us from historical oblivion is the reason for PAFO's existence.

PAFO views the history of our fatherland as the "cake" and the history of our great accomplishments in America merely as the "icing." But if there persists the brainwash that our African past was one of ignorance and savagery, then the "cake" is spoiled and we will discard everything—the "cake" and the "icing."

PAFO aims to help you, the student, to repair and offset the psychological damage our captivity wrought. Over the generations, the damage has intensified. Therefore, we think it is our bounden duty to immediately start the process of healing and repairing. That's why we agree with Thomas Huxley when he said, "Perhaps the most valuable result of all education is the ability to **make yourself** do the things you **have** to do when it ought to be done, whether you like it or not. It is the first lesson that ought to be learned; and however early a man's training begins, it is probably the last lesson that he learns thoroughly."

Another lesson was learned about two thousand years ago when the old Roman Empire was teetering on the brink of destruction. They came to Cicero and said, "Oh wise one, what must we do to preserve Rome?" After some reluctance on Cicero's part and beseeching by the Roman governing hierarchy, Cicero said, "In order to restore Rome to its former greatness, you must clean up the moral decay, and your children must be respected as children. Adults must take their rightful place because that is what made Rome great in the first place. We must teach our people they are a nation of winners. Do not talk of the defeats. We must glorify our ancestors and above all we must not let others write or paint us in a light that we would not want to be shown or known." He also added that, "There was very little that was more important than for any people to know their history, culture, traditions, and language; for without such knowledge one stands naked and defenseless before the world." This is why the late President of the U.S. John F. Kennedy agreed with and echoed Marcus Tullius Cicero.

Now that we have told you about our raison d'etre, we want to better prepare you for session III.

In order for you the reader to get a better understanding, we will acquaint you with the following.

There are several theories of evolution which attempt to explain how the various factors have worked together to produce the actual process of change. The principal theories are: (1) natural selection, (2) use and disuse, (3) mutation, (4) orthogenesis, (5) isolation, and (6) hybridization, and laws.

1. **Natural selection** was promulgated by Darwin and is also known as Darwinism. His theory is a matter of common observation that like produces like-that the offspring of most living things resemble their parents. We recognize that cats beget cats and not dogs; but if we examine a litter of kittens, we find that no two of them are exactly alike. In other words, they vary. Looking at the world around us, we notice that more plants and animals come into existence than can possibly survive; and that from this prodigality of nature there results a struggle for existence. In this struggle, the living forms best suited to the various environments in which they dwell will survive; all others will perish; this is to say, only the fittest will survive.

2. Next to Darwinism, the most famous explanation of evolution is **Larmarck's theory** of the inheritance of acquired characteristics, also known as the theory of use and disuse. In his first edition of his famous work, Lamarck expressed his theory in the form of two laws; and in the 1815 edition, the two laws were expanded into four.

3. Professor Hugo deVries is generally recognized as the father of the **mutation theory of evolution**, although the same principle was formulated independently by Professor Lester Ward. The mutationists

claim that evolution proceeds by sudden large changes rather than by gradual small ones.

4. The **theory of orthogenesis**, ably advocated by Professor Henry Osborn and Dr. Robert Broom, attributes purpose to the evolutionary process. The ortogeneticists believe that a mysterious life force permeates all living things, and causes them to evolve in certain predetermined directions.

5. The **theory of isolation** is based on the idea that, if a group of animals or plants of the same species are allowed to intermingle freely, there will be little or no variation away from the type; but if the larger groups are broken up into several smaller groups, and these are prevented from interbreeding, each group will vary in different directions.

6. In 1916, the Dutch biologist J.P. Lotsy wrote a book with the title What is a Species? in which he argued that evolutionary progress had been brought about largely by the crossing of species, and the resultant development of fertile hybrids.

1st Law: Life, through its own forces, continually tends to increase the volume of every body which possesses it, and to increase the size of its parts, up to a certain limit determined by life itself.

2nd Law: The production of a new organ in an animal body results from a new need supervening and continuing to make itself felt and from a new activity which this need arouses and maintains.

3rd Law: The development of organs and their functional capacities is constantly in ratio of the use which they receive.

4th Law: Everything which has been acquired, impressed upon, or changed in the organization of individuals during the course of their life, is preserved by generation, and transmitted to the offspring of those which have undergone the changes.

END OF SESSION II

SESSION III

WHITE RACISM—ANTHROPOLOGICAL DEVELOPMENT AND ITS EFFECT ON PEOPLE OF COLOR

The late brother, Doctor William Hansberry*, Louis Leaky and other top anthropologists of the world confirm that the oldest fossils of mankind were found in Africa. One of the principal digs is an area in South East Africa. This area is known as Ol'Duvai Gorge near Lake Victoria in East South East Africa (where Tanzania is today). It is in a strip of land on the coast of the Indian Ocean, two hundred miles in width and five hundred miles long.

The shadowy beginnings, but yet steady and slow advancement of mankind from Cambriam, Paleozoic, Mesozoic and Cenozoic eras, point to Africa as the greatest stimulation of Homo Sapiens. This greatest stimulation, which occurred in the Cenozoic era during the epoch called the Pleistocenic period, came about because the evolutionary processes were never slowed down in Africa, as in Asia and particularly in Europe. The oldest fossilized remains of human beings are found in Africa. By this evidence, we know that Mother Africa was the cradle of civilization.

Very briefly, we want to say that fossilized remains were considered the better way to trace the human tree. There were of course many unanswered questions, such as being reasonably sure that you had a human bone or a primate.

Radio carbon fourteen was one of the earlier methods used to determine the age of the fossil. Potassium—Argon later was used in the dating process of fossilized remains, and you must remember that the age

---

* See Hansberry in the Appendix entitled *The William Leo Hansberry Notebook*.

of the bones are very important to know.

Fortunately, bones are no longer the only evolutionary clues available.[3] In recent years, biochemists have learned to investigate human ancestry through living cells. By analyzing the DNA molecules of two animals and measuring the differences in the sequence of their components, they can gauge how long it has been since the two diverged from a common ancestor. DNA research has become the best hope for answering questions the bones have not.

According to the leading anthropologists, Ol'Duvai Gorge is a place in Tanzania, E.S.E. Africa, where nature preserved the remains of the most known direct line of "Mankind," millions of years ago, and we call him "Homo Habilis," or "Able Man." Before Homo Habilis, dating back approximately twenty-five million years ago, his ancestor was another creature known as Proconsul or Dryopithecus. He is considered the granddaddy of both ape and man.

This Proconsul line eventually produced, by way of mutation and selection, other ancestors of mankind, called Ramapathecus, Kenyapithecus and later, the Ethiopian ape-like men. The most important link of this evolutionary chain was Homo Habilis, who could make tools and build shelters. As he did these things, his brain enlarged a little. It is said, that these developments took millions of years, and as the brain enlarged, and the body evolved, a more direct progenitor known as Australopithecus evolved. Most anthropologists agree that Australopithecus dominated because of his ability to make weapons for his protection. Not having the predators' natural weapons such as teeth and claws for tearing, he had to develop tools and weapons. With weapons of stone he began evolving into a killer creature becoming carnivorous, and not a vegetarian, like the gorilla, monkey or other primates. Taking a good hard look at this subhuman at that time, he had the same thin lips, protruding large ears and straight hair as the ape or anthropoid. In Siberia, in 1961, substantial evidence was found in a chunk of ice, showing the physiognomy of Australopithecus, as he lived more than two million years ago, along with the mammoth and other prehistoric animals.

THE CHELLEAN AXE SCIENCE

The strip of land referred to above is conceded by all leading anthropologists as being the place man broke through his bestiality and

[3] *In Search of Eve—*. Rebecca L. Cann, professor of genetics at University of Hawaii at Manoa, in Honolulu.

became man, asking what only man asks, "Who am I"?, "From whence came I"? And "Whither go I"?

At this time in this strip of land in East South East Africa, called by Robert Ardrey in *African Genesis* as the "womb of all mankind," generally conceded ancestor of *all* mankind had all evolved to the same point. But over long millenniums some of the Australopithecine began trekking from the "womb." Thousands stayed but others thousands left, taking four paths from the "womb." These paths have been traced by a French scientist named Chellean.

What he did was to identify the main weapon of Australopithecus. It was the hand-axe chipped into a definite shape by the Dawn Man. As he wandered from the "womb", Australopithecus discarded some axes, dropped some fighting and lost others. Chellean traced four paths from the "womb" defined by these particularly shaped age-old axes. This method of tracing paths is called the Chellean Axe Science.

One of these paths Chellean traced led to Asia. Another path
led to Europe over what must have been a land-bridge across the Mediterranean Sea.

THE EFFECTS OF THE GLACIERS

In Europe the Australopithecine evolved gradually until the four great ice ages that swept down from the North Pole in three to four miles high ice sheets.

Each glacial period lasted tens of thousands of years followed by a gradual warming period lasting the next tens of thousands of years.

In the unbelievably numbing bitter cold of these glacial periods, Australopithecus, had no clothing, no fire and little shelter except mountain caves. The septum of his full African nose narrowed through natural selection. After all, the Arctic cold when breathed not warmed through a narrower and narrower pair of nostrils, the African lungs could not tolerate the icy air reaching it. Those fuller spaced nostrils gradually were *selected out*, and only those with the narrowed nostrils were left. The narrowed septum and nostrils today affects the speech of the descendants of the European Australopithecine. The speaking and singing voice is definitely nasal.

Other things happened to the European Dawn Man in the frigid wastes of Europe.

For one thing the numbing cold over tens of thousands of years slowed down evolution.

MUTATION AND NATURAL SELECTION IN EUROPE

Mutational changes slowed down in all living things in Europe's cold including man. We must understand what mutation is.

Mutational changes result from penetration of tiny radioactive particles into the reproductive mechanisms of living things. The particles come from nuclear fission. Our sun is a constantly exploding nuclear holocaust.

Inside the reproductive mechanism the particles wreak minor havoc among the orderly systems of reproduction determiners, altering forever the resultant offspring.

When the offspring emerges with its changes, physical, mental or both, its chance of survival depends on the environment. If the environment is gentle, thousands of the changelings survive to pass on those mutational changes. But, as in Europe, the environment was terribly hostile, few of the mutationally changed offspring survived. There was then but little mutational change during the Ice Age.

Another factor minimized mutational change in Europe. And that was the angle of the sun. The sun is a giant hydrogen bomb, raining radioactive particles over the entire solar system. As the result of ninety-four million miles of distance from the earth, the dispersal of the particles produce only tiny mutational changes called micro-mutations.[4] The rain of these particles decrease in intensity and number the further from the equator plants and animals are, because the energy directed from the sun is at a less and less direct angle.

Thus, the two factors, fewer radioactive particles from the sun and the intensely hostile environment slowed down mutational change of all plants and animals in the frozen glaciated continents of the north.

In Europe there was little speciation or changes of plants and animals.

The European Australopithecine were no exception. Caught in the four great glacial periods, these creatures who wandered to Europe with unevolved hair, profuseness of bodily hair, close-set eyes, large movable ears, thin lips, undeveloped buttock muscles, huge torsos and short legs, changed but little over the hundreds of thousands of years. Thus is the European today, changed but little from the Dawn man.

[4]Macro-mutations changes occur when there is a nearby nuclear explosion such as Hiroshima. Macro-mutations are big, sudden changes in the offspring such as two heads, six fingers on each hand, etc.

MUTATION AND NATURAL SELECTION IN AFRICA

The story differed widely in Africa. There, conditions were perfect for uninterrupted mutational change. The angle of the sun was direct and produced maximum numbers of particles to enter the reproductive mechanisms of plants and animals, insects, birds, and fish.

The climate and environment were salubrious, maximizing chances of survival of the changed offspring.

Thus, over the thousands of generations of micro-mutational changes, the *African Australopithecine changed dramatically in physical ways.

Where lived his first cousin the ape, early Dawn Man, Australopithecus, had scant protection for his body in the later African Homo Sapien.

According to some outstanding paleontologists there is no evidence that shows that true African Homo Sapien with his majesty of color, hair and superb athletic physique did not emerge prior to twenty thousand years ago. Thus, even under practically perfect climatic conditions, it took millions of years of straining for perfection to produce the truly evolved Homo Sapien, the unmixed Black man.

Let us examine some of the physical characteristics of ours which was the basic cause of our bondage and is today the cause of shame of too many of us who do not yet understand who we are.

HAIR

Let us look at hair under the microscope both literally and figuratively.

Straight hair is the hair of the ape, the cousin of Dawn Man, Australopithecus, and is called *unevolved* hair.

When that hair of the ape, the European or Asiatic is examined under the microscope it is seen to be cylindrical, and capable of absorbing water. It is soft and loose affording no protection to the scalp.

It is round cross-sectionally, because it emerges from a round hole in the scalp called a follicle.

Strangely enough, a baby of true Black parents while in its mother's womb has round follicles from which cylindrical or unevolved hair shafts emerge. Sometimes the unevolved hair persists many months

---

* Australopithecine — plural of Australopithecus

after birth (to the delight of uninformed parents). Gradually the follicle (the hole) squeezes out of round to an elliptical shape and the hair shaft undergoes a marvelous transformation. The new growth emerges from the elliptical hole or follicle as a ribbon. An oil-based chemical compound is fed to the shaft at the roots from the sebaceous gland and gradually the hair shafts evolve into a cloche-like protective covering for the most important part of the anatomy—the human brain. The human brain is the greatest accomplishment of all evolution of any species and thus requires the greatest protection.

The fact that true Africoid people are the *only* humans on the planet that have this maximal, protective covering for their brains is reason enough for us to presume the value placed on the African's brain by nature. Maximum protection equals maximum value in the evolutionary sense.

In addition, there is a portion of the brain not covered by the skull. It is, that part of the brain in all Homo Sapiens that grows down beyond the skull in the back of the cranium and is called the *medulla oblongata*, the small somewhat pyramidal last part of the vertebrate brain continuous posteriorly with the spinal cord.

It is very vulnerable to blows. It is especially vulnerable to a karate chop, except in evolved man, the true African. In the African man a muscle has evolved which overlays and protects the medulla. In the African woman there has evolved an especially strong and wiry hair (somewhat jocularly called the "Kitchen") which protects her medulla.

No other Homo Sapien has this special protection.

Our hair then goes through all stages from the ape-like unevolved hair. When it begins to evolve uninformed Black parents say, "Oh, it's going 'back'." Actually, it is going "forward." In this course we shall always refer to our hair as "evolved" or "human" hair.

When we look at "evolved" hair under the microscope we notice four things.

First, the hair, automatically as it evolves, begins to become alive and raise itself from the scalp. This forms a "halo" to affect a cushion against blows or falls. This arises from the chemical flowing from the sebaceous gland.

Secondly, to strengthen the cushion effect, the hair shaft automatically forms waves with a spring-like characteristic.

Thirdly, each hair shaft grows hooking tendrils on each side, hooking on to the adjacent hair shaft. This forms a woven halo to protect against penetration of objects which could penetrate the skull and damage the brain.

Fourthly, the shape of the hair shaft is not cylindrical, but ribbon or flat shaped. This provides for the ability to grow the tendrils for the weaving effect.

Those tendrils are so strong in truly evolved hair that the teeth of ordinary combs will break when attempts are made to destroy the tendrils by combing through the hair. Strictly speaking our hair should not be combed.

2. Protection Against Head Lice

There is a head louse against which there is absolute protection when our hair is not too unevolved. That louse is known scientifically as the genus *Mallophaga* that infests the heads of non-African haired peoples. Even our Puerto Rican brothers and sisters are infected by this louse dubbed in street-talk as "cooties."

Schools, even as recently as this *current* year, are being closed because of the infestation of the *Mallophaga*, in non-Black children. Newspaper articles suggesting the medicines to buy to control the infestation are constantly being written.

They tell us that the agonizing bites of the lice, tear the hairs from the heads and eyebrows on non-Africans. Curiously enough, the African-American, even if exposed, doesn't become infested.

Hospitals, in areas of cities that treat white human derelicts use Black nurses to tend the white alcoholics who are brought in for treatment. It is the *evolved hair* that keeps the louse out of our scalps.

A Reason For Evolved Hair

True Black men with evolved hair must have been mighty few twenty thousand years ago, and only in Africa, where mutation never slowed down. Where mutational change is protective to the species, as is evolved hair, selection for protection increases geometrically. Today, Africoid hair has increased to more than seven percent of world population.

However, we must not forget why hair is on the head in the first place. Protection! And nature went *all out* to protect the African brain. Could it be that nature is trying to tell us something?

A strange-looking brother said to me once, "One day, when we have shed our brainwash, have shed the foreign religions of Islam and Christianity, pure light will emanate from our children's head." I had never seen him before and have never seen him since.

Could it be that he was trying to tell us something about our brain's evolution?

BACKGROUND OF THE BRAINWASH AGAINST AFRICAN PEOPLES

Webster:

"Brainwash"—1: a forcible indoctrination to induce someone to give up basic political, social, or religious beliefs and attitudes and to accept contrasting regimented ideas. 2: persuasion by propaganda or salesmanship.

The rich plantation owners of the Old South had a communication system to keep each other abreast of techniques to control our father and mothers. Their troublesome captives fought like tigers to be free, spilling their blood in a torrential stream for us, their descendants. The communication system among the rich planters was in three publications, *The Farmers' Register, The Southern Planter and The Southern Cultivator* so found Kenneth Stampp, in his meticulously documented book, *The Peculiar Institution*. Kenneth Stampp is the University of Southern California's Department of History head.* They exchanged information in these publications over the generations on how to control us and the society-at-large.

They, the planters, had to do something to suppress the ever-occurring armed rebellions of our fathers, the strikes, the sabotage of farm machinery, the thousands of fires, and work stoppages.

The planters had to do something to suppress the rising abolitionists' movement.

The planters had to preserve and extend the most profitable venture in history—our captive and forced labor.

They did.

They brainwashed the total society, including millions of our fathers and mothers.

They made the total society believe that our physical characteristics were badges of degradation—our hair was bad, our color, they made us believe, was wrong and our features, the society and we were conditioned to believe, were terrible.

They made the whole society believe that we deserved the brutality we received.

*Published 1956

We still believe it and so does the rest of the society.

The rejection of us by all of us is fundamentally based on hair, color and features, added to the conditioned belief that we ancestrally came from a primitive barbaric existence.

That is why PAFO is going to great lengths to explain the facts about our physical characteristics and African cultures—to get this "monkey" off our backs.

The rejection by us and the rest of the society (whites) of our physical characteristics is just one reason we are despised by all of us. The other reason as pointed out by Stampp is the belief by all of us that our fathers and mothers came from a primitive, jungle-like existence.

These twin brainwashes are the root causes of racism. That is why we are going into fine detail about them to free first, our minds, because, if the mind is not freed, the whole person is in psychological chains.

So that we can observe from a closer point in time for better understanding let us look at what these twin brainwashes have done to us since the Emancipation Proclamation. Then we can go on with the discussion of our physical characteristics.

After the so-called Emancipation Proclamation, Black people thought their former condition was eradicated. All of the various jobs, obstacles that they ran into such as jim-crowism, segregation, low paying jobs, lynchings, just to mention a few, would someday be overcome. What took the place of chattel bondage, was economic enslavement and its many spinoffs. Social scientists, who have studied the race problem here in America, have all concluded, that the basic cause is the result of a white racist society. According to Knowles and Prewitt, in their book *Institutional Racism in America,* the analysis of the delivery of benefits (although never equitably distributed in any society of Europe) discloses that those benefits invariably are slotted *overwhelmingly* in favor of whites. The Kerner Report reinforces Knowles and Prewitt.

But this is only one of the thousand manifestations or symptoms of THE PROBLEM. THE PROBLEM: i.e. (Programmed contempt of the African's intrinsic worth) is traceable to a book written in 1795 at the University of Gottingen in Germany by a so-called authority on race named Johann Friedrich Blumenbach. In his book (De Generis Humani Varietate Nativa) he stated that the white or Caucasian was the first and most beautiful and talented race from which all the others had degenerated to become Chinese, Negroes, etc. Blumenbach included Egyptians among his Caucasians. The "Negro" as a degenerate "non-human" was immediately seized upon by Europeans and racist America to justify their brutalization of Africans. Gottingen created the myths that provided the intellectual framework for later slanted and distorted research. THIS IS HOW THE PROBLEM AROSE AND FLOURISHED FOR ALMOST TWO HUNDRED YEARS.

Let's look at the bottom line of how the sickness of racism is fueled. The fuel that is used to perpetuate racism is based on a diabolical myth appertaining to Black people's anthropology and their ancestral homeland (Africa). In short, these whites, either directly by inference, by innuendo and any other method have said African Americans are part ape or three-fifths of a human. The subconscious of all has been inundated by this doctrine, especially in America. This is the justification by which they legally and illegally murder, plus all other indignities that we suffer as a people.

We are depicted as misfits of society (except the few that perhaps may be in sports, certain few politicians may escape, and of course, those of us in the entertainment world). However, even these are not solely exempt unless they dance to their tune.

We (of PAFO) believe there is great hope of solving the problem through deprogramming the entire society.

How we are attempting to do this is through positive imagery. That's why our family produced the video called, *The Songhai Princess*.

Positive stories about the grandeur of Africa and its inhabitants at this time is the only equal counter that will neutralize the Willie Horton syndrome. (It was illegal to single out any one race in such a paid for advertisement to buy votes). Of course, you still have negative imagery in various Black shows.

It seems to us that if the problem is concededly a white problem then the searchlight should be turned on whites. Another spinoff of white racism is median income that has been steadily widening over the decades, even though the educational gap has been steadily decreasing. The percentage of the gap from 1970 to 1980 has widened to forty-eight percent according to a study by Wattenberg and Scanmon in *Commentary Magazine*.

SOCIAL DARWINISM AND WHY THE INHUMANENESS OF WHITES

We Blacks have tried every conceivable avenue that we thought would work to change our condition for the better. The basic reason for failure is that the "Seven Veils of Illusion" do not deal with the root cause. The Seven Veils of Illusion are education, economics, laws, politics, housing, jobs and time. Undergirding this basic reason for Black failure in a white racist society is the lack of knowledge of first the all-important "Corrected History," and secondly physical anthropology; for without this knowledge we never will learn the *name of the game.* Rooted in the historical approach of "Why the inhumaneness of whites" which includes their greediness, selfishness, and sadistic tendencies is that ingenious version of the rationale for extermination of pigmented peoples by non-pigmented people best known as "Social Darwinism."

Social Darwinism extended the biological evolutionary process and natural selection to a struggle between different races, and in that conflict, so goes the theory, the stronger more advanced and more civilized, would naturally triumph over the inferior, weaker, backward and uncivilized" peoples. Knowles and Prewitt come close in directing the searchlight to "why," but fall short in explaining that type of thinking in the first place. We will venture two major hypotheses.

The first is based on the impoverishment of European soil through many millennia of glaciers that scraped away fertile top-soil.

The geologists tell us that as late as 40,000 years ago a glacier covered Europe, destroying most top soil, trees, and root systems. Then during the warmer periods (inter-glacials) dawn-men of Europe (Australopithecus) came down out of the caves of mountains and over the millennia of the inter-glacial periods developed a survival pattern that persists to this day. This survival pattern, deeply ingrained, expressed itself in ways including but not limited to the following because of the lack of natural resources. The impoverishment of the soil and hostility of climate spun off (1) Extreme acquisitiveness of the Europeans, (2) Eternal warring on each other, (3) Super-exploitation of the few natural resources, (4) Seeking of new sources.

Secondly, let's take a look at how climatic and environmental conditions pervade the psyche. Let's look at the Chinese whose environment was much friendlier than the Europeans'. For centuries they had invented and used what is now called gun powder for fireworks and other festive occasions, but never used it for killing. In a short time after the Europeans were introduced to it, they found a way to use it as a destructive weapon.

The same thing happened when they learned the art of melting iron ore and the art of sailing, from Africans. Europeans used these new discoveries to acquire control over other continents of these indigenous people. In 1591, Europeans formed an alliance with the mixed North Africans (Moors) and attacked the highly developed and rich Songhai Empire in trans-Sahara West Africa, with the gun, which was the ultimate weapon of that day.

According to the Research Task Force of the Black Learning Centers of Philadelphia, Pennsylvania, its Historical Review of November 1973 chronicled the following (summarization):

(1) At midpoint of the time elapsing from the European Expansion (mid sixteenth century) to the present shows that in terms of percentage of world population, Europeans and their descendants in whatever part of the globe constitute only 20% of the world population. (2) Europeans and their migrant descendants have been involved directly in the slaughter of ninety-five million human beings out of a total of one hundred and twenty-five million humans who have been killed. (3) Europeans and their migrant descendants have not only physically slaughtered 75% of the total slaughtered, but in addition have destroyed every other culture into which they have come in to contact and controlled.

The question arises whether or not this pre-disposition to kill is genetic or whether it is a European-enculturated proclivity (bent, disposition or inclination). There have been advanced at least four theories on this question. The final resolution will determine the course of action of eighty percent of the people of this planet. If there is some uncontrollable genetic, inborn inherent tendency to murder humans, then the method of self-protection of the other 80% is clear, Europeans must be annihilated. If this proclivity to murder is not inborn, then there must evolve some change method, such as disarming, plus psychotherapy, on a mass basis.

Scholars are fairly evenly divided among the four theories. There are two theories supporting the approach that the European's proclivity for human murder is non-genetic, (i.e. enculturated) and two supporting that it is an inborn (genetic) trait.

The following two support enculturation.

THE SINGLE BONE THEORY

This theory is that because of scarcity of natural resources of Europe, the few arable land plots and the few hunting ranges all led to fierce fighting for control. This fighting persisted over thousands of centuries.

In the book *Barbaric Europe*, published by Time & Life Publishers, 1973, chapters are spent documenting the historical fact that the *"European Society was organized for the one aim of making warfare* (P. 16)."

This constant warfare over the centuries led to the unquestioned superiority of Europeans in the art of killing other human beings. This absolute concentration on the honing of the skill in murder, explains the advancement of weaponry of murder by the white race over the races who were concentrating in areas of cultures and science for enhancement of the quality of human life.

Coupled with the highly developed art of mass murder were the unfulfilled needs of the Europeans from their impoverished continent. This coupling effect led to the destruction of Africans, East Indians, American Indians, peoples of Australia and other islands of the sea as they, the Europeans, bled the natural resources of those lands and carried those resources back to their impoverished people.

In order to make some kind of rationalization with their so-called Judeo-Christian ethic, many excuses had to be invented to explain away their habit of mass murder, their blood thirstiness. Terms were invented such as "Manifest Destiny," "European Westward" or "Settling the West," "Saving the World for Democracy," "Stopping Communism" and one projected by the most advanced Europeans in their slaughter of twelve million in gas ovens was called the *"Ultimate Solution."*

THE CRESS THEORY

The second theory supporting enculturation is one advanced by the former Howard University psychology professor Dr. Frances Cress Welsing in her book, *The Cress Theory of Color Confrontation.*

This theory says in capsulized form that:

Skin pigmentation is normal for humans. The Europeans, upon coming into contact with pigmented peoples, recognized their own abnormalcy. They therefore projected their own feelings of inferiority onto the people they really regarded as superior. They reinforced their projection to the ultimate, by attempting to wipe out (murder) the object of their projection of their own inferiority.

The other portion of the Cress Theory states that Europeans were frightened upon realizing that not only were they physically inferior (non-pigmented) but also numerically inferior (out-numbered). This raised anxiety levels to uncontrollable heights and resulted in mass slaughter of people of the world in order to psychologically reaffirm some degree of self-assurance. This is much like a person who kills out of a fear-craze.

THE GENETIC THEORY OF THE DAWN MAN SYNDROME [5]

The third theory states that the proclivity of Europeans (and Euro-Americans) to kill is inborn and is the result in the European and their migrant descendants of lack of evolutionary development. It is called the "Dawn Man Syndrome." In short, the Dawn Man Syndrome states that the European is the undeveloped Dawn Man, (evolutionarily speaking), whose hunting and killing instincts are uncontrollable through long bloody centuries of genetic compounding, aided by technology. The Recapitulation Science[6] shows that Dawn Man, Australopithecus or some off-shoot, was non-pigmented with loose, straight hair, profuse bodily hair, large protruding ears that could wiggle, thin lips, close-set eyes, undeveloped buttock muscles and short legs.

Dawn Man became a meat eater by necessity, most likely because desiccation (drying up) of the forest world from which he originally came.[6] He first hunted for food, and meat to be eaten on the spot. His developed brain led him to hunt and kill for meat supply for storage to be eaten in the future. The killing for food was *later* extended to killing for control of *hunting ranges* that led to *genetic selection* of the best hunters and killers, coupled with natural selection. The Dawn Man Syndrome catches up all of these impulses in the white man that is based on his inborn, inherent tendency to murder other human beings.

THE PRE-FRONTAL CORTEX THEORY

The fourth theory is that promulgated by the National Institute of Mental Health (N.I.M.H.) which also implies that the impulses of the European to murder is genetic. We call the observations of the N.I.M.H. the "Pre-Frontal Cortex Theory."

Its observation is based on the fact that *homo sapien* has three brains inside his cranium. Note that all of mankind are *Homo Sapiens*, which is the single surviving specie of the genus HOMO and of the primate family *hominidae* to which we belong. The Latin words "Homo Sapien" means man, the wise. The oldest of these three brains is called the *old*

---

5 Horite—Read Genesis Chapter 36 (Bible). Horite and or Troglodyte was a high anthropoid dwelling in caves. E'sau of the Bible went up in Mt. Seir and dwelt among them. Consult older dictionaries.

6 see PAFO's evolutionary chart pertaining to the Miocene.

mammalian brain that controls reflexes such as breathing and heart beat. The next oldest is the *new mammalian brain*, which is the center of specie preservation.

One component of the *new mammalian brain* controls the areas of the mating instinct. Another component is that which controls the impulses for the protection of the females and the young. The specie preservation switchboard center is controlled by the *new mammalian brain.*

It goes into operation also when two mammals of the same specie are fighting. When one is losing, an impulse in his brain forces him to signal defeat to the winner. The wolf's or dog's signal is to throw over his hind leg, exposing his unprotected belly. In the wolf or dog, this signal triggers the new mammalian brain of the winner, and the winner must stop the fight before the death of the loser. Thus, this acts towards preserving the species. In man, the signal is to put up his hands.

However, even though this specie preservation instinct in the new mammalian brain is present in all men, in most men, a short circuit takes place by the pre-frontal cortex.

This portion of the brain composed of gray cells on the outside the largest portion of the total brain called the cerebrum is known as the pre-frontal cortex. If spread out, it would look like a gray sheet about an eighth of an inch thick about the size of a newspaper tabloid sheet.

It is the center of abstract thinking, *envisioning* the finished product, the center of creative thinking, mathematical reasoning, cold and logical, incapable of impulses of warmth, compassion and love. It developed very recently in the evolution of man (Homo sapien) and is almost entirely absent in all other animals.

Since the newer brain is a product of relatively recent evolution, its synchronization or meshing rate with the new mammalian brain is also based on the evolutionary *stage of development of the particular race.*

Now the N.I.M.H. says that man's propensity to kill his own specie comes from the fact that no matter if the loser gives the winner the man-signal that he is defeated, the trigger mechanism in the new mammalian brain of the man holding the machine gun, *does not mesh with the pre-frontal cortex* and he pulls the trigger of the gun anyway.

Hence, in the Vietnam War, a Lieutenant Calley could murder babies, old men and helpless women who not only had their hands up in surrender, but were praying to him for mercy.

This did not trigger the mechanism in the new mammalian brain of the white leaders to stop the slaughter, so they kept on murdering anyway. This theory states fairly emphatically, that the retarded evolution of the European causes less synchronization, hence more murders. The unspeakable horror of the murder by the most advanced nation of the Europeans, the German nation, of twelve millions in the gas ovens of that nation speaks clearly to that point.

The tendency to kill others is evidenced by the Euro-American's preoccupation with capital punishment (killing) of African Americans. An example is told in this story. Our story starts in the House of Representatives in the state of Pennsylvania. A state representative (D) on April 25, 1973, delivered a speech on the floor of the State House during a debate on capital punishment House Bill 700. The speech was delivered by a Black man, David P. Richardson, Jr., representing the 201 legislative district of Philadelphia. Here are excerpts of that historical speech. "Mr. Chairman, I should like to quote from two eminent American citizens, Dr. Louis L. Knowles in the Doctorate of Ministry program at the University of Chicago and professor Kenneth Prewitt, associate professor of political science, University of Chicago, who, in their book *Institutional Racism In America*, page 58 and I quote; 'On page 77 they end their analysis of racism in the administration of justice in America with these words: *the cultural myopia of white society permeates our judicial system, making it inherently incapable of delivering justice to people of color*. Gentlemen, the hard cold facts, end product of the depth of racism has produced the statistics as quoted on page 132 of the international library of *Negro Life and History*—1969 year book, that of the 3,859 prisoners executed since 1930, 53.5 percent were Black. According to the United States Census of 1970, Blacks constitute twelve percent of the population and are convicted of sixteen percent of the crimes punishable by death as outlined by house bill 700. Then even assuming that those convictions were arrived at equitably, fairly, without bias, the bias of execution weighs 570% greater probability for execution of Blacks than for whites. The basic problem as pointed out in the report of the National Advisory Commission On Civil Disorders (March 1968) is white racism—individual and institutional....White racism is responsible for those conditions that lead to the crimes by Black people which you are anxious to punish. The pretex of the bill is thinly veiled. It is not to stop crime because *history* shows that capital punishment is not a deterrent, but a pretext to satisfy the blood lust of Europeans in America against Black people. In closing I would like to go back to the Mother country of America about a Queen of England, who had pick-pockets hung in the market square so people could watch. As you know this only increased the pick-pocketing, and also increased the crowds. In fact, those who came to watch would set it up for pick-pockets to pick their own pockets so they could watch other brutal inhumane hanging." Mr. Richardson voted, "no," on that bill. (Full speech is available upon request.)

PAFO tends to hold to Theory number one, which states that the European's proclivity for murder is enculturated because of the glacial impoverishment of Europe's soil. We therefore contend that white people can be trained to become humanistic and can be curbed from their propensity to kill with mass psycho-therapy.

Unfortunately, this sickness of the Europeans is infectious and has spread to us. Therefore, we should stop them from spreading their poison to us. This is why we continue to study these various sciences so we can better cope with Black survival.

RECAPITULATION SCIENCE

We mentioned this earlier in this chapter—the following will explain. The recapitulation science declares that the embryo of an animal, while in its developmental state before birth, and while in its mother's womb, goes through each and every stage of evolution that all of its ancestors had gone through all the way back to the primal cell, the amoeba. In Western culture, this idea was first propounded by Dr. Ernest Heinrich Haeckel (1834-1919), a great zoologist in Germany. What he didn't know was that his great works would prove *conclusively* that the disdained Black man is the farthest advanced of all mankind.

Dr. Haeckel, a disciple of Darwin, first advanced this idea as a theory. He kept and preserved in alcohol, human embryos and foeti that had aborted which were in various stages of gestational development. What he found, was that these various stages of development corresponded precisely with the various stages of development of *mankind* from the amoeba up to now, in evolutionary development.

However, it wasn't until the early 1960's that this theory was actually proven. It was proven by an experiment executed by Life Magazine.

The scientists connected with that periodical, inserted a tiny camera into the uterus of a pregnant woman, and it took photographs of the developing baby during the whole nine months. What these pictures

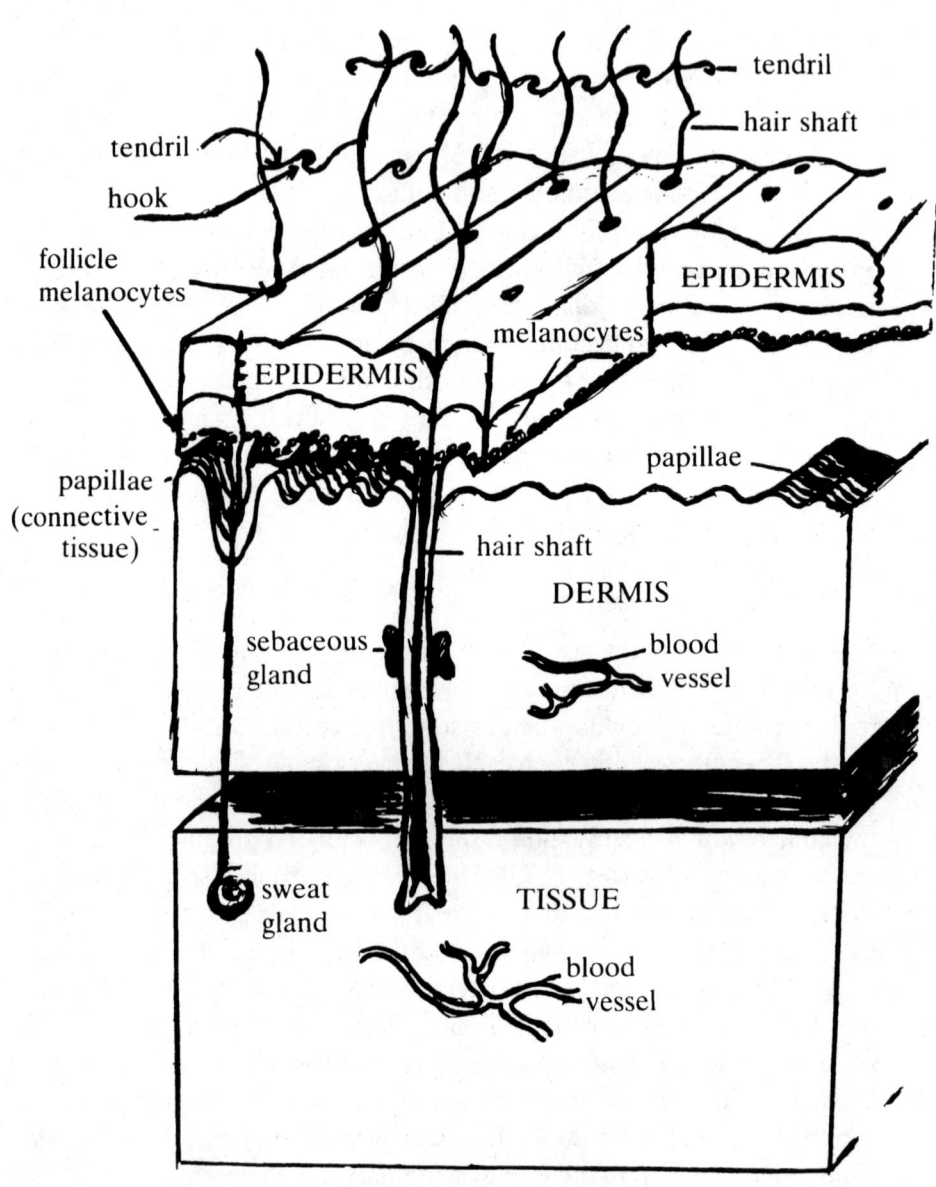

Cross-section of piece of human skin and scalp

showed in living colors was that the tiny baby goes through early first stages that man went through. It develops gills, then loses them, develops lungs while going through the amphibious stage, then finally develops the mammalian four chambered heart. The pictures showed the more than a billion year journey of man's evolution, encapsulated in a mere nine months.

The important thing for us to understand is that the pictures showed that at the eighth month in the mother's womb, the baby had reached Dawn Man's stage with unpigmented skin. *If there is hair before birth* it of course is straight or unevolved, and the buttock muscles are undeveloped. The most surprising thing to the scientists was that the eight month old foetus of Africans of pure blood was *white (unpigmented skin) with straight hair and undeveloped buttock muscles.*

We know just through our own observations, that many of our babies (Black) are born with Dawn Man characteristics, and do not acquire their richer pigmentation until *many months after birth.*

Inductive experimentation discloses that the ears are the earliest indications of the ultimate skin color of the child.

It is therefore proof positive, that the African foetus goes *through* the white, straight-haired stage on its evolutionary journey to *our more advanced stage. If* as white pseudo-scientists try to say that the white man is farther advanced, then by all scientific data, the *white foetus* would have to go through the Black-skinned, evolved hair stage that *it does not do.*

HAIR AND SKIN COLORS

On the page facing this is a drawing of the cross-sectional view of a tiny piece of scalp and skin magnified thousands of times, adapted from the World Book Encyclopedia.

Examine the pictures of the hair shafts and note the tendrils that hook onto each other that make for the weaving together of the hairs. This weaving is designed to impede penetration of objects into the scalp and brain.

Note the upright stance of the hair as it rises from the scalp in a wave-like shape to provide a springlike halo to protect the scalp and brain. Together with the tendrils, the upright, wave shape produces a *woven halo* of maximal protection.

The purer the African blood, the more tendrils per centimeter of length of hair, the more coil-like effect, the greater protection per centimeter of growth and thus the less need for long hair to achieve maximal protection.

The hair of the African automatically stops growing when it achieves the precisely correct length for maximum protection based on the closeness of the weaving effect and the strength of the hair coils.

The hair of the African is spaced between the shafts to provide ventilation for the scalp.

Note in the picture the location of the sebaceous glands on either side of the hair shaft. These glands supply oil for nourishment to the hair shaft, the oil moving up the hair shaft by capillary action.

We can help this flow by stimulation of the scalp through frequent brushing outward to the ends of the hair shaft. From time to time PAFO will supply to you information for proper care of your evolved hair.

WHY THE BRAIN IS SO WELL PROTECTED

One may wonder why the force of evolution went to such great lengths to protect the brain. The basic reason is because it is the quintessence of all evolution—the human brain. If man attempted to build a computer to even come close to the capacity of your brain, the huge conglomerate of tubes and wires, diodes and triodes, condensers and coils, transistors and resistors, would have to be housed in a huge building three square blocks in area, three stories high, and would need the waters of the Niagara Falls to cool the intense heat generated by it.

You can have substituted any organ in your body but the brain and you would still be you. You can have false hair, false teeth, false eyes, false or someone else's kidney, even someone else's heart and you would still be you. But substitute just one small part of your brain and you would lose your identity. Hence nature's forces of evolution housed this marvelous creation in a protective sac, floated it in a protective liquid to absorb damage jarring, covered it with a bony shield called a skull, covered the skull with a special rubbery mesh of tissues called a scalp then covered the scalp with hair. Evolution made a slight mistake by failing to cover the medulla oblongata with the skull. This portion of the brain controls respiration, circulation of the blood and digestion. But evolution corrected its mistake in the true African as set forth back on page 1 of this Session. First, nature caused the exposed medulla to be covered with a special set of muscles and fatty tissues. We call this the "medulla over-lay" because it lays over and covers the posterior end of that exposed portion of the brain. When you see an African, especially, those who are more fully evolved, one sees rolls of fatty tissue just above the collar at the back of the neck. This is not usually too visible in the less pigmented and of the younger African male; and of course the Orientals and the Europeans. However, in the older of the Orientals and some Europeans, mainly those involved in athletics, there may appear underdeveloped muscle tissue over their medulla.

Secondly, the forces of evolution made no error when it evolved the ultimate of hair to protect the African brain; the ultimate, beautiful hair of the African.

HAIR GLOSSINESS

Only animals and humans with animal or unevolved hair have shiny hair. The true African hair that is healthy is not glossy.

The unevolved hair is shiny, not because it is oily or even healthy, but because the outer layer of that type of hair, called the cuticle is made of tightly overlaid cells that overlay each other like scales on a fish. These cells reflect light just like the scales on a fish reflect light.

The true Africoid hair also has an outside cuticle, but the cells overlap loosely. Thus, light is not reflected but is absorbed between the overlapping cells. The light that is absorbed by the hair shaft sends vitamins to the inner core of the shaft aiding in keeping it alive and healthy.

However, our conditioned pre-occupation in trying to appear as Caucasoid as possible leads our unenlightened people to heavily grease their hair to artificially gain this glossiness. In addition, they use hot combs to burn the tendrils and kill the weaving effect as well as the spring effect preventing the protection of the brain. The heavy grease clogs up the interstices (openings) of the cells of the hair shaft's cuticle, preventing the absorption of the health-giving vitamins from the light.

The basic fact to remember about our hair is that the evolutionary forces producing our hair sought to afford maximum protection to the potentially most advanced organ ever produced by evolution—the African brain.

We also must remember that the unevolved hair of the ape is the same physically and chemically (by use of spectrum analysis) as the Europeans and the Orientals.

We must learn all about our physical characteristics in order to neutralize the three centuries of brainwash.

MERELY SAYING "BLACK IS BEAUTIFUL" IS MEANINGLESS WITHOUT KNOWLEDGE OF OUR HAIR, SKIN COLOR OUR FACIAL FEATURES AND OUR DEVELOPED GLUTEUS MAXIMUS (BUTTOCK MUSCLES).

SKIN COLOR

While the knowledge of the evolutionary superiority of evolved hair is important to have, the how and why of the various hues of skin color of Africans is fundamental to our regaining our personhood. Hair differentiation is easily masked, but not skin color. Hair! One can fry it, dye it or buy it—but not skin color.

It was on color that the European built a whole language for glorification of white and degradation of black, for reinforcement of a brainwash for control of us.

We must understand that only in the language of our chief oppressors, the English speaking peoples, is the color "black" a word of opprobrium (of absolute wrongness). In the English language we speak of "black sheep of the family," "Black Tuesday (stock market crashed," "black-ball (a negative ballot)," "black market, black magic, black character, devil's food cake (black or chocolate)." There are one hundred and twenty-three synonyms for "black" which are negative, and only one positive (the profit of a business).

On the other hand there are ninety-nine synonyms for "white" and all are positive: "fair, high character, honorable, angel food, white lie, virginal, chaste, sinless, etc."

The English language developed the greater number of these synonyms for "black" and "white" deliberately during the early years of our captivity.

While some may say that night is black and is equated with fear and negativeness, we are reminded that in Japan the highest honor in the art of karate is the Black Belt and it gets just as dark at night in Japan as in America.

It was not until our degradation in America that our color was a badge of degradation. Down through the ages our color was a badge of triumph. Over twenty-five hundred years ago, Herodotus, the Father of Western History remarked in his chronicles regarding his visit to cities in Africa that those people had skin the glorious colors of the setting sun and that "truly the very gods must have made their homes among the Africans."

The true Africans range in color from golden caramel *up to* the rich, bluish black.

For many years it has been known that rich pigmentation afforded absolute protection from agonizing and cancer-inducing sunburn, but it was not until the last decade that many investigators in separate studies found and are still finding an ever-lengthening list of advantages. Foremost among these investigators are the PAFO people. A group of investigators was an international team of European and Euro-Americans.

This team has been having biennial conferences for the past decade investigating the question of "Why Europeans did not have this evolutionary protection?" Out of such studies came the knowledge that aerosol expellants of such liquids as deodorants, insect repellents, etc., could pierce and destroy the ozone layer enveloping the earth.

This has frightened whites, because the ozone layer filters out much of the ultra violet rays of the sun. Whites get skin cancer now if exposed to too much of this particular radiation even when now it is mostly filtered by the ozone layer. This group of scientists found that if this protective ozone layer is even partially destroyed, whites would perish from mass skin cancer, while having virtually no effect upon pigmented people. That is why aerosol expellants are now being replaced by pump action expellants.

Their findings on a number of advantages of pigmentation are published in books kept at various libraries of the world in various languages. The books that the authors have studied are kept at Logan Square Free Library in Philadelphia. Their findings are included, *infra* (below in this book).

MELANIN

Melanin is a brown liquid chemical secreted from cells located in the epidermis of the skin giving color and protection to the skin.

If you scrape off some dead skin from the sole of your foot you will note it has a dead, lifeless, whitish gray color. There is no melanin to give those pieces of skin a look of life. In fact, there is very little melanin produced for the sole of the foot or the palm of the hand because the skin is highly specialized for thickening and toughness. The point here is merely to give you what color the skin is without melanin.

Look at the diagram on page 54. Note that the drawing of the highly magnified piece of scalp is divided into three layers. The two layers on top comprise the skin. The top layer is the *epidermis* or outside skin. Even though itself is very thin, there are microscopic layers of cells. The bottom layer of cells of the epidermis is made of cells called the *melanocytes*. Now here is a very curious point. The scientists say that *all races have the same abundance of melanocytes*. A logical question would be, "Then why don't all races produce an abundance of melanin?"

Many scientists say that in order for these cells to produce melanin and other pigments, there must be present a hormone and an enzyme. The *melanin stimulating hormone* (M S H), under the bitter cold of the glacial periods failed to fully evolve in both the Asians and the Europeans. But all races have the enzyme called *tyrosinase* which provides for the production of melanin for hair and eye-coloring only and not for full body production. The enzyme *tyrosinase*, acts as a catalyst which is produced by living cells. In chemistry, a catalyst is a substance which produces a chemical reaction without itself being permanently affected. (See *African Origin of Biological Psychiatry* Dr. Richard King, and *Melanin: The Chemical Key to Black Greatness* by Mr. Carol Barnes.

While melanin, fully developed, is a very deep color of brown, Africans have another protective agent that is yellowish in color that is reputed to be an excretion of the melanocytes but an earlier evolutionary development. The later development of the excretion included all of the advantages and then added on some other advantages with the most advanced deeper colored melanin. The earlier evolved excretion of the melanocytes, carotin, is the incomplete evolved melanin which the melanocyte cells of the Asiatic people excrete. What is amusing is the haughtiness of some poorly pigmented Black people who have only the carotid stage of melanin.

Again look at page 54. You should note that the melanocytes are like little factories producing a continuous stream of the chemical melanin.

Scientists are discovering more and more advantages of melanin. The more melanin (or richness of pigmentation), the greater the following advantages:

---

7 An internal secretion produced by the endocrine glands (ductless) of the body which exercise a specific stimulatory psysiological action on other tissues or organs. In this case, it is the melanocytes.

1. PROTECTION against aging.
2. PROTECTION against harmful radiations.
3. PROTECTION against air-borne abrasives.
4. PROTECTION against long immersion in water.
5. PROTECTION against harmful effects of cold.
6. QUICKER muscular responses.
7. BETTER sight.
8. INCREASED information from the environment or "Vibes."

ADVANTAGES OF MELANIN

1. PROTECTION AGAINST AGING

Aging is something that happens to all of us; a natural and so far irreversible process. Surprisingly, and despite the fact man has long attempted to retard the aging process through both science and superstition, it is only recently that aging as a biological phenomenon has gained widespread attention. Now it appears that Gerontology, the study of the aging process, is coming into its own as a field of medical research.

One of the more interesting investigations into the aging process and one of particular interest to Blacks, is being led by Dr. Leon M. Edelstein, Director of the Department of Dermatology and Dermato-Pathology, at the St. Vincent Hospital in Worcester, Massachusetts. For the past seven years, he has studied the possibility that melanin, the substance that colors the skin might be an age retardative.

"Up until recently, melanin had been thought to be a fairly inert pigment," says Dr. Edelstein, "and that it wasn't terribly important except for its ability to protect the skin from harmful effects of the sun, such as skin cancer or rapid aging. *Now people have gotten interested in melanin because the pigment can absorb a great deal of energy and yet not produce a tremendous amount of heat when it absorbs all of this energy.* Therefore, it's conceivable that it could be transforming this harmful energy into useful energy."

According to Dr. Edelstein, melanin can absorb tremendous quantities of energy of all kinds, including energy from sunlight, energy from X-ray machines that treat cancer, and energy that is formed within cells during the metabolism of cells. His theory is that melanin, in addition to its ability to neutralize the potentially harmful effects of these energies, might also be able to use them in a positive way—in slowing the aging process.

For instance, black and white mice are used in the experiments on aging conducted by Dr. Edelstein. Researchers have found that black mice are able to absorb large doses of Dopa (dihydroxyphenalanine), a substance causing the development of melanin, while white mice are adversely affected by the same substance.

Foods that provide essential ingredients for longevity are milk, beans, carrots, mushrooms, radishes, red wine, eggplant, and bananas, which release high levels of anti-oxidants and melanin when they break down chemically.

"*We feel very strongly* that because of the potential functions of melanin, individuals who have increased amounts of it within their cells have the potential to function more efficiently."

One of the obvious reasons why melanin retards aging is protection of the skin from wrinkling. This protection is afforded by the abundance of oil that melanin triggers from the body to rise to the skin and keep it from wrinkling. It is disheartening to see our sisters keep wiping this valuable oil from their skins, putting oil-soaking lotions and powder on their skin and *thus hastening wrinkling*.

Dr. Edward Robinson, Elaine Richardson, and Calvin Robinson's grandmother, a gorgeously richly pigmented lady, had fewer wrinkles at age ninety-one than those of us less richly pigmented descendants had at thirty years of age.

We must cease putting oil-drying alcohol and after-shave driers on our faces.

2. PROTECTION AGAINST HARMFUL RADIATION

We noted in an above section, the ability of melanin to absorb harmful radiation, and not only to absorb it, but to store and use its energy harmlessly. One radiation from the sun is ultra-violet rays in poorly pigmented people, agonizing sunburn and skin cancer. Because of melanin's ability to neutralize the harmful components of these rays into bodily energy, points up just a few characteristics of this marvelous chemical.

We note that white people seem to be developing many devices to produce year-round tanning of their skins. While we may say that imitation is the sincerest form of flattery, we must remember that tanning for whites is a status symbol. This symbolizes the appearance of the leisure class.

3. Protection Against Air-Borne Abrasives

Munitions manufacturers of gunpowder, noted during World War II that white workers had tremendous absenteeism and skin cancer, while having no such effect on Black workers. The same is true in plants that utilize large amounts of gypsum and asbestos. Sand whipping through the air in desert areas, causes the skin of whites to develop cancer, while the skin of Blacks remain unaffected.

4. Protection Against Harmful Effects of Cold Air

Melanin protects against frost bite, which if unattended, results in gangrene.

Dr. Edelstein, above, notes the ability of melanin to absorb large amounts of energy, stored to be released when harm threatens the skin.

The skin has tiny capillary openings covering the epidermis, hundreds in an area the size of a quarter. These openings are regulated by tiny muscles. They are there, not to protect the skin, but to keep the body's blood constant at 98.6 degrees.

When the weather is hot, the capillary muscles expand and open the capillaries to the outside to cool the blood.

When the weather is cold, the capillary muscles contract, to keep the blood away from the chilling weather and closer to the warming chemical furnace within our bodies.

This leaves the skin unprotected in non-pigmented peoples. But the combination of stored energy and the lubricating oil from the melanocytes goes far in protection of harmful frostbite.

A relative by marriage of PAFO's Robinson family, Dr. Herbert Frisby, a trained scientist and Arctic explorer uncovered the truth of who was the first man at the North Pole. He found and scientifically proved that it was an African American, Matthew Henson who trekked the Arctic wastes and planted the American flag at the exact point of the North Pole.

Matthew Henson went with Admiral Perry over the years from 1892 to 1909 and he, the only Black man in the party, suffered no frost bite. The reason the good Admiral was unable to make the last few miles was because he was incapacitated from—you guessed it—frost bite.

5. Protection Against Long Immersion in Water

Skin unprotected by melanin absorbs water and is damaged by long immersion.

Because of the continuous lubricating oil excretion of pigmented skin, as well as most likely the release of the stored energy, the pigmentation affords long-term protection against such immersion.

6. SPEEDIER MUSCULAR RESPONSE

For many years it was believed that the chemical, melanin, moved only outward to the surface of the skin.

Now, the scientists investigating this evolutionary advancement for skin protection find that the melanocytes, these little melanin producing factories, also send this chemical along the neural (nerve) and muscle-feeding channels.

In Dr. Edelstein's experiments at the Department of Dermatology and Dermato-Pathology at the St. Vincent Hospital in Worcester, Massachusetts, he found that "...individuals who have increased amounts of (melanin) within their cells, have the potential to function more efficiently. This is especially important in muscle cells and cells such as the cardiac muscles. It's conceivable that this may be in part one explanation for the remarkable physical ability of many Blacks.

7. MELANIN PRODUCES BETTER SIGHT

During World War II, a study was made in 1942 to determine what soldier groups should *man* the anti-aircraft guns, especially at night. Sharpness of sight, distance of sight and *depth* of sight were scientifically tested.

Not amazingly to us who know, these white doctors found that eye color made a marked difference, even among whites; the darker the eyes, the better the sight.

Amazingly, however, they found that Black soldiers, *even* with the *same* color of eyes as a brown eyed or black eyed white soldier, showed a *significancant superiority* over whites.

We must remember that the lens of the eyes are operated by muscles, and the melanin in these muscle cells make for more efficient precise "fine tuning" of these lenses, hence better sight of Black persons.

Consequently, anti-aircraft gunners stationed in Philadelphia, Pennsylvania and around the *world* were Black.

Especially is this ability most pronounced at night. We can see better at night and have less color blindness than whites, and not as susceptible to eye disease as they.

8. Melanin Provided Information to the Brain

The bio-scientists who were referred to above, have warned their white brothers about the danger of fluoro carbons destroying the ozone layer and thus causing mass skin cancer among whites. They also found in their experiments that what Black people call "vibes" results from the ability of the melanocyte to transmit certain positive or negative signals to the brain that is picked up from surrounding environment.

Using modern techniques of the electron-microscope, they discovered that a certain enzyme called *yalmum* within the melanocytes picked up the movement of a body near a richly pigmented person, or picked up negative or positive mental radiations from considerable distances and transmitted this information to the cerebrum to be interpreted there.

They discovered this by experimenting with a South American amphibious creature that had a large black pigment patch on his head and its long tongue could catch silently flying insects that were *behind* it. They surgically removed this patch of pigment and the creature could not catch enough insects to feed itself. As a matter of fact, the scientists had to feed him to keep him alive. Months later, nature restored th pigment and he finally could begin to adequately feed himself.

One final observation on melanin. Do not get confused with an oft-repeated myth that our rich color came from being under an African sun for thousands of years until the tanning became permanent. That is a myth.

Tanning comes from the *surface* of the epidermis becoming charred. Pigmentation comes from a chemical that is *within* the epidermis.

Pigmentation is the result of millions of years of evolution to this high point in that process.

Just remember that the Eskimo is brown-skinned!

FEATURES AND OTHER STRUCTURAL CHARACTERISTICS

The Nose

It was not been scientifically established that the broader flair nostrilled nose of the African enables us to breathe better.

What has been established is that there is no equal to the African in producing beautiful tones in speaking and singing.

The nose, mouth, throat and chest are the resonant chambers of the voice that is produced in the larynx and swells it to great proportion. The fuller the resonant chambers the more pleasing the tone.

The ancestor of all mankind, Australopithecus had the broad rich tone emanating from the full resonant chamber of the nose.

However, after many of them migrated to what is now called Europe, natural selection killed off *all* except those which had the *more* pinched noses. The reason is simple: The lungs of the Australopithecine developed originally in Africa, and were developed to receive only warm air.

The inside of the nose is lined with an abundance of blood vessels, carrying the heat from the internal furnace to warm the cold air being inhaled on its way to the lungs. The narrower the nostrils and the longer the passageway, the more the blood could warm the inhaled air. Wide nostrils were death in the bitter blasts over tens of thousands of years in three mile high seas of ice. Hence *nature selected* out those more adaptable to the Arctic environment, and marked for death those whose noses could not warm the icy air, thus leaving only those who produced the more pinched and longer noses.

And so these unclothed creatures, with no hearth to warm themselves, survived to beget the pinched-nose Europeans. The penalty paid is the nasal, unresonant tone of the Caucasians' speaking and singing voices.

In a sense, with their small resonant chambers, they are the "violins" in the stringed ensemble" of Homo Sapiens. The African is the "cello," which is a violin with full resonant chambers. And in a stringed ensemble you need *both* the violins and the cellos (which is short for *violoncellos*) to make beautiful music (If they only understood that).

Our full noses produced the "Voice of the century" Marion Andersons, our Paul Robesons, Leontyne Prices, Nat King Coles, and we could go on and on.

THE GLUTEUS MAXIMUS BUTTOCK MUSCLES AND THE LIPS

The Gluteus Maximus was not only a survival development when he hunted, but also a maneuverability when hunting and when he was the hunted. The buttock muscles development is in direct proportion to both running speed, jumping and maneuverability. It is most highly developed in the Africans.

LIPS

Dawn Man, Australopithecus, (meaning Southern ape-man) had thin lips like his cousin the ape. After the migrations over the hundreds of thousands of years of hundreds of thousands from Africa, the Australopithecine, caught in the glacial ages of Europe had their evolution slowed down and failed to evolve fuller lips, pigmentation and other advanced evolutionary characteristics.

Those Australopithecine who remained in Africa evolved fuller lips along with other advanced characteristics. The fuller lips came about this way based on inductive and deductive reasoning.

Lips are sex-readiness signals. During heightened sexual emotion, blood rushes to the various erotic parts of the body, one of which is the lip area, causing the lips to redden and swell. This signalled sex-readiness to potential sex partners from these *two* changes.

As pigmentation increased, however, the reddening was covered over in the African and the size of the lips only remained—the larger the size, the greater the readiness. The African females who developed this lip-sized signal to the greatest extent were most avidly pursued. Over the millennia, through natural selection in Africa, fuller lips became the standard of beauty.

European females do not consider themselves even dressed acceptably unless they brightly redden their lips, (the red for blood color).

Most, with ape-like thin lips paint the lips outside their natural lines to make them appear fuller and thus swelled with sexual desire.

IS EVOLUTION STILL GOING ON?

Of course it is. But it's so slow in Homo Sapiens, that it is imperceptible within a generation or two or three.

We have knowledge that in South Africa, the true Black Man is still evolving at a faster rate than any other portion of the human family. A quote from the New York Times and reprinted in Jet Magazine in 1958 "White South Africans Calls Black Man Superior"—White supremacists in South Africa were shocked to hear white scientists declare that Blacks are the most advanced type of humans. Addressing an exclusive Roadepoort Rotary Club, Dr. M.W. Jeffreys told his astonished listeners, "If you can swallow it, the Black people are the true humans and you are the unevolved specimen of an original white ancestor, primitive man. The Black Man is the newest species of man." To support his thesis of Black superiority, Dr. Jeffreys, a University of Witwatersand anthropologist, noted that (1) Gorillas have very thin lips and straight hair, (2) Whites have straight hair also and lips just a little fuller than the Gorilla, (3) that the Black Man has lips much fuller or larger (human) than both and no straight hair. (4) that the Black Man's heart is an improvement over that of the whites and other races as well. A large extra branch from the left coronary found in a number of examined Black people's heart provide a better blood supply, and probably accounts for relative infrequency of coronary thrombosis among these Blacks.

Whites are thick-skulled with heavy bones resembling earlier mammals. Blacks have thin skulls and slender bones, yet the bones of the Black man's are *stronger*. Another quote, this time from a Philadelphia, Pennsylvania newspaper the *Bulletin*, "In 1958, a team of anthropologists from Harvard University were puzzled because, at birth, the blood fat levels of Blacks and whites were seemingly identical. Yet on the average, a Black man's veins from age fifty-eight to seventy are supple and unchoked. Of course, this was before the dramatic change in the eating habits of Blacks. There were increased smoking habits, as well as the excessive intake of salt, sugar and alcoholic beverages. And this does not take into account the processed foods of which we have become addicted to; thus, cutting down our intake of fresh vegetables and fruits.

Yet even with this seemingly disregard for observing health rules, Blacks have less arteriosclerosis, while the whites' veins are choked and old usually starting before age forty.

THE BLOOD

It is generally known that the job of the blood is basically to carry nutrients to, and waste from all tissues of the body.

The blood is made up of cells and plasma; of which plasma is the fluid part of the blood or lymph without the corpuscles.

There are four classical blood groups: A-B-AB-O, of which is present in all homo sapiens. However, a new system called DIEGO, has been found in American Indians, Japanese, and Chinese. All three of these groups have arrived at the carotene stage, with the Indians being just past it.

Yet, there is a new antigen called Js, found in the Blood of Blacks in the year 1953. This is an independent system discovered by E. Giblett in 1958.

In 1979, according to the American Red Cross the valuable *U Negative blood* which has the absence of this antigen occurs only in the Black population as well as *Duffy A, Duffy B negative* and *JSB negative antigen*. (For further information contact ARC's Blood Services Penn-Jersey Region, Phila. PA). An antigen is a protein which stimulates the body to produce antibodies but which is not normally present in the body.

RH FACTOR

It is a substance in the red blood cells of most persons. Red blood cells that contain the Rh factor agglutinate (clump), if they come in contact with an antibody called *anti* Rh, this reaction can produce serious illness or death. Persons who have the Rh factor are *known as Rh Positive*. Those *lacking* it are *Rh Negative*. The Rh Factor was discovered in the Rhesus monkeys in 1940, and was named Rh for the monkey by Karl Landersteiner and Alexander Wiener. All races have the Rh Factor—even cattle, mules, horses, pigs, etc., but the purer the African blood, the Rh factor disappears.

In a later chapter, PAFO mentions the effect that pure African blood has on diseases such as gonorrhea and syphilis. The French explorer and medicine man Dr. Finot, and the missionary Dr. Livingston, upon examination and experimentation, had found that these two aforementioned diseases died out when it made contact with pure African blood.

There was a television series called "The Immortal," back in the late 1960's and early 1970's. It was about a man (white), whose blood was so powerfully endowed with special life giving elixirs, that if only a small amount of his blood were injected into a seriously ill or wounded person, almost immediately that person would start to heal.

Highly evolved pure African blood was in the veins of two Black brothers of Alabama. One brother was especially endowed, while the other brothers' blood was not quite as potent.

Jet Magazine of June 1967 on its cover, had this caption—"Man lies down on hospital table, gives a quart of blood worth 12,000 dollars."

On the inside pages, the story unfolds to the amazement of its readers, that the Lewis blood has the ability to immunize most people having various kinds of blood disorders and diseases. Some of these diseases include a disease derived from the Rh Factor called "erythroblastosis fetalis," Also, there were various kinds of anemia and hemophilia, not to mention an increased healing ability of flesh wounds, afforded by this marvelous blood.

PAFO is not trying to teach racial superiority, since in reality there is only one race, but we are only attempting to focus the searchlight of inquiry on the truth. The truth is that one segment of the human race may or may not develop more improved physical or mental attributes depending on the geographical location of each segment of the human race.

END OF SESSION III

The Great Hall of Columns in the Temple of Karnak

The Sphinx

The face of the Great Sphinx of Giza—one of the largest statues ever made—has the head of a Man and the Body of a Lion, symbolizing the triumph of the mind over Man's lower animal Nature.

SESSION IV

AFRICAN CONTRIBUTIONS AND THE EXISTING SOCIETIES—B.C.

As evolution continued, generally changing Australopithecine into Homo Sapiens, which really began before the Ice Age; we find a direct correlation between the evolving creatures and their migrations within Africa and into the other lands.

The four great rivers of Africa, in the early migrations of "Man," played a great part in determining the directions of those migrations. It was not until (man) had learned to store water before he could feel safe in leaving the fresh streams. The early Stone Age men of Kenya, Tanzania, Ethiopia and other early dawn men, lived for many hundreds of thousands of years within reach of the survival sources of both the Congo and the Nile. They fished and hunted along those streams for food and began widening the areas known to them. Often the search for food led them downstream, and new settlements in new areas were a result. In the course of hundreds of thousands of years through the migrations of short distance of thousands of Stone Age families, settlements had been made along all four major rivers, and the first movements of African Stone Age people into what is now known as Europe and Asia were taking place. As yet, there were no cities; no agricultural communities. The nomadic movement of hunting and fishing peoples continued for more than a million and a half years. Many migrated westward and found food along the rivers of Siberia and Russia, the Indus, the Tigris and the Euphrates. The geological readings indicate that the stone age inhabitants of East Africa were experiencing four major pluvials[1], the rest of the inhabited world was going through the

1 Floods of great magnitude

Ice Age and other climatical conditions. By this time, the African segment of Homo sapiens was moving toward mastery of the environment. His skills were more varied; he began to domesticate animals, to weave and to make pottery.

Community development began some 37,000 years B.C. at Jos Plateau, of what is now known as central Nigeria, in the Rift Valley of south central Africa near the great falls of Kalambo.

However, it was not until 6,000 B.C. that settled agricultural communities first appeared. Jericho was one of those first cities built in Asia Minor, in the valley of the river Jordan. Another was around Fayum Lake, near the Delta of the Nile River. The settled stone-age communities existed around 4,500 B.C.

Egyptian civilization developed as a result of the natural rich soil deposited by the overflow of the Nile. They found they could plant seeds, grow food and have a surplus. With a surplus of grain food, people came from surrounding areas, which developed a new kind of social relationship, with a division of labor and a new way of living, through the building of cities. As the communities grew, the people of the Nile developed a central government in the era 4,200 B.C. and thereby began the first 365 day solar, lunar and stellar calendars.[2]

Circa 3,000 B.C., the First Dynasty of Egyptian Pharaohs was founded by Menes. Five hundred years later, the surplus of wealth was so great, that Cheops built the Great Pyramid.

On this note of the Pyramid, let's consider this observation as quoted from PAFO's *Cultural Genesis*, (Chapter II).

The ancient civilization of Egypt, spread from south to north, and there is seemingly no doubt, that the earliest center of civilization in Africa (Al-kebu-lan) was the country watered by the upper Nile. The principal state of this Ethiopian country, bore the well known name of Meroe. The ground belief is that the civilization of Meroe precedes that of Egypt.

It is enough to say very briefly, that on the site of the city of Meroe, there exists remains of temples and pyramids from which archaeologists have drawn the conclusion that the pyramids were a form of architecture native to Meroe, and only afterward brought to perfection in Egypt. The carvings of the monuments of Meroe show a people in possession of the arts and luxuries of civilization, and having great knowledge of

---

2 John Jackson, *"Introduction to African History."*

science. On the base of one of the monuments, a zodiac has been found. This remarkable spot is regarded by the ancients as the cradle of the arts and science, where hieroglyphic writing was discovered, and where temples and pyramids had already sprung up, while Egypt still remained ignorant of their existence.

It was Meroe at that point in time that was chiefly responsible for the transmission of iron technologies to many cultures and other countries in Africa. The beautiful wrought iron grilles, balconies and gates of Charleston, South Carolina, Savannah, Georgia and New Orleans, Louisiana came to the United States by way of contemporary African nations who were the recipients of the knowledge from ancient Meroe.

To get the proper picture in timing these important events, we are looking at Meroe about 11,000 B.C. Other Ethiopian civilizations preceded Meroe, but we want you to know, that all of these people were Black people.

THE GREAT CONTRIBUTIONS OF AFRICAN WOMEN IN DEVELOPING CIVILIZATION

Pardon the seemingly redundancy of our digest for promulgating the intellectual prowess of our illustrious ancestors, but the truth must rise again.

We live in a world, today, which continues the gross distortions of science and the solutions of the problems of humanity. It is further implied, in this propaganda, of history that the problems experienced by Black people the world over, today, are due to some inherent inferiority of Black skin to deal seriously with the complex issues confronting contemporary civilizations or that they lack the capacity and determination to solve their social and intellectual problems.

Therefore, the central role of African people in the transition to modern society continues to be conspicuously absent from the history books. Under these circumstances, it is difficult to accept the fact that African people, in general, and Black women, in particular, have made an invaluable contribution to the development of contemporary civilization—in fact, laying the basis for it!

The basis for the future for African people can only be found in an accurate re-evaluation of the very beginnings of their past that had been established thousands of years ago by African women. More and more modern Egyptologists and anthropologists have increasingly taken the informed position that nothing new has been invented over the last ten thousand years of human history. What we are saying is that the scientific foundations for modern civilization had been established long before the coming into existence of European society. *These foundations were laid by African women thousands of years in a country now known as Egypt.*

Somewhere around 4,000 B.C., a people who became known as Egyptians burst upon the world stage. It is generally agreed by many writers, including us, that these Egyptian people had no uncivilized or primitive period in their history. Their appearance as a completely cultivated and highly technical people from the very beginning was at one time a major mystery of history. The noted Egyptologist E.A. Wallis Budge has stated that "We are to seek for the origin of Egyptian religion and especially of its central figure Osiris with his ritual of death and resurrection not in Asia, but in Africa (Alkebu-lan). I became convinced that a satisfactory explanation of the ancient Egyptian religion Aait (Maat) could only be obtained from the regions of the Sudan. Sudini beliefs are identical with those of ancient Egypt because the Egyptians were Africans and the modern people of the Sudan are Africans...Osiris was, we believe an African though not necessarily a nilotic god, and the birthplace of culture seems to have been the upper Nile." This is the region where the goddess Ater-Tshema-T was worshipped. *It is clear from Budge that the Egyptians were Africans and not eastern Semites nor extraterrestrials and that their greatness came from Southern Africa.*

Gerald Massey, one of England's greatest historians, tells us that the earliest wise men came from a place in southern Africa named Kent (Khentiu). This location is identified with the Egyptian goddess, Nekhbit, who came forth in the south and as such was the opener (organizer-ruler) of that region. She was also a goddess of the cardinal points that identifies her with what we now call the science of astronomy. Massey places Khent as being in the Great Lakes region of south central Africa near Uganda that he says was known as the inner land Ta-aakhu the feminine abode and the birthplace. All of this tells us that at the very beginning of the record of human achievement an African woman was a ruler-organizer-astronomer in the south near Uganda. *She is one of a long line of distinguished African women who would lead the travel of civilization from its southern origins until it arrived in the north in a land now known as Egypt.*

Contrary to a misconception that prevails in some quarter, these people were not always known as Egyptians. Massey states that among the Egyptians, there was an old record which listed thirty dynasties in one hundred and thirteen descents that lasted for 36,525 years. Before Meroe, about 10,500 years, the African Homo Sapiens was on the cusp of receiving melanin in abundance. He was in the process of evolving out of the carotine stage that visibly was noticed about thirty-seven thousand B.C. or 17,500 years before the melanin stage got fully underway.

The thirty dynasties were in three series. The first series of princes was that of the Auritate. The second was that of the Mestrateans and the third of the Egyptians.

These facts are significant in many ways for they seriously challenge the extraterrestrial interventions theory and at the same time they begin to lay a firm foundation for reexamining the role of Africa's daughters in the origin and spread of civilization. Egyptian historian Manetho has left a record which states that a race of demi-gods and kings ruled over Egypt before the unification under Menes. Sir Norman Locker indicates that a Black woman whose name was Hathor was originally a personification of the path of the sun. The names of these people were grafted into the religions of Christianity, Judaism and others. Many of Europe's scholars have commented on the character of this early society ruled by African women in southern Africa. After many years of study, A.H.L. Heeren formed the opinion that there did exist a time when this classic ground was the central point of civilization of the world. Also when its inhabitants must have possessed all that constitutes an opulent and mighty refined and cultivated nation. Agustus Le Piongeon writing on Ancient Egypt says "It seems to have burst upon us at once in the flower of its highest perfection." *This circumstance compels us to assume that the skill of these first artists of Egypt was a portion of that civilization which its first settlers brought with them when they relocated themselves in the Valley of the Nile.*

According to Massey, the first form of physical geography was founded on the female figure Gebit, the woman, and that the naming of the hinder thigh Khepesh. It was the sign of the constellation of the great mother was done by a people who lived far to the south of Egypt. In her form of Neith, she was the goddess of writing. Of all the early religious deities who came down the Nile River from the southern interior of Alkebu-lan none have had a greater impact on European history as the goddess Isis Ast ur-t-mut-neter. She makes her appearance at the very dawn of history as the perfect woman the personification of being brilliant, Black and beautiful in the fullest meaning of the terms. Budge gives a Greek translation of a poem of this great Black goddess: "I am Isis, the mistress of every land and I was taught by Hermes. I am she who governs the star Kuon the god Ast-Septit. I divided the earth from the heavens. I made manifest the paths of the stars. I prescribed the course of the sun and the moon...seshet."

In modern scientific terminology, persons who divide the earth from the heavens and make manifest the paths of the stars and prescribe the courses of the heavenly bodies, are known as astronomers.

These few lines hint at the scientific role played by African women from the most remote times. Budge writes that, "It is said that Isis discovered many medicines and the she was greatly skilled in the arts of physics...." On the racial identity of this great goddess, Budge states "...The legend which exists in Egyptian texts tells how the goddess, after she conceived Horus, retired to the swamps of the Delta and how being alone there she brought him forth...." In this, as in many other respects, tradition regarded Isis as an African woman. We believe that by now you may be aware that the female principle preceded the male. Africa's recognition of this important point clearly shows that Africans' regard for the woman is above all other nationalities and religious dogmas. Before the incursions, Africans had always prodigiously extolled their great sense of love for all of its citizenry irrespective of gender. The matrilineal system (Southern Cradle) is a clear expression of that deep sensitivity that ruled Africa.

Since the female principle preceded the male, one would expect a female measurer or layer out of the stars to have appeared before the male god Tooth. We find that as we go back in time, she was Ashen or Antes and sometimes, she was known as Sheshet. In Egyptian language, it means she was the goddess of writing, the original astronomer or mistress of the laying of that foundation. There was Tekhi, the goddess of months or the measurer of times. According to Massey, she was the registerer of the celestial chronology, and like the book of Enoch, the recorder of the luminaries of heaven together with their generations, classes, periods, powers and names. It has been clearly established that about six thousand years ago, there was a mass movement of Black people bringing civilization up from southern Africa. G. Michanowsky tells us that about 4,000 B.C. there was a gigantic stellar explosion or supernova in the southern constellation Vela. Cyril

Fagan records that the first point of Aries retrograded into the thirtieth degree of the constellation Taurus in 4,152 B.C. Victor Clube and Bill Napier, have concluded that it appears that they were once a part of a single gigantic object ten to 20,000 years ago which underwent a series of disintegrations.

These events from deep in space may have been the signal for the death of one age and the birth of another. There was, they reasoned, a way to be certain. They must move to a part of Africa that afforded an unobstructed view of the heavens above and the horizon on earth. They began to construct land—telescopes now known as temples to provide precise measurements of the positions of the heavenly bodies. This meant a move into the barren ground of lower Egypt. It is certain that the coming of the second sun (supernova) and the appearance of the cosmic serpent was responsible for the building of so many temple observatories and pyramid observatories along the Nile River from sixteen to thirty degrees north latitude. The Greeks called the land Agyptus; the Romans latinized it and called it Egypt. The Black people who lived there called it Kemit and Ta Mera. They drew the land as a right triangle of thirty-six, fifty-four and ninety degrees. This right triangle allowed them to calculate in terms of half degrees all of the trigonometric functions of angles between zero and thirty-six degrees. Livio C. Stecchini says that since the angles of thirty-six degrees is two-fifths of a right angle and one-tenth of a full circle, these astronomer-priestesses could calculate the trigonometric functions for all angles. The ancient Egyptian astronomer-priestess used the obelisk to calculate the polar and equatorial circumference of the earth to a high degree of accuracy. These world wide geographical calculations were done under the goddess Neigh. She was the goddess of weaving who in an esoteric way represented the calculating of latitudes and longitudes. Her sacred city is Sais. A much later time in Egyptian history, about twenty-seven hundred years ago, Sais became the capitol of Egypt. When the great goddess Isis and Neith ruled supreme, there in her temple was carved the words "I'm all that was is and yet to come." In the Fourth Century, the so-called Church Universal (Catholic) through Constantine and later on by Theodosius I and the Emperor Justinian switched the color of the Madonna and Child to white. In the process, they corrupted the Holy African Cross that was a symbol for the temple of Sais by hanging people on it. Neigh's sacred city of Sais that housed the cross represented the geometric calculations chiefly during the overflowing of the Nile very early in Egypt's history. It was also representative of the human figure.

Massey states that the Typhonians[3] who were the most learned of Egypt and the builders of the pyramid were acquainted with the real length of the cycle of precession of the Equinox and that they discovered the motion of the apsides or longer sides of the earth's orbit. Moses Cotsworth says that they could measure the length of a year to 365.24219 of a day. Early African people expressed many of their views about the universal forces (NTU) in terms of the mysterious marvels of the female principle.

Walis Budge said, "When male is replaced with female, it relates the Maat principle in dealing with celestial math calculations." This means that the female principle is the one that reckons in heaven the counter of the star Urshu, the enumerator of the earth and the measurer of the earth. Her knowledge and power of calculations measured out the heavens and planned the earth and everything which is in them. This African goddess was also a part of those who invented astronomy and astrology, the science of numbers, mathematics, land surveying, medicine and botany. Liveo Stecchini says that in the reign of these astronomer-priestesses that they analyzed curves by dividing the area under a curve into a series of rectangles that is the basic principle of integral calculus. It appears that in analyzing the curvature of the earth, they used rectangles six feet wide; and this was thousands of years before Isaac Newton or Gottfried Leibniz appeared on the scene.

According to Herodotus, two Black women are credited with being the founders of Delphi and Dodona in Greece. They would use an abacus type of device for calculating in terms of trigonometric angles. In order to obtain the right lengths of the second and minute of the sidereal time, one must take as reference a degree of latitude further north than Egypt. The degrees at the latitudes of Dodona and Delphi provided the correct values.

After successfully establishing both research centers in Greece, these early African female scientists began to instruct Greek females in techniques of ancient Egypt's sacred mathematical and astronomical sciences. This would be the beginnings of the *Oracles of Dodona and Delphi*.

Let it be known that long before this knowledge from Egypt could

---

3 Astronomer-Priestess

become part of Greece's consciousness, there had to be years and years of a series of indoctrinations. The Greeks were barbaric and totally ignorant of any type of civilization except the law of the jungle. Space and time would not permit us to tell how difficult it was to get through the wall of mental stolidity.

Therefore, it was very necessary to use a form of superstition based in mythical fables and the claps of thunder. Finally, the subconscious was able to translate portions of this knowledge to be absorbed on the conscious level.

Democritus is supposed to be the first to formulate the atomic theory but modern research causes us to seriously question this. Higgins writes, "We are also told by Demetrius, in his treatise on succession that Democritus travelled to Egypt for the purpose of his education and received the instruction of the priests. We also learned from Diogene and Herodotus that he spent five years under the instruction of the Egyptian priests and that after the completion of his education he wrote a treatise on the sacred characters of Meroe."

Based on the information here, it is quite apparent that Black Africa is not only the "Cradle of Civilization," but African women were its founders and leaders. This was during an era in which terrestrial movement controlled the existence of enlightened people. At that time, Black women, as scientists were revered even more than men but only for those particular endowments. Before the onslaught of the incursions into Africa, African men and women enjoyed the bliss of the highest obtainable level of a social relationship. It was the effect of the incursions to a good degree that began the relegation of African women to positions of less importance. Yet it never sank to the level of other countries that restrain their women from scientific or other endeavors, including politics.

We aforementioned that Egypt's first dynasty was organized by Menes, a little more than five thousand years ago. However, Egypt had more than sixty kings prior to Menes, which was during the period Egypt was divided into two or more kingdoms. However, it seems that the dynasties weren't counted until Menes made Egypt one kingdom. The forerunners of these great Africans that spawned such great civilizations were none other than the Twa people, also known as Pygmies.

Somewhere between the building of the "Great Pyramid" and the rise of the great empire of Meroe, the Sphinx was built some thousands of years before the pyramids.

An early great African, Imhotep, was a scientist, architect and medical genius. Imhotep lived during the third dynasty and was worshipped as a god in Greece for three thousand years. He, along with other great Africans, promulgated the concept of the ancient African-Life Forces—Philosophy of all peoples "Oneness," and their unity with the forces of the natural world. In this philosophy, ancient Africans scientifically concluded that all things are made up of "energy," (not solid matter). This was millenniums before Caucasian physicists laboriously decided that a solid piece of steel is simply tiny spinning bits of energy with spaces in between.

It was **Imhotep** 4,600 years ago, and **not** the much later Hippocrates 2,300 years ago, who was the **father of scientific medicine**. The very symbol of medicine used today (the intertwined serpent surmounted by the winged sun), is African. Of Africa's fifty countries, Egypt only, has been accorded detailed study and honor by white historians. They tried to brainwash us into believing that the Egyptians were white, or as they called Indo-Europeans.

Ancient Africans gave the world, the first alphabet, as well as the system of units of measure and balances that we use today. Carpentry was transformed during the Bronze Age when many metal techniques developed to high levels such as casting, welding, soldering, and riveting, just to mention a few.

African contributions include the chisel, saw, hammer, wheel and many other tools and items. In the literary world, Africa led the way. The proverbs of Pathhotep appeared 2,000 years before the Book of Proverbs appeared in the Old Testament Bible. Lyric poetry was inscribed on walls within the pyramids. Epic poetry, commemorating events and the lives of ancient African kings were written. In 2100 B.C., short stories were written in Africa. There was *The Shipwrecked Sailor, The Tale of Two Brothers, The Eloquent Peasant* and many more. To the chagrin of some white people, Europe itself was named after a beautiful Black princess named Europa. Her father, Agenor, was a Carthegenian/Phoenician. Carthage was where Hannibal, that great general came from.

In Karnak, Egypt, stands the great temple of Amen. Karnak[4] is one of the architectural wonders of the world. There are eighty thousand

---

4 Karnak-Arabienaive (African name IPET ISUT = the holiest of places)

statues, 140 gigantic, decorated columns supporting a solid granite roof. The main temple is a thousand feet long and three hundred feet wide. In the words of one of our mothers, Queen Hatshepsut:

> "You who shall see these mountains in later years, and shall speak of my works, you will say we did not know it was possible to make a mountain of gold. To aid them, I gave them bushel after bushel of gold as if it were sacks of grain...for Karnak is heaven's image on earth."

(Nefertari-Ahmes, a Kushite was the grandmother of this queen)

Kush eventually conquered Egypt in 720 B.C. With the discovery of smelting iron, mankind buried the Stone Age. Black Kush raised Africa out of the Stone Age with their techniques, processes, arts and crafts. Their descendants spread over Africa, especially to the region known in our time as the Western Sudan, from which we here in America mainly come. Some of the outstanding families that later left Egypt and came to the Sudan, were the Dogans, the Bozo and the Minianka. This happened around the fifteenth century. They refused to stay in Egypt because the Islamic religion was being forced on them as well as Christendom. They preferred the religious concepts of our ancient fathers and mothers as any good indigenous African might do. A later session tells about the great knowledge they brought to the Western Sudan with them.

THE CARTESIAN THEORY[5]

A student of comparative history can see without difficulty that various people scattered all over the world often develop similar institutions without ever having had any contacts whatsoever. This is equally true of the most isolated groups. Similar circumstances may produce similar ideas and culture patterns—all of which may confirm the Cartesian theory about the equal distribution of common sense among all mankind. By simply "doing what comes naturally," one society may evolve a life system not unlike another society ten thousand miles away across distant oceans. Therefore, neither the "External Influence" theory nor that of the common origin of a widely segmented people should be hastily affirmed. We hold this to be true even in the study of one race in the generally same environment of one continent. The evidence must still be conclusive.

---

5 Descartes, Rene—1596-1650. A philosopher, mathematician and scientist. Many scholars considered him the father of modern philosophy. His philosophy became known as the Cartesian Philosophy.

Origin of African Democracy

The foregoing observations suggest that the Constitution of any people or nation, written or unwritten, derives from its customary rules of life, and that what we now call "democracy" was generally the earliest system among various peoples throughout the ancient world. What was a relatively new development, was absolute monarchy.

Among the Blacks, democratic institutions evolved and functioned in a socio-economic and political system that Western writers call "Stateless societies" or "Societies without chiefs." When these societies were referred to as "primitive" democracies, the writers are in fact doing the very opposite of what they intended. Because, far from being just a descriptive term for backward peoples, "primitive" also means "the first, " the beginners. Moreover, many of these "stateless societies" were states in fact without necessarily conforming to a predetermined Western structural pattern of a state. Indeed, what is called a "stateless society" in African would hardly be classified as such in the West, for the Western definition of a state does not include the requirements of one man as its executive head—a state being any collection of people occupying a given territory, and living under their own government independently of external control.

These facts are set forth at the outset because both the constitutional system and its offspring, African democracy, originated in "chiefless societies." And, what is even more significant, democracy reached its highest development here where the people actually governed themselves without chiefs, where self-government was a way of life, and "law and order" were taken for granted.

The basic structural outline of these states remained the same throughout Africa. There were the usual variations and exceptions. The amazing thing was and is the uniformity—amazing how the most basic elements of ancient Black civilization could have been held on to, continent-wide, by all of these dispersed and isolated groups in spite of the continuing impact of unimaginable forces of destruction.

The lineage ties and responsibilities and the age-grade or age-set system were the earliest institutions through which the African constitution functioned, and out of which its democracy was born. It was a network of kinsmen, and alleged kinsmen, all of whom descended from the same ancestor or related ancestors. All men live in the same community or state, but they were often scattered far and near in separate and independent societies.

The ancestor from whom they claimed descent was always "great" because of some outstanding deed or extraordinary achievements. These generally grew in magnitude as time and the generations passed, thus causing the true achievements to be overlaid by the false claims growing out of praise songs. Each generation of poets and storytellers gave the imagination full range in romantic glory. Myths were born in this manner, and the later concepts of both royalty and divinity gained support from the same source. In contiguous independent chiefdoms the lineage was the powerful factor in providing the basis and incentive for the later formation of kingdoms and empires. No people in African history used the concept of kinship ties more effectively than the Lunda in the remarkable expansion of their empire. Even more remarkable than the territorial expansion of the Lunda empire was their idea of a nation as one big brotherhood. Accordingly, instead of first attempting to conquer and annex by force, they would approach independent states and seek to demonstrate from oral history that all of them were merely segments of a common lineage—all brothers in fact. It appears that the majority of states believed in the principle of a common ancestry and readily became members of the empire; some required more facts before they were convinced; still others were not convinced or preferred to remain separate and independent anyway. These were generally conquered and given a lower status in the nation than those who united voluntarily.

We are considering lineage before the rise of kingdoms and in particular, the lineage as the governing and organizing force in states without chiefs or kings, where community consensus was the supreme law that anyone could ignore only at his peril.

There were interesting aspects to the many situations where a large number of these chiefless states were scattered over a wide territory, each independent of the others, yet all fully aware (and unlike those in Lundaland, had to be convinced) that they belonged to a common lineage. Kinship found expression in trade and in temporary confederations when attacked by external foes (those not considered to be members of their lineage).

There were quarrels and warfare between these member states of the common lineage. The highly humane aspect of African warfare that puzzled many Western visitors doubtlessly developed from the widespread recognition of lineage or kinship ties. For in the much heralded "tribal wars" the main objective was to overcome or frighten away the adversary not to kill at all if it could be avoided. Hence, the hideous masks and blood-curdling screams as they charged. Even when the enemy was defeated or completely surrounded, escape routes were provided, the victors pretending not to be aware of them. Indeed, there are reports of "rest periods," called when neither side seemed to be winning. At such times the warriors on both sides might meet at the nearest stream to refresh themselves, kid each other, and laugh at each other's jokes until the drums, gongs or trumpets sounded for the resumption of the battle. This was traditional Africa. How did it change to warfare to kill each other, lineage or no lineage? How did it happen that even now in our modern and "advanced" civilization some of the most murderous and inhuman of wars are fought by Blacks against Blacks? This is because of our decreasing concept that we are in fact one people? It's quite clear that in early Africa "war" was not much more than a frightful game when among themselves. Was the radical change brought about by the death-dealing incursions from Asia and Europe? Yes, because those incursions were designed to eventually rob Africans of their land. This raises other questions of great urgency: Are they really civilized today? Have they not substituted the trappings of civilization—our triumphs in science, technology, and the computer "revolution"—for civilization itself?

Suffice it is to say here that the steady weakening of lineage ties and its spirit of unity was also a weakening in sense of brotherhood and unity among the Blacks. Today it really finds little expression except in various language or tribal groups, and they maintain it more and more as a cohesive force to be used against all others.

Lineage, then, was the most powerful and effective force for unity and stability in early Africa, and this was so true, that a state could be self-governed without the need for any one individual ruler, chief or king. Everyone was a lawyer because just about everyone knew the customary laws. Therefore we were a nation governed by laws.

We know that the big question in your minds is how did all of this change? Was the death dealing incursions from Asia and Europe responsible, or was the African himself the cause of his own downfall?

There are many reasons for the downfall of the African. But, by far, the most devastating was the Euro-Asian and Arabic invasions, along with their brand of religions.

Unmistakenly, Africans were not the root cause of their downfall. When we analyze the development of the minds of mankind as a whole we find that nature, and geography had the final say.

Checking back in Session III, we find that those Australopithecine that went into Asia and Europe had a very difficult time to survive. Over the millennia of the glacial period they had developed an extremely high degree of acquisitiveness and aggressiveness. This acquisitiveness and aggressiveness was in the direction of constantly making war because of Europe being so impoverished and a scarcity of food during the Ice Age. The Ice Age also scarred Asia, but was not as devastating as it was in Europe.

The Asian incursion into Africa began in pre-historic times for the subjugation of the whole race and continent. Then came the Arab hordes who are white people, the so called Semitic division of Caucasian and are blood brothers of the Jews. Then the Romans started the destruction on North Africa (Carthage) in 146 B.C. However, when we speak of the destruction of North Africa, we are talking about the change over from a black population to an Arab and Berber population. The mixed breeds mainly mulattos, (also called Almoravids) along with the Berbers, by the seventeenth century had changed North Africa from Blackamoor to Moors. They, like the Europeans, contrived to exterminate, subjugate, and take over Black Africa. This is why we say that this mentality evolved out of the difficulty of survival during the Ice Age. It seems to have made all other nationalities develop a *far reaching* plan to ensure the survival and power position of their unborn generations. Their pretense of loyalty and friendship to Blacks when Blacks were in power proved then and as now, to be our undoing.

Contrary to the Arabs, whites, Berbers and Asians who were part of the Australopithecus who were caught in the grip of the Ice Age, only those that remained in Africa developed away from the killing instinct and extreme acquisitiveness. The African environment, as opposed to the Asian and especially the European environment, was not hostile for survival. Fruits and vegetables were considerably plentiful and with the African development of agriculture, it gave us time to think and plan for civilization. We developed a spiritual resilience and trust in mankind because we subconsciously feel that other races are like our own.

As a people (probably because of the lack of this particular knowledge) we don't realize that Asians, but whites especially, are not nearly developed spiritually as Blacks. The hundreds of unending killings and warfare penetrated deep into the psyche of Europeans to give him the kind of mind he has today. Likewise, the Black man's psyche on the whole, so far, has not coped with white treachery. We always feel that he will change, and as a result Blacks always wind up behind the snowball.

Since the mid-Sixteenth Century and up until recently there has been an intensification of physical external forces against Black Africa causing mass migrations of the peoples of the smaller African states and the splitting up of the people in the larger states. This became possible because of superior weaponry. As a result, the take-over of the reigns of civilization through the blocking out of African's accomplishments made almost total conquest easier. It is no wonder that Blacks are bewildered on their own history because the Arabic and European names then, as well as now, used by Blacks causes confusion. Remember, the Arab was just as big a slaver as his European counterpart. Therefore, Black Africans should get away from using any names except Black Africans (check Session X). We are confused on the color of the Pharaohs, because of the amalgamation, the Christian and Islamic brotherhood myths. Blotting Blacks out of history was easy since the takeover, and with just a wave of the pen, black Hamites, and even Cushites like the Egyptian are no longer African. They carefully catalogue African history in such a way that a history becomes the history of the Arabs and Europeans. The American History Association says the first period is from the fall of the Roman empire to (700 A.D.). The second period of African History is the period of Arab invasions and Islamic civilization (700 A.D. to the coming of the Europeans in 1500). The European period from 1500 to 1960 is subdivided in 1880 to mark the period of colonialism, and from the White viewpoint, there is no Black civilization. Before their first classification, the American History Association eliminated four thousand years of Black African civilization, and if you please, all of this was done under the heading of African History. As you can see in just this very brief sketch the European, Arab, and Asian death-dealing incursion caused Africans to forget the kind of democracy and lineage concepts that were traditionally African. PAFO says all Black-*MINDED* Africans no matter where they live in the world should return to the African MAAT concept of Black religion.

Note: Consult *Destruction of Black Civilization*, by Chancellor Williams.

END OF SESSION IV

DR. JOSEPH S. CROOM, Founder of the 20th Century Bible Research School of Theology. He was a great inspiration in the very early years of the authors.

"Lord give us men in the image and likeness of God.
Men of pure hearts and clean hands, and not men of fraud:
Men who love liberty and will fight to win.
Who will dare and die and their lives gladly spend—
　　　Lord give us men!"

From the poetic pen of J.S. Croom

WESTERN SUDAN STATES EARLY ELEVENTH CENTURY

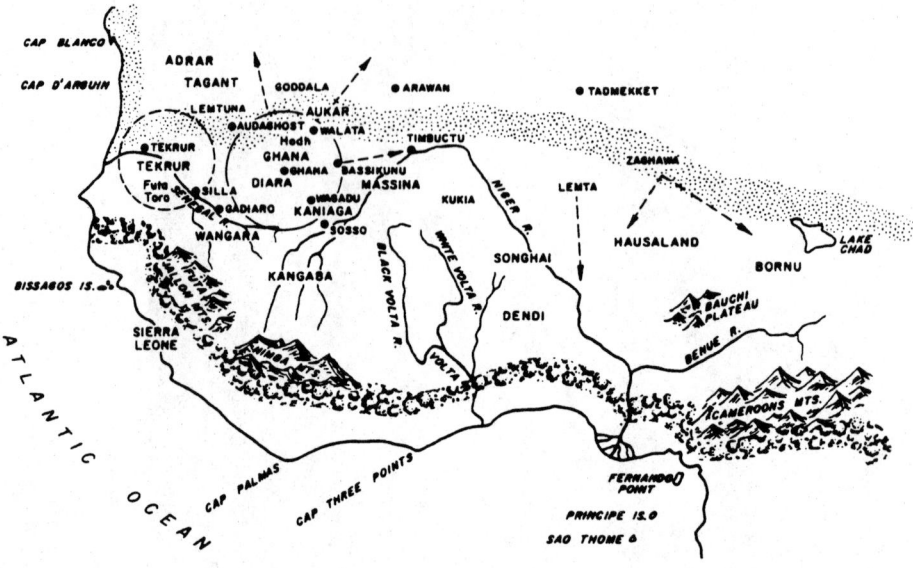

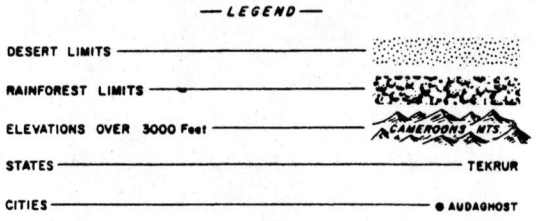

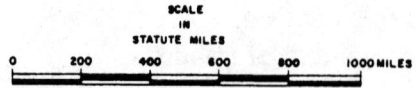

SESSION V

THE DEVELOPMENT OF THE WESTERN SUDAN

PRE-GHANA
What eventually became Ghana was first ruled by the Berber Dynasty. The Berbers, nomadic, fierce desert tribesmen were from the northern part of Africa. Finally, about 732 A.D., local rule returned to the Soninke people, when warriors of the Sosse clan executed a successful revolt against the Berber Dynasty.
GHANA (300 A.D. - 1100 A.D.);
    Control extending from the Senegal River to the Upper Niger River.

I. CLANS—Great families linked to one another, finally growing powerful enough to wage war and expand into empires. African nations are comprised of a confederation of many clans.

II. NATIONS—A consolidation of clans. ("Tribe" has been used in a manner that diminishes the magnitude of the consolidation, so we must use "nation" instead of "tribe" when referring to our history).

III. POLITICAL ORGANIZATION (Development of)
    A. The empire was divided into provinces
        1. The Upper Niger and Upper Senegal regions were those provinces. The conquered areas were controlled by allowing the conquered king to be a puppet, king, etc.
    B. Governmental Organization and Resources:
        1. Judicial System:
           a. Lower Court
           b. Higher Court
           c. Supreme Court
           d. Religious Freedom

C. Principle of Succession:
   When the king died, the heir to the throne was his sister's son. This was know as the matrilineal system.
D. The *king* was commander-in-chief.
   (An Arab scholar, El-Bekri, wrote that the king could put 200,000 warriors, with more than 40,000 being archers, on the front within 48 hours).
E. Economy
   1. Agriculture: cotton, sorghum, millet
   2. Mining: gold, salt
   3. Barter: Trade was the life blood of this early civilization. The exchange of such Ghanaian goods such as cotton, for metal ornaments, leather goods, plus all types of foodstuff which Ghana did not raise.
F. Religion:
   1. Songs, prayers, dances of observances.
   2. Belief in a creator who caused all things, and that the magic power from this creator could be used for good or evil.
   3. Belief in lesser gods.
   4. Priests were the religious specialists. (See Legend of magicians or those who made Ouagadou Bida intercessions).
   5. From 900 to 1000 A.D. the Islamic religion grew in importance to Ghana. Along with Islam, came the Arabic language.
G. Education:
   Generally various groups trained children in the specialty of the particular group. This was very effective in the Ghanaian highly organized society.
H. Written Language:
   1. It was not until about 733 A.D. that the intrusion of the Moslem faith brought the Arabic language to Ghana. Probably had this not happened there would not have been any preservation of the Ghana Empire on record. However, there were written languages before the Arabic language that West Africans had used. But here again the incursions were hindering factors.
IV. GHANA'S FALL
The leader Abu Bakr hammered at the gates of Koumbi, in an attempt to capture Ghana. King Bassi and his successor, Tenka Menin held out

for about ten years (1106 to 1077). The city was finally destroyed.

Although the Almoravid destroyed the power of Ghana, after Abu Bakr's death, their power fell apart, and in the break-up of the Ghana empire many states broke away, one of which was Mali. In one last desperate attempt to recreate Ghana, a powerful King of the southern branch of the Soninkes attempted to reestablish Ghana around the city of Sosso.

The King, Sumanguru, a member of the Keitee Clan, reconquered Ghana but the kingdom only lasted for five years. In 1235, he was defeated by the forces of a rising new power headed by Sundiata, meaning "hungering lion," a Prince of the Keitee clan, and a member of Mali, (a Mandingo Kingdom).

Sundiata's lion-like determination is what earned him his metaphorical name, "Hungering Lion."

When he was born, he had an affliction that rendered him a cripple. This affliction is credited with saving his life. His life was spared, when a brainwashed King of Ghana sought to eliminate all newly born male children in the kingdom. Prophesy had it that the King of Ghana would be replaced by a strong young prince. His army lieutenants fanned out through the country side, to kill children two years and under. When the King himself saw this crippled child, his heart had pity on him. He simply could not conceive how a cripple could ever be a threat to him.

As time went on, the child's parents sent out a call for doctors to try and cure him, but to no avail did that pursuit pay off. After Sundiata was about four or five years of age, he made a vow that he would cure himself.

Enduring excruciating pain in his attempt to walk, he finally was able to walk, he finally was able to walk a little with the aid of a cane. Each day, week and month he became stronger. He became an expert swordsman and about the age of fourteen or fifteen he fled Ghana. He developed and built a well trained army and returned to Ghana to drive out the brainwashed King. He did much to heal the old wounds by laying the proper spiritual foundation. He believed in the kinship ties of all African people as being "one" people just as the great Lunda people did.

MALI'S RISE

Sundiata never knew defeat because after defeating the Sosso, it left Mali as the most powerful state in the Western Sudan. He left the job of extending the boundaries of the new Malian Empire to his many followers, and some of the generals of his army. Sundiata devoted his attention toward laying a firm foundation on which Mali could grow and prosper.

To digress for a moment: Pan African Federation Organization endeavors to lay a firm foundation to not just build an organization but to build a nation. (See succeeding chapter for details).

Sundiata moved his capital from Kangaba to Niani (Ne-ah-nee) the city of his birth. He worked to reestablish the all important central government that would provide peace and order throughout the empire. He regained control of the gold fields of Wangara, also the restoration of the important salt trade. Next, the all important agricultural industry had to be fully developed, realizing no empire could be powerful if it couldn't feed its people.

Mali became one of the richest farming regions in all West Africa. Sundiata directed Mali towards the road to power and prosperity.

END OF SESSION V

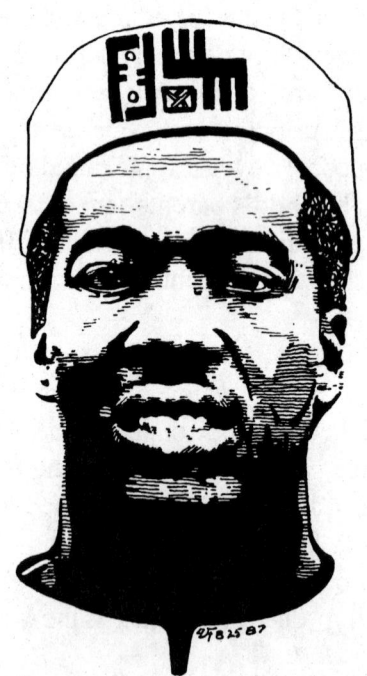

Sundiata King of Mali defeated Sumanguru of Ghana in 1235 A.D. Sundiata means "Hungering lion." He was afflicted as a child. His indomitable courage to overcome his affliction earned him that name.

SESSION VI

SAGA OF THE MANSAS AND THE FAMOUS HAJJ

After Sundiata's rule, his successors proceeded to establish one of the greatest states that Africa had ever known. The rulers took the proud title of Mansa—which means emperor or sultan.

Sundiata had several sons and one of them was name Wali. He expanded the kingdom eastward and westward during his reign from 1255 to 1270. He made a pilgrimage (Hajj) to Mecca, on the Arabian peninsula.

SAKURA

Mali fell upon some sad times after Wali ruled, with another one of Sundiata's sons (Karifa) going insane. Yet when in desperate need, strong leadership came on the scene. At this point, Sakura came on the scene breaking the legitimate line of succession of the Mali kings. During his fifteen year rule, he extended Mali down along the Gambia River to the sea; he had heard many tales of that sea. In his boyhood, it was known as the world's end and also believed to be where the world began—in the water. During the beginning years of Sakura's reign, he embraced the Islamic Faith and took the name of Abubakari the II in 1296 A.D.*

Abubakari the II had visions as a child of finding the end of the world, and as a king, he wanted to make that vision a reality. He called for all in his empire who knew the waterways and had experience in sailing to aid him. All sizes and manner of boats were built; two hundred master boats and two hundred supply boats. Abubakari called his captains together and issued the following orders: "Do not return until you have reached the end of the ocean or when you have exhausted your

*PAFO wonders why Sakura would name himself after an Arab who destroyed so many of his African people. (see page 90).

food and water." They went away, and only one came back after a very long absence. The captain explained to the King about the disappearance of all the ships in front of him, his being the last one, he turned his ship around because of fear and headed back to Mali.

This news, made Abubakari more set on his desire to search the sea and to find new land. He assembled a fleet that dwarfed the first expedition and pairing off men and women by the hundreds. He would command the new expedition and keep in touch with his captains by means of the talking drum. In 1311 he conferred the power of regency to his brother, Kankan Musa, based on the understanding that Kankan was to assume the throne if after a reasonable lapse of time the king did not return. Abubakari II took leave of Mali with his fleet down the Senegal River heading west across the Atlantic. He took his griot[1] and his history with him never to return.

THE BLACKS OF DARIEN

It is not too far-fetched to assume that the first American historian Peter Martyr reports on a meeting between the Spanish explorers and the Blacks of Darien. Blacks were found in the province of Darien and other South American and Central American islands. There is mounting evidence of Pre-Columbian art, pottery and skeletal remains of Africans all of which has a profound effect on native population. In the two expeditions of Abubakari II, roughly eight hundred ships with not less than one hundred people on board. Even with only half surviving and in three hundred years of multiplying, could become a formidable force.

The fourteen-ton stone heads with African features are proof that the Africans reached Central America. They were deified by the Olmec Indians for bringing them agricultural, architectural and medical science. Dr. Ivan Van Sertima's great work, *They Came Before Columbus* documents their successful trip.

Kankan Mansa became Mansa Musa and officially took the throne of Mali in 1312 A.D. His total rule was twenty-five years. As the fame of Mali spread across the Mediterranean Sea to Europe, Mansa Musa's name became known throughout the world. He extended the boundaries of Mali by diplomacy and war. Gao was one of those City-States that Mansa Musa, through his lieutenants, persuaded to become part of the

---

1 Griot—Court historian by memory only.

empire in 1325. Of course, this happened when Mansa Musa was on his hajj. He promoted trade and commerce and encouraged the spread of learning. He was a lover of the arts, designing, architecture and literature.

Some of the fleet of Mali's special navy sailing down the Senegal River, heading across the Atlantic. The ships were laden with men and women. Sakura, King of Mali gave orders to his captains to not return until you reach the oceans end or your food was exhausted.

MANSA MUSA'S FAMOUS HAJJ

PAFO's aim is not to glorify a religion that is not indigenous to the African people. The only religion that we would glorify would be "MAAT," because it is truly African (Alkebu-lan). There are two reasons why we will relate to you this religious hajj. First, to show you the true sincerity of our West African forebearers. That sincerity being reflected by pursuing, with vigor and fidelity, those things we perceived or thought to be right and true. Secondly, the hajj was a part of the West

African history that showed how rich Western Africa was and is.

Mansa Musa's Hajj was the most fabulous on record. In fact, it was so great that it flabbergasted people through the countries that he traveled on the way to Arabia. Even after one hundred years, the descendants of those people continued to talk about it. The journey was more than five thousand miles round trip. Imagine the amount of food, water, medicine and money it would take for such a trip.

There were assembled about one hundred camel-loads of pure gold dust, with each load weighing three hundred pounds. By today's gold prices of four hundred to five hundred dollars per ounce, we will project an amount of approximately one hundred sixty million dollars.

Included in his entourage were many members of his family, close friends, doctors, teachers and his local chiefs of the Empire whom he wanted to honor. Altogether, there were sixty thousand people in his caravan.

All along his route he gave away little bags of gold. He was extremely generous to all of those who performed any type of service. Mansa Musa entered Egypt in July 1324, and was an immediate celebrity and sensation. He gave away so much gold, that the over abundance upset the economy of Egypt for twelve years. Mali covered an area equal to that of Europe. The political subdivisions within were well organized. Some of the territory was under the direct control of the Mansas. Mali was divided into provinces; each province was administered by governors or ferbas. Each important town in the province had inspectors or mayors called Mochrifs (Mo-krifs). The financial system was basically taxes, trade and commerce. Mali was a land of plenty. On the agricultural phase of their system fertile soil grew sorghum, rice, taro, yams, beans and onions. They raised poultry, cattle, sheep and goats. They also grew cotton for making clothes, and one of the most useful noncultivated medicinal liquids and a red dye that came from the Boa tree. Every large city or middle-sized village had its own craftsmen, woodcarvers, silversmiths, goldsmiths, coppersmiths; trade was a major industry.

Being the greatest power in the Western Sudan, Mali took over the trans-Saharan gold-salt trade. Musa protected the all-important trade route between the Maghreb and Western Sudan by establishing friendly commercial relations with the ruler of Fez in Morocco.

Why was salt so important in those days? Fact 1—There was no refrigeration. Meat had to be preserved in hot weather, salt was a preserver. Fact 2—Remember that when one perspires a lot, we lose a tremendous amount of body salts and liquids; thus resulting in weakness and possible dizziness. Therefore larger amounts of salt must be ingested. Fact 3—Salt was used for sterilization of surgical instruments.

Another great source of revenue was copper. Many parts of Northern Africa drew their supply of copper from Tagedda that was under Malian control. Trade was so good that even the so-called common people in Mali were well off. There were many great cities in Mali. Niani, the great capital of Mali-Walata (founded by the people who fled Koumbi) was the gateway to the Sudan for the trans-Saharan caravans coming from Maghreb. There was Gao, which became the capital of the oncoming Songhai Empire. There was Timbuktu; sitting at the great bend of the Niger between Niani and Gao.

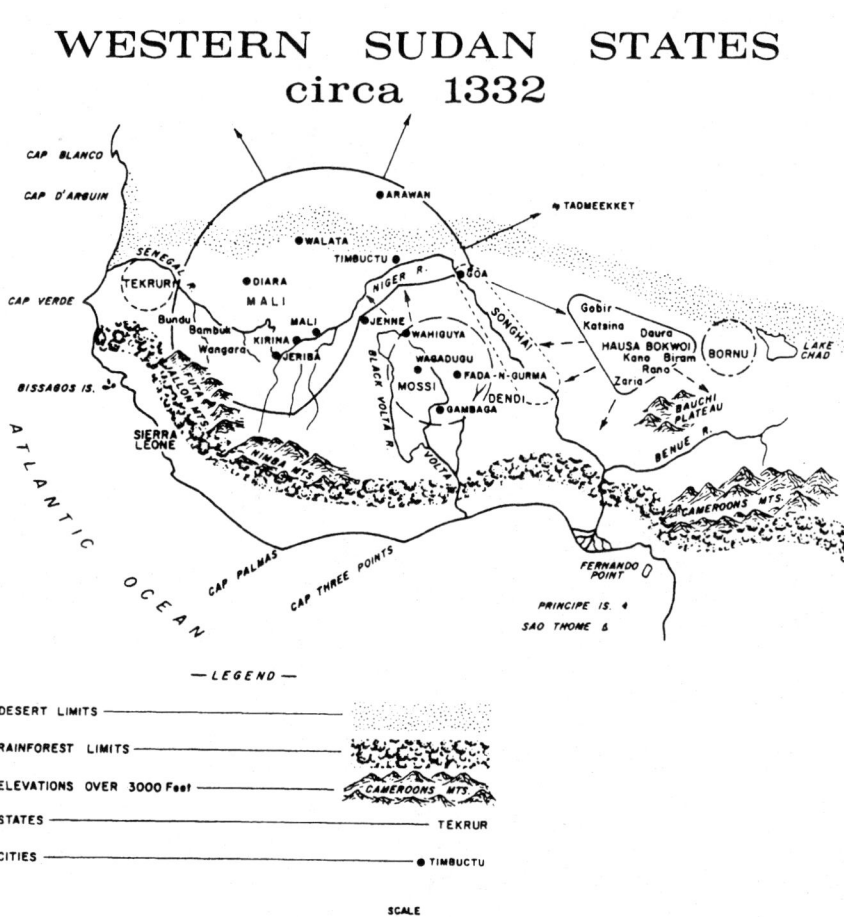

Mansa Musa died in 1332, and was succeeded by his son, Maghan. Maghan didn't have his father's ability and wisdom and because of this, the Mali Empire lost Timbuktu. Maghan only ruled 4 years and died. He was succeeded by his father's brother Mansa Sulayman, who did much to repair damages done by Maghan. In 1351 Sulayman followed Mansa Musa's example and also made a Hajj to Mecca. He began to reassert Malian control, but died in 1359—and thus the last of the able Mandingo emperors. His successors were too weak to hold the empire together, and at the same time the two princes that Mansa Musa brought back with him from his Mecca journey had escaped from under the rule of Maghan. These two Songhai princes built a strong dynasty called Songhai which surpassed Mali as the most powerful and important state in the Western Sudan. It became larger than all of Europe.

In 1481 Mali made one last bid to fight off the challenge of Songhai by attempting to make an alliance with a European power. The alliance was never made and Mali's fate was sealed. This is not saying that Mali was destroyed as a people; but only as a major power. In the overlapping historical saga between Mali and Songhai, we will show you how intertwined these two powers were. Let us look at Session VII as each nation competes for center stage.

END OF SESSION VI

SESSION VII

SONGHAI'S BEGINNING

The Songhai people themselves, were farmers, fishermen, hunters, craftsmen, traders and warriors. They were a confederation of people who came to dominate the middle Niger around the region of Dendi. The first large Songhai settlement was a town called Kukya. It became the capital and attracted people from the surrounding regions. Looking on a map of Africa today, Kukya in the area of Dendi country would be near what is now the northwest frontier of Nigeria.

THE CAPTURE OF KUKYA

Between the seventh and ninth centuries, a group of Berber nomads swept down from the north, and captured Kukya. The Songhaians developed and founded a settlement that became known as Gao. Moslem traders settled in Gao, and began spreading Islam. From the eleventh through the fourteenth centuries, Songhai's biggest problem was the maintenance of its freedom and independence from the growing power of the neighboring empire of Mali.

When the Malian emperor Mansa Musa returned from his famous Hajj to Mecca by way of Gao, to see the city and its king (Dia-Assibai); Mansa Musa took two of Assibai's sons back to Niani as hostages against rebellion. Read the story of these two princes of destiny in the following pages.

SULAYMAN NAR AND ALI KOLON

It was in the period that the main components developed for the foundation of establishing Songhai's beginning that had as its capital, Gao, the great industrious city.

Gao was located downstream from Timbuktu on the Niger River. A mighty city-state, it had refused to become part of the Mali empire that angered Mansa Musa to no end. Because Gao was a large city manufacturing iron works, gold, silver and tin tools and agricultural implements, he needed to bring Gao into the fold so that he could standardize the weights and measures, as was done later in Songhai.

While Mansa was away on his Hajj, his son was busy extending the boundaries of the Malian empire. On his trip back home, Mansa Musa was delighted to hear that his soldiers had a "welcome home" gift for him. What they had done, they had persuaded the city of Gao to become part of the Malian empire.

King Assibai came from the palace to the great gates of the city and surrendered his sword to Mansa's son, Maghan. He was so happy, he made a detour to see his gift of the city of Gao, the capital of the Songhai people.

As Assibai escorted Mansa Musa to his palace, Mansa Musa's eyes fell on two handsome young men, about fifteen years of age. They were the favorite sons of King Assibai, born just hours apart but two different mothers. The elder, Ali Kolon and the younger, Sulayman Nar.

King Assabai could not conceal his love and affection for the boys which proved to be his undoing. Mansa Musa said, "Now, King, I know you have promised your loyalty to me, and that you will pay the taxes I shall impose for our mutual benefit, but I shall need some insurance for your promised loyalty. I shall take these two princes back to the capital of Mali, Niani, with me."

The King was anguished. He pleaded to Mansa Musa to spare his boys. But Mansa was adamant. "No harm will befall them," Mansa Musa said. "They will be treated as royal hostages. They will be treated as my own sons. But you must always remember to obey my edicts and remain loyal to the Malian empire."

The two boys bid tearful goodbyes to their father and mothers as they mounted the handsome camels that were grandly outfitted for so royal a pair. They began their sad, two hundred mile journey to the royal city of Niani, vowing to themselves and whispering to each other that one day they would return to Gao or die trying.

The boys' eyes were as big as saucers as they neared their destination for they saw such wealth and splendor they had never seen before. The great farms of Mali spread out as far as their eyes could see. There were great farms of Sorghum, rice, taro, yams, beans and onions. There were huge herds of cattle, sheep and goats. There were poultry farms of so many chickens, that the boys felt they couldn't begin to count them. The cooks on the caravan prepared bounteous meals of thick hippopotamus steaks, beef steaks, and for variety, expertly prepared wild buffalo steaks, elephant and crocodile.

When the boys passed through the cities and large towns, they saw the industrious people of Mali skillfully put their country's resources to use. Each large city or middle-sized village had its own craftsmen, woodcarvers, silversmiths, goldsmiths, coppersmiths, blacksmiths, weavers, tanners and dyers.

The boys saw the great caravans of camels hauling the salt and gold to and from Mali and places north of the Sahara.

Even all of this opulence and excitement didn't change the boys' desire to escape. They watched for every chance.

But Mansa Musa called together his twelve most trusted calvarymen. His words were brief and to the point. "Don't let them escape."

When they reached the golden city of Niani, the boys could scarcely conceal their delight at seeing the beautiful homes, two and three stories high made of polished stone, sitting on tree-lined avenue. They could scarcely conceal their pleasure at seeing the beautiful Malian maidens, dressed in their shining, colorful clothing, their finely-wrought leather shoes their hair in amazing designs.

The boys were assigned to special apartments in the huge royal palace. Though they couldn't see their guards, they knew that they were being watched. They were allowed to ride for miles, but they knew that they were being followed at a respectful distance. If they went a little too far, all of a sudden, five or six guards would suddenly appear and lead them gently but firmly back to the palace.

The years went on. Ali Kolon and Sulayman Nar learned how to hide provisions in secret places along the route back to Gao.

Then one day, in 1332, Mansa Musa, the great emperor died. During the confusion, the boys, mounted on fast horses escaped.

Too late, they were spotted by their guards who gave chase. Over the next six days, they rode in desperation. The guards, trying to catch them, rode as though their very lives depended on it.

But Ali Kolon and Sulayman Nar made it back into the city at the last instant, just as the huge gates closed against their pursuers.

The two boys, now safe, found out to their sorrow that their father had died the year before of a broken heart. Ali Kolon was hailed as the successor to the throne which he assumed under his self-named title of "Sunni" which means "replacer."

This established a new dynasty or succession of rulers of Songhai.

The new king of Songhai, Sunni Ali Kolon, dreamed of expanding his small city-state of Songhai into a huge empire that he hoped would someday eclipse and swallow up the Malian empire.

He worked very closely with his brother Sulayman Nar in laying a firm foundation for empire building. They knew that the African traditional religion was in jeopardy because of the encroachment of the many enemies of Mali, especially the Arabs who were our traditional enemies.

Ali Kolon along with his brother taught the concept of the Lunda people which was that kinship found expression in trade and federation especially when attacked by non-African invaders.

During the one hundred and thirty-two years leading into the reign of Sunni Ali Ber, the descendants of Ali Kolon and Suylayman Nar reigned supreme. The African system of justice, economics and scholarly pursuits were being fed by the roots which drank the spiritual nourishment and wisdom of our illustrious ancestors.

END OF SESSION VII

SESSION VIII

SONGHAI'S EXPANSION

PART I

Sunni Ali Ber ascended the throne of Songhai in 1464 and with the capture of Timbuktu in 1468, Songhai became an empire. In the city of Timbuktu, there was the great University of Sankore, with its thousands of students from all over the known world. In 1433, Timbuktu was invaded by Tuareg nomads; their leader Akil, after having captured Timbuktu chose not to live in the city. Ammar was the King of Timbuktu. His duty was to collect taxes, of which one-third was for himself and the rest to be turned over to Akil.

SUNNI ALI BER MARCHED INTO TIMBUKTU WITHOUT OPPOSITION
JANUARY 20, 1468

However, Akil began demanding a greater portion of the taxes. Ammar had sent a letter to Sunni Ali Ber in Gao and boasted that Timbuktu could repulse any kind of attack. Meanwhile, Chief Akil often double-crossed Ammar and rode into town and seized all the tax money after Ammar had made the collections. Ammar then plotted to get even with Akil, but he needed Sunni Ali Ber's help. He sent a secret message to Sunni Ali Ber offering to hand him the city if he would come to drive out Akil. He also hoped that Sunni would forget about that boastful letter. Sunni Ali immediately ordered his army to march at once on Timbuktu. Akil and Ammar watched from the top of a hill as this huge army moved towards the city. It so unnerved Akil that he decided to flee; and many of the scholars and professors and citizens fled also. They fled mainly because of wrong information about Sunni Ali Ber reportedly being a savage. Sunni was cruel, but mainly because

Sunni Ali Ber I. His ability on the battlefield humbled all those who stood against him. He married the beautiful Queen of Jenné after the seven-year war.

WESTERN SUDAN STATES EARLY SIXTEENTH CENTURY

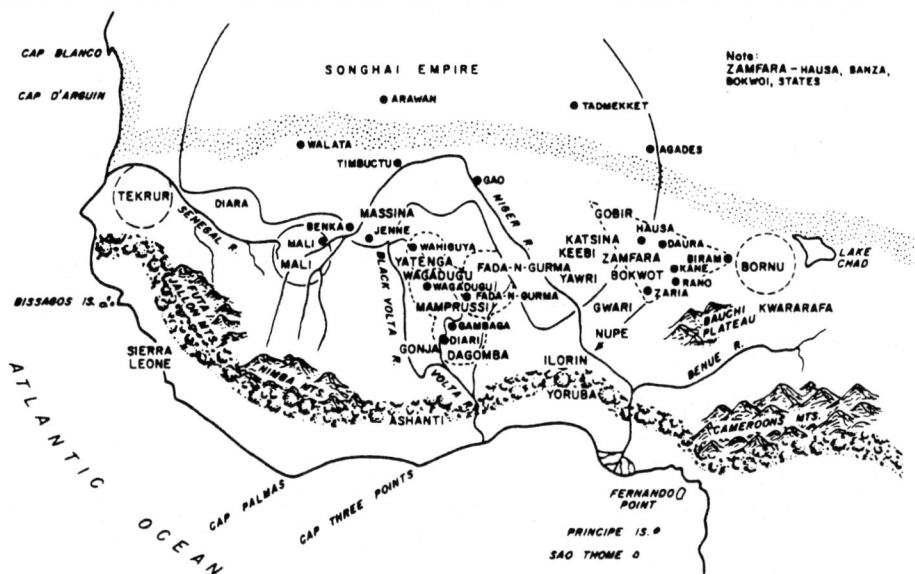

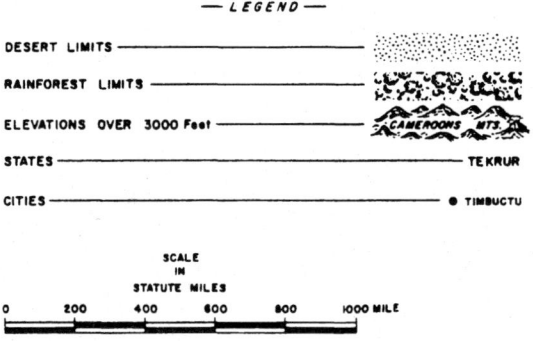

Timbuktu was allied with the Tuaregs, who were his bitterest enemies. This was the result of decades of Tuareg-Songhai rivalry for control of the Middle Niger. Most Moslem writers of history described Sunni Ali Ber as a tyrant, because of the humiliating treatment of Moslem scholars at Timbuktu, particularly since Sunni Ali was supposed to be a Moslem himself. His ability on the battlefield humbled those who stood against him. He also was generous, but above all else, he was an able ruler with a real talent for organization and government.

When Sunni Ali Ber marched into Timbuktu, he assumed control without opposition on January 20, 1468. The Tuaregs never invaded again.

END OF SESSION VIII

SESSION IX

THE BEAUTIFUL CITY OF JENNE

O What a beautiful city
O What a beautify city!
Twelve gates to that city of
Hallelujah.

These were the words that began a song that our fathers and mothers sang during our time of remembrance and tears on the plantations of the old South.

They were singing of an ancient city in West Africa from which thousands of its citizens were brought across the stormy Atlantic—in the holds of ships—in chains. The city—Jenné.

If we could go by time machine back to the Fifteen Hundreds, back to West Africa—back to the Beautiful City and walk along its tree-lined avenues, we would forever be redeemed by the experience.

The sights of sophistication and beauty would, at first, clash with the mental pictures and attitudes with which we have been inundated all of our lives.

We would be delighted to see our mothers and fathers dressed in the velvet tunics and flowing robes as described by eyewitnesses of that day.- Leo Africanus and Es'Sadi

*We would marvel at the architecture and design of the multi-stories homes of polished stone.... "without cement" as Vlahos speaks in his *African Beginnings.*

We would see people coming in and out of the banks, depositing and withdrawing money and cashing checks.[1] *Checking accounts* were noth-

---

*1 The African Past (by Englishman Basil Davidson), also *Before the Mayflower* by Lerone Bennett.

University of Jenné. Mathmatics Department head conferring with Dean of Law School about recent large increases in student enrollment.

ing new to Fifteenth, Sixteenth and Seventeenth Century West Africa. One of the last great emperors, a brilliant and enlightened legislator made many improvements in Songhai. One in particular was in the banking and credit systems. Yes, they had credit even then.

We would see scholars of all nationalities and colors, wending their way to the fourteen hundred faculty of that great university of Jenné, to study law, medicine, history, astronomy, higher mathematics and, as Bennett's *Mayflower* quotes, "...to check their Latin and Greek manuscripts...".

We would turn onto the wide commercial thorofare where would be located the foundries manufacturing out-put in iron swords and agricultural implements — the shops with their works of glass, gold, ivory, copper, tin and silver, as mentioned by Katz in his book, *Eyewitness*.

With respect to the implements; iron implements, iron was first smelted in Africa, according to John Hope Franklin in his book, *From*

17th Century Jenné of West Africa showing front view of Bank of Jenné.

Slavery to Freedom. On page 27, he goes into detail to prove that the use of iron was developed very early in the *economy* of Africa. He says, "From Ethiopia to the Atlantic, there is much evidence of adroitness in the manufacture and use of iron." Different clans, with the Songhai empire of which there were ten to sixteen clans, specialized in metallurgy.

An early carving, from the Songhai empire depicts a mounted warrior encased in armor, manufactured in Songhai. His beautifully caparisoned (decorated) horse had portions of his head and body encased in steel armor. But, the amazing thing, according to some of these books, is that the armor was woven from steel with such fine smelting skill, that it was extremely light and flexible and practically impenetrable. According to the author, Basil Davidson, in his book, *The African Genius,* iron was smelted and developed many centuries before in Africa, before Europe and China.

As night would swiftly come, the sound of violins would be borne gently in the balmy breeze. We would turn in that direction and come presently to the night clubs "...with their orchestras of violins, harps, guitars, flutes, bugles and bagpipes," as described by Quarles in his, *The Negro In Our History*.

Our strange dress would hardly warrant a glance from the crowds engaged in dancing, chess, fencing, and gymnastics. It is because our African parents were cosmopolitan and welcomed strangers in strange dress.

Speaking of clothing and dress, many shops of various types and materials were located in the Songhai cities. One city, that specialized in this, was the city of Kano. According to the accounts of a German traveller, in the nineteenth century, he said that Kano exported to Timbuktu, alone, three hundred camel-loads of clothing annually. The cotton clothing was woven and dyed in Kano. Some were in the form of robes and dresses of all colors and in plaid of various colors, as well as black.

Not only were there a great number of shops in the larger cities, but as Lerone Bennett, in *Before the Mayflower*, writes on page 22, that shocked Songhai historians: "Most of the people of Timbuktu amused themselves with music and singing in night clubs. Orchestras were the rage with both male and female singers. The dress of the women was extravagantly luxurious. Men and women were fond of jewels and the women dressed their hair with bands of gold."

The time has come for us to find our way back down the broad avenues to our time machine. We are saddened to have to go.

The orange glow of the setting sun dances on the manmade waterfalls and lights up for fleeting moments the thousands of rich colored flowers on the tapestries of hanging gardens in the city's park we are passing.

We re-enter our time machine. We are transported in an instant back to here and now.

Fortunately, we can share with you, the reader, more than just the inadequate work pictures we have just created. We have recreated a tiny bit of the memory of the Beautiful City. It is recreated in the buildings of Boys Town of the House of Umoja in the city of Philadelphia, Pennsylvania. And, on the first floor of the Martin Luther King building is a tiny replica of a portion of that city called Jenné—The Beautiful City.

JENNÉ WAS FOUNDED IN THE THIRTEENTH CENTURY

Jenné (Jen-nay) was founded sometime in the thirteenth century by the Sonikes in the declining years of Ghana's Empire. Jenné was in the backwaters of the Bani River, which was a tributary of the Niger some 300 miles southwest of Timbuktu. Jenné's attractiveness was due to the beauty of the waterways and the imaginative designs of many of its buildings.

Protected by treacherous swamps, it could only be reached by way of narrow twisting canals and streams. This made Jenné easy to defend. Many past kings of Mali, including Abubakari made ninety-nine attempts to capture Jenné, but their endeavors always ended in frustration.

Learning flourished within Jenné as in Timbuktu, Gao and Walata with their universities of high repute and thousands of professors. Many of these learned men lectured and conducted research on various subjects. Some of those disciplines were medicine, surgery, (such as the removal of cataracts on the eye, the transplanting of limbs and the study of bacteria.

NURSING AND CARE OF THE SICK

The care of the sick goes back into the dim past, when late Dawn Men called on the mother of his clan to cool his forehead with water from the brook.[2] It is not too far a stretch of logic to imagine that the Shaman or medicine man or so-called witch doctor, in Stone Age societies, had persons who aided him in administering to the sick and the hurt, who later became known as "Nurses." In the ancient societies of Western Africa, temples were built to placate evil spirits thought to be responsible for disease and death. Back in ancient Egypt, the history of nursing and the care of the sick is found inscribed on papyrus, on steles and obelisks. The writing was in hieroglyphics, the translations of which were happily resolved by the finding of the famous Rosetta Stone in 1799 by troops of Napoleon. The finding was the basis of the true study of Egyptian Hieroglyphics. The stone of polished black basalt was inscribed by priest in three columns. One was in hieroglyphics, one in

---

2 *Cultural Genesis* (Chapter II, J. Weatheraux—Ancient Africa)

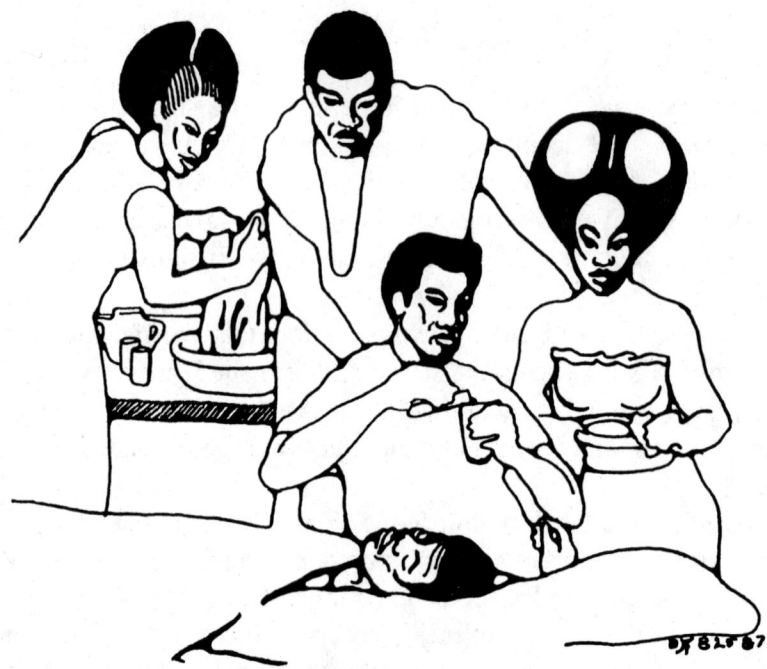

One of the Songhai's hospitals. The scene of course is doctor, nurse and attendants caring for a sick person.

the everyday spoken language of the Egyptian, (demotic—cursive) and the third in Greek. Champollion spelled out the sounds of the Egyptians (about 1820) and compared the language with the later Koptik. The stone was found at Rosetta in the delta of the Nile by M. Boussard. It was inscribed in 198 B.C. in the reign of Ptolemy Epiphanes (now in the British Museum). It declares the benefits conferred on Egypt by Ptolemy V as the son of Ra, the beloved of Pitah and the living image of Amen.

Imhotep, the chief physician to the court of King Zoser, Pharaoh of the third dynasty of Egypt, scientifically propounded more than two hundred prescriptions for various diseases. The Papyrus Ebers written about 2500 B.C., lengthened the list of seven hundred prescriptions for all kinds of diseases arranged in sections according to the different organs to be treated. In West Africa during the period called the Middle Ages in Europe, caring for the sick through training schools was operated under the aegis of the emperors of the Songhai Empire. An Arab traveller and historian, Ibn Battuta notes that at the College of Medicine of the University of Sankore, in the city of Timbuktu, his blind brother was made to see by an operation removing cataracts from his eyes.

Leo Africanus, noted historian of nine volumes on the Songhai Empire directed to be written by the Pope, his adoptive father, wrote in 1578, "Here in Timbuktu, there are great scores of doctors, judges, priests and other learned men, bountifully maintained at the king's cost and charges."

The art of physical healing was only part of the science of the physicians of West Africa, who were also taught the art of emotional and mental healing. The authority of the practitioner was high coming from a broad knowledge of herbal medicine plus psychological insight and intimate understanding of local circumstances. Of course, there is much more on the evolution of "Nursing," but we are just touching on it so that you can see that the background was Black. (Reference at bottom page)[3]

PERSONIFICATION OF BLACK RESPECT OF ACQUISITION OF JENNE AND SONGHAI'S EXPANSION

Sunni Ali Ber realized that the capture of Jenné was not an easy task. He devised a plan of siege instead of direct attack. The siege lasted seven years, seven months and seven days. During the period of no rain, the Songhai Army camped just outside of the city to cut off supplies. With a naval fleet of four hundred large ships, Jenné was cut off during the rainy season. After seven years of stubborn resistance, Sunni was ready to quit. Even some of his men urged him to give it up. Just at that time, he received a message from one of Jenné's captains that Jenné was about to collapse due to such an effective siege. The ruling council of the city decided to deliver Jenné into the hands of the Songhai King. The Queen Mother of Jenné rode into the Songhai camp to surrender to Sunni Ali, but Sunni Ali greeted the ruling Mother with great respect, inviting her to sit at the side of the Songhai monarch. At this time, a tradition began, and it gave the kings of Jenné the privilege of sitting on the same with the king of Songhai, a sign of mutual respect and regard. Sunni Ali Ber marched into Jenné at the head of his army,

---

[3] Research by Elaine Richardson—Her final paper as an undergraduate at Temple University (Philadelphia, Pennsylvania). Reference: William Osler, *Aequanimitas* (Philadelphia). V. Robinson, *The Story of Medicine*, New York: Tudor Publishing-Goodnow *History of Nursing* (Phila. and London. *The World of Africans & Afro Amer.* Ibn Battuta, *Travels in Africa* (Haklyut Collection: Paley Libr. T. Univ.) Basil Davidson: *The African Past. (Before the Mayflower:* L. Bennet)

Beautiful Queen Dara of Jenné. She married Sunni Ali Ber shortly after Jenné's surrender to the Songhai Emperor. The symbol on her headress is the letter H in hieroglyphics and was not a negative symbol. It was at the top of the Great Pyramid of Gizeh and is considered a symbol of life.

the troops did not pillage the town. Songhai people have always admired courage. Sunni Ali went out of his way to show the people of Jenné that he had no grudge, and he was extremely kind to all. To seal the bond, he proposed and married the beautiful Queen Mother of Jenné.

ACQUISITION OF JENNE

The year of the capture of Jenné was 1473. Shortly after the addition of Jenné, the Songhai Empire replaced Mali as the dominate power in the western Sudan.

Sunni Ali Ber realized the importance of the Niger River in commerce and military operations. Like Mali, he divided his empire in provinces and placed each under the control of a governor.

At that time, the people of the western Sudan were beginning to meet new visitors. Prince Henry "The Navigator" sent Portuguese ships and sailors down the west coast of Africa, establishing a number of coastal trading posts.

European explorers and traders seeking to get into the Sudan from the coastal regions, found their way barred by rain forests and the mighty Songhai armed forces. Raids to get slaves from the Songhai Empire were repulsed time and again. This brought about the distrust of our people against all Europeans. Contrary to what the uninformed of our people say, we of the Western Sudan, the Songhai people did not sell our people to any European. Also, the Europeans could not crack our defense through the Fifteenth and Sixteenth Centuries. Raids were made by the Europeans, and was somewhat successful in other areas of Africa at that time, but not in Songhai. Now, this is not to say that there were not isolated instances of kidnapping by European commando raids.

Sunni Ali Ber's reign was coming to an end, and also his life. He died in 1492. In death, as in life, the career of Sunni bore many resemblances to that of Mali's, Sundiata. Both of these rulers were fearless warriors who prepared the foundations for great empires.

Arabic writers of history hated our father Sunni Ali Ber. One reason was that he was too steeped in the great African philosophy-religion—Ma'at. Another was that they never forgave him for his ignominious defeat of the Islamic general, Akil, who had held Timbuktu in an iron grip of tyranny. But the Songhai people revered him almost like a god, calling him "the most high". He was very much like two earlier freedom fighters, Queen Kahina of Numida, a Black Jewish African and her cousin General Kuscila of Mauritania. Together they fought Arabic invasions and practically stopped the spread of the Arabic religious concepts (Islam) circa 695 A.D.

General Kuscila was an original Moor (called later Blackamoor), and a follower of Ma'at. However, by the time of the Moorish civilizing of Spain (beginning in the 700's), Islam had begun to have a great grasp on their minds.

Queen Kahina, a believer in Judaism, but like her cousin, she also believed in the Africa-for-Africans as her first priority. Arabic military leaders were so demoralized by Kuscilla and Queen Kahina's military prowess, that they made a decision to team up with the Europeans and as a result, Islam and Christendom began a steady spread in Africa. Some historians of that period say that one of the things the Arabs did which would have infuriated Queen Kahina, was the robbing of Egyptian graves, and the grinding up of the mummies into a fine powder and selling it as a sex potion. It was also alleged that the Arabs used the mummies for firewood.*

There has been on-going systematic brutalization and contempt by the Arabs against Africans down through the centuries. Even today, there are documented reports of Berbers and Arab militia forcing Africans into captivity. The New York Times of July 20, 1994, told of the Berbers and Arab militia holding ninety thousand Mauritanians in physical bondage. The article said that even though those African Blackamoors of Mauritania are Moslems, it makes no difference to the Arabs. It is the Arabs' contempt of Africans. Yet we know that the Moslem law forbids enslavement of fellow Moslems, but that doesn't count when the victims are Africans. The Arabs believe in the *race-first-only* doctrine.

*The Rape of the Nile — Bryant M. Fagan — 1975

END OF SESSION IX

SESSION X

THE SHORT REIGN OF SUNNI ALI BER'S SON

Sunni Ali's successor to the throne of Songhai was his son. He was a Moslem, but in name only, i.e., he did not do a good job of pretending. This irritated the Moslems, and all efforts on their part to convince him were rejected. Sunni Ali II vigorously defended the traditional African religion that was his traditional and sovereign right and for that he was dethroned in 1493.

Perhaps a little more background on this subject matter would give you more insight to the Arabic-Islamic influence on African people. If you will check back to the fifth session of this text you will find that the Arabs tried in vain to militarily conquer us, but were unable. After all of those battles, some of them settled in Ghana bringing the written Arabic language and the Moslem religion (Islam) to the Western Sudan. Much of the written language of Western Africa was replaced.

THE REASON THE ARABIC LANGUAGE WAS ACCEPTED

When the Arabic language came along, it was during a period of thirst for world-wide knowledge and therefore Western Africa accepted it (the Arabic language) as a godsend, but was later to regret it. The Arabic language, unlike any other language in the world, had a three-way advantage in its spread. It was the language of religion and learning and the language of trade and commerce. The trade and commerce use, made it more widespread among Blacks than it would have been otherwise. Arabic therefore, was the language used by Black scholars in West Africa whether they were Moslem or not. All this made the widespread revival of learning in Africa appear to be an entirely Moslem affair. To be able to read and write again for the advancement of higher education was far more important to Africans than the vehicles of religion as a media, whether

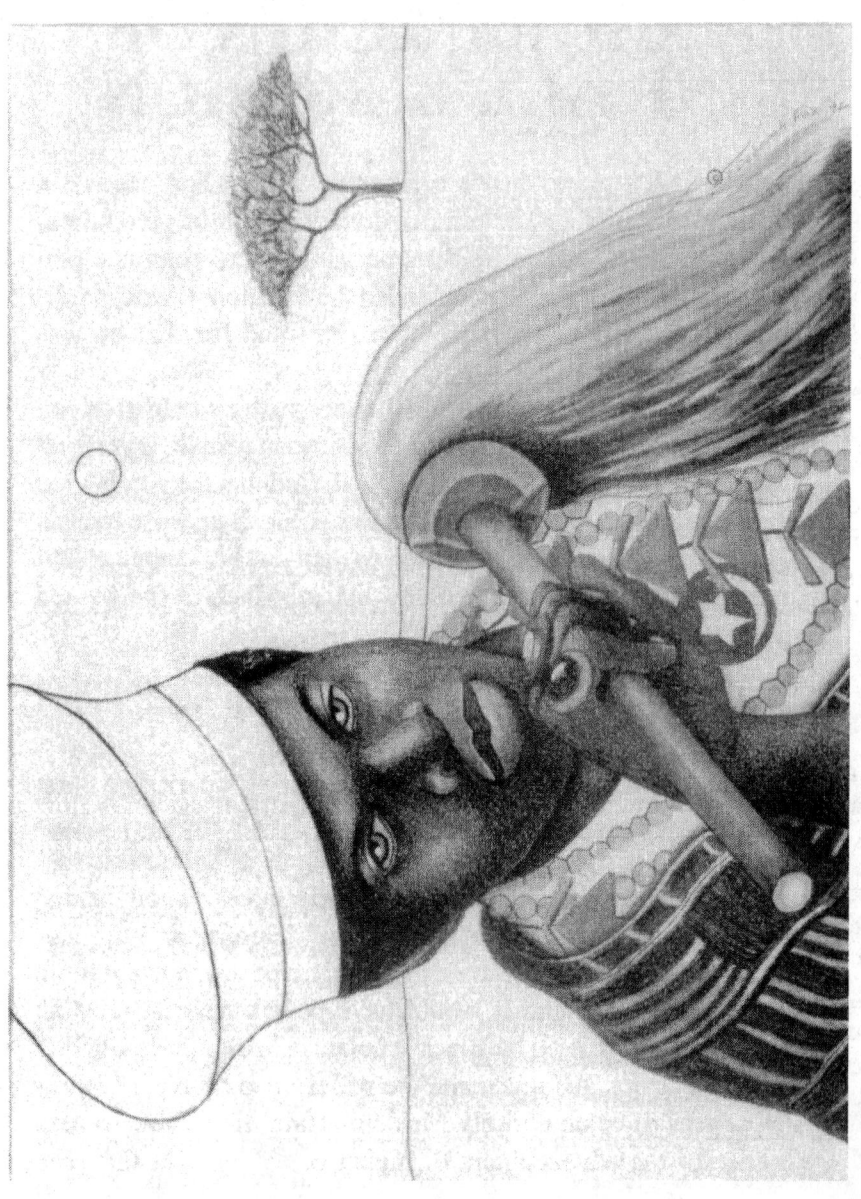

Askia Muhammad Touré the Great. He built the empire internally and externally. Internally, his success was measured by the unity and love that the Songhai people had for each other, and externally, their love for learning.

Travelers always felt safe in Africa's indigenous populated countries and Songhai was no exception, and this was on the loneliest roads and streets.

Moslem or Christian in orientation. Now we want you to note that the *masses* of the Blacks did not embrace Islam. A few did, when it was expedient; because the rulers, notables but particularly the *merchants* were devout Moslems. The Arabs generally controlled the trade and commerce market and always looked with disfavor on non-Moslems or those not in sympathy with their cause. They set the stage for the revolt that put an end to Sunni Ali Ber's rule.

The Sunni incident reminds us of that which happened to Kwame Nkrumah of Ghana and Patrice Lumumba of the Congo. When Blacks don't dance to their tune, then we are campaigned against. Most of our Black rulers in Ghana, Mali and Songhai even though they played the expediency game, always put the needs of the people as the first priority above being a Moslem. The only thing we of PAFO have against religion other than the traditional African religion, is that the other religions have separated and divided Black people. Islam and Christendom have Black people at swords edge, never being able to concentrate as a whole on the ills that so greatly affect us as a people. We have some who say, "get your soul saved," and away with the rest of this earthly tradition. It is certainly nothing wrong with getting your inner-self cleansed of wrongdoing to your brother or sister by renewing your determination to treat them right; but we as Black people, must learn to love RACE first by actually looking out for each other, for which we admire the white Jews.

This is just what Askia Muhammad Touré did when he ascended the throne of Songhai in 1493. He was religiously sincere and very faithfully committed to Africans. Askia made a hajj in 1495. He was accompanied by five hundred horsemen, one thousand foot soldiers, and he took three thousand pieces of gold with him.

After the hajj, he undertook a series of so-called holy wars to bring the Islamic faith to kingdoms where the people continued to worship ancient Gods, which may have been a mistake. However, he did put an end to the dangers of constant raids on Songhai's northeast frontier by the nomadic Tuaregs. He had numerous military victories with only a few minor setbacks.

To strengthen the Moslem faith and to administer Moslem justice (in place of the traditional laws) throughout his empire, Askia appointed Islamic judges to every large district. By this time, Songhai had become a huge empire, characterized by order and prosperity. The vigor of commercial and scholarly activity in the empire served as tribute to the skill and wisdom of Askia the Great. It has been said, that as huge as the empire was, travelers were as safe in any part of the Empire (which was larger than all Europe) as though he were in the King's court. For one thing, there was no delinquency among children. Then of course that meant that the parents were not delinquent in their duties. We were always good people long before Islam, because we were African. In ancient African tradition, we had established and developed the extended family concept, where every adult male and female in the Empire, was considered father and mother of every child. Also, in our Songhai governmental structure, there were family counseling agencies throughout the Empire, which helped to reduce divorces to a bare minimum. Adult delinquency in the main is largely responsible for children's delinquent tendencies in the United States of America.

We know that everything has an end, and the end was becoming visible. After Askia's death in 1538, his sons followed each other to the throne. Their misrule didn't have much impact on the decline of our empire. By the empire being so closely knitted to the foundations laid by the first Sunni Ali Ber and reinforced by Askia Muhammad's wisdom, that even with Askia's sons not doing all that was necessary for the perpetuation of the empire, it was still too strong for a successful invasion by foreigners at that time.

THE NEWS OF SUDANESE GOLD

The news of Sudanese gold, for years was drifting back to Europe and other countries. Also, the quest for slaves to be taken to what they called the "new world" was becoming more demanding. With things not completely right going on at the Songhai palace of the rulers, the Moorish Sultan of Morocco after a fierce battle, won the salt mines from us in 1588 at Taghaza. Right here and now, we will tell you about the Moors, mainly because some Blacks in America through the genealogy line, err in thinking they are today's Moors. We implore you to closely peruse the next few lines.

The original name of Egypt and by extension Africa was "Chem" or "Kemet" which meant both "the Blacks" and "the land of the Blacks". "Chemistry" means "the study of the Blacks" which the ancient Greeks did. According to some historians, Africa or Af-ree-ka meant "occupier" in old Egyptian and was the name applied to the Greeks who occupied the land when Alexander (so-called "The Great") conquered Egypt in 323 B.C. As amalgamation became more and more widespread, only the Berbers, Arabs and Coloureds in the Moroccan territories were called Moors, while the darkest and black skinned Africans were called Black-a-Moors. Eventually, "Black" was dropped from "Blackamoor." In Northern Africa—and Morocco in particular—all Moslem-Arabs, mixed breeds and Berbers are readily regarded as Moors. The real African Blacks, having had even this name taken from them, must contend for recognition as Moors like Africans in America must contend for recognition as Americans.

Mauritania is specifically where the Blackamoors originated, and they did spread in that whole northern region of Africa. PAFO believes that we should shed a little more light on the Blackamoors. When they were in possession of the great Egyptian knowledge and culture, they spread it throughout portions of Asia, Asia Minor, Europe and other parts of Africa. Dr. John Jackson, in his *Introduction to African Civilization* said that, "While they (Blackamoors) were occupying Spain in 700 AD, they established schools, libraries, hospitals and other great science centers and much more." He said the Western world had never seen such greatness in terms of knowledge. He warned that because the Blackamoors used the Arabic language that later students would tend to think it was an Arabic affair and not an African initiative. Just as African American inventors and medical geniuses who, of course speak English, could in some distant future be taught that these geniuses were white English. (Jealousy spawned by a programmed disdainment creates this American illness.)

The mixed breeds, and, in particular, the Arabs have always tried to take credit for the knowledge that lifted Europe (Spain) out of their intellectual degradation and that's why they dropped the word "Black" from Moors. Thereafter, when Africans were bludgeoned into a deep cultural sleep, some dreamed they were from Asia originally. Others dreamed the color Black was a curse. Others dreamed that following the religious concepts of our enemies would free us. When this cycle of slumber was about to be at least neutralized, we were invaded by the Europeans and brought here to America, and generally got off the track of our own realism. Some of us did not go to sleep and began to fight these myths that had been taught to us and the world.

AFRICAN ORIGIN OF SO-CALLED ARABIC NUMBERS

The zero to nine of the so-called Arabic numbers originated in Africa. In the book, *African Presence in Early America,* Dr. Ivan Van Sertima has a photograph on page 13 of his 1987 edition, of a room

THE SHORT REIGN OF SUNNI ALI BER'S SON

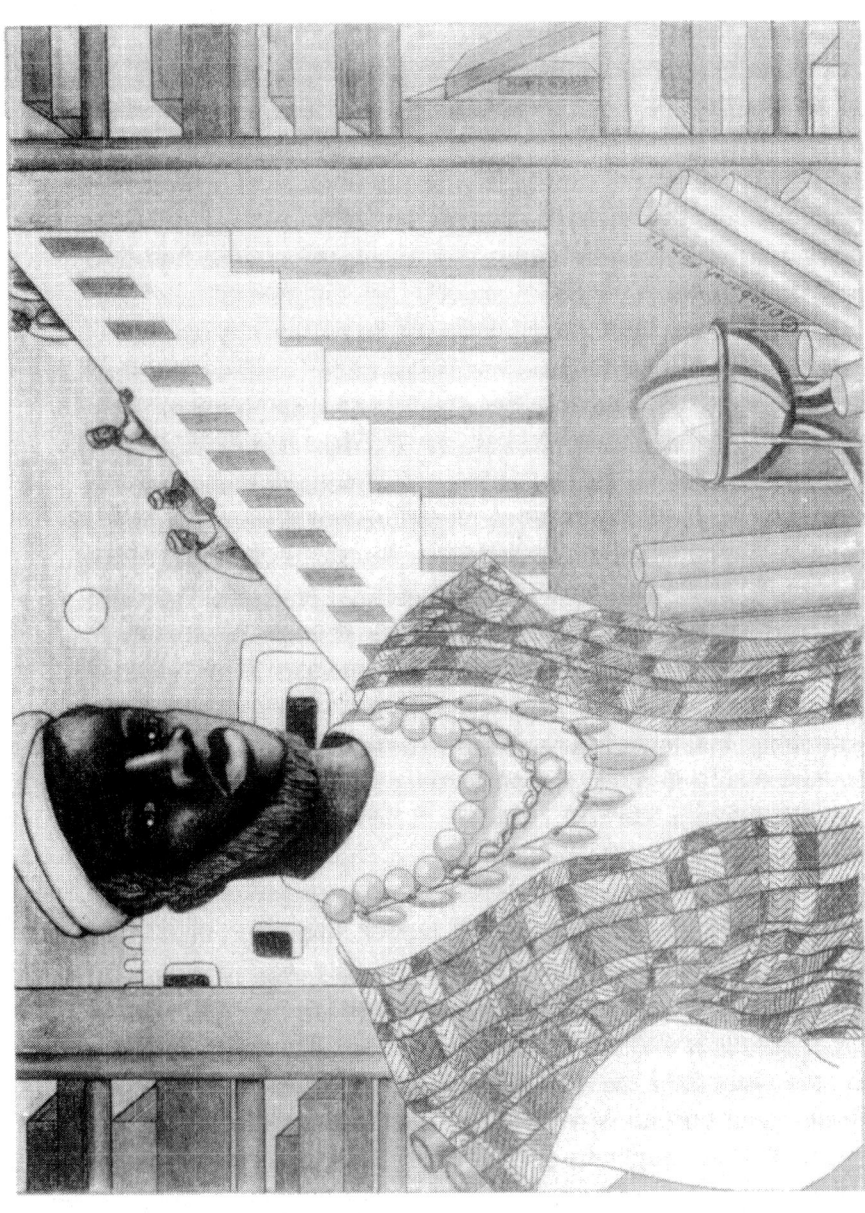

Ahmad Babo—Born 1526. He was the biographer and lexicographer. He was the last president of the University of Sankoré which was in Timbuktu. Babo, along with other learned men were kidnapped and carried to Morocco to work for our enemy.

found in the step-pyramid of Pharoh Djoser, in which the numbers as we know them are found. The numbers are individually carved on a wall, each within a square. The step-pyramid was built 4,900 years ago, in Sakkara in Egypt's Third Dynasty by Djoser's physician/architect, Imhotep.

This numbering system, which the Pan African Federation Organization is renaming "African Numbers," found its way thousands of years later through conquests by the Egyptians to India. The World Book Encyclopedia records that the Blackamoors in its conquest of India after 622 A.D. learned about this "new" numbering system, adopted it and took the numbers to Spain which was the "African Numbers" first introduction into Europe.

At the time of the Blackamoors' rescue of Spain from its ignorance, Roman numerals were being used instead of today's number system. The existence of the so-called "Arabic" now "African Numbers" system gradually replaced the inadequate Roman numeral system. Historian John Weatherwax and Dr. Josef Ben Jochannan allude to the fact that the Arabs and the Europeans plagiarized the accomplishments of Africans.

(We are indebted to mathematician, electrical engineer, inventor, historian, Spencer Rawls of Philadelphia for his research in the above.)

The Pan African Federation Organization considers it our bounden duty to correct the falsehoods told over and over again about our illustrious ancestors. It is incumbent upon us to truthfully and honestly separate the history of the Arabs and any other people from the history of Africans. If we don't, we will continue to be confused at home and abroad.

African people must begin to put the unvarnished truth of history and the fervency of foreign religion in its proper context.

Even though the Great Askia and his sons had appointed Islamic judges to every large district so as to strengthen the Moslem faith in Songhai, *it did not stop the invasion which occurred in 1591*. England supplied the guns for a hand-picked army of Moslem-Moors led by Judar Pasha, and on orders from the Sultan Ahmad Al Mansur, the attack was on. They sought the gold mines of Wangara, but they never found them. The Moslem Army was being paid by Europe to attack, thus making them a mercenary army while the Europeans attacked us by way of the sea.

They never would have dared, had it not been for the intervention of the gun that was invented in the early 1500's. It was the gun, and that alone, that gave the European nations along with the help of the Moors the edge, to eventually defeat us.

THE CONSPIRACY

There is a very interesting, but disturbing story about the use of the gun and how it was involved in the eventual downfall of the Songhai Empire. The story also involves a controversy between various history scholars who were divided on whether there was a betrayal against the Songhai government and the people of Songhai. PAFO's research shows that not only was there a betrayal, but the Sultan Ahmad Al Mansur was a strong force in that conspiracy.4 To be sure there were other African leaders who helped devise a plan of confidence to keep guns out of the Songhai Army's hands, keep in mind how devout a religious man, Askia and his sons were. The government officials were pressured because of their extreme devotion to Islam. The game was "two Islamic brothers should not use guns of the Europeans against other Moslem brothers." Real men," they said, "met on the battlefield with sword and shield face to face." Yet the Moroccans, Berbers and Arabs were all involved in the gun trade and its distribution. Since this, in reality, was a confidence game, PAFO says that this set Songhai up for the betrayal of the century. Proof was when the Sultan Ahmad Al Mansur gave the order to attack, it came on the heels of the Songhai Army giving up their guns. PAFO must point out that all other ethnic groups put **race** first and everything else second or third. We hope that we, as Africans, have now learned our lesson. We see how other nationalities protect themselves which is their god-given right, which is not for short-term but long-term as well. By the acceptance of foreign religions and rejection of our own over the long haul, our power as a major nation began a steady decline, even with all of our religious piety.

We are some of the most powerless people on the planet. Looking back on Cicero's time, his advice added another two hundred years or more to Rome's power as a nation. Of course we know that Rome turned back to her wrong ways and finally went under.

It is abundantly clear that the vast majority of Black Africans and particularly of the Western Sudan responded bravely against the European-Moor conspiracy. They enjoyed the advantage of the gun. However, in all other aspects of the conflict such as generalship strategy and battle tactics, it is clear that we, Africans, more than held our own against the graduates of the best military academies of Europe. Africans armed only with spears, bows and arrows and swords, displayed greater valor than whites and the Moors firing guns from a safe distance. A king of the Nedebele observed that..."A gun is a weapon of a coward."

WHY DIDN'T AFRICANS INVENT THE GUN?

Some have asked, "Why didn't we, the African, invent the gun?" We answer this truism by showing that the MIND will produce whatever it concentrates on. In our Songhai Empire, we were concentrating on how to cure the diseases that plagued mankind. We had developed by then, immunizations against typhoid fever, smallpox and other bacterial diseases just to mention a few. We were transplanting limbs, successfully treating people with gout and other ailments. We were scanning the skies in our thirst for greater knowledge in astronomy. We had developed a means of empire communication through our then unique mailing system. We were turning out doctors of law and philosophy from our four great universities— "Gao, Sankoré, Walatta, and Jenné" with their thousands of professors. While we were doing all these beautiful things, the European then as he is today, was looking for the *ultimate weapon,* and so he found it. While we were searching for the greater means for enhancing life, they were searching for the greater means for destroying life. Great numbers of our learned men perished during that period. Some escaped and others did not.

AHMAD BABO

Now the most famous African scholar during this period of the beginning of Songhai's destruction that also was the height of our intellectual flowering, was the last president of the University of Sankoré, Ahmad Babo, born in 1526. He was the biographer and lexicographer, he told us in his series of biographies about the Euro-Asian-Moorish (white-out) from ancient times to then, of Black indigenous African peoples' accomplishments.

There seems to be no question at all about Babo being the greatest and most prolific writer and scholar in the Sixteenth Century. In the Moslem destruction of Songhai, the main centers of learning with all their precious libraries and original manuscript were destroyed first. Then the age-old practice of seizing all men of learning and skilled craftsmen for enslavement and service to the conquerors. Foremost among these captured and carried off to Magreb was Ahmad Babo. There he was treated as an honored guest and instructed to use his great learning in the service of his conquerors, the Moors.

Whether Babo continued to write and publish any more books is uncertain. Let's suppose, that four or five of his forty or more books had escaped destruction and had come down to us, or even just one. Here we are considering what we have lost from just one man, *let alone the countless others whose works were erased along with their names. The brutal interruption by the Moors during the flowering of our learning in West Africa is fact, because they run through the entire field of Black History.*

As Eleanor Hoffman said in her book on *The History of the Moroccans and the Land of The Moors*, "The onslaught of the Moorish attacks was an extremely stunning blow by the Moslems. They amassed close to fifty thousand men with muskets to invade Timbuktu. Then the European expeditionary force invaded from the south and west. The heroes of those battles that the Songhai Army spawned were many, yet in the end we had to capitulate to overwhelming odds."

In Timbuktu, Jenné, Gao, Walata and other Songhai cities, the brutality was one ugly picture; wholesale slaughter, rape and looting by the Moorish Pashas. The Moors burned the books of the University of Sankoré and all of this was done in the name of Allah just like lynching in America was done by white Christians. As we mentioned earlier, the real indigenous Moors (Blackamoors) would not be stupid and burn their own books.

Africans who embraced a form of Judaism, as well as other beliefs were killed along with the traditionalists of Maat. All were sold into bondage that did not escape. Because many of the Moors looked like Africans to outsiders, it seemed like it was the indigenous-minded Africans who were killing Africans. It was the mixed breeds (Moors) Berbers and Arabs that were doing the killing of Africans and remember, they were killing those Africans that were of the Islamic faith. For the amusement of these so-called fellow brothers in the faith, our fathers and mothers were put into pits. There they released ferocious lions on them that tore our foreparents to shreds.

Here again, race, was a factor just as it is today. Some Africans, living in America today, believe that we Africans, must have committed some sin for the punishment that we suffered, and are yet suffering. Yet many travelers, like Homer and Herodotus, after spending considerable time in Africa, could only praise us for our just acts towards mankind our wisdom and beauty....PAFO thinks that if we cannot name the sin that we were alleged by some to have committed, then stop confusing people with falsehoods.

One fact is, that the general enslavement of Africans began during the very period when Western Africa was the very center of culture and learning. The Moors, as well as the whites, proclaimed Africans to the world as savages. Another fact is that the Black African Moslems were not spared destruction by the Moslem Moors. You can just visualize Universities' study structure consisting of faculties of law, medicine and surgery, letters, grammar, geography and art. Here, art had to do with the practical training of manufacturing, building, and other allied crafts. The basic training expertise, was through the apprenticeship system of various crafts, and now it was being destroyed.

In 1911 and 1912 French administrators at Timbuktu and Kayes, obtained copies of material as pertaining to the last days of our empire. The author of these manuscripts, Mohammad Kati, was born in 1468 and lived for 125 years. The material, *The Tarikh-al Fettash*, along with the writings of the grandson whose name was Abderrahman Es-Sa`Di was an eyewitness in the beginning of the empire's decline. In Abderrahman's material *The Tarikh Es-Sudan*, he said:

> "I saw the ruin of learning and its utter collapse in Songhai and because learning is rich in beauty and fertile in its teaching; telling men and women of their land, ancestors, their annals, the names of their heroes and what lives they led. I asked for divine help and recorded all that could be gathered on the subject of the Songhai Princes of the Sudan, their adventure, history, their achievements and their wars."

He prayed that finally these manuscripts would somehow, someday find their way into the hands of the remnants of his people. He wept for us, the unborn, because he had a vision of the terrible scourge which was to come.

END OF SESSION X

SESSION XI

THE INCURSIONS OF AFRICA AND ITS EFFECTS ON AFRICA'S "RACE FIRST" TRADITION

The effects of the invasions or incursions of Africa were two-fold. It was not just occupation of the homeland with the rapes of our women and the castrations of the African male, but the superimposing of their religion and subculture on us. One might ask, "What does religion have to do with negative effects on an invaded people? After all, what is wrong with European religion and the religion of the Arabians?" To answer those questions, a simple "Nothing is wrong" would suffice. We are saying there is nothing wrong for either of those two ethnic groups. However, there was a difference insofar as *indigenous* Africans were concerned.

At that time, religions of the Europeans and Arabs were used to subvert, subjugate, persecute and exterminate indigenous African people to take over their land and their physical persons. When Africans gave up their religious beliefs and became Christians or Islamic, *they had to deny their own traditions*. As Chancellor Williams in *Destruction of Black Civilization*, also John Jackson in his *Introduction of African Civilization* said that "As the conquering hordes of Asian Arabs carried the banner of Islam, the cry was "Believe or die by the sword." In Christendom, it was the same. Africans died at the hands of Constantine and Theodosius I when they did not accept their version of Christianity. In other words, they had no choice.

We think that we must make it clear about the structure of the original African religion because to most Africans, at home and in America, there is a dearth in the knowledge thereof. We give a few hints in Session XVI and also in the appendix of this book. Now we are going to give you another dimension to this great understanding to life's mystery call **Maat**.

The structure of **Maat** was based on the laws of the universe that bind men and stars together. These laws are immutable and if one jot or tittle were removed, heaven and earth would pass away. The laws involve the physical and the spirit of mankind as well as the rhythms of the celestial and our interaction with them. This includes conscious and subconscious that in reality is the oneness. There was and is only symbols that the ancients used to reflect the expressions of the developing humans. Each stage was characterized by certain words that gave credence to a particular development. Also, the use of images of certain animals, such as lions, falcons, etc. figured into this total universal scheme of the original African concepts.

However, due to these early and recent incursions into Africa, the original concept has been greatly misinterpreted. Early European invaders never did understand and as a result the term mystery system evolved.

The devastation of the incursions and occupation and the mixing of all kinds of foreign religious skewed that original concept.

In the original, there was not a so-called god of this or a god for that. The so-called god for this or that were only symbols. Example: the call of thunder (Thor) was the principle of cold air rushing in to fill a vacuum created by the heat of the lightning flash. As a result you have thunder. Another might be vibration of marching feet in perfect step or rhythm that can demolish a wall or bridge.

These principles are laws, not beings or gods. Remember that Pharaoh Akhenaton promulgated the "one god" concept of which Judaism is the offspring; yet the concept is not understood. The cutting of ourselves, making houses for these gods are not true, original African, but a misinterpretation of the concept. While we were in the throes of fighting off invaders, struggling for bare existence and trying to rebuild the destruction wrought against us, we lost a lot of our concepts about the religion of our forepoarents.

This loss manifests itself even in other ways than in the above mentioned material. Let's look at the difference in perception of the African nations in the so-called names of the gods. Each name of the so-called gods actually represented the adoption of an early universe and mankind. As James Allen says, in his book, *As a Man Thinketh*, "That mankind is a growth by law and not a creation by artifice."

The African nations that were strong enough to resist the religious and physical onslaughts were classified as pagans or heathens. PAFO feels that there is a need for an explanation of the shrinking away from various religious doctrines. Let us be as objective as possible as we journey in pursuit of the truth.

Truth can bind people as well as liberate depending upon various time factors. That's why this particular session is so important as to show how the undermining of African indigenous-minded people took shape and why.

The mind, if bound with cords of lies, half truths, inferences, etc. cannot respond to truth even when it's being presented. Another name for being bound is brainwashing. In Session XXIII, in the "Truly Understand Brainwashing" section, we give an account of how brainwashing works. We believe that it affects the individual person and also as a whole we blame ourselves for our own victimization along with our enemies. We also mention in Session XIX how awesome and devastating this power is, but never why.

This particular brainwash, to most African Americans and Africans, as well, is the type that kills the image of the positive self-worth and race-worth of so many of us. However, this particular negative self and race-worth is mostly manifested when the question about products sold by white people were in direct competition with products sold by Africans. Let's again, in our mind, review the scenario of the brainwash in the following light:

Intellect and logic cannot override the turned-off positive electric switch that of which subtle negative brainwashing creates. Therefore, when we replace negative imagery of African Americans into the true positive concept within the screen of our mind, then we will have the needed positive picture.

Carrying this a step further, we want to just emphasize the serious repercussions of how these incursions inflicted us. Even today, we are denying the great wisdom of our forebearers. We have been brainwashed to believe that we indigenous thinking Africans put African women down. Nothing could be further from the truth. In Session IV, we gave some briefs of the great wisdom of African women and how they created the first great civilization.

Books were written to destroy the female African and her rightful place. When these writers found that in Africa, the Black woman was heralded as truly great, they hastened to demean all women, making them to be only subservient. That was not the true African beliefs and concepts and that is why we believed in the Matrilineal Social System, and not the Patriarchal System.

In session V, we give a brief account of our Matrilineal System.

HOW THE MATRILINEAL SYSTEM WAS USED AGAINST US AFTER THE HORDES OF ASIANS INVADED AFRICA

No other society or religious group practiced the matrilineal system as we, Africans,, in ancient and early modern times. African religious concepts and ancient African history are tied in together with the African female.

Very briefly, we will give you a glimpse of the summary of the two-cradle theories.

SUMMARY OF THE TWO-CRADLE THEORY

Dr. Cheikh Anta Diop, the historian, presents us with the concept, nay reality, of what he terms the two-cradle theory. This theory, when correctly understood helps to understand the history of humanity. But more importantly, it gives us insight into factors that contribute to the destruction of African civilizations.

In succinct form, the theory sets forth the following: There are two basic cradles from which humanity developed; the southern cradle representative of Africa and the northern cradle representative of Eurasian continent. The southern cradle is characterized with an abundance of vital resources, a sedentary agriculture character and matriarchy. This cradle valued the matriarchal family, territorial state, the emancipation of women in domestic life, the ideal of peace and justice, goodness and optimism. Its favored literatures were novels, tales, fables and comedy. Its moral ethic was based on social collectivism.

The contrasting northern cradle as exemplified by the culture of Aryan Greece and Rome, valued the patriarchal family, the city-state, moral and material solitude. It defied women's rights and subjugated them under the private institutions of the patriarchal family. In this system, a husband or father had the right of life and death over a woman. Men, in this region, long remained a nomad, wherein the practice of cremating the dead was developed. The ashes were placed in urns to transport dead ancestors. Its literature was characterized by tragedy, ideas of war, violence, crime and conquests. Guilt and original sin and pessimism all pervaded its moral ethic which was based on individualism.

It is not hard to visualize the subsequent consequences when these two cradles met. The aspect of matriarchy that was most dangerous to the African was that ascent to the throne of a nation or empire within Africa, went through the son of the king's sister. That is the rightful heir to the throne in the southern cradle was the king's nephew by his sister. Access to the throne, by foreigners was achieved through marriage to the king's sister.

Dr. Chancellor Williams has noted that those from the northern cradle exploited this practice to gain control of African empires. Yet this is not the central focus at this point. Many will undoubtedly assert that most of Africa today is a patriarchal society and rightly so. But the error lies in misunderstanding that this is not an indigenous African practice, but a foreign and alien practice that has crept insidiously into African culture and society by what would appear to be the most harmless of indulgences—religion.

Dr. Diop correctly attributes the rise of patriarchy in Africa to the external factors of Islam, Christianity and the secular presence of Europe in Africa. Thus, for those who argue that Islam—and we might include Judaism, another patriarchal religion—is germane to African culture have no intelligent line of reasoning when attempting to justify many of the practices of Islam in Africa. Most noteworthy, the treatment of women in Islam. This treatment is not one common to the African prior to the incursions of the Arabs with their brand of religion. It is clear from their treatment of women that this is a religion that finds its practices in patriarchy hence northern cradle inhabitants. PAFO will further state that we have no fight against those of our people who practice Islam or Christianity. We are just not for those people who invaded our land and forced us to take a path that has dethroned us.

The incursions were so numerous, that they produced several different nationalities or "races." Therefore, in the continent of Africa you have today, the Arabs and/or their offspring mixture in Libya, Algeria, Morocco, Egypt, Mauritania, Spanish Sahara. These lands, today, are peopled by mulatto children of the Arab and African women (Almoravids). Berbers Euro-Asians, Afro-Euros and Afro-Asians. The overwhelming majority of these people are loyal to the Arab-European fathers, never to their African mother's people.

Before these more recent incursions, there were much earlier incursions. They occurred from three to five thousand years ago. Recent, being defined about 600 A.D. until now. Keep in mind that there were other Asians besides the Arabs. There were the Hyksos, Mongolians, Persians, Assyrians, Hitites, Syrians, Israelites, (but not the Falasha Jeudi) and many others. Impartial historians usually told history as it happened as best they could. We are speaking of such men as Basil Davidson, Chu & Skinner and Josephus who substantiated the occurrence of these incursions.

We, the authors of this book occupy a unique position, because a lot of this history was handed down to us by our grandmothers and grandfathers. Not only were we only to keep it alive until we were able to authenticate by some renowned historians. But we are in the process of writing the biography of several of those ancestors through the ship records that was carrying prisoner-of-war cargo.

Let's take a peek at how the incursions affected Egypt. When one looks at the various portraits of the Egyptian Pharaohs, and sees the strong Asian, Arab, or European strain, you can be sure that was during a period when the incursions had taken place. No one explains this better than Chancellor Williams, in our opinion.

The undermining of African civilization and unity of alliance between indigenous African States was a tactical maneuver to wrestle the continent out of our control. In the Epilogue of this book, we will outline the problem and the possible solution so that we may proceed to deprogramming the entire society.

END OF SESSION XI

SESSION XII
WESTERN AND CENTRAL SUDAN SOUTHWEST AFRICA-(ANGOLA) & QUEEN NZINGA

THE FALL OF THE SONGHAI EMPIRE

The Songhai Empire in 1595 lost the ability to totally control all of its vast territory after fighting against the two-pronged attacks from the Moors in the north and the Europeans from the west. The invaders, even with their guns and cannons, were still not strong enough to penetrate past the inner western and central states, which by this time saw the necessity of fending for themselves. These were the former colonies of Songhai, which had to remain consolidated and form new states known as Hausa and Kanem Bornu. *In the central Sudan, a large degree of safety and security was reestablished.* Some of the trade routes of the sub-Saharan were reopened. The Yoruba, the Ibo, Nupe, Borgu and the Jukun were also developing powerful state structures. The most powerful of which was Kanem Bornu, as it maintained the strength and leadership needed to preserve independence from the Moroccans and Europeans.

For more than seventy years the remains of the Songhai Empire resisted the very slow advance of captivity and eventual enslavement wrought by continuous war by an enemy with superior weapons. Slowly, security gave way to fear and violence succeeded tranquility. However, in the Songhai remnant, complete invasion did to come to the interior until the Nineteenth Century. What really hastened the breakthrough into our interior, was the inability to get enough guns to effectuate a turning of the tide. Yes, we captured prisoners with their weapons, but we couldn't replace the bullets. A direct result of the conspiracy to keep guns out of the Songhai army's hands.

Security gave way to fear, and did cause some of our people to compromise their honor, and helped the invaders capture some of our own people. This did not happen on a large scale, but it probably helped to hasten our final collapse.

This part of our plight reminds us so much of other nationalities under similar circumstances. We remember the white Jews of Germany who were being exterminated by the Germans in the early 1940's. The Jews, while waiting execution and prosecution, were trying to curry favor from their Nazi captors. They would make their prison garb resemble the uniforms of the Nazi S-S or German soldier. Some of them informed on one another and thwarted attempts of their fellow prisoners to escape. Therefore, it is a human weakness to look out for self. When this happened, even though on a small scale, it was enough to set greater captivity into play.

QUEEN NZINGA OF ANGOLA

Fighting was going on all over Africa; resisting the enemy. This included South Africa's Shaka The Zulu followed by his nephew Cetshway, who would not let the white man in Zululand. But no where East or South of Songhai was there anyone greater in resisting the white advance to take over Africa and her people, than Queen Nzinga.

Because Black women have never really received the credits due them, PAFO wants the world to know that they are the greatest. Also, that the world should know that Africa has used some of the best military strategy in defending their homeland, and that African women figured very prominently along with their men, and here is the story of one of those great African women.

"The Black Terror," as she was called, came in the form of a death defying Black Queen, named Nzinga. Whoever heard of a woman general, leading her armies in person? The truth is that she was the greatest military strategist that ever confronted the armed forces of Portugal. Her tactics kept their commanders sweating in confusion and dismay. Her aim was nothing less than the total destruction of the slave trade. To this end, and what alarmed them most, was that she had developed a system of infiltrating Portuguese Black troops with her own men, causing whole companies to rebel, desert and join her armies in what she called a "War of Liberation." Portuguese casualties were always

ANGOLA AND QUEEN NZINGA

Her loyal followers provided her with seating when the Portuguese governor refused a chair. She refused an offer of peace because she knew she had the strength to do so.

heavier than reported, for she staged surprise attacks with lightning speed, always aiming first to capture guns and cannons. Even though Queen Nzinga surrounded herself with armed guards on these long marches, she never knew how many Black soldiers were her own men!

In 1622, a new governor was sent from Lisbon to make peace. Portugal had been appointing "governors of Angola" for more than forty years without having control over it. The peace conference was held at Luanda. The Black delegation was headed by the country's ablest and most uncompromising diplomat, Anna Nzinga, not yet Queen, but sister of the King, the woman power behind a weak King, and the one responsible for inspiring the people to continue the war of resistance when every hope was gone. She herself had become their last hope. Even before the peace conference began and with it the risk of wrecking it, the governor's caucasian arrogance could not be restrained. The governor had decided on a studied insult at the outset by providing chairs in the conference room only for himself and councilors, with the idea of forcing the Black princess to stand humbly before his noble presence. He remained seated, as she entered the room. Nzinga took in the situation at a glance with a contemptuous smile, while her attendants moved with a swiftness that seemed to suggest that they had anticipated this stupid behavior by the Portuguese. They quickly rolled out the beautiful Royal carpet they had brought before Nzinga, after which one then went down on all-fours and expertly formed himself into a "Royal throne" upon which the princess sat easily without being a strain on her devoted follower. Yet she rose at regular intervals, knowing that other attendants were waiting for the honor of thus giving to these whites still another defeat. She was so loved by her people that it was believed that all would die to the last man and woman following her leadership. Such were the men, who gladly formed a human couch before the astonished Portuguese for their leader.

She faced the Portuguese governor and spoke as a ruler of the land, and not as a subject of the King of Portugal. She did not recognize the man in the big chair as governor because she did not recognize the existence of a Portuguese "colony of Angola."

Nzinga became queen in 1623, and went into action at once.

Nzinga's greatest act, and probably the one that makes her one of the greatest women in history, was in 1624 when she declared all territory in Angola over which she had control was free country, all slaves reaching it from whatever quarter were forever free. *Since it was clear to her that white power in Africa* rested squarely on the use of **Black troops against Black people,** she undertook the first and only carefully organized effort to undermine and destroy the effective employment and use of Black soldiers by whites, the first and only Black leader in history who was ever known to undertake such a task. She had carefully selected groups of her own soldiers to infiltrate the Portuguese Black armies, separating and spreading out individually into Portuguese-held territory and allowing themselves to be "induced" by Portuguese recruiting agents to join their forces. The quiet and effective work of Nzinga's agents, among the Black troops of Portugal was one of the most glorious, yet unsung, pages in African history. Whole companies rebelled and deserted to the colors of the Black queen, taking with them the much needed guns and ammunition, that she was unable to secure except by swiftly moving surprise attacks on enemy units. The Queen's armies were further strengthened by runaway slaves who streamed into the only certain haven for the free on the whole continent of Africa.

There was so much unity and patriotism and so much fanatical devotion to this "terrible Black Queen," as she was called by whites, that internal subversion was almost impossible. To the Portuguese, Queen Nzinga had passed the last word in unheard-of audacity when she was able to influence scores of basal chiefs to rebel against them and join the cause of their own race. This was too much. **This woman had to be destroyed.** The Portuguese marshalled all of their forces on land and sea to crush Nzinga. They captured her island stronghold in the Cuanza River in July, 1626, dividing her forces, and by a swift encircling movement designed to capture the Queen, cut off her main supporting regiments and forced her not only to retreat but to withdraw from her country. With Nzinga's flight from Angola it appeared that the Black menace was over and victory complete. Any child in the most distant bush could tell you that their Queen was "just away on business." All Angolan Kings and Queens were so African that they could not be *tricked* out of their African names. The Queen herself had dropped "Anna" from her name, when she discovered that baptizing a Black into Christianity meant surrendering his soul and body not to any Christ, but to the white man.

In November 1627, she crossed the borders back into her country as the head of a strong army, made stronger as her loyal chiefs. The wildly cheering people, including her fanatically devoted freed men, flocked to her as she swept forward to recapture the Cuanza stronghold held by Philip I and put him in flight. The Portuguese continued to be *amazed* at this display of *Black unity*, and under a woman's leadership at that. Black unity was now seen clearly as Black Power, and that meant an unconquerable people. They were resolved to break that unity and the power that developed from it. The Portuguese retreated to their strongholds on the coast giving the Dutch threat as an excuse, and not the threat of being annihilated by the Queen's forces.

The Portuguese regrouped and strengthened their forces for an all-out war to destroy Nzinga at this time, not to cease fighting until they had Nzinga or her body. They began by giving orders and offering a big reward for her capture, dead or alive. Their slave troops, still the backbone of the Portuguese armed forces, were given special inducements of land and freedom for her capture. Realizing that such an all-out attempt to capture her meant that countless thousands of her people would die in her defense, she outwitted the Portuguese again by slipping out of the country, instructing her lieutenants to spread the word everywhere that she had fled the country, mistakenly entered the territory of an enemy, and had been killed. To give point to the story, there was real weeping and mourning throughout Angola, because the masses believed the story to be true. So did the Portuguese. The Bishop could celebrate a **special mass** in celebration of the **special blessing**, and the colony of Angola could now be organized after fifty years of obstruction.

In 1629, the Portuguese stood shocked when Queen Nzinga "burst upon them from the grave" sweeping all opposition before her. The Portuguese were completely defeated. She had not only retaken her own country, but had become Queen of Matamba also, have replaced the weak queen there. Nzinga was now an empress of two countries. She now redoubled her campaign against slavery and the slave trade by making both Ndongo and Matamba havens for all who could escape from the slaver. The few chiefs engaged in slaving in nearby states now stood in fear of her wrath.

Nzinga *knew* that every white man in Africa was an enemy of the Blacks. It was a matter about which there was no room for debate in her mind. Even the holy robes of the priests in Angola not only covered their real mission as agents of the Portuguese Empire, but also covered their lust for the Black bodies of their helpless so-called slave girls.

Nzinga continued her campaign against th Portuguese, winning victories everywhere a battle was joined. The Queen was further outraged over the success of the Portuguese in capturing both of her younger sisters. This gave the enemy a most powerful bargaining weapon. Yet, she continued to reject all of their principal demands, with the result that her sisters, to whom she was deeply devoted, remained in captivity for many years. Nzinga was particularly ruthless with captured Black chiefs where were allies of the whites. She did not hesitate to sell such chiefs and their followers into slavery.

In 1663, as a dull Autumn sun lengthened the shadows over the palace grounds where thousands stood in tears, the sun slowly went down behind the Angolan trees and darkness spread over the land. In the heart-torn state of national mourning, the Queen's Council permitted two priests to come in and perform the last rites of the church. Since the Queen had renounced the Catholic Religion many years before her passing, this appearance of priests in the royal bedside, may be explained either as a once-a-Catholic-always-a-Catholic theory, or as an attempt by Catholic Portugal to give the appearance of final victory on all fronts.

And so it is written in the official documents of Portugal, that Nzinga returned to the church that had baptized her "Anna." Yet she was one of the very first of the Blacks to see that the Portuguese conquests, the trade of prisoners-of-war, and the church were all inseparably; one and the same. The long years of warfare had been equally against all three, the unholy Trinity. She never surrendered to any. In 1983, three hundred and twenty years after her death, her people, now Catholic themselves, do not believe she ever returned to the church.

We feel that specific information about the Black armies controlled by the Portuguese as well as the Arabs, should now come to the fore, even though we mentioned about the effects of the incursions in part back in Session IV and Session XI.

SLAVE CHILDREN OF THE ARABS

During the period of the earlier incursions, as well as this period, Black women were raped by the Arabs and other Asians. Arabs are basically a white people. They are not of the Euro-Caucasian people, but white just the same. As the hordes of Asians and Arabs continued to invade Africa and kidnapping African women, having children by them, they created a new breed or race whose loyalty was to *their fathers' race* and not to their African mothers'. Islamic tradition says the child is of the fathers' race. Here is a clear case in point where you can see that a foreign religious concept imposed on Africa's children did irreparable damage to us physically and mentally. It is no small wonder that we became confused and that confusion continues down until today for too many of us. This is how foreigners were able to raise a Black slave army. Those children were reared in that tradition. Their complexions ranged from light-skinned up to dark brown and even black. This helped to break the strength of the true or indigenous African. Thus, you had Black complexioned troops fighting with the Europeans and the Arabs; so the question was asked back in Chapter III, was the African himself the main cause of his downfall? The answer is "no." It was because of external forces. Yet things might have been somewhat different if we Africans, weren't so trusting of the other races.

A very great demand for labor was needed during the Industrial Revolution taking place in England and America.

The white world conspired against us, with one concern and that was to forever keep guns out of our hands. Psalms 83:3 in the Bible says, "They consulted together with one concern and said let us cut them off from being a nation that their name may be no more in remembrance." We were indoctrinated with their almost irrevocable brainwashing and then forever supervised by white people. Even though slavery existed centuries before, in Europe, Africa and Asia, never had it broken *every* link between the captive and his own culture and smashed the very structure of his society. Through mass murder and dispersal of those deemed suitable for servitude, many African societies came to a complete and final end. That Africa, and particularly Western Sudan Africa has recovered at all from the loss of tens of millions of her people, the smashing of scores of societies and from the *debasement* of those structures which remained, IS THE WONDER.

Finally en mass, we were marched to the waiting ships to be taken to the West Indies, America and England. Only the strongest, the youngest, the healthiest, the most beautiful and the most intelligent were taken by the force of the gun. The lame, the maimed, the sick, the elderly, the extremely nervous and the weak were left behind.

The whole of Africa was almost completely ravished, but particularly the Sudan, but even those who were left (without the gun), were valiant and stubbornly resisted the murdering invaders, making them pay in blood for every one of us they were able to capture. They forced those of us who were left from our choice farmland, driving us into what is tantamount to barren reservations. They took our stone homes and forced us to live in huts (the negative image of Africa that has been and still is projected by a people that had to perpetuate their "superiority imagery").

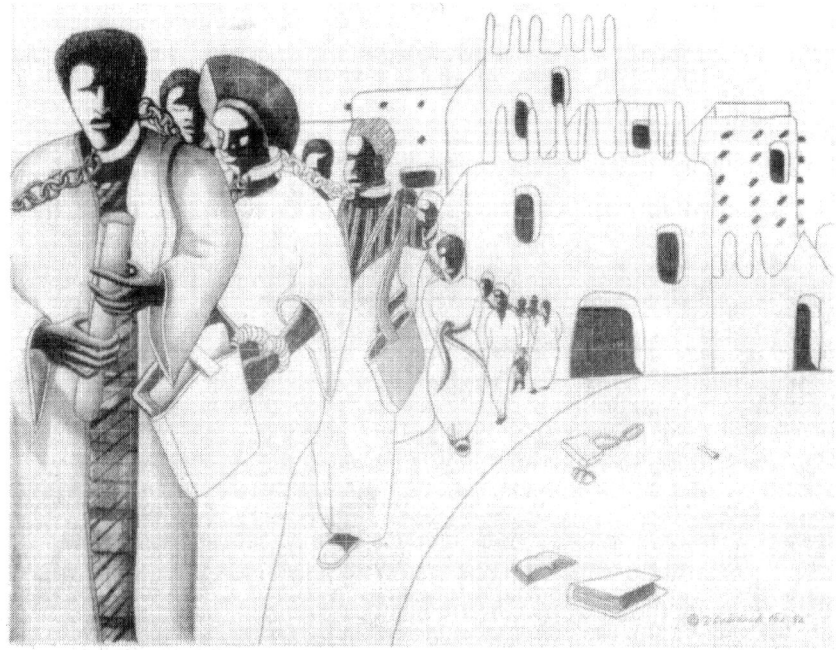

Picture of some of the university students, citizens, and children just snatched from classrooms and homes and were forced into the infamous Coffle Line.

THE MIDDLE PASSAGE

Profits were so huge that white men became fanatical in their quest for riches. It is said that a smart merchant could turn a cargo of Black flesh into profits up to *5,000 percent above cost*. Our flesh financed the *entire* Industrial Revolution. (A later chapter reveals this phenomenon). The record depicts that during the period between our involuntarily leaving our beloved Mother Continent and brought, by force, and violence, to America by way of the Middle Passage, that millions of our ancestors lost their lives during that voyage. Some jumped overboard rather than submit to captivity. Many more died from disease, shipwrecks, piracy and starvation. It is said, that for years the sharks never knew a hungry day. Blacks of today can only imagine, at best, the torture to which our fathers and mothers were subjected. The humiliations and weariness from the long march to the sea, their nakedness before these barbarians who really didn't know culture. We, the foundation of culture, and refinement, the cradle of civilization, the teachers of the world, being sold to the highest bidder—and this was just the beginning.

END OF SESSION XII

Africans fought with great valor on the field of battle and after capture, we still fought. This included the Coffil Line. The ordinary citizen, as well as the army often ambushed the slavers who were marching our mothers and fathers to the waiting ships.

SESSION XIII

BRIEFS ON THE MIDDLE PASSAGE AND THE TRIANGULAR TRADE

Who benefited from the atrocious acts of the initial captivity, the Middle Passage and ultimate barbaric servitude?

In 1517 Bishop Lascasas advocated the encouragement of immigrants to the new world, by permitting Spain to import twelve Blacks to each of the West Indies Isles. The trade in prisoners-of-war to the new world was then formally opened. Dutch, Portuguese, French, or English each at various times held a monopoly on the trade, depending upon who bid the highest.

THE POWER BEHIND THE WORLD SLAVE TRADE WERE THE ROYAL FAMILIES

The traders and merchants were the ones that stood out front, although the power behind the scene were the members of the royal families. In 1667, civil war broke out in England between the merchants and aristocrats—for an increased share in the profit of the p.o.w. industry. This was big business, the biggest in world history.

We were forcibly being loaded on ships. We, the very essence of culture and civilization and all that it entailed—to be taken away from our beloved Continent. Let's attempt to visualize the sailors who were trying to keep things moving by brutally beating our people for the least infraction, such as pausing or looking around. Some were being branded with a red, hot iron, while others were made to lie on the ground for fitness examination. This went on after long marches to the coast day after day. Thousands died on the way, others were shot while attempting to escape.

We were loaded on these ships, like logs, shackled together, only twelve to eighteen inches apart. On a great many of the ships where the stacking quarters were small, there was hardly head room.

THE MIDDLE PASSAGE WAS THE CROSSROADS AND MARKETPLACES OF DISEASES

Just imagine, if you will, an approximately forty to fifty day voyage of the most extreme cramping, the almost indescribable stench of waste matter left to encrust on our person, and on others. The captors also had the beastly gall to lust after some of our mothers by forcing relations with them. Many of our mothers were brave enough to resist his sexual thrust and died on the spot for doing so. The Middle Passage was the crossroads and marketplaces of disease. Gonorrhea and Syphilis came to America by way of Columbus and other white explorers. Gonorrhea and syphilis, along with tuberculosis almost annihilated the Indian. Even in our physically weakened condition, we showed a very remarkable resistance to those European diseases. As Finot, along with Livingston in J.A. Rogers, *From Superman to Man*, said: "Syphilis and gonorrhea does not seem to be able to penetrate the blood of Black people, as long as there is no foreign genetic intrusion."

One may wonder how this is possible that one group of humans are immune against two such widespread diseases.[1] Two leading scientists at the Institute of Technology in Pasadena discovered a property of proteins that would become the foundation for later work in evolutionary biology. They discovered ways in which hemoglobin, the primary blood protein, differed from one primate species to another in an attempt to learn why some primates never contract malaria, sickle-cell anemia or other diseases. *They found a correlation between the degree to which the hemoglobin molecules of two species differed and the evolutionary distance separating them. It is therefore reasonable to conclude this is applicable also within the human family.*

Thousands of us rather than submit to bondage, refused to eat, thus starving to death. Falconbridge, a ship doctor, wrote that he saw glowing coals of fire put on a shovel and placed so near our lips so as to scorch and burn them. In many cases even this did not persuade us to eat. Then we were flogged day after day, and sometimes this had the required effect. Yet, there were still others of our fathers and mothers that even after all of those atrocities, still refused to eat and became sub-

---

1 Rebecca L. Cann, Professor of Genetics at University of Hawaii at Manoa, in Honolulu. *In Search of Eve*.

One of the many factories which manufactured instruments of torture which provided employment for thousands of white people. For over a century and a half, the factories were located mainly in England and New England.

ject to a new kind of torture called the "speculum oris" or mouth opener. It resembled a pair of dividers, with notched legs and a thumbscrew at a blunt end. The instrument was forced into the mouth, breaking teeth as it went in. There was a turn-screw which acted as jaw pryer forcing the mouth wide open and holding it open. Our parents had a choice of hot coals or food to be forced down.[2]

There were many other instruments of cruelty that were employed against us to force us into submission. These instruments of torture were manufactured in New England and Britain, employing thousands of white people for over a century and a half. Many times our parents had the ability to hold their breath and will themselves dead. Finally, after about two months of this gruesome voyage of torture, we reached the planned destination where started the system of profit. They analyzed their cost in food, payment of sailors, etc. This is known as the Triangular Trade: Africa, The West Indies, New England or England.

By the Eighteenth Century, all trading in Africa had specified methods of purchasing and handling the traffic trading post of factories. The goods were cotton of all description, utensils of brass, pewter, and ivory, boxes, and beads of many sizes and shapes. Guns and gun powder, whiskey, brandy, rum and a variety of food stuffs were some of the most important items being exchanged for P.O.W.'s.

Then the captives were transported to the plantation in the West Indies. There the ships were unloaded. Their captives were exchanged for minerals and food. The ship left the West Indies with minerals and other products for sale in Europe. By this triangular system three separate profits were making an all time high mark-up in Europe. *The first profit was selling the consumer the goods to the ship-owner, the second was selling captives to the planters and mine owners of the Americas, while the third and biggest was realized on the sale of the West Indian cargoes in Europe. It was largely on the steady and stupendous profits of circuitous enterprise that France and England would ground their commercial supremacy.*

END OF SESSION XIII

---

[2] The speculum oris, manufactured in a factory owned by Brown and Savitts in Boston, Massachusetts was especially profitable. Our research shows that the money made in supplying the torture instruments for Brown paid for his building a large university that took his name — Brown University.

SESSION XIV

BREAKING IN THE CAPTIVES FOR PLANTATION WORK IN THE NEW WORLD

A new experience was about to unfold after that terrible sea voyage. Only the strong survived to face this new horror.

Our mothers and fathers were first used on the tobacco plantations of the Caribbean Islands. By 1639, the European market had become so gutted with weed that the price decreased sharply, and a great loss was sustained by the West Indies planters. Some turned to cotton and indigo, neither of which proved as profitable as they'd hoped. The Dutch suggested that they should try sugar. All this required much hard labor to clear the field, and plant the crop so that there was no let up in the importation of our people from the homeland. We were kept in a constant state of terror.

THE REPORT OF SIR HANDS SLOAN

After a tour of the Island in 1766 Sir Hands Sloan reported that we were severely punished for the tiniest infraction of overly harsh rules. **They used such excruciatingly painful acts as nailing us down on the ground with crooked sticks on each limb, then applying force by degrees from the feet and hands, burning them gradually up to the head.** For crimes considered of a lesser nature, gelding (castration) or chopping off half of the foot with an ax. These punishments were suffered by our foreparents with great constancy. For running away we were put in iron rings and great weights on the ankle, or a cruel device-about the neck, (iron rings with two longnecks riveted to them or a bit in the mouth). We were whipped until our flesh was raw, and often killed as a warning to others who were thinking about running away.

WHEN THE OVERSEER WAS IN CHARGE

When the overseer was in charge, the P.O.W. was mostly the victim of a person whose only interest was in getting more out of us for the captor. Captives were constantly being brought in from Africa, and the overseers found it necessary to develop a practice of breaking in the newcomers. In some areas they were distributed among the more seasoned captives, whose duty was to teach the new arrivals the way of life in the New World. In other places they were kept and supervised by a special staff of guardians or inspectors who were experienced in breaking in the Blacks who might offer resistance to adjusting to their new environment. *The mortality rate was exceedingly high, with the estimation of death running to as much as thirty percent, in a season period of three or four years. Old and new diseases, change of the elements and food, extreme exposure, suicide and excessive flogging were among the main causes of the high mortality rate among the new comers.*

Only the strong survived...and we are their children.

The overseers did not distinguish between men and women in their work requirements or in applying the lash for any dereliction of duties. Pregnant women were lashed severely when they were unable to keep pace with the other workers. Women who paused in the field to care for their babies whom they carried on their backs, were lashed with a cart whip. They were accused of idling away their time. Food on the whole, was insufficient. The planters did not often encourage any type of diversified agriculture, which would have provided food for the workers. When this was done at all, P.O.W.'s were often given small plots of land far from their houses, that they could cultivate in their spare moments. The time for such activities was usually Sunday. They were so fatigued by the labor of the week that they were hardly capable of working at all, even on the traditional work day. On many islands the Black population outnumbered the white. For example: As early as 1673, there were ten thousand Blacks on Jamaica Island and only eight thousand whites.

Because of the influence of the many planters in England at that time, it was possible for the passage of an act regulating Blacks on British plantations. This passage referred to Blacks as wild, barbarous, savage of nature, to be controlled with strict severity. Our parents were not to leave the plantation without a pass; much like South Africans' apartheid of today. They were not to go away on any Sunday under any circumstance and were not allowed to carry any weapons. If a captive struck a white he was seriously whipped, and for the second offense he was to be branded on the face with a hot iron. If the captors accidentally whipped a captive to death, he was not subject to fine or imprisonment. In some of the French colonies the laws were similar. **When Ogie and his associates were found guilty of conspiring to revolt in the last decade of the eighteenth century all were crudely executed. Their arms, thighs, legs and back bones were broken with a club on a scaffold. They were fastened around a wheel in such a manner that their face was turned upward to receive the full glare of the sun.** The cruel treatment was designed to prevent uprising and running away, but it was unsuccessful against this mighty people.

END OF SESSION XIV

SESSION XV

OUR FATHERS AND MOTHERS IN REVOLT AGAINST THEIR CAPTORS (ALSO THE MAROONS)

In the previous chapter (session) we saw the extreme cruelty perpetrated against us to discourage and prevent running away and revolting. Yet, all of this did not stop the uprisings from taking place.

You would not wonder why we dared to fight at such great odds, if you knew our glorious past. We of the former Songhai Empire were free, Black, beautiful and ingenious. We were endowed with the spirit of freedom then and now. We were also very strong in our psyche.

On almost every island, there is a record of some of the most serious revolts against the plantation system, and every where there is evidence of many escapes. When the British took possession of Jamaica in the seventeenth century, most of our foreparents escaped to the mountain, and were frequently joined by others of our people. By 1730, these ex-captives under Cudgo their powerful leader had so terrorized their captors, that Britain was compelled to send additional regiments to protect them. Haiti had its revolt as early as 1620, but their most celebrated freedom fight took place in 1803 under the dynamic leadership of Toussaint L'Ouverture. (See Haitian Revolt.) Haiti also had its "Maroons." (Those who were fugitives from captivity or descendants of fugitives). As early as 1620, the outlawed colonies grew to such proportions that the colonial government recognized it in 1780. The Maroons kept in constant touch with the other segment of our people and incited many to revolt. It is conceded that they were largely responsible for the Haitian uprisings in 1679, 1691 and 1704. As we recall an article on the Maroons in the Philadelphia Tribune (Black newspaper on February 9, 1982), our hearts filled with pride at the bravery and the ingenious methods our fathers and mothers used in fighting the slave system. The word Maroon was a term that evolved from the word "Cimarron" which is Spanish for runaway or unruly. It initially referred to cattle or other animals that were difficult to domesticate. Escaping into the interior of their captive country, Maroons selected locations that were difficult to find and economically unfeasible for the European colonist to cultivate. Easily defended, these communities were often inaccessible with false trails and natural barriers (swamps, sheer cliffs, etc.) creating hazards for any who were not completely familiar with the terrain. Should the enemy succeed in finding the carefully hidden trail, it was booby-trapped and approached single file only. Escape routes were equally well hidden with secondary camps developed in caves or sink holes to enable the Maroons to effectively withstand any siege of their main village.

Extraordinary defense techniques were developed by the Maroons to overcome the colonists, generally superior weaponry and manpower. The colonists' armies were composed of their own men, plus mercenaries, Indians, captives and sometimes a few free Blacks. Many of the captives were willing to fight for their promised freedom and often proved to be the better soldier. In Cuba, they trained dogs to hunt fugitives and to flush out the hidden Maroons. Guerilla warfare was the tactic used so successfully by the Maroons, while the colonists insisted in marching in proper formation and regimental clothing supported by the drum to give cadence to the march.

Usually armed with sticks, clubs, rocks, bows and arrows, spears, knives and other rudimentary weapons, the Maroons would lie quietly in wait when the general alarm was given. Camouflaging themselves with leaves and twigs, they blended into the underbrush or tops of trees. Ambushing the foe, they would hit and run with devastating results on the moral human life and economy of the country where the resistance took place.

Maroon settlements could be found throughout Latin America and the Caribbean (and even in the United States—most particularly in Florida and South Carolina). They became fierce fighters whose ability to plan and fight ("fight and flight") made them a source of terror among the colonies. These various settlements developed standards for existence that enabled them to survive in their hostile environment. Any inter-tribal or cultural difference that could possibly cause defeat was quickly forgotten. They learned early that *unity* was their key to becoming permanently free.

The Black militarist of the "New World" during the Sixteenth through the Nineteenth Centuries were generally insurgents *reacting* to cruel enslavement by the European powers. In the middle of the eighteenth century, recalcitrant Blacks of Haiti found a fearless leader in Macandal, a native African, who announced that he was the Black Messiah sent to drive the whites from the islands. He carefully laid his plans for the coupe d'etat, but by accident the plot was discovered, and Macandal was executed. At the time of his execution, he warned his enemies and comforted his friends by telling them he would return, more terrible than before. Many Blacks and some whites believed that Toussaint L'Ouverture was the reincarnation of Macandal. These revolts showed that docility of the Black man in the New World is a *myth*. There were four hundred recorded revolts. In the New World the Black man proved beyond a shadow of a doubt that he would die for his freedom.

We would be remiss if we didn't speak of the hundreds of revolts taking place on mainland United States of America. Some of the most celebrated revolts were as follows: In 1800, a Black man, one of our foreparents, named Gabriel Prosser had plans so well organized that with the enlistment of fifty to sixty thousand captives, had there not been a betrayal, the history of our people in this country might have been written much differently than what we know it today. Let us look in to the story of how this forefather of ours planned for our freedom.

He was a man of few words and his dark impassive face looked as if it were carved from ebony. He belonged to Thomas Prosser of Henrico County from whom he had taken his second name. Mostly folks called him Gabriel, and the revolt that he organized became known as "the great Gabriel conspiracy." Of all the revolts in the South, some historians consider Gabriel's the most significant in its effects upon the ever tightening codes of captivity. Certainly it spread fear of the captives in an ever-widening circle from Richmond throughout the entire white South. And there might have been a most frightful massacre in the city of Richmond had it not been that the elements intervened on the night set for slaughter.

Gabriel Prosser. A six foot, two inch man with such persuasive oratory that he was able to recruit thousands of our captive fathers and mothers in a bid for freedom.

Gabriel had planned his revolt very carefully, and he must have been a man of great persuasive powers to be able to swear so many people to secrecy in so dangerous an enterprise. His African followers were said to number well over a thousand. There were in Virginia in 1800 about 347,000 captives, of whom some 32,000 were in the city of Richmond and its surroundings. But the white population of Richmond was considerably less. Some of these were French and some were Quakers—minorities, to be sure, but of liberal tendencies.

As early as April, Gabriel began to make active plans for revolt at the time of harvest when the grain would be ripe, the gardens full, and fruit hanging from the trees. Then, he reasoned, for Africans who would be no longer dependent on their captors, there would be plenty to eat. In his own mind he set the date of the revolt for the very end of August, and on the first of September, he planned to occupy Richmond, killing all of the captive owning whites, but sparing the French, the Quakers, and the poor old women who owned no captives. Throughout the summer he met secretly with groups of his fellow captives, never gathering twice in the same place or at the same time. Sometimes groups would meet in the smokehouse, again in a tannery, sometimes in a cabin, others in a grove, sometimes at a crossroads late at night. Gradually, Gabriel had several hundred men and women of bondage sworn to uphold him in a might bid for freedom for all.

Gabriel thought that if enough Africans could be united to seize Richmond from the whites, other captives in all the surrounding countryside would join them in taking over the houses and lands of the so-called "masters" throughout Virginia. Then he would set up an empire of newly freed captives with himself at the head. Behind those wide eyes in his impassive face there was a very great dream—freedom for all within the entire area with which he was acquainted. Gabriel was illiterate, but he had heard about France, and he had heard the slogans of the American Revolution. He had heard, too, of the Declaration of Independence. And if he had never heard of any of these things, Gabriel was still the kind of man who would have wanted to belong to himself, not to any other man. Even if he bore his captor's name, he did not love his captor.

Gabriel was a giant of a man. He was six feet two in height. He had a friend, Jack Bowler, who was equally as tall and physically as powerful. Together with Gabriel's brother, Martin, they planned to lead a three-way invasion of Richmond between midnight and dawn on the first of September; each to conduct a group of captives by a different route into the city. From any sharp tool available that they could find, or steal away from white tool houses, they made weapons. They cut blades of scythes in half and made from each blade a pair of cutting irons capable of severing a man in two. They made bayonets of kitchen knives. They fashioned clubs, stole firearms, tied slingshots to forked branches. For Gabriel and his lieutenants, it was a summer of feverish activity. When they would be ready to march, every man would be armed with something, at best a gun, at worst a club or a stone. With their crude arms, they planned to take the government arsenal in Richmond.

Whenever Martin was present at a secret meeting of captives, he expounded on the Scriptures, and quoted that part of the Bible that declared that God would strengthen a hundred to overthrow a thousand. And the assembled captives would shout, "Amen!" for they believed that God was on their side. Meanwhile another of Gabriel's brothers, Solomon, busied himself with the making of cut glasses. Of the crude weapons of these Virginia captives a white witness later said, "I have never seen arms so murderous." In reality they had very little with which to fight for freedom—by the end of summer only a few muskets, a peck of bullets, ten pounds of ammunition, some pikes, and twelve dozen scythe-swords. Clubs and stones did not count much, and what were fists and bare hands to subdue an arsenal? But of audacity and courage they had a very great deal.

On the last night in August, a Saturday, the captives agreed to meet in Old Brook Swamp at a point six miles outside of Richmond, there to receive their orders from the young leader, Gabriel, and by sundown those who could get away so early had started for the appointed place from plantation to mansion, country cabin and city shop. According to an account written later by Thomas Wentworth Higginson, these were Gabriel's plans for the meeting in the swamp: "Eleven hundred men were to assemble there, and were to be divided into three columns, their officers having been designated in advance. All were to march on Richmond under the cover of night. The right wing was instantly to seize upon the penitentiary building, just converted into an arsenal; while the left wing was to take possession of the powder-house. These two columns were to be armed chiefly with clubs, as their undertaking depended for success upon surprise, and was expected to prevail without hard fighting. But it was the central force, armed with muskets, cut glasses, knives, and pikes, upon which the chief responsibility rested; these men were to enter the town at both ends simultaneously and begin a general carnage....In a very few hours, it was thought, they would have entire control of the metropolis....For the insurgents, if successful, the penitentiary held several thousand stand of arms; the powder-house was well stocked; the capitol contained the State treasury; the mills would give them bread; the control of the bridge across the James River would keep off enemies from beyond. Thus secured and provided...in a week it was estimated they would have fifty thousand men on their side, with which force they could easily possess themselves of other towns."

None of this ever happened. Instead on the Saturday night of the planned rendezvous in the swamp "the most furious tempest ever known in Virginia burst upon the land...Roads and plantations were submerged. Bridges were carried away. The roads were rendered wholly impassable. The Brook Swamp, one of the most important strategic points of the insurgents, was entirely inundated, hopelessly dividing Prosser's farm from Richmond; the country Africans could not get in, nor those from the city get out." The fields turned to bogs, the roads to rivers. From early evening on the rain came down in torrents, the wind howled and lashed the rain into stinging blades of water. In the stormy dark, pitch black and waterfilled, it was impossible for the captives even to see the roads, and short cuts across meadows or paths through forests were utterly indecipherable. Only a few hundred men were able to slosh through water or wade through mud up to their ankles to get to the appointed meeting place in the swamp. Gabriel's expected thousand dwindled to a miserable soaked group of faces that he could not even see in the dark and the rain. For any of them to reach Richmond that night would have been impossible. There was nothing for him to do but dismiss them, and before they could reassemble, they were betrayed.

The captives who betrayed them were named Tom and Pharaoh, and they belonged to a Mr. Moseby Sheppard whom they considered a kind "master." Tom and Pharaoh did not wish their master to be killed, so on the very day that Gabriel's great meeting was planned, they told Sheppard all about it. Sheppard, in turn, notified the authorities. And, Governor James Monroe, of Revolutionary fame, late that afternoon called for a troop of United States Cavalry to guard the city, appointed three military aides to conduct the defense of Richmond, and ordered cannon, wheeled into place around the capitol building. Even as Gabriel's followers, that evening, were hurrying through the dusk toward the swamps, the city was prepared to blow them to bits should their plan be carried out.

But it was only the next day when the full scope of Gabriel's plot became known that panic swept the city and martial law was declared. The whites were aghast at the unsuspected danger that had threatened them. As the news spread the whole state of Virginia became alarmed. Plantations turned into armed camps and in all the cities military patrols were doubled. Everyone realized that had it not been for the unusually terrible storm of the night before, a great deal of blood might have been shed and many lives taken. In the white churches of Richmond that Sunday, God was thanked for having spared their lives from Negro slaughter. Providence had protected Richmond by tempest, by thunder, lightning and rain. God, the whites felt, was on their side.

Quickly the authorities proceeded to take vengeance on the helpless Negroes. From Tom Pharaoh and other docile frightened captives, mostly house servants, they extracted all the names they could have those implicated in Gabriel's plans. Some captives were hanged without trial no sooner than they were caught. But to expose in full "the conspiracy" the governor ordered a series of trials for the hundreds of suspected captives who were rounded up. For Gabriel himself, who had escaped, a reward of three hundred dollars was posted. Jack Bowler surrendered. Other leaders were captured. But nobody would tell where Gabriel had gone; and the soldiers could not find him in the bog of Old Brook Swamp.

When the trials began in Richmond, Higginson writes that, "Men were convicted on one day, and hanged on the next, five, six, ten, fifteen at a time, almost without evidence." There were so many captives put to death, until various masters began to complain at the loss of so much expensive property. Able plantation hands and good servants were not always easy to come by, even through purchase; and among the followers of Gabriel had been some of the most intelligent and hard working captives of the region. Finally, the courts were urged to give fewer death sentences, lest they decimate the best of the captive population of Henrico County. In mid-October, as the excitement began to die down, the *New York Commercial Advertiser* reported from Richmond, "The trials of the Negroes concerned in the late insurrection are suspended until the opinions of the Legislature can be had on the subject. This measure is said to be owing to the immense numbers who are interested in the plot, whose death, should they all be found guilty and be executed, will nearly produce the annihilation of the Blacks in this part of the country." Jail sentences, chains, public whippings, and other punishments were meted out to many. Innocent and guilty alike suffered, for captives had to be taught the lesson that freedom was not meant for Black men and women, only for whites. But the two captives who betrayed Gabriel, Tom and Pharaoh were quickly pardoned for their loyalty to their so-called "master."

As to Gabriel, he too was eventually captured. They found him in the hold of the schooner Mary when it docked at Norfolk after a trip from Richmond. They brought him back to Richmond in chains. And so important did they consider this prisoner that the governor himself interrogated him. But Monroe reported that Gabriel "seemed to have made up his mind to die, and to have resolved to say but little on the subject of conspiracy." It had been Gabriel's plan to make a flag for his army of freedom and to inscribe on this flag Patrick Henry's famous slogan, "Liberty or Death." But Gabriel never had a chance to make the flag. However, he must have remembered, as he sat on trial in

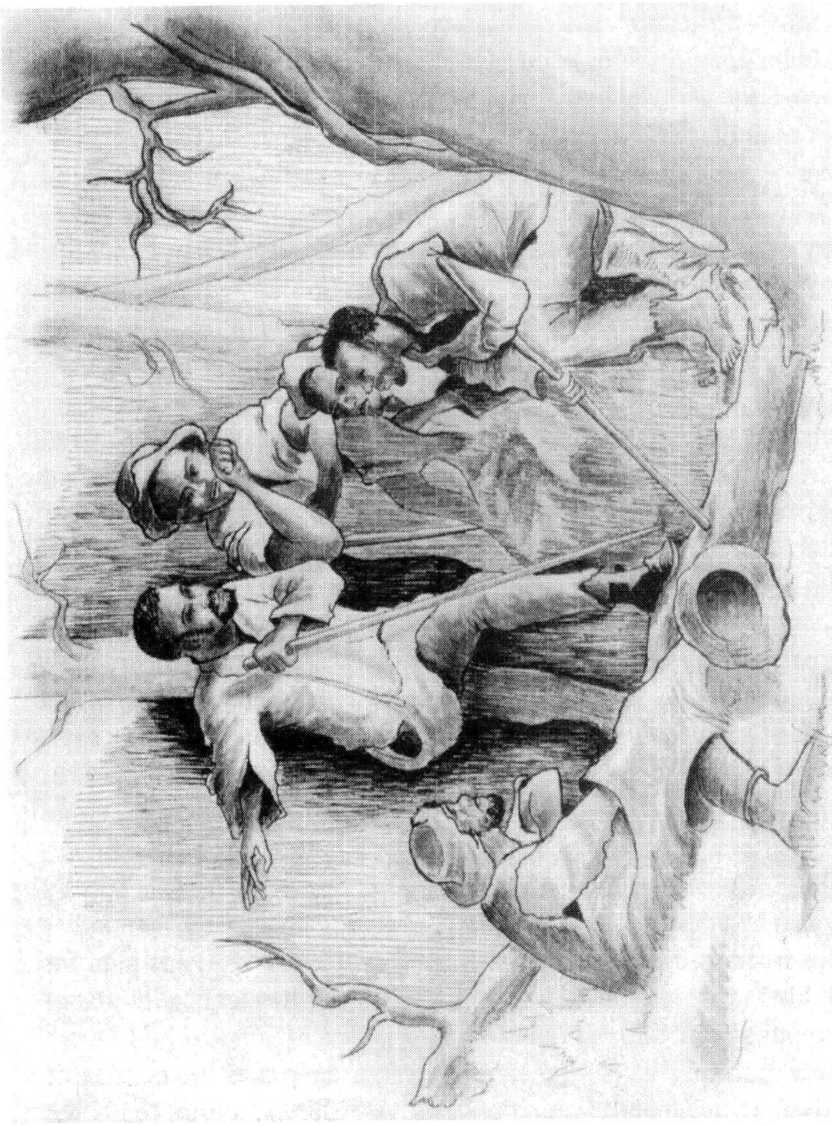

Denmark Vesey with stick in his hand, maps war strategy with his top aides and his chief lieutenant, Peter Poyas.

Richmond, what would have been emblazoned on his flag had the rebellion succeeded and the captives taken Richmond.

Except for the informers—and there were only three whose names were remembered, Sheppard's two captives and another called Ben Woolfolk—little information could be gotten from the men brought to trial. Indeed, some refused to talk at all in court. Their very silence frightened the captors, astonished the prosecutors, and shook the composure of the judges. Said one captive calmly when ordered to testify, "I have nothing more to offer than what General Washington would have had to offer, had he been taken by the British officers and put to trial by them. I have ventured my life in endeavoring to obtain the liberty of my countrymen, and am a willing sacrifice to their cause; and I beg, as a favor, that I may be immediately led to execution. I know that you have predetermined to shed my blood. Why then all this mockery of a trial?"

Gabriel's process took more time than any of the others, but from him, so newspaper accounts of the time indicate, the court learned almost nothing. *The Norfolk Epitome* reported, "The behavior of Gabriel under his misfortunes was such as might be expected from a mind capable of forming the daring project which he had conceived." Another account declared, "When he was apprehended, he manifested the greatest marks of firmness and confidence, showing not the least disposition to equivocate, or screen himself from justice." The *United States Gazette* added that the man displayed "the utmost composure, and with the true spirit of heroism seems ready to resign his high office, and even his life." Gabriel went to his death without naming anyone implicated in his plans. On October 7, 1800, he was hanged.

Gabriel Prosser undauntedly went to his death, but is believed by many that his ideas and spirit might have possessed the body of another famous freedom fighter named Denmark Vesey. In 1821 his plan for Black liberation and mode of operation was almost identical to that of his famous predecessor's, Gabriel Prosser.

There burning, in Vesey's breast was a deep and unquenchable hatred of African captivity and captors. A brilliant and hot-tempered man, he was for some twenty years a captive. He travelled widely and learned several languages; he learned also that slavery was evil and that man was not meant to be in bondage to man. Vesey reached a point, it is said, he could not bear to have a white person in his presence. The plan this firebrand conceived is one of the most elaborate on record. For four or five years, he patiently and persistently played the role of an agitator. Men he saw, must not only be dissatisfied, they must be **so dissatisfied** that they would **act.** Vesey was interested in **action.**

He told his fellow captives that their lives were so miserable that even death would be an improvement. Vesey buttressed his argument with quotations from the abolitionist Toussaint L'Ouverture and the Bible. He would read to those who were still in chattel from the Bible how the children of Israel were delivered out of Egypt from bondage. But he warned that God helped those who helped themselves. It was necessary to strike the first blow. Always, everywhere, the words of Joshua were on his lips..."And they utterly destroyed all that was in the city, both men and women, young and old, and ox and sheep and ass with the edge of the sword." This volcanic man, witnesses say, never rested. If he saw captives bowing to white men in the street, he would rebuke them. When the captives replied, "But we are captives," Vesey would comment with bitter sarcasm, "You deserve to be a slave." (Showing, beyond the shadow of a doubt that it takes the strong to make the weak stand up). With that type of philosophy, Vesey gained a vice-like hold on our people throughout Charleston, South Carolina. Many of our people feared Denmark Vesey more than they feared the whites. After reaching this point, Vesey switched from the role of agitator to organizer. He organized lieutenants and other sub-leaders for his army of liberation. Peter Poyas was a first-rate ship carpenter boarding on genius. It is said that ice water must have run through his veins. He was undoubtedly the coolest gambler in the history of Black freedom fighters. This is what made him Vesey's top chief Lieutenant. In this remarkable organization Peter and Vesey perfected a cell-like organization. (Check the Vesey story in some of the references listed in the back of this volume).

On November 11, 1831 an African captive, Nat Turner born in the state of Virginia was hanged for the same reason that Prosser, Vesey and Poyas were hanged. That reason being a burning desire to free our people. And because of only one or two of our people selling out to the murderers for personal gain, they all died.

Nat Turner's name was feared by whites throughout Virginia and even in North Carolina. He too was great in his quest to free our people. This happened in a generation of crisis in which the issue of Black captivity, almost severed the nation. His arm of vengeance did much to bring that crisis to a head. Nat Turner's insurrection was a landmark

Nat Turner his arm of vengeance did much to focus the issue of Black enslavement which almost permanently severed this nation. The sacrifices all these great ancestors did, hastened the day of our physical redemption.

in the history of the American system of Black extermination.

We would be remiss if we didn't mention another kind of insurrection, that lent so much to that great struggle for our freedom that was going on during that period.

In 1844, a vigilante committee was founded by a daring young man named William Still. He was a major conductor of the Underground Railroad and also chairman of the militant Vigilance Committee. They would meet in a house in Germantown (Philadelphia, Pennsylvania) to discuss various strategies.

Among those with William Still, there was this marvel of a woman; they called her "MOSES." She came out of the night, silently, stealthily, mysteriously. Nobody knows how she came or when she came. Suddenly, inexplicably, she was there, on the edge of the slave quarters, singing a song, old as the night and deep as the hopes of man:

Harriet Tubman. She became known as Grandma Moses. Here is a drawing of her at a younger age with a deep expression of concern. She was troubled over the plight of her people. She was struck in the head by an overseer for trying to prevent two of our people from fighting.

> Hail, oh hail, ye happy spirits,
> Death no more shall make you fear.
> Grief nor sorrow, pain nor anguish.
> Shall no more distress you there.
> Around him are ten thousand angels
> Always ready to obey command
> They are always hovering around you.
> Till you reach the heavenly land.

Harriet Ross Tubman (c. 1823-1913) was born to captive parents in Maryland. Her childhood memories, like those of other captive children, were mostly of hunger, mistreatment and hard work. At about fifteen years of age, she intervened to protect another captive, and was struck in the head by a two pound weight hurled by the overseer. The injury caused her to suffer sleeping seizures and dizzy spells for the rest of her life. In 1844 or 1845 she married John Tubman, a freedman. Several years later when she was determined to escape to the North, her husband refused to join her. Her two brothers who started out with her, lost heart and returned. She went on her way alone and made her way to freedom. For the next decade, all of her amazing energies and talents were devoted to rescuing her family, all neighbors and other captives. In all, she made nineteen rescue trips to the South. She was a legendary figure with a $40,000 reward on her head. It was her pride that of the three hundred or more captives she rescued as a conductor on the Underground Railroad, *she never* lost a single passenger. She always carried a pistol, with which she spurred on laggard or despairing fugitives, telling them, "You'll be free or die!"

Harriet Tubman was more than a brave abolitionist. She was a militant Black leader and a revolutionist, dedicated to winning Black freedom. She was respected and befriended by Black and white abolitionist leaders and was known for her exploits in Canada and Great Britain as well as throughout the North. She was unique among Black women in her military role. She fully supported John Brown's plan for the raid on Harper's Ferry, but was prevented by illness from joining him as she had planned. During the Civil War, she worked as a nurse, spy and a scout. Her position was unique, in that the several times she commanded troops both Black and white, on scouting raids of the most spectacular of which she rescued 756 captives.

She was fighting that war in the fiftieth year of her emancipation when she had her last vision. "I am nearing the end of my journey," she told the members of the A.M.E. Zion Church of Auburn, New York." I can hear the bells ringing, I can hear the angels singing. I can see the hosts a marching." Soon afterwards, on March 10, 1913, Harriet crossed her last river and went. If there is any justice in the universe, to her reward, with bells ringing, angels singing and the host marching; we say her reward was in her services she rendered to our people. A verse in the Bible says "They that might be the greatest among you, let them first become the servant."

All of the great men and women giving their lives, sweat, tears, their love and concern for us, their children, hastened the day of our *physical* redemption. Their great sacrifices were the forerunner of those great debates on the "slavery" questions that resulted in the abolition of chattel bondage in the United States of America.

Had it not been for the great outpouring of love and devotion of our people for their brothers and sisters and themselves included, the so-called "freedom" as we know it today probably would not be.

Here we were a people with the loss of their original leadership command, and in a hostile land after being torn from the safety of their national protection became united in love, deprivation, long suffering, anguish and respect for mutual protection.

END OF SESSION XV

This is a picture of a so-called slave cabin. It was cramped, airless, crudely construced. For centuries our fathers and mothers slept on dirt floors. The cabins were extremely overcrowded which increased our death rate.

SESSION XVI

THE LIFE STYLE OF BLACKS, AND UNMITIGATED PRESSURES TO DESTROY BLACK FAMILIES DURING BONDAGE

The Life Style of Blacks,
and the unmitigated pressures
to destroy our Black Family
during our bondage.

Although the television series of "Roots" did a magnificent job of awakening us to some of the horror that we suffered during our captivity, it was at least a thousand times worse. The motion picture *Farewell to Uncle Tom*, which used a lot of Kenneth Stampp's book *Peculiar Institution*, really told how our living conditions were, which coincided with what our great-grandparents had told us.

We lived amid conditions consistent with our almost total lack of power. The majority lived in cramped, airless, and crudely constructed shacks without the most basic provisions for security and sanitation. There were no windows, floors, or insulation. It was not uncommon to find entire P.O.W. families existing in one-room cabins under the most crowded and unhealthy circumstances. In most instances, during the centuries of our physical captivity our fathers and mothers slept on dirt floors. Some of the groups with one hundred and fifty captives and upward were cramped into only twenty-four huts measuring sixteen by fourteen feet. This also attributed to the premature deaths of so many of our mothers and fathers. To make more profit, they gave us the cheapest and the poorest food. A peck of cornmeal and three or four pounds of salt port or bacon, comprised the basic weekly allowance of most adult captives. We were in a constant state of chronic hunger most of our lives. It was only due to the power with which our blood was endowed, which came from the fathers and mothers before, that really kept us alive. Contrary to the false rumors about pork meat making us grow strong and was good for us, actually, it had just the opposite effect. We survived and multiplied not because of this pork, but in spite of it. All of these conditions opened the door to a host of diseases and sent our death-rate soaring.

We were first brought here (the weak of mind, spirit, and body had been selected out), and now we had come to this. We originally had the world's strongest traditions of family life and cohesion in our proud past. This is why the captors never hesitated to dissolve our families, especially when large profits were to be made. This meant that husbands, wives and children could be separated with impunity. The displaced African family was not important. The captor superseded the father as the authority in the P.O.W. cabin. In fact, the father was as powerless as the children in this dehumanizing structure. The father could do nothing if his wife was whipped or raped by the captors—even if in the father's presence and in the presence of the children. We can say, that the status of the Black male resembles that of his male captive predecessor in some rather alarming aspects, inasmuch as few Black men can really "protect" their families or themselves from the aggressions of a racist society. Considering the degree to which the captor went, to dehumanize and robotize Blacks here in this country, is a "wonder" that we survived at all. There was no limit to the kinds of cruelties and humiliations imposed upon us by their code laws. An historian, Stanley Elkins, had concluded that the whites had succeeded in reducing the Blacks to the level of dependency of infants, much as the Nazis were later to do to the hapless Jews, who were herded into their dreadful World War II concentration camps. But the Jews' HOLOCAUST lasted for only ten years while the **AFRICANS' HOLOCAUST LASTED FOR THREE HUNDRED YEARS.**

Not only were these tactics used here in the United States, making us like dependent infants, but throughout the African continent of which whites controlled.

In Liberia, for instance, the Euro-American teaching of Christianity, the American language, the use of American currency and general political policies, have made these Blacks think like whites. The so-called Liberians were the ex-captives that were taken back from the United States and placed in that particular location in Western Africa.

The apparent success of the white control of Blacks throughout Africa came about, first as a result of the military take over, through long bloody wars. Secondly, as each city was conquered, it was painful for our foreparents to be removed by force from their beautifully built brick and stone homes with inside plumbing and running water facilities. We were forced to build and dwell in the now familiar huts. But these huts are of a special construction and insulated for all types of weather conditions. However, whenever there are any kind of pictures shown of Africa from years ago and even today, they only want you to see those huts. We who know our history and the white man's game, know that the lies told about us must be perpetuated in order to justify the injustices practiced against us. When narrating a movie on African life, they never show the cities unless there are white people being portrayed in a power position and the Blacks being subservient to them. We are *always* doing a so-called tribal dance or being carriers on some white man's African game hunt.

THE "WHITE IS RIGHT" CONCEPT

Let us now consider what really forced Black people down from their position of high world respect for ourselves. Looking at it as objectively as possible, we cannot say that it was only because of the gun, but rather the philosophical follow-through of the "white is right concept." **Then they introduced the doctrine of respect, love, obedience and honor to white people who were and are relentlessly taught in every facet of African life at home and abroad.** There were published pamphlets in every conquered African country where schools were set up to teach this doctrine. They forced African people to rename their children from African names to their so-called Christian names. To really put the nails in the coffin, they teamed up with the Arabs and projected the white God concept, giving the African the Bible and the Koran, further indoctrinating us into false concepts against Africa's traditional religious concept of Maat (NTU).

Having lost this, the *God of our fathers*, we, Africans of the ensuing generations down to today cannot communicate with our true past, thus winding up confused, which prevents us from putting our ethnic program together.

As we have pointed out in previous chapters, that the contempt against Africans as a whole was taught on a "must" basis. This contemptuous teaching was designed to make the world society and particularly the society of the white world feel that any atrocity they committed against us was justified. By teaching their people that we were a bunch of jungle bunnies, nymphs of nature, so childlike that the whites were ordained to put us in captivity and take over our land.

This teaching was designed specifically to make us feel contemptuous of ourselves—which we are. If we really knew from whence we came, what we did in terms of achievements that spells out who we are, we wouldn't have that hate for each other or envy and feeling of strife. Yes, it was our knowledge in all fields of civilized endeavor, bringing mankind from the depth of ignorance into the marvelous light. As we aforementioned in the "Looking Forward" of this text, "they had to rewrite the history books to correspond with the brainwashing. Had this not been done, the great knowledge of Black Africa and especially the Western Sudan would have become common knowledge. This would have resulted in our minds being free and the resistance to captivity in the United States of America would have been a thousand times greater."

As we mentioned in Session Ten, that we were scanning the skies for greater astronomical knowledge, a point to ponder, because how could supposed savages know about the science of astronomy. This brings to mind the special knowledge that our grandparents knew about the science of agriculture. The knowledge of planting in accordance with the moon, stars and the time of the month. This was not something that was dreamed up, but it had come down through the blood and in the genes. Even with all the massive brainwashing perpetrated against us, some of our forefathers' and mothers' genius still got through. And what that was, that came down to us among other things, was the Maat Concept.

Our people expressed their religious beliefs through the concept defined as Maat that they considered as a divine order established at the time of creation. This order is manifested in the normalcy of phenomena. In all African societies, it manifests itself as justice and in an individual's life as truth. Maat is this order, the essence of existence, the concept of harmony with the divine order of the universe.

To the ancients, space was of life and death importance. This is evidenced by their mysterious megalithic monuments that were tuned to the rhythm of the star cycles, which they realized were the pulse of life affecting vegetation growth, animal migrations and mating cycles correlated with the positions of the moon, stars and the sun.

"In a mountainous area of the Republic of Mali, approximately two hundred miles south of Timbuktu, live several large African families: the Dogon, the Bambara, the Bozo and the Minianka.[1] In striving for greater calendrical accuracy, the astronomer priest of various families such as the Dogon, incorporated the rising and setting of certain stars or groups of stars into their calendar for greater accuracy and community harmony, which fosters greater mental development among the African peoples. This is why we say in PAFO's "Purposes and Goals," that power is organized energy or effort.

The complex knowledge of the Dogon of Mali about the Sirius Star System is sending shock waves around the scientific world. Not only did Western Africans plot the orbits of stars circling Sirius, but have revealed the extraordinary nature of one of its companions "Sirius-B," which they claim to be one of the densest and tiniest of stars in our galaxy. Sirius-B is not only the smallest type of star in the sky, it is also the heaviest. It consists of a metal the Dogon calls sagala, which is a little brighter than iron and so heavy that all earthly beings combined strength could not lift a cubic yard of it.

They say there is another star besides Sirius-B (po tolo) orbiting Sirius called "emme ya" which is larger that it but four times lighter and travels along a greater trajectory in the same direction and in a period of fifty years. This "emme ya" (sun of women) has a satellite called "nyan tolo" (star of women). What is really astonishing, about these ancient Africans revelation is that Sirius-B (po tolo) is invisible to the unaided eye.

This is why M.I.T. Professor Kenneth Brecher in his essay, *Sirius Enigmas*, was so startled by the complex and incredibly precise knowledge of the West Africa Dogon people about the orbits and trajectories of stars within the Sirius System, exclaimed rudely; "THEY" (Africans) have no business knowing any of this." PAFO KNOWS that as this knowledge of our people becomes more and more widespread, the white racists desperados will continue to try to say that somebody from outer space taught us all of this. Now you can more readily see why it was important during our physical captivity as well as now to blot out

---

[1] Ivan Van Sertima, *Journal of African History*.

our true history. They just simply couldn't afford the truth to be known, not only to us, but to their own people as well.

They portrayed us as animals, with no supposed civilization except perhaps on the lowest level of neolithic existence.

The television version of *Roots* projected this, when Alex Haley finally found Kunta Kinte. By that time, our original cities had been destroyed, thus forcing us into a different type of living conditions, especially since our choice land was taken. Let us now resume the plight of our people in the United States.

CAPTIVITY ON MAINLAND UNITED STATES (1638-1862)

Forced Black labor throughout the plantation system at best, was a continuing horrible experience for our mothers and fathers. Working from sun-up to sun-down whether they were feeling ill or not didn't matter, and because of these hardships, we sparked off many small insurrections as well as big ones. Those that inspired us to revolt such as Gideon Jackson, Frederick Douglass, Harriet Tubman, Robert Purvis, James McCrummel, James Barbadoes, Samuel Cornish, Theodore Wright, Peter Williams, just to name a few, caused the whites to fear us more and more. They were ordered to arm themselves, thus causing our mortality rate to go even higher. The whites more and more began to feel that their power of life and death over us made them indeed superior beings. When this happened, it affected the psyche of the white race then, and even down to this present time.

They didn't know that behind this arming of the ordinary white person to keep our people from running away or to resist continued captivity—was to protect the investments of none other than the planters and textile manufacturers.

Seven percent of the total population of the South in 1860 "owned" nearly three million of the three million nine hundred and fifty-three thousand captives.

This was nearly as great a concentration of ownership as the best agricultural land. This means that in a country predominantly agricultural, the ownership of labor, land and capital was extraordinarily concentrated. Such peculiar organization of industry would have to be carefully reconciled with the new industrial and political democracy of the nineteenth century if it were to survive. Five million whites who had no captives were united in the interest of the captors of our people.

Some were overseers and drivers and dealers for our foreparents. Others were hirers of whites and Black labor, and still others were merchants and professional men forming a petty bourgeois class, and climbing up to the planter's class.

The mass of poor whites were economic outcasts, and the domination of property was shown in the qualification for office and voting in the South. The Southerners and others in the Constitutional Convention asked for property qualification for the presidency, federal judges and senators. Most Southern state governments required a property qualification for the governor, and in South Carolina, he had to be worth ten thousand pounds. Members of the legislature had to be land-holders. The wealthiest planters controlled the representation in the House, and taxation in the other or the use of federal appropriation and taxation combined. The Southern Planters held this control until the Civil War. Political power was equivalent to two million freedmen in the North. They fought bitterly during the early stages of pre-Reconstruction to retain this power for the whites. There was another motive which more and more strongly as time went on, *compelled the Planters to cling to our captivity, their political power was based on it*. The espousal of the doctrine of Black inferiority by the South was primarily because of the economic motives and the inter-connected political urge necessary to support the captive industry. The third motive was brought about by periods of panic arising from doubt of its ability to maintain its power and control. The South had chosen eleven out of sixteen presidents, seventeen out of nineteen attorney-generals, twenty-one out of thirty-three Speakers of the House, and eighty out of one hundred foreign ministers.

The Civil War clouds were beginning to form with the growth of the abolitionist movement and the resultant so called great "slave debates" which was sparked by some of our great freedom fighters. Let us say here and now, that the North in general did not support the abolitionist movement to the point that they would take up arms against their southern counterpart for Blacks. Lincoln also let it become known that his only concern was to save the Union. If it could be saved by freeing some, he also would do that, but if it would take the freeing of all the Blacks to save the Union, he would do it. The North was afraid that "slavery" would spread on a wholesale basis into the North and threaten the jobs of the northern worker. You see, we, the descendants of the Songhai Empire were skilled in many crafts; we were carpenters, brick layers, stone masons, designers, coppersmiths, and everything that had to do with the building trade. If "slavery" were to spread to the North, then white northern building contractors could never compete with the captors with his skilled captives. This fear of unfair competition (as they put it) is what really put the teeth in the abolitionist movement. The captors wanted to extend their power through the increased importation of African captives, and the North wanted it stopped. Here again, profits and those who sought them, played a major role that was to help shape the destiny of Blacks, whites and Indians.

The South was winning the war, and this caused Abraham Lincoln to issue the Emancipation Proclamation on September 22, 1862 in order to legalize our fathers' bearing arms. Thousands of our fathers joined the Union forces against the South and another quarter of a million in the role of spies, nurses, suppliers, orderlies, messengers and a host of other duties that were necessary to speed the war to a successful conclusion. Many Black soldiers were decorated for their bravery and extraordinary brilliance on the battlefield with twenty-one Congressional Medals of Honor. By an act of Congress, on July 28, 1866, provisions were made to accommodate a number of Black soldiers who had served in the force. As a result, the Ninth and Tenth Calvary Regiments and the twenty-fourth and twenty-fifth Infantry Regiments were created.

END OF SESSION XVI

SESSION XVII

THE CIVIL WAR

The War Between the States of the United States of America, commonly referred to as the Civil War, began early on the morning of April 12, 1861, by the firing by Southern soldiers on the Union-held and garrisoned fort in the harbor of Charleston, South Carolina, called Fort Sumter. Before the war was over, on April 5, 1865, five hundred and twenty-five thousand American servicemen had died; more than all the servicemen of America had in all of the wars fought by America before the Civil War and after the Civil War combined. The firing on the federally-held garrison put into action the previously announced threat by the Southern States that if Lincoln won the election, which he had just done, the South would secede from the Union. Lincoln had said before the election:

"A HOUSE DIVIDED AGAINST ITSELF CANNOT STAND. I WILL PRESERVE THE UNION AT ALL COSTS."

The South, by attacking and starting the war felt that it could, in a short while, force the North to give up some of its national power, allowing captivity to spread to the territories, and enforce the infamous Fugitive Slave Law, which meant for the North to carry out with more fervor the return of Black persons who had escaped from the terror and oppression of the South. This promise to the South had not only been made in the Constitution of the United States, but also in a law of 1850.

The weapon the South thought that it could use to force the North to not only stop the war but give up some of its considerable national power, was based on something the North desperately needed as well as Great Britain. With its warm climate and nearly four million Black captives, the South had a seeming unending abundance of—cotton—for the mills of the manufacturing North and Great Britain.

It is absolutely incorrect to believe that the North fought the war to free the Black captives. Lincoln said in his inaugural address on March 1, 1861:

Abraham Lincoln: We will quote Abraham Lincoln as he supported the following amendment to congress, "I support this amendment to the constitution which will forever deny congress the right to abolish slavery in the states." Documented in the book, History of the Labor Movement in the U.S. *by Foner.*

"I HAVE NO PURPOSE, DIRECTLY OR INDIRECTLY TO INTERFERE WITH THE INSTITUTION OF SLAVERY IN THE STATES WHERE IT EXISTS. I BELIEVE I HAVE NO LAWFUL RIGHT TO DO SO, AND I HAVE NO INCLINATION TO DO SO." To demonstrate his attitude even more dramatically three days later, he supported an amendment to the Constitution:

"I SUPPORT THIS AMENDMENT TO THE CONSTITUTION WHICH WILL **FOREVER DENY** CONGRESS THE RIGHT TO ABOLISH SLAVERY IN THE STATES;."

The author, Foner, in his *History of the Labor Movement in the United States*, said that in one month three states had endorsed this evil proposal, but their firing on Fort Sumter put an end to the proposal.

You do not have to be a scholar of history to read in book after book that it was not the intention of the North to end the captivity of our fathers and mothers, but only to preserve the Union with so-called slavery in it. James Ford Rhodes reduced it to two words—African captivity.

W.E.B. DuBois said in his *Black Reconstruction* that the very idea of fighting the war to free Black people was absolutely abhorrent to the white Northerner and was voiced in the popular ditty of that time:

"To the flag we are pledged, all its foes we abhor,
And we ain't for the nigger, but we are for the war."

Not only was the idea of fighting to free Black people abhorrent, but the idea of the Black man fighting to help the North in its endeavor to preserve the Union was also loathsome to the white Northerner. When Black plantation captives escaped to Union camps, expecting to find welcome for their proffered services as fighters or workers, the Northern soldiers most often beat them, or held them while his Southern so-called master beat him to the insulting jeers of the soldiers. Congress PASSED A LAW in July of 1861, requiring that all "slaves" were to be returned immediately to their so-called masters upon claim.

In the North, Black volunteers were told to not only keep out of the recruitment centers that they flocked to by the thousands, but were set upon and beaten and in many, many instances killed. Petition after petition from African Americans flooded both the state and federal administrations. A petition from prominent Black leadership of Philadelphia in May 1861 offered ten thousand able-bodied "colored citizens to bear arms...." Among them was famed Philadelphian, Octavius V. Catto who was later killed by a white mob. Buildings and schools have been named in his honor. To all of these petitions, if they were replied to at all, came the official Lincoln administration response, "This is a white man's war," Secretary of War Cameron said in August, 1861:

"THIS DEPARTMENT HAS NO INTENTION AT PRESENT TO CALL INTO THE SERVICE OF THE GOVERNMENT ANY COLORED SOLDIERS."

For a year and eight months of the war, the Lincoln administration was able to keep our fathers out of the war—but not 100% effective. Dr. James McPherson, professor of history at Princeton University, author of *The Negro's Civil War*, said that thousands of poorly pigmented Negroes (mulattoes) passed for white and went in white regiments during this period. While the exclusion was very effective in large cities, in small towns some Black volunteers were occasionally accepted. The first blood shed in the Civil War was a Black volunteer from Pottsville, Pennsylvania whose townspeople allowed him in their regiment. As they were passing through Baltimore six days after the war started, April 18, 1861, a crowd, infuriated at the sight of a Black man in uniform attacked his contingent with brickbats and laid his face open to the bone. The people of Pottsville marked his grave with the following inscription:

> "In Memory of Nicholas Biddle—His was the proud distinction of shedding the first blood in the late war for the Union, being wounded while marching through Baltimore with the First Volunteers from Schuylkill County."

Our fathers' attempts were met with hostility and jeers. Lincoln said as late as August 1862, in reply to a petition:

> "I am afraid that if we gave Negroes guns, the rebels would have them in two weeks."

In spite of the violent exclusion, in spite of the lynchings and humiliation, the rejections, the scoffers and the jeers, we will show and prove by records that this despised and rejected human being, the **African warrior**, who eventually won the war, won his freedom, and who, at the same time preserved the Union.

How could this happen? Again we must rely on the documented history contained—not in the textbooks, but in the writings in the **National Archives**—and in the books written based on the records in the War Department of the United States of America.

HOW BLACK SOLDIERS WON THE CIVIL WAR

The records show that during the spring and summer of 1862, the North began losing the war. The Confederates, sensing victory, turned sharply on the offensive. Washington was threatened with invasion. Just outside of Washington, the North lost the Second Battle of Bull Run. The Union Army was being chased and humiliated on every turn of events. On the political front, the Republicans were losing battle after battle. McPherson said:

"IN JULY AND AUGUST, DEFEATISM WAS SLOWLY CREEPING OVER THE NORTH. DESERTIONS BY THE THOU-

SANDS OCCURRED."

The beaten and humiliated generals were crying for help. Generals came to Lincoln. General Benjamin Butler said,

"MR. PRESIDENT, THE NORTH IS LOSING THE WAR. THERE STANDS A BLACK FORCE WAITING IN THE WINGS OF HISTORY, WAITING TO RUSH ON STAGE TO SAVE US."

But Secretary of State Seward said,

"WE MUST HAVE A GENERAL EMANCIPATION DOCUMENT BECAUSE TO USE THE BLACK MAN WITHOUT PERMISSION OF HIS OWNERS, WE WOULD BE USING ANOTHER MAN'S PROPERTY AND THAT WOULD SET A FEARFUL PRECEDENT. TO LEGALLY USE THE BLACK MAN AS A FIGHTING MAN, WE WOULD HAVE TO LEGALLY FREE HIM. BUT, MR. PRESIDENT, I BELIEVE THAT IT WOULD BE INAPPROPRIATE TO PERMIT NEGRO SOLDIERS TO COME IN NOW WHILE WE ARE LOSING THE WAR, BECAUSE HISTORY WOULD MAKE MUCH OF THE FACT THAT WE HAD TO ASK THE NEGRO TROOPS TO SAVE US WHITE FOLK. WE SHOULD AT LEAST WIN ONE BATTLE BEFORE WE ISSUE THE DOCUMENT TO ALLOW THEM TO FIGHT."

General Butler said,

"WE'VE LOST ALL THIS YEAR'S BATTLES."

President Lincoln replied,

"WE DON'T WANT HISTORY TO THINK THAT WE HAD TO STRETCH FORTH OUR HAND FOR HELP TO THE NEGRO. WIN FOR US ONE MAJOR BATTLE, THEN WE WILL ISSUE AN EMANCIPATION DOCUMENT AS A FIT AND NECESSARY WAR MEASURE. THEN YOU WILL HAVE YOUR BLACK HELP."

The Confederates had pushed into upper Maryland in the western part of that state in early September. Now was the time for the battle for which Lincoln had asked. On September 17, 1862, near the Antiem Creek the second bloodiest battle in the total war was fought. After it was over, twelve thousand Union and ten thousand Confederate troops lay dead. Lincoln, anxious for any semblance of victory of the North, signed the Emancipation order on September 22, to allow Black troops to be used legally by the North. This was the fit and necessary war measure. Black troops would be allowed to fight at last, beginning January 1, 1863. This was the day for which the eager, angry and intrepid Black warriors had been waiting. This was the day that they would say in one voice—"Let me at them!"

Congress had sensed that there would be inevitable admission of Black troops because of the fervor, and enthusiasm, the ardor and passion of the petitions from Black people pouring in. So they passed THE LAW OF JULY 17, 1862, specifying that if they were admitted, they were to receive less than half the amount white soldiers were paid. They would have to pay for their own laundry while the government paid for the white soldier's laundry at $3.50 per month. Black families of volunteers were not to receive any subsistence as would white families, and Black volunteers were not to receive any bonus.

In spite of such degrading discrimination, our fathers came by the thousands. Now, with no law barring their entry. Black captives of the South left the plantations by the tens of thousands. Dr. Lerone Bennett, in his *Before the Mayflower* stated the fact that more than 300,000 came from the plantations. Two hundred and ten thousand of these served in labor battalions, building fortifications, digging trenches, serving as cooks, teamsters and servants. More than ninety thousand were organized into regiments of infantrymen, artillerists and calvarymen.

Northern African Americans contributed more than eighty-six thousand fighting men with Pennsylvania leading the way with nearly twenty-five thousand volunteers. The border states is credited in War Department records as having contributed forty thousand Black volunteers.

How do we know this?

In reply to a Civil War Veteran's inquiry as to the number of Black men in the army, we have this letter from the archives of the Library of Congress written by the Chief Arnosworth, Chief of the Record and Pension Office, War Department, Washington D.C., dated September 13, 1895. THE OFFICIAL RECORD SAYS, "AS REGARDS THE WAR OF THE REBELLION, IT IS SHOWN BY OFFICIAL STATISTICS ON FILE THAT 178,975 COLORED SOLDIERS WERE EMPLOYED, WITH 7,122 OFFICERS, PRINCIPALLY WHITE, MAKING A TOTAL OF 186,097 OFFICERS AND MEN." OF THE NAVY—BENNETT WRITES: "OF THE 118,044 SAILORS, 29,511 WERE NEGROES." This makes almost two hundred percent more Black naval volunteers, than white in proportion to population.

The overall Black involvement of servicemen and labor battalions in direct Civil War involvement was over 500,000 Black persons.

Dr. McPherson states that these figures of the War Department are too low. In actuality, Black involvement was much higher. The actual figures can never be known for two reasons: One is that an unknown number of light-skinned (poorly pigmented) Blacks melted into white outfits. The other is that the Army had a policy that when one Black trooper wa skilled another was put in his place under the same name. Many more African Americans would have enlisted if conditions had been near equal. The spirit of would-be volunteers was chilled by the well-publicized treatment of scorn, derision and violence at the hands of white fellow Union soldiers. It was also chilled by the fact that the white soldier's families received full subsidies, while the Black soldiers received half pay, no bonus, hand-me-down uniforms, non-functional equipment and their families received no subsidies. Then to add to the fears of some half-hearted, the president of the Confederacy, Jefferson Davis, made this announcement:

"ALL NEGROES WHO ARE CAPTURED WILL BE EXECUTED."

Added to all of this was the hostility of Northern whites against Black soldiers. Woe betide any uniformed Black caught in Boston, New York or Philadelphia by white mobs unless he was in company with many of his fellow soldiers.

The A.M.E. Christian Recorder of July '63 stated: "ON JULY 13, 1863, New York's white population erupted into four of the bloodiest days of mob violence ever witnessed by the metropolis. The immediate object of the mob's wrath was the draft enrollment office. The city's helpless Negro population bore the brunt of this violence. Dozens of Negroes were lynched in the streets or murdered in their homes. The Colored Orphan Asylum was burned to the ground. It seems that the fury was sparked by their having seen regiments of colored volunteers pass through New York on their way South, infuriating the whites of New York. How did these scorned and handicapped warriors become the pivotal factor and win the war for the humiliated and beaten North? Historian Bennett said, "They fought in 449 battles. This is based on the battles listed in Part 8 of the Volunteer Army Register of the United States."

It was the impassioned and gallant way that they fought. The New York Herald wrote in its editorial in May, 1863: "The Negroes advanced as grim and stern as death—fought with desperate gallantry (one never saw such fighting) and when within reach of the enemy struck about them with pitiless vigor that was almost fearful. They never shrink nor hold back no matter what the order. Through scorching heat and pelting storms...they marched with prompt and ready feet."

During 1863, Black troops fought in hundreds of battles and turned the tide of battle from Southern victories to a balancing of the scales. They won grudging admiration from fellow white officers and foes alike at Fort Wagner where more than fifteen hundred brave, Black troopers were slain. They did themselves proud at Millikens Bend up the Mississippi, at Olustee, Florida and Port Hudson in May of 1863. Too, in 1863 Black troops fought and won battles in South Carolina against overwhelming odds in battles in which ferocious, specially trained dogs were sent against them.

Christian A. Fleetwood, one of those warriors, a hero of battles in 1863, was a literate Baltimorean volunteer, whose papers are at the Library of Congress. His biography at that Library tells of his determination and strength of character. A simple statement in his diary mirrored the feelings and the motivation of most African American men who had volunteered:

"DECEMBER 31, 1863: THE CLOSE OF THE YEARS FINDS ME A SOLDIER FOR THE CAUSE OF MY RACE. MAY GOD BLESS THE CAUSE, AND ENABLE ME IN THE COMING YEAR TO FORWARD IT ON."

He vowed that he would free his people or answer to God, the reason why!

He bid goodbye to his loving mother and his friends. His beautiful fiancee tearfully asked him:

"WHY DO YOU HAVE TO GO BACK? YOU HAVE FOUGHT IN NUMEROUS BATTLES. ANYWAY AMERICA WILL FORGET WHAT WE ARE DOING LIKE THEY HAVE FORGOTTEN THE THOUSANDS OF BLACK SOLDIERS WHO HELPED WIN FREEDOM IN THE REVOLUTIONARY WAR. LIKE THEY HAVE FORGOTTEN THE BATTLE OF NEW ORLEANS IN THE WAR OF 1812 WHERE GENERAL ANDREW JACKSON PRAISED BLACK TROOPS FOR SAVING AMERICA'S HONOR. YOU AND I ARE NOT IN SLAVERY. WE'RE FREE."

Fleetwood replied,

"BUT YOU AND I ARE NOT FREE. NO BLACK IS FREE FROM THE CONTEMPT AND LOATHING OF HIS FELLOW MAN. I CAN SEE THE WAY WE'RE LOOKED AT. THE HATRED. I GO TO FIGHT TO WIN RESPECT AND HONOR OF ALL BLACK

PEOPLE NOT JUST THE BLASTING OFF THE CHAINS OF SLAVERY OF MILLIONS OF OUR PEOPLE. I SHALL FIGHT TO WIN RESPECT AND HONOR FOR US, AND OUR CHILDREN, AND OUR CHILDREN'S CHILDREN. WILL YOU WAIT FOR ME? WILL YOU MARRY ME WHEN I RETURN? 'TILL DEATH DO US PART? LET'S NOT SAY GOODBYE. LET'S JUST SAY, `TILL WE MEET AGAIN.'"

He was resolved that he would lay his very life on the altar in the coming battle trials so America would not again forget what her soldiers of ebony had done for her. He was determined that he would rid America of the contempt that its citizens had for him, even though he was considered free. He went back to camp after his Christmas leave.

In a few months into 1864, a battlecry was born which spurred him and his hundreds of thousands of Black compatriots to even greater heights of passion for their common cause. It happened in Tennessee. It happened on April 12 at Fort Pillow that was garrisoned by a small contingent of African American troops. They were overrun by a tremendously superior force of Rebel troops. The Union forces surrendered that evening after an intense, valorous but hopeless fight. The Rebels were led by Lieutenant General Nathan Bedford Forrest, later the creator of the infamous Ku Klux Klan. The Rebels finally overran the fort shouting, "Kill all the niggers." A later Congressional investigating committee said that Forrest's men murdered three hundred soldiers, women and children after they surrendered. At Memphis, a few days later Black troops fell to their knees and swore remembrance. After April 12, 1864, African American troops entered all battles with the cry, "Remember Fort Pillow." Poet Laureate Paul Lawrence Dunbar memorialized the massacre in his famed poem *THE COLORED SOLDIERS:*

> And at Pillow! God have mercy
> On the deeds committed there.
> And the souls of those poor victims
> Sent to thee without a prayer.
> Let the fullness of thy pity
> O'er the hot wrought spirits sway
> Of the gallant colored soldiers
> Who fell fighting on that day!

Two months later Fleetwood's Fourth Brigade shouted "Remember Fort Pillow" along with three Black regiments, as they carved a mile-

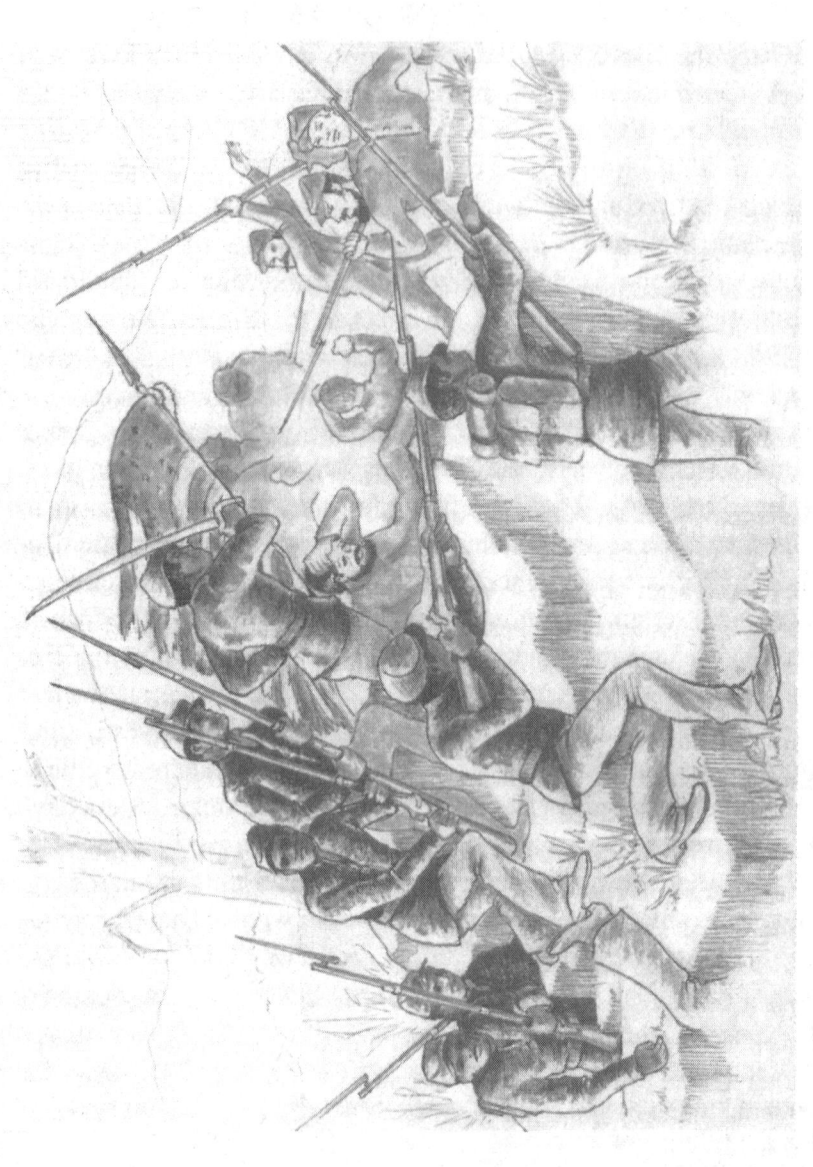

Scene of the Battle of New Market Heights, Virginia. African Americans stormed up steep hill in the face of cannon fire and well positioned Confederate troops with rifles. Black troops were given rifles with no caps, and only bayonets. Their will to win for us, their descendants, was so great that they took the hill, but with great loss of life.

wide swath in the Confederate lines in the June 15th Battle of Petersburg. Memories of this important battle are located just outside of the historic city of Petersburg, twenty-two miles south of the Confederate capital, Richmond. Memories of this second of eight battles of Petersburg are preserved at the Petersburg National Battlefield. The actual sites of the battles are in this huge park, the artillery displayed that was actually used. The park is kept by the National Park Service. Sergeant Fleetwood's diary of June 15.

WEDNESDAY, JUNE 15, 1864: UP AT BREAK OF DAWN AND UNDERWAY TO JUST OUTSIDE OF PETERSBURG, OUR DIVISION WENT INTO ACTION. CHARGED WITH THE 23RD. TOOK FIRST BATTERY. LAY UNDER THEIR FIRE ALL BALANCE OF THE DAY. ADVANCED BY DEGREES IN LINE. ALL OUTCHARGE AT 7 P.M. CAPTURED 7 BATTERIES."

At the actual site of a battle that was taken by Fleetwood's 4th Brigade, we met Park Ranger John Davis of the National Park Service, an expert on the siege of Petersburg and historian Dr. James Smith. THIS is just one point in a mile-wide breakthrough of the Confederate lines, where just one of the seven batteries was captured.

THE BATTLE OF NEW MARKET HEIGHTS, VIRGINIA

The God of his fathers was with Sergeant Fleetwood that day while around him fell 135 of his 4th Infantry as recorded by the War Department. He fought at various battles all summer long, with passion and valor, like a man possessed. But the battle that carved for him a golden niche in history's hall of fame happened on September 29. It was the Battle of New Market Heights. New Market Heights was a high, sharply inclined hill. It overlooked and defended the important New Market Road, which led straight to the heart of the Confederacy, its capital—RICHMOND, only five miles away. New Market Heights was considered an impregnable defense of this road. New Market Heights stretched for nearly a mile overlooking the road. On that hot September morning in 1864, more than a thousand Confederate troops were on top of that hill. About two hundred yards to the west of the road lay a wide creek, called Four Mile Creek. Any attack of the Heights would have to come across that creek which would be in range of the cannon that could shoot accurately eight times that distance.

Sommers, the acknowledged expert of this portion of the Civil War says in his most detailed account of this great battle written in his book *Richmond Redeemed*, that twice before, white divisions had tried to cross this creek to take the Heights, which you can't see now because of the trees and foliage. During the Civil War, the Confederates had stripped this whole area for perfect view. The two attempts of huge white divisions failed each time. Then General spoke up.

"SEND IN THE NEGRO TROOPS!"

Nearly four thousand of our fathers responded to the urgent call. The 4th, 5th, 36th and 38th United States so-called Colored Infantry, according to the Record and Pension Office of the War Department responded. In the 4th, was Sergeant Major Christian A. Fleetwood. His diary describes the events leading up to that fateful day of September 29, 1864:

"WEDNESDAY, SEPTEMBER 28, 1864, WE MOVED BY GUNBOAT TO JONES LANDING. WE MARCHED AT TEN TO DEEP BOTTOMS CAMP. JUST WEST OF THE JAMES RIVER. FOUR OTHER BRIGADES JOIN US. WE HAVE TO CROSS THE JAMES RIVER ON PONTOON BOATS. THE BOATS ARE FASTENED TOGETHER."

"THURSDAY, SEPTEMBER 29. UP AT 4:30 A.M. I CAUTION MY MEN TO BE SILENT. IN THE MOONLIGHT, WE MARCH ON SILENT FEET TO FOUR MILE CREEK JUST AS DAWN IS BREAKING. AS WE START ACROSS, THE CANNON FIRE FROM THE HEIGHTS BEGINS."

Dr. Edward Robinson whose video shows him at New Market Heights speaks. "This is the creek that thousands of African American troops crossed by wading and half swimming from the other side. This is Four Mile Creek. The water is clear now. In 1864, over a century and two decades ago, this was water was red with the blood of hundreds of African-Americans who, on September 29th were being ripped apart from the cannon on hills about two hundred yards behind me. Here I stand at the very spot on which some our fathers who made it across that creek were blown apart. This ground is hallowed by their blood.

"IF THESE STONES COULD SPEAK, WHAT A STORY THEY COULD TELL.

"But just below the surface of the ground lay poignant reminders of that day so long ago—bullets that rained down on the Black troops have lain undisturbed for over a century. To tell us about that is local resident Mr. Eugene B. Cooley, Sr. Here is a button with the blue uniform.

"This area which approaches New Market Road is called Chaffin's Farm. Just about here the Union color bearer had his brains blown out. He was the second color bearer to die after crossing over Four Mile Creek. But Fleetwood grabbed the flag before it hit the ground, held it aloft, rallied his men and dashed ahead toward the New Market Road. Lead death rained all about them, men falling right and left of Fleetwood. After wiping out the sharpshooters to the left and right of them, the Union soldiers got within rifle-range of the cannoneers on the Heights which kept the Rebels busy ducking for cover on the heights. Now their chance to dash across the road and begin the upward climb. I am crossing the road.

"I AM HERE STANDING ABOUT ONE-THIRD UP THE HILL WHICH OUR FATHERS CLIMBED ON THAT DAY ON SEPTEMBER 29TH. THE CANNON BARRELS POKED OUT OVER THE EDGE OF THE HILL UP THERE. THE REBELS WERE SHOUTING THEIR BLOOD-CURDLING YELLS AND OBSCENITIES FROM THE TOP—JEERING, YELLING, 'NIGGERS COME ON UP, IF YOU DARE.

"What greeted their eyes were the frises, which were obstacles strewn along the face of the hill, with its sharp pointed eight-feet long poles and abatis placed about eight or ten feet in front of where I am now standing, over which the Black troops had to climb and become sitting ducks for the artillerists on the top of the hill. Still they came on, defying the death all around them. Fleetwood led the charge up the hill holding the flag high in the air. The Rebels on the top of the hill saw that there was no stopping the warriors coming on relentlessly at them. They cursed; and all that could do so, turned and fled along the top of the hill toward Richmond. We wondered why there were no monuments or markers, but we understand that the land is under negotiations for purchase by the county to make this whole area a park.

BLACK SOLDIERS CAPTURE NEW MARKET HEIGHTS

"At last the road, New Market Road was free for Union soldiers to travel upon. The capture of New Market Heights made this possible because of the intrepid valor of our fathers, the Black soldiers. Because of this road now being open, the inner defense of the rings around

Richmond had been pierced. The final months of the war lay just ahead, because of this major battle and the outstanding valor of our fathers. Of the twenty-one Congressional Medals of Honor awarded Black soldiers during the entire war, thirteen were awarded because of this one battle. This was the battle from which Christian A. Fleetwood was awarded his Medal of Honor. Here we see the medal of honor and the letter from the War Department."[1]

"The medal of honor has been highly prized by servicemen for a century. President Harry S. Truman once told the men to whom he presented the medal, "I would rather have that medal than be president of the United States.""

"The big obstacle was now cleared. Other Black troops came up the road about two miles to Fort Harrison and fought a major battle that same day. A mystery surrounds this charge led by General Ulysses S. Grant himself. Captain James Richard, a former commander in the Nineteenth United States Colored Troops, in 1894 made this revelation in his book for the Providence: Soldiers and Sailors Historical Society.

" 'THE WORLD'S STANDARD OF HEROISM IS THE SPARTAN GREEKS AT THERMOPYLAE, BUT THE ASSAULT OF COLORED TROOPS AT THE CRATER AND THE ASSAULT AND CAPTURE OF FORT HARRISON AT NEW MARKET HEIGHTS WITHOUT FIRING A GUN (THE CAPS HAVING BEEN TAKEN FROM THE GUNS) USING BAYONETS ONLY; WHERE GENERAL BUTLER SAYS HE COUNTED 543 BLACK HEROES DEAD IN A SPACE NOT 300 YARDS LONG, CHALLENGE GREEK, ROMAN, OR ANY OTHER HEROISM.'"

The question is, "Why did they take the caps from the Black soldiers' guns making them fight against bullets with bayonets only?" This was one of the dreadful odds we overcame.

While African American soldiers were winning praise and admiration from those who hated them, both Northerners and Southerners, the South was being vanquished by their despised former captives on every battlefield. The Rebels were being beaten by Black soldiers in Charleston, South Carolina by the 21st United States Colored Infantry, the 54th and 55th Massachusetts Infantry. They routed Rebel forces in Georgia and Florida. They went up against overwhelming odds in Louisiana and Mississippi and vanquished their foes. On April 30,

---

1 From the video, *How African American Soldiers Won The Civil War,* by Studio II Productions, Inc.

General David Hunter, Commander of the Department (Union Forces) of the South, reported to Secretary Stanton: "I am happy to be able to announce to you my complete and eminent satisfaction with the results of the organization of Negro regiments in this department...(they) possess remarkable aptitude for military training...and are imbued with a burning faith that now is the time appointed by God, in His all-wise providence for the deliverance of their race." From Maryland to Florida, as far west as Mississippi, Black troops achieved outstanding victories in 449 battles until finally, the South decided that it would swallow its pride and authorize the enlistment of Blacks as soldiers. On March 13, 1865, President Davis signed a "Negro Soldier Law," the dying gesture of a crumbling nation. Before any regiments could be organized, Richmond had fallen and the war was over.

Of a value difficult to calculate was the work of hundreds of thousands of Southern African Americans as spies for the Union. Of tremendous help was Harriet Tubman, famed underground railroad heroine.

Allan Pinkerton, the chief of the United States Secret Service said: "I found them ever ready to answer questions and to furnish me with invaluable assistance. I never hesitated to employ them..."

After Richmond has fallen on April 2, 1865, Lee evacuated and retreated westward. To add insult to injury, it was an all-African-American corps that chased General Lee's tattered army from Petersburg to Appomattox Court House, where they made Lee surrender. It was the all-African-American Twenty-Fifth Corps moving forward at double-quick time while Lee's troops were running in confusion. Both Black and white Union troops witnessed the last gesture from Lee's troops as their white flag went up. As historian, Lerone Bennett says in his *Before the Mayflower*, "Cheers rang out from hill to hill and thousands of blue caps filled the air," on that memorable day—April 5, 1865.

Lincoln admitted, in a letter of August 26, 1863:
SOME OF THE COMMANDERS OF OUR ARMIES IN THE FIELD WHO HAVE GIVEN US OUR MOST IMPORTANT SUCCESSES, BELIEVE THE EMANCIPATION POLICY, AND THE USE OF COLORED TROOPS, CONSTITUTE THE HEAVIEST BLOW YET DEALT TO THE REBELLION.

General Ben Butler said,
"WITH YOUR BAYONET YOU HAVE UNLOCKED THE IRON-BARRED GATES OF PREJUDICE, OPENING NEW FIELDS

OF FREEDOM, LIBERTY, AND EQUALITY TO YOURSELF AND YOUR RACE FOREVER."

With general after general praising Black troops, Fleetwood could not even imagine that America would forget what the African American soldier had done for America. He could not even imagine that the heroics of a quarter of million Black servicemen plus a quarter million spies and labor battalions would be systematically and efficiently erased from the American and the world's minds. That it was done is described in the preface to the 1984 edition of Higginson's book *Army Life in a Black Regiment*; the preface written by historian Howard N. Meyer.

We quote, "in the mid-1860's it was widely understood that Black soldiers in great numbers had contributed mightily to the victory of the Union side in the Civil War. A century later, few Americans were aware of their contributions, as I learned when my 1962 edition of *Army Life in a Black Regiment* was published. An expression of surprise even came from the school board president of a great northern city, 'I had not known that any Negro soldiers fought in the Civil War,' he wrote."

In his novel 1984, George Orwell coined the word "unperson" for individuals whom the regime wanted to be forgotten. His parable about the Ministry of Truth and its *"memory hole"* for the disposal of unwanted facts has been simplistically supposed to apply only to a totalitarian society. Unfortunately, it also can apply to a democracy. (Americans have found that) (the) presentation of an altered view of the past made the injustices of the present seem more acceptable." General after general admitted that, "If it were not for African American troops, the war would have certainly been prolonged or not won at all by the Union." Secretary of War, Stanton, wrote that, "The hardest fighting of all was done by the Black troops." Yet with all the evidence that the Civil War was won by the Black troops, why were they consigned to America's *'memory hole'*?" I think that the real answer is that both the South and the North were intolerably embarrassed. There would have had to be an agreement made between the South and North to keep the heroics of a half a million participants in the war out of America's school textbooks for four generations, out of sixty thousand books on the Civil War, out of 125 films by Hollywood and television—not a mention made, not a battle of Black participation out of 449 battles fought by our fathers. The embarrassment? The North was embarrassed because, IT WAS FORCED BY ITS IMMINENT LOSING OF THE WAR IN 1862 TO HAVE TO CALL BLACK TROOPS FOR HELP.

THE CIVIL WAR 193

Details of the statue's foot, face, crown, hand, and flame.

Picture of original model of the Statue of Liberty

THEN LINCOLN HAD TO APOLOGIZE PUBLICLY WHEN THE HEROICS AND VALOR OF BLACK TROOPS MADE HIM EAT HIS WORDS THAT THE REBELS WOULD HAVE THE BLACK SOLDIERS' GUNS IN A FORTNIGHT. THEY WERE EMBARRASSED BY THE FACT THAT OUR FOREFATHERS FOUGHT SO VALIANTLY, WINNING TWENTY-ONE CONGRESSIONAL MEDALS OF HONOR, 36,847 DIED ACCORDING TO THE WAR DEPARTMENT.

The number dying and according to Dr. McPherson, 31,000 maimed, was a big sacrifice of blood. Perhaps these are reasons why the North refused to allow little Black kids and little white kids learn the true story of the Civil War. I can understand the embarrassment of the South. To really understand that feeling, you must understand that for two hundred years, the South had used every method known to man to turn our fathers into frightened, servile zombies, and had actually believed that they had—perfect "Uncle Toms." When lo and behold, the Rebels found themselves being whipped even when in superior numbers by their now non-pretending former captives. Then, of all things, the proud and Rebel-revered and almost worshipped General Lee being chased for miles by Black troops. It was too humiliating to allow future generations of white children to know this horror. It was equally unpolitical to allow future generations of African Americans to know this. To know this they would feel proud of their race, and that is not good for control. So both the South and the North had too much embarrassment to allow the TRUTH to interfere with power.

The myth that President Lincoln freed Black people stands now stripped and naked, revealed in all its baseness and lies. As we have witnessed here, our fathers, the African American servicemen paid with a river of their blood for our physical freedom, but not only that, saved the Union.

It is clear now why Southern whites unleashed their waves of frenzied hatred at Black people after Rutherford B. Hays withdrew Federal troops from the South in 1877. It is now clear why, without apparent cause thousands upon thousands of our fathers and mothers were lynched all the way up to the period following the First World War. The South was furious that our fathers had whipped them in fair battle so soundly that it was humiliating, and in doing so had exploded their basic tenet that the African was not a man, but a "thing." Then even at the last, as the final *coup de grace* Black troops had actually chased their hero, the god, General Robert E. Lee and pinioned him in his death throes at Appomattox Court House in ignominious defeat.

There had to have been a conspiracy between the South and the North to have buried, so completely, the real story that the Black soldier was THE pivotal figure in winning the Civil War. They could not even imagine that the reason the de-emasculation did not work was *because* we were of African lineage. Our fathers were not so far removed (as we are now) from the cultural memory of the dignity and world respect that we enjoyed for centuries in our Songhai, West African homeland. That story is of the beautiful cities, of homes on tree-lined avenues, the great universities of West Africa, are also buried in America's *"memory hole"* along with this story of HOW BLACK SOLDIERS WON THE CIVIL WAR.

Think of the severe psychological damage done to four generations who grew up without the pride of knowing that their fathers saved the United States from disintegrating. (Twenty-one years of northern schooling, and I have never heard of it). So not only were we denied the birthright of that knowledge to push us to our full potential, but the larger society grew up despising us not only from a programmed belief of our biological inferiority, but despising us because they believed we contributed nothing to the world nor to America.

While Black Americans won their own freedom by rescuing the beaten and demoralized white troops of the North, we are pragmatic enough to realize that this little episode of ours cannot change the commonly-held belief that Lincoln freed us. But in the harbor of New York, on Ellis Island, there stands a monument today that we hope will constantly remind all Americans of what was buried in America's *Memory Hole*. And that fact is that the Statue of Liberty is in the harbor of New York because Black servicemen won the Civil War and freed us African Americans from the long night of physical bondage.

According to Dr. Jim Haskins, a member of the National Education Advisory Committee of the Liberty-Ellis Island Committee, professor of English at the University of Florida, and prolific Black author, points out to what stimulated the original idea for that 151 foot statue in the harbor. He says that what stimulated the idea for the creation of the statue initially was the part that Black soldiers played in the ending of African bondage in the United States. It was created in the mind of the French historian Edourd de Laboulaye, chairman of the French Anti-Slavery Society, who, together with sculptor Frederic Auguste

Bartholdi, proposed to the French government that the people of France present to the people of the United States through the American Abolitionist Society, the gift of a Statue of Liberty in recognition of the fact that Black soldiers won the Civil War in the United States. It was widely known then that it was the Black soldier who played the pivotal role in winning the war, and this gift would be a tribute to their prowess. Suzanne Nakasian, director of the Statue of Liberty, Ellis Island Foundations' National Ethnic Campaign said that the Black Americans direct connection to Lady Liberty is unknown to the majority of Americans, Black or white.

During the summer of 1986, a nationwide celebration of the Statue of Liberty took place in the United States, and was widely televised. The television production coincided with the big business financing of the renovation of the century-old Statue. The whole celebration had to do with the landing of European immigrants in America, their feelings, their emotional ties to the Lady in the Harbor, how they felt, and what it meant to them. No mention was made to our knowledge about the real reason for the Statue of Liberty—the celebration of winning of the war by Black soldiers. News reporters had the audacity to ask Black Americans how they felt about the celebration. I was called and asked. I told the reporter, (MY NAME IS LISTED) the history of the statue. Not one word that I say, or any of my colleagues saw, recorded what I had told the reporter. It seems incongruous, that ABC with all of its international connections, with all of its resources could have *overlooked* this history that is recorded in all of the reference books.

The World Book Encyclopedia, mentions that the statue was presented to the United States government because of the end of slavery in the United States, but it states, "At the feet, but seldom seen, is a broken shackle. It symbolizes a people winning their liberty"...When I quoted that I asked my questioner, what people in the United States had just won their liberty? Certainly, it was a bit late for such a monument to be presented for congratulations for the United States for their winning *their* liberty from Britain a whole century before, "It symbolizes a people winning their liberty." Who is the "their" people? It was the Black American.

When the statue was presented to the United States Minister to France in 1884, it is said that he remonstrated that the dominant view of the broken shackles would be offensive to a United States South, because since the statue was a reminder of Blacks winning their freedom it was a reminder to a beaten South of the ones who caused their defeat, their despised former captives.

This Black connection is never mentioned in the history books. That story, too, is buried in America's *Memory Hole*. Oddly however, the American Committee's White Statue of Liberty has been gradually turning Black, a chemical transformation that baffles everyone.

PROOF OF DOCUMENTS

1. You may go and see the original model of the Statue of Liberty, with the broken chains at her feet and in her left hand. Go to The Museum of the City of New York, Fifth Avenue and 103rd Street (212-534-1672).

2. Check with the New York Times magazine, part II—May 18, 1986. Read the article by Laboulaye.

3. The dark original face of the Statue of Liberty can be seen in *The New York Post*, June 17, 1986, also the *Post* stated the reason for the broken chains at her feet.

4. Finally, you may check with the French Mission at the United Nations and ask for some original French material on the Statue of Liberty, including the Bartholdi original model.[2]

America's cover-up of our fathers' role in winning the Civil War makes the Watergate cover-up pale, by comparison, into historical insignificance. But, until that and other important truths about Black Americans are widely and dramatically revealed, America can never live out its golden creed of Liberty and Justice for all. It cannot climb to either world human rights leadership or world industrial leadership with hatred and scorn of so large a population as our race with its corrupted history festering in its loins. However, corrupted history, like a festering sore can be healed in the bright sunlight of TRUTH. Then perhaps America's golden creed can be realized. Then perhaps the dream of Dr. Martin Luther King can be fulfilled.

END OF SESSION XVII

The essence of this documentary on the Statue of Liberty was presented on the floor of the House of Representatives in the state of Pennsylvania by State Representative (D) David P. Richardson, Jr. Current President of National Black Caucus of State Legislators 9/9/87 & 10/7/87.

2 Research by Jack Felder, from *The Black American*. Volumes 26 & 27.

A stage coach arriving in the South after Civil War with truly concerned educated, Philadelphia, Pennsylvania African Americans, from the Institute for Colored Youth (I.C.Y.) to help rewrite state constitutions. Hundreds came to help.

SESSION XVIII

THE PERIOD OF THE BLACK RECONSTRUCTION

In the first years of freedom, Black leaders and the Black masses raised a clamorous cry for land. So did Charles Somers and Thaddeus Stevens, and other radical Republicans. The original cry of "forty acres and a mule" seems to have come from Stevens who suggested the breaking up of large plantations and the distribution of land to the freedmen in forty acre lots. But Stevens' program was too radical for Americans who tried as usual to do too much with too little. For fifty years or more, the freedmen chased the pipe dream of forty acres and a mule. Thousands of freedmen were defrauded by operators who sold them colored pegs, which, they say could be used to mark off the forty acres. Thousands more bought halters for the mules that they never received. It was fashionable in come circles to sneer at the seemingly stupidity, of the Blacks who clung to the "forty-acres and a mule" myth so long. Theirs was a brave and just dream that they held onto for so long, and that no one heeded the cry of their hearts that called not for sneering, but for weeping. Land reforms, as Myrdal and other modern scholars pointed out, were indispensable prerequisites for a lasting peace. The failure of the abolitionist and the radical Republicans to achieve the basic objective doomed Reconstruction from the start, and paved the way for our present conundrum (our unsolved riddle of believing we are free). This tragic period of aborted hope began with a promising political revolution. Blacks were elected to the legislature of every southern state. Lieutenant governors were elected in Mississippi, Louisiana, and South Carolina. Twenty Blacks were sent to the House of Representatives. Two Blacks were elected to the Mississippi Legislature, and a prominent Black politician, P.B.S. Pinchback served briefly as Governor of

Louisiana. During the heyday of Reconstruction, in the years between 1867 and 1877, Blacks took steps towards oneness. A series of political gatherings of a frequency and intensity unparalleled in American political history were held in the old "slave" states. Contemporaries said there was a camp meeting excitement and religious intensity about the huge alfresco (open air) political meetings held by ex-captives in Black areas. On registration days, freedmen thronged the court house, virtually mobbing the registrar in a frantic effort to get their names on the book. After their names were taken, a South Carolina paper said, "They went on their way rejoicing." The leaders of this revolution were typical American political types. Some, like Robert Brown Elliott of Eaton were handsomely educated; others like Beverly Nash pulled themselves up by their boot straps. Most were educators, lawyers and preachers; but some were like Blanche K. Bruce, the first Black to serve a full term in the United States Senate from Mississippi (1874-1881), and James Napier a well-to-do planter.

BLACKS MAINLY REWROTE THE CONSTITUTIONS OF THE SOUTHERN STATES

There was a lot of work to do after the conclusion of the Civil War. In order for African Americans to be better protected in the former "slave" states as they were sometimes called, the state constitutions had to be greatly altered. This was done by Black men and women of the South who had bought their freedom, had travelled and had earned good money. Concerned educated Blacks from Philadelphia, Pennsylvania, by the hundreds, came South to help draft the constitutions of the southern states. Those constitutions were excellently documented, and sent the white south screaming and crying into the modern world. "Slavery" and other forms of servitude were abolished, as was the ancient custom of imprisonment for debt. The property rights of women were protected, and divorce laws were written. Black politicians were largely responsible for pushing for the most important innovation in Reconstruction government. They established public school systems for poor and rich Black and white. The constitutions of Mississippi and Louisiana, incidentally, called for integration of the school systems. Although Black Republicans relied on political tactics, direction was not neglected.

We want to make a slight digression for a moment just to update you on general concern of Blacks in the United States of America for each other's plight. There were many concerned Black people in New York

City, Boston and to some degree other smaller northern towns where there was a sizeable Black population. However, Philadelphia, Pennsylvania seems to have led in establishing Black America's first high school. Allen B. Ballard, professor of political science at City College New York in his book, *One More Day's Journey,* said "Philadelphia Blacks were never content to leave education to their children in the hands of white people." Private schools were established throughout the 1800's—some three hundred and fifty of them. There were about 1,000 students in public schools and 748 in charity schools. A Black woman, Sarah Mapp Douglas was largely responsible for creating a preparatory school for the capstone of Philadelphia Black education. It was called, "The Institute for Colored Youth" popularly known as (ICY). The Institute had an all Black faculty that was highly qualified. Black Philadelphia community out of its own degradation had created a semi-autonomous school system that ran from the kindergarten to high school inclusive. The ICY's curriculum emphasized the classics. Final exams were given in Latin, algebra, geometry, physiology and trigonometry. They wrote on such subjects as the Rosetta Stone and Radicalism vs. Conservatism.

The graduates of the school who went South during the Reconstruction taught their classes about the greatness of Africa. Most all Philadelphia Blacks, including ICY students were connected to the underground railroad. Belonging to the underground railroad was considered a high point in the life of Black people who were considered anybody in that day. Most Blacks were somebody then, **because they had true love for one another which made them somebody.**

ICY was actually the forerunner of Cheyney State University that is now near Philadelphia, Pennsylvania. Then as now, Black schools (colleges) become the source of inspiration for African American leadership. As opposed to white colleges where so much frustration overtakes the Black student by overt and subtle racism, Black colleges become the haven that is needed to realize the intrinsic values of the Black student.

On Black campuses our Black students are surrounded by positive and supportive faculty. They are spurred on by a tradition of excellence. Students usually acquire the discipline and determination that take them as far as their talents will allow. We are sorry to say that Black colleges enroll only sixteen percent of Black college students. Yet with that small percentage that the Black colleges enroll, they produce thirty-seven percent of all Black college graduates. So one can see how a positive environment can enhance the academic prowess of people. The overwhelming majority of Black national leaders state and local, were nurtured in the warmth of Black educational institutions as well as such organizations as the Black church, U.N.I.A. and the Black masons.

We give this short synopsis about African Americans in the 1800's on how they wanted to interlock their destinies physically, morally, and spiritually in order to help free the minds of our brothers and sisters. We think that Blacks of the 1980's and 1990's should take a page out of the history of our fathers and mothers of the 1800's.

Certainly Dr. Martin Luther King did, when he used direct action to force implementation of the Federal Laws for Black people's rights, and remember he graduated from a Black college. We mentioned, that during the "Reconstruction" period we used direct action in the rice fields and cotton fields, and Black women played a crucial role by going on strike. In New Orleans, Charleston and several northern cities, Black leaders organized sit-ins, ride-ins and walk-ins to force compliance with the laws. In May of 1871, Black leaders in Louisville, Kentucky organized a ride that attracted national attention. The campaign began on May with street cars and Blacks sitting in white sections. Louisville whites counter-attached by overturning the street cars and smashing windows, but the campaign continued, until the company instituted a new policy of integrated seating. Reconstruction and all of its various facets taught a supreme lesson for America—the right reading of which might mark a turning point in our history. For ten years in these United States, for one hundred and twenty months, a part of America tried democracy. Little Black and white children went to school together. All over the South in those years, Black and white shared street cars, restaurants, hotels and dreams. Never before, never since had there been so much hope. A Black mother knew that her boy could become governor. The evidence of things seen, the evidence of things heard, fired up millions of hearts. Black mothers walked ten, fifteen and twenty miles to put their children in school. They sacrificed and strained, they bowed down and worshipped the miraculous ABC's from which so many blessings could flow with God's help.

The sky or at the very least the mountain top was the limit. Had not Blanche Bruce been suggested as a possible Vice-Presidential candidate. Black mothers, bending over wash tubs, could hope; Black boys in cotton fields could dream. The millennium had not come, but there were some who believed it was around the next turning. The sun rose and the sun set and for ten years, the Constitution of the United States had meaning from Maine to Mississippi.

NIGHT QUICKLY RETURNETH

The climate of Northern opinion changed as soon as the Northern victory had been solidified beyond recall, beyond the power of the South to alter or disturb the voices of compromise and conciliation. There were demands for a political settlement from the Northern business interests, who said the political trouble in the South was impeding the establishment of a national domestic market. The Northern sentiment crystallized in 1874 and 1875, and newspapers periodically started hammering away at "Blackism" and alleged corruption. The conservative Northern press said the South was tumbling and rolling about in the "Black Sea of Blackism." A new slogan came into being ("Emancipate the Whites"). The counter-revolution came to a head in 1876. Small wars were fought by white and Black men in South Carolina, Louisiana and Florida. In these states, both Republicans and Democrats claimed victory and established governments. Both sides incredibly evoked the words of the Declaration of Independence. As it happened the presidential race between Republican, Rutherford B. Hayes, and Democrat, Samuel J. Tilden, hinged on the dispute of electoral votes from South Carolina, Louisiana and Florida. Hayes claimed these states and the Presidency and the electoral commission supported him. It was necessary for both Houses to certify the result. The Democrats had a majority in the House of Representatives. As inauguration day approached, a group of southerners in the house launched a filibuster that prevented the orderly counting of the electoral votes. If the Democrats could hold out until the end of inauguration day, America would not have a President. Disorder or perhaps war would be inevitable. The Republicans and the Democrats got together in order to get the Presidential race settled. They did not hesitate to sacrifice all of the ten year gain of Blacks that was made during the Reconstruction Period. They met in Georgetown at a plush hotel in the Wormly House that was a fashionable hotel owned by a Black businessman. The agreement gave the South "Home Rule" and Hayes the Presidency. The essence of the bargain of 1877 was a defacto suspension of the constitutional safeguards that protected the rights of Black people in the South. The bargain was signed and delivered, the South called off the filibuster and Hayes was elected. On April 10, 1877, the federal troops were withdrawn from Columbia, South Carolina and the white minority took over the state government. The Reconstruction was finally overthrown by a violent counter-revolution led by the **Klan**, the red shirts and many other terrorist groups. The key elements in this counter-revolution was not the South, but the North; not the terrorists, but the businessmen of the North. It was impossible for Reconstruction to have succeeded if it were not backed up by force. The North used force the first years of Reconstruction because of interest in solidifying its national unity.

Democracy worked better for our people in the South than it did for our people in the North. But when profits were in jeopardy, our feelings, our gains and our security, were no more thought of, than the killing of rodents. Therefore, we say that since we have no other way to judge the future but by the past. Let us then let history be our criterion to man our own destiny.

POLITICAL INTRIGUE/THE NADIR OF SEEMINGLY BLACK HOPE 1867-1877 AN AGE OF TERROR AND BETRAYAL — 1877-1901

Every generation seems to produce its own leader to deal with the problem of those times. From 1877 even until the present, the plight of Africans living in America and elsewhere seems to be a time-continuum of man-made nightmares.

The first twenty-two members of the House of Representatives of the U.S. Congress, plus lieutenant governors, were elected in Mississippi, Louisiana and South Carolina. P.B.S. Pinchback, an African American served briefly as governor in Louisiana. It was during this brief period that African Americans took steps toward oneness, 1867 to 1877. Those elected African American officials fought the whites continuously. They fought against white corruption and trumped-up charges of office misconduct and they were victorious. They registered thousands of Black people to vote. Many died in that attempt. Black homes were burned, people had to flee for their lives.

Finally after the voting tally was confirmed, we find that an African American named Blanche K. Bruce was elected to serve a full term in the U.S. Senate, from Mississippi, the first to beat the white opposition. He served from 1874-1881. Check above about this man. In that super-hectic time, African genius came through with flying colors, winning major social advances. Black politicians were responsible for abolish-

THE PERIOD OF BLACK RECONSTRUCTION

ing all forms of involuntary servitude and imprisonment for debts. They passed laws protecting the rights of women, the right for them to actually file for divorce. They established for the first time public schools for the rich and poor.

When the Reconstruction Period came to an end, it came with a cruel violence. (Check Session XVIII for details). PAFO feel that we owe a deep debt of gratitude to our fathers and mothers of that period who pioneered in the paths of race honor, fidelity and courage for their descendants to emulate.

It is incumbent for us to always remember:

Hiram R. Revels, Senator, Mississippi, 1870-1871.
Blanche K. Bruce, Senator, Mississippi, 1875-1881.
Jefferson P. Long, Congressman, Georgia, 1869-1871.
Joseph H. Rainey, Congressman, South Carolina, 1871-1879.
Robert C. DeLarge, Congressman, South Carolina, 1871-1873.
Robert Brown Elliott, Congressman, South Carolina, 1871-1875.
Benjamin S. Turner, Congressman, Alabama, 1871-1873.
Josiah T. Walls, Congressman, Florida, 1873-1877.
Alonzo J. Ransier, Congressman, South Carolina, 1871-1873.
James T. Rapier, Congressman, Alabama, 1873-1875.
Richard H. Cain, Congressman, South Carolina, 1873-1875, 1877-1879.
John R. Lynch, Congressman, Mississippi, 1873-1877, 1881-1883.
Charles E. Nash, Congressman, Louisiana, 1875-1877.
John A. Hyman, Congressman, North Carolina, 1875-1877.
Jere Haralson, Congressman, Alabama, 1875-1877.
Robert Smalls, Congressman, South Carolina, 1875-1879, 1881-1887.

The betrayal of the Northern industrialists who influenced the government to withdraw the Union troops, laid the foundation for the murdering of so many African Americans.

Yes, thousands were killed during the post-Reconstruction period. Therefore PAFO dedicates this tiny portion of their book to those first great elected officials who will forever live in our memories.

A few of their spiritual descendants have surfaced in succeeding generations such as: the late great Mickey Leland, a person fully dedicated to aiding African people anywhere in the world. There is John Conyers the Black congressman who introduced a bill (HR 40) to create a commission to study the reparations due Africans in America for a payless captivity, for the murder of millions and for physical and spiritual brutalization after we won physical freedom.

We must remember the late Herbert Arlene (D), Pennsylvania's first Black senator. He was responsible, among other things for aiding Dr. Edward Robinson to establish an authority to lend up to $200,000 to Black businesses. Also, there is State Representative, David P. Richardson, Jr., who measured on accomplishments of state legislators, stands head and shoulders above all state legislators when thoroughly analyzed by PAFO. He is heralded as one who can't be bought, is fearless, strong and has a spiritual resiliency. His fifty-three page record of 2,489 documented bills and resolutions that he sponsored and co-sponsored over his first 22 years, are too numerous to mention, and at this writing, he is just 46 and still in office. We'll mention a few:

H.B. 1783—Prohibiting investments in corporations doing business in South Africa (helping Mandela get elected).

H.B. 1919—Establishing African American Reparations Study Commission.

Other house bills preventing electric and gas cut-offs on weekends.

Other house bills preventing the word "illegitimate" to be placed on any state papers or documents describing a child born to unwed parents.

H.B. 200—Act 17 of 1993—This bill eliminated the placing of liens by the state against the real property of recipients of public assistance. (Many thousands were helped by this bill)

More of these spiritual descendants will surface as time goes on.

END OF SESSION XVIII

State Representative David P. Richardson, Jr.
of Penna. — 201 legislative district
1973-Present

SESSION XIX
THE CONTROLLING MACHINES

A ruling class often subjected to periods of panic, arising from doubt of its ability to maintain its power, may be expected to develop a complex and thorough system of control.

THE VARIOUS METHODS OF SUPPRESSION AND OPPRESSION WERE INSTITUTED

The American slavocrats did develop numerous psychological, social, judicial, economic and militaristic methods of suppression and oppression. One of the most basic devices of control was fostering of belief in the innate inferiority of the Black people. Theologians asserted all sundries, including telling our people that we were the accursed of God. Either the descendants of Cain or else the "Snake" (Nachash) who tempted Eve and who was really the Black man.

The ethnologists, sociologists, and historians offered alleged proof of the natural inferiority of Black people and the necessity of filling God's ordained role of a "slave" to the white man. Laws and propaganda emanating from colleges, pulpits, politicians and the press continually and consistently drummed out the concept of the alleged inferiority of an entire people.

Year after year, generation after generation, the poison was deliberately and copiously administered to the captives themselves from childhood to the cemetery; so that we were ever aware that our most heinous crime—that for which there was no forgiveness—was to forget our—so-called "place," or to become "uppity." The branding was done early, all at once. They tried to convince the captives that God had willed that they occupy their lowly position. They were told that unless they perform all their tasks well that they will suffer eternally in "hell." Specifically, they were warned not to be saucy, impudent, stubborn, or sullen. Nor were they to alter their behavior, even if the owner was mean, cross or cruel, because that was the Lord's concern not theirs. They were to take all punishments without showing anger.

To summarize, one may say that the tiny minority of savage decision-makers of the Southern States were not content to depend upon social inertia or the powers of their own leadership to maintain their dominate position. Every trick, rule, regulation and device was called into play. They succeeded in debasing an entire people via psychological, intellectual, and physical methods. The inculcating and glorifying of the most outrageous deeds were buttressed by theological, historical and anthropological theories, dividing the victims against themselves, by utilizing spies and traitors. They completed the oppression by establishing an elaborate police and military system, and the enacting of innumerable laws of suppression. The developing of a social order, within which, the institution of Black servitude became so deeply imbedded, that it was true that to touch one was to move the other. This indissoluble linking of one with the other epitomizes the entire method of control and was at once its strength and its weakness.

The power structure used the best anthropologists and theologians of that day to demean the Black man. They kept saying the Black man was in the ape stage, and that he positively is not equal with the white man or the Asiatic. They also compared the anatomy of the Black man with that of the ape, and that his intelligence was on the same level with the apes. We were proclaimed as being childlike and therefore forfeiting claim to equal treatment to other men. Possessing no such claim, Blacks must be taken in hand by superior people (whites) and shown the path they must trod. The Christian whites told our fathers and mothers that they were inherently inferior and had accomplished nothing in all history. Racism was also incorporated into the Christian religion by the white theologians. In effect, to say, that when you doubted their racism you were contradicting the Bible, since they said God had cursed the Black man to be black and had doomed him to everlasting servitude to the white man. So, according to their so-called, white scientific minds, they began to twist the word "black" until the life and beauty was gone from it. It became the "nightmare." When the banks went up in the 1930's, it was a "black, dreadful day," instead of a "white, dreadful day." When a black cat crosses your path it's "bad luck" instead of "good luck," as it used to be. The good guys wore white hats, the bad guys wore black hats; black is grim, distorted, grotesque, satirical, "black comedy," "black humor." There is coercive terminology used—such as "black mail" (we say "white mail").

An illegal market is referred to as a "black-market" (we say "white market"). In the dictionary there are 123 synonyms that are negative for the word "black." Black is: bad, dirty, soiled, evil, wicked, worthless, immoral, sinful, wrong, inferior, poor, unsound, unstable, disagreeable, corrupt, vicious, abominable, hateful, horrible, base and pernicious, etc. Because of this type of mind-twisting, we became race-haters. The power structure also began to propagandize the Blacks and themselves with the word "white." They say that white means: good, pure, beautiful, spotless, superior, etc. By their white standard that to which we began to adapt, we became white inside, hating our Black outside, and dooming us to self-destruction. We developed an inferiority complex that deepened over a long uninterrupted period of time. That complex is very dangerous to the human personality. It defines what we can and cannot do, thus encouraging a very negative picture of ourselves. This is the work of the racist society to destroy our self-image of wanting to be Black.

We do not want to seem redundant, but because this particular phase of our subject matter has such great effect on our people, we feel that we should give a little of the historical roots of racism. White people as well as Black people probably do not know this, because the real controllers of this society are the ones who throw the rocks, but hide their hand.

HOW THE ENGLISH LANGUAGE WAS USED TO HURT BLACK PEOPLE

By the time the first English colonist arrived in the New World, they had already inherited a host of associations tied to the word "black" which became important as men put *language* to use in first defining and later justifying the status *they desired for the nonwhite*[3]

Before the close of the fifteenth century, the words "soiled" and dirty first became linked with "black." By 1536, "black" connoted "dark purposes," "malignant," "deadly"; by 1581, "foul," "iniquitous"; by 1583, "baneful," "disastrous," and "sinister."

Before the end of the sixteenth century, Englishmen associated "smut" with "to mark or make dirty." In compound nouns, tags and epithets connotations: In 1532 "blackguard" meant variously "scullions and kitchen knaves," the devil was established as the "Black Prince" by 1563; by 1590, pagan practices fell under the title of so-called "Black Arts," a term that derives from the medieval latin word "nigromantia,"

---

3 *White Racism* by B. Schwartz and R. Disch.

itself a distortion of the Latin word "necromantia." Hence for the Elizabethan, "Black Arts" was linked with "magic," "Necromancy," "death," "secret," and "devilish." As was in the true African religious concept of "Maat" which the European and the Arab societies took careful pains to denounce African religious beliefs as "pagan." Also, if you were not a Moslem, they considered you an infidel and were put to the sword. As you may recall, this started with deadly seriousness in 382 A.D., and slowly intensified, especially from the sixteenth century on.

In many of Shakespeare's plays, such as *Othello, Love's Labour's Lost, Macbeth*, and others, the negative use of the word "black" is used as well as its synonyms. This shows how well planned this virulent scheme to erase Black people from the annals of mankind.

This control mechanism was imposed on our people during the days of our physical bondage, which was a very strong poison in our very soul and mind. If you stop and review in your mind, for a moment, this "Control Machinery," you will readily see how deep this instrument of mind destruction could and did penetrate far into the recesses of our subconscious mind. Sociologists and psychiatrists have stated time and again, that what has been done to our people, in both mind and body, would have driven any other completely out of their minds.

After Reconstruction, and the re-establishment of white Southern rule, America, along with her Allies, prepared the people of Europe and America to accept an additional role that they were about to play. The preparation came in the form of superintensification of destroying virtually all of the true history of Black people. The rewriting of the history books made Black history almost impossible to find. Instead, history books portrayed white people as the leaders of all cultural advancement; and Blacks were depicted as having no history, a nymph of nature, "so child-like". Blacks were made to be less than human, by the whites, so as to justify anything they were doing to us.

The Europeans were preparing to justify the partitioning of Africa, which was what the Berlin Conference was all about in 1884. The world greedily wanted the wealth of Africa, in order to enrich Europe and America. Almost every European power had a piece of Africa. They stole the gold, diamonds, precious metals and stones. They went into Egypt, and into the tombs of the Pharaohs and carried back to Europe the treasures of the Africans. England was the primary plunderer of Egypt. The wealth of Africa was so stupendous, that England became the leader of Europe, dictating the policy of the economic world market; thus giving England the name, John Bull.

America has programmed her people to believe that Africans were not only docile and child-like, but also incapable of organized warfare. We felt that this episode about a West African lady will add to the mounting evidence that the white world's top echelon just plain lied.

This story is relevant particularly because many of our grand and great-grandparents had heard something about this story. The authors of this book heard about this fine lady.

By the late 1800's, the effects of the dual invasions of the Arabs and Europeans began manifesting themselves throughout the continent.[4] This can be best demonstrated by the story of Sarraounia (Sar-roon-a).[5] Sarraounia, an African Queen, ruled over a territory located in the present day Niger.

The reason the story of Sarraounia is so important is so we can see clearly for the first time the dual oppression Africans were fighting against, was for the right of self-determination and to free their land of foreigners.

The external oppression came in the form of a French invasion expedition which had as its goal to move through the Sokoto Nation in the upper regions of Nigeria with the final destination being the country of Chad. The internal oppression came in the form of the Sokoto Nation that had already suffered a defeat at the hands of the Arabs and had been converted to an Islamic Nation at least fifty years earlier. The adoption of the Arab ideology was quite evident in Sokoto's mentality towards the kingdom of the Azan headed by Sarraounia. Here are some of the manifestations of that mental attitude. The Islamic Africans had four problems with the Azan people.

1. A woman (keeping in mind the Islamic philosophy that women were considered property) ruled the Azan Nation. As you can see true mainstream African philosophy in practice, treated our women with high respect.

2. A woman who had defeated them militarily when she resisted efforts by the Moslems to be converted to Islam.

3. She was not Islamic. Her god was of the traditional African concepts, of which should be all indigenous Africans, at home and abroad.

---

4 Basic source of reference, The Dry Wind From the North (English translation). The original French was, L'Harmattan by Abdoulaye Mamani.

5 PAFO collaborated with V. White (Fumi) and R. White.

4. The African Moslems considered her a pagan. Her appeal for help from them to defeat the French fell upon deaf ears.

Here, an event that has occurred many times in our history shows itself in this nineteenth century scenario. Africans, sometimes called Sudanese, were still unaware of the European's intent. They allowed their desire for additional women and cattle to lead them to join the French Army as mercenaries.

Let us look at the reason why the French were in West Africa in the first place:

This particular time period is just after the Berlin Conference in 1884. As you already know, the Berlin Conference was all about the partitioning of the continent of Africa. This was an attempt to make up for the loss of the African slave trade. Practically every European country took a slice of Africa. France came to take the Western Sudan. The slave trade had left Africa so weak, generally speaking, that the Europeans had little trouble in taking what they wanted. They did this of course with the help of the Arabs and the converted Africans from their traditional religion to Islam/Christendom concepts. Had Africans realized like President Lincoln did, that a house divided against itself can't stand, they would have automatically put the African's interest first before a religious concept that was not of their ancient fathers and mothers.

The Black troops under the direction of French officers with cannon and rifles, moved through the Sokoto Nation leaving in their wake destruction never seen before in the Sokoto Nation. The further the French-lead African army moved in to Sokoto the more they heard of the powers of this lady whose name was Sarraounia. It was known that anyone who went against her would surely be defeated and bad luck would follow them. The French writers and Azanian griot's said that she was not only brilliant, but also very beautiful.

The captured women of the Sokoto nation knowing the power of Sarraounia planned and executed successful escapes that were attributed to the powers of Sarraounia. The French captain in charge, full of hope for power and glory pushed the men into greater danger by deciding to attack Sarraounia. The French knew that if they did not conquer or destroy Sarraounia, that it would be seen as a sign of fear on their part. The Arabs and the Europeans vowed to never leave an African as a model for Africans to immortalize.

They used extreme brutality against those captured African villagers, and this greatly influenced the decision of those factions of the Sokoto

THE CONTROLLING MACHINES 213

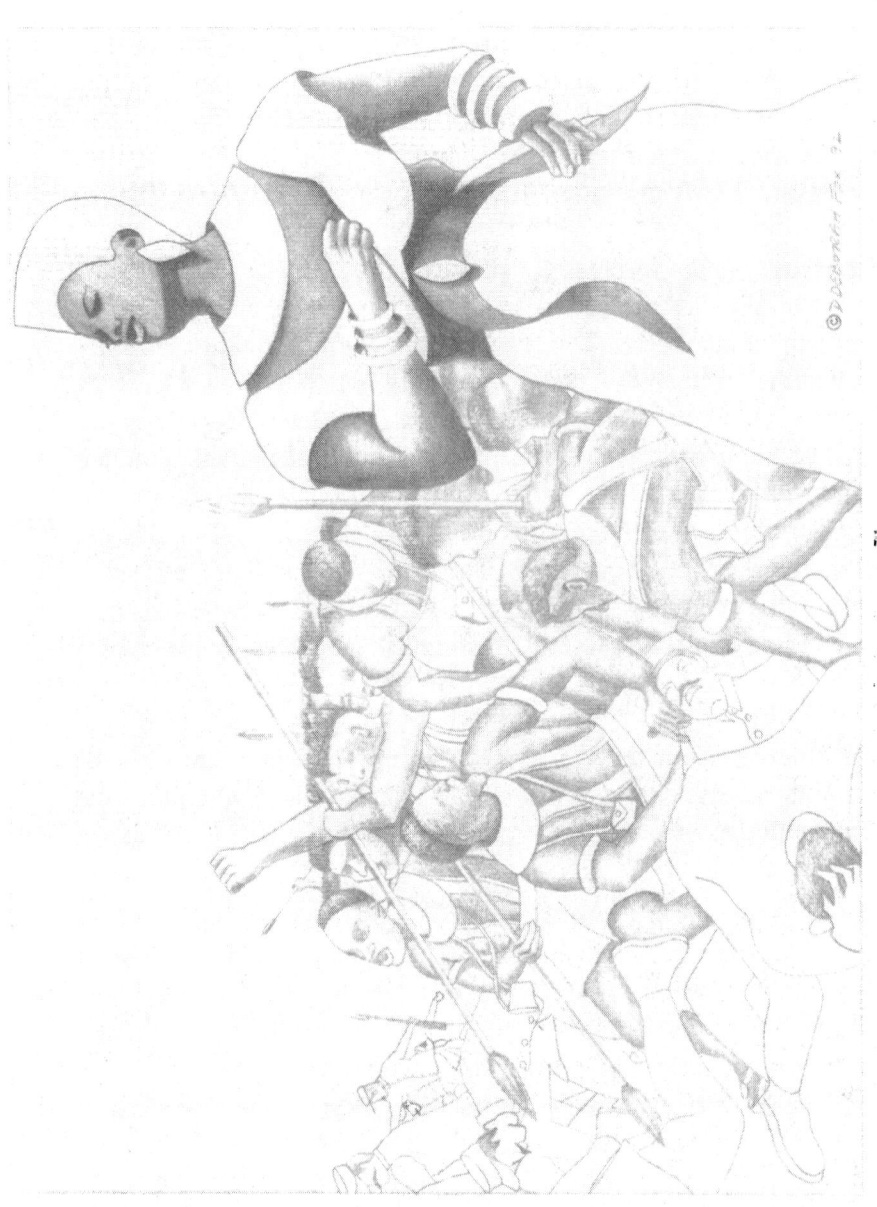

Sarraounia and units of her army sizing up the pending battle with French-led soldiers.

and other bordering nations to join the Azanian Army. Many Africans compared her genius with that of Angola's Queen Nzinga.

With this added strength Sarraounia prepared for the invasion of the French held areas. More and more Africans joined Sarraounia as they beheld the unwonted mass murder and torture that this French-led army inflicted on the African people. The following plan ensued:

1. Destroy as much ammunition as possible prior to the actual battle.
2. Then pull the infantry into the castle causing as many casualties as possible.
3. Then retreat to the forest to finish the battle.

Steps I and II were so successful that the French-led army never followed them into the forest. The pressure was so great on this mercenary force, that they retreated in disarray, leaving Niger.

Victory was Sarraounia's along with the combined efforts of those who joined her in trying to free Africa. Sarraounia reminded them that even though they were of so-called different nationalities, customs and religious concepts, they were welcome to stay in the Azan Empire, and maintain their separate beliefs. The one thing she said that they had to realize was the enemies of Africans do not distinguish between us when they are killing us, so we shouldn't distinguish negatively between ourselves. She said our combined strength and genius can defeat our common foe.

The Azanian griots tell the story of her exploits down through the generations, so that posterity can tell the story of those who faced the foreign challenge.

A SAD COMMENTARY

While the story of the Azanian empire finally ended up on what appeared to be a positive note this was not the general trend for the rest of Africa. Africa was being deluged by the most subtle brainwashing ever imposed on a nation of people along with terrible physical brutality. Back in Session I (Illustration of the Black Psyche), we talked about a small number of people who were able to control hundreds of people by brainwashing them. We are not trying to do an overkill of the brainwash doctrine, but we feel that it is very important to understand how really it can take one over. The danger is in the underestimating of its power.

It was not until the 1960's that African nationalist's struggle became so widespread that the Colonial powers were forced to acquiesce to the demands for African independence. The independence was of varying degrees. The Colonial powers maneuvered to retain almost direct control as well as indirect control. They (Colonial Powers) greatly influenced financial, transportation, communication and other essential services. Let us carefully examine this new kind of bondage as PAFO calls it.

The leading government in this new bondage against Black Africans is the Apartheid Government of the Republic of South Africa. Supposedly free African countries are so hamstrung by the way of military and economic coercion, that they are virtually ineffective. Here is where the power of imagery as well as the physical power combine. And as it combines, we absorb it into our mind, we become practically one with our enemy. The following will show how we manifest oneness with the enslavers of Africans. When whites were calling the shots directly in certain countries, they classified mixed breeds as coloureds and were given a higher status in the financial and social arrangement of the countries that practice it. Certain Black-governed states also followed the South African lead of intra Apartheid giving Asians and less pigmented Africans a much higher rating status over the very well pigmented. This has been observed by many visiting American blacks who say to those African- run countries, "How dare you do this when only yesterday you were in the same condition?" PAFO knows that the Mission schools contributed to this mindset because those schools carefully avoided teaching about the slave trade. We found that White America made sure that the worse African American films were shown in Africa. As a result, many Africans thought that African Americans, in general, were not serious. PAFO says that total concentration on deprogramming must be a priority here in America first.

In the meantime, America was preparing to expand her borders, which expanse was to be perpetrated through the taking over of pigmented people. This included the islands of Cuba, Puerto Rico, the Philippines, the Virgin Islands and Hawaii. This was done after a war was provoked, and Spain was driven out of the hemisphere. Harsh treatment was awarded the new nations of the country, by the wholesale imposition of white racism. This coincided with the deal that the North and the South made to put the Black man in sort of a new bind called "Neo-Slavery." After a taste of semi-freedom, experienced during Reconstruction, the Tilden-Hayes Compromise called for a reconditioning process of the Black man; not only to blunt his aspiration for so-called equality, but to utterly destroy even the germ seeds. This is when the Knights of Columbus, White Citizens Council, Ku Klux Klan, the laws of the land, judicial, executive, and legislative, plus the white citizenry rode roughshod over the Black man. This was climaxed between 1884 and 1895. Those eleven years were known in Black History as the years of the "Terrible Nineties." In this period, lynching of our people was an every day occurrence in all of the confederate states. Conservative estimates showed that at least three to five of our people were lynched each day in those states. They were lynched in the North also, but not nearly on the same scale as in the south. In this period, more of us were lynched then, than from 1895-1930, a period of thirty-five years. Advertisements were frequent in the Southern newspapers and on posters of coming lynchings. White women were urged to come, especially if pregnant, so were Black (would-be) leaders. The reason was obvious, they thought that fear and inferiority could somehow be transmitted into the unborn foetus, and likewise leadership and superiority. This barbarity was reminiscent of the old Roman Empire days, when scores of lions were let loose on defenseless people. Thus, in this country, they would send fifty men to drag one or two defenseless Blacks out of a house to lynch him. Why were there whites bent on killing us? There were two main reasons why many whites were enraged and humiliated in response to Black Reconstruction. Andrew Jackson, for one, bemoaned the fact that Blacks had taken Richmond, calling the incident "a citadel of racial treason taken possession of by a lot of soldiers of African descent led by a Dutchman." Now where is that bragging chivalry of the South, which flattered itself that one of them could whip five Yankees in the beginning of the war, when now fifty thousand of them run from a thousand Blacks?"

The other reason was that the Blacks fought back, as in the case of the Cane Hay Massacre, which occurred in South Carolina, October 1876. A mob of whites was forced to retreat and several were killed by defending Blacks. A rumor in 1882, alleged that Blacks had held a recent meeting and planned "an immense stake burning of oppressive whites." At Phoenix, on November 8, as some Blacks led by Tom Tolbert prepared to vote, a local "ne'er-do-well" attempted to stop them. Blows were exchanged, shots broke out, and the interfering white was killed and Tom Tolbert wounded. The Black people, expecting trouble, had buried their arms nearby. In the melee after the guns had gone off, doubt and fear beset them, and they debated about whether or not to fight back. In the end they did, agreeing with Charles White that "we can shoot as long as them white folks can." It is reported that our women stood and shouted at some of the men who were retreating, to "go back and shoot those white folks."

END OF SESSION XIX

SESSION XX

THE POST RECONSTRUCTION FREEDOM FIGHTING ORGANIZATIONS AND INDIVIDUALS

With all due credit to Booker T. Washington who espoused a doctrine of separate but equal and of "casting down your buckets where you are," he unwittingly opened the door for the Supreme Court to favor Plessy of the *infamous case of Plessy v. Ferguson. This is when the Supreme Court wrote into American law the doctrine of racial separation and classification.* This ruling tore at the Thirteenth and Fourteenth Amendments and at the Civil Rights Bill of 1875. It gave the individual states the power to administer the money for schools and other public conveyances and accommodations, and in addition, it didn't forbid white individuals from discriminating. Some may disagree with the fact that Booker T. Washington, under the circumstances at that time, did what he thought was best in face of so much maiming and killing of our people. We were gripped by a fear that produced reactions into several directions, of which Booker T. Washington took the more passive position and others decided to withdraw from the situation by going to Canada, Mexico or Africa. *But there were yet others like IDA B. WELLS BARNETT, an intrepid Black woman editor who walked the streets of Memphis with two guns strapped to her waist and organized the first effective opposition to lynching.* She was also one of the founders of the NAACP. We salute our beautiful, brave women in Philadelphia, Pennsylvania that made a vow to put a stop to gang youth violence while Black men (so-called) peeped from behind safe doors saying, "We can't do anything to stop it." We salute our beauti-

Ida B. Wells Barnett. She walked the streets of Memphis with two guns strapped to her waist. She organized the first effective opposition to lynching.

ful brave women of old and new history who showed our emasculated men that somewhere along the way, one must take a do-or-die stand. (In supplementaries pertaining to ovations to our Black women, we shall give some insight on such personalities as Mammy Pleasant, Sojourner Truth, Mrs. John F. Cook, Mrs. E. Carter, Mrs. J.E. Holmes, and Fallaka Fattah just to mention a few).

More than a million Black farmer organized a Black Farmers' Alliance and cooperated with the Populist Movement. Black Women organized the National Association of Colored Women. The National Afro-American Council called for a day of fasting and meditation. E.J. Waring, the first Black lawyer in Baltimore called for law suits against those inhuman atrocities. His idea was singularly modern. "We should organize the country over, raise funds and employ counsel. Then if an individual is denied some rights or privilege, let the race cause and test the case in law." Forty-eight years later, another Baltimore lawyer, Thurgood Marshall would take this idea and make it into a thing of beauty. There were some in this age like Ida B. Wells Barnett who believed the time for talk was past. They wanted to fight fire with fire. There were some who wanted an all-Black state. Edwin P. McCabe, the author of this idea had an interview with President Harrison, but the project never got off the ground. The Black State idea germinated because a whole generation of Black leadership had been killed before their very eyes. The first was merely a prolongation of the vain search for freedom that seemed to forever elude their grasp like a tantalizing will-o-the-wisp, maddening and misleading the headless host. The holocaust of war, the terrors of the Ku Klux Klan, the lies of the carpetbaggers, the disorganization of industry all contributed . Also included was the contradictory advice of friends and foes. It left them bewildered with no new watch word beyond the old cry for freedom. Then like now, we had diverse kinds of ideas that all think is the solution. **THERE IS ONLY ONE SOLUTION! AND THAT IS TO DEPROGRAM THE TOTAL SOCIETY.**

Out of this maze of confusion wrought against us by these so-called people came such organizations as the Niagara Movement by W.E. Dubois. Let's not leave out Frederick Douglas who started the *North Star Newspaper*, NAACP, Urban League and the Honorable Marcus M. Garvey (Father of the Modern Struggle) all of the aforementioned figured very prominently in the unending struggle for Black survival. Black people sought freedom and escape from persecution in many ways. Some of us psyched ourselves into work and scientific achievement. We invented, according to conservative estimates, more than sixty percent of the inventions during the Industrial Revolution. The ideals of liberty demanded for its attainment powerful means of which the Fifteenth Amendment was supposed to give. Now before the ballot was supposedly achieved, it was looked upon as a visible sign of freedom, we now regarded it as the chief means of gaining the liberty with which the war had partially endowed us. We thought that anything was possible through the power of the ballot. Yet the decade slipped away and left the half-free excaptives wondering, but still inspired. A new vision began to replace the dream of political power, because with Blacks, "hope springs eternal."

In their time as in the present time, those in the forefront of the battle for Black survival, thought they had gained some ground in alleviating the harsh conditions of Black people. We are not going to debate this point because we're dealing in relativities insofar as to whether or not we have gained. We look at the staggering loss of life that our people suffered from the point of invasion of our empire, the take-over of our land, the loss of our culture, traditions, language, almost resulting in the crushing of our manhood. This lessened our ability and sense of responsibility in protecting our women and children, **and finally the ultimate in our lost manhood, made us not *want* to *identify* with Africa, but with white people**. We can say, that since the so-called Emancipation Proclamation, Black people bought and owned up until 1913, which was forty-eight years after the Civil War ended, 550,000 homes, operated 937,000 farms and conducted some forty thousand businesses. We had accumulated seven hundred million dollars, and more than seventy percent of us were literate. We had forty thousand churches, 35,000 teachers and one million seven hundred thousand Black students in public schools including some colleges. This showed beyond the shadow of a doubt, that we, at that time had not lost our desire and reverence for learning.

It is therefore with a great deal of trepidation that we suggest that a statement and belief about which we have heard over and over again is incorrect. That statement and belief is that "We, (Black people in the United States) have made *progress*." We take exception to that statement. Our view is that Black people in America have made *no progress*.

We hear certain pontifically announced statements over and over and over again so that most of us come to accept the statements as having validity without applying some analytic reasoning to the statements. Once our senses become saturated with the statement, it becomes what people (whom we accept as knowing what they're talking about) say, that the belief of the statement is "internalized." Then, these "experts" say that when a statement comes to be believed, then internalized, the chances of upsetting the belief in that statement is minimal indeed, especially when intellectually attempting to upset the belief.

It is, however, incorrect to use as a *referential* point of progress for Blacks starting from a situation that is against *Basic* Laws of Humanity in the first place. We must not agree with our oppressors, when they insist that we have made such progress.

The generally accepted meaning of the word "progress" is, in this context, a greater achievement measurement of a particular state of affairs at a point in time against similar, or the same components of the state of affairs at a prior point in time.

"Progress" is measured against a certain referential point in time, PAFO's primary thesis is that one cannot have, as a referential point in time, a set of circumstances that contravenes universally accepted laws.

The primary pivots of our argument against our having made or (have battered obstacles so as to have) "progress" is that the prior point in time or referential point against which our present state of affairs is measured by those who say Blacks have made "progress" is an incorrect point in time from which to measure. The point in time that is usually taken is the era of our captivity (so-called "slavery"). We maintain that our captivity is an incorrect time-point from which to measure "progress" because chattel captivity contravened universally accepted laws. The reference point should never have occurred in the first place, therefore should not be the point against which to determine "progress." That means, that whatever point of reference occurring during our captivity and beyond in America in the past that you choose, the state of affairs that existed is an incorrect point from which to measure. Our statement just made, we admit, was made with the full knowledge that we are battling against a whole "set" of conditioned beliefs, and allows us to suggest a corollary to that statement: IT FOLLOWS, AS DAY FOLLOWS NIGHT, THAT THOSE WHO IDENTIFY WITH THE PERPETRATORS OF A CRIME WILL SEEK TO PROMULGATE STATEMENTS THAT ALLEVIATE THE WEIGHT OF GUILT ASSOCIATED WITH THAT CRIME.

In essence, we are saying that the total society follows the lead of those who control the media of communication and, thus, all are conditioned in the same mould concerning internalized beliefs. This American society set the conditions of that point in history. The state of affairs of the oppressed people, which state should never have existed should not and logically cannot be the standard from which to measure "progress."

Perhaps an example that is out of the conditioned context of this subject may clarify this point:

It is said that during the European's animalistic gas-oven extermination of human beings, a high point of ten thousand Jews exterminated per week was reached. We think that few would agree with a statement made subsequent to that high point of ten thousand persons-exterminated-in-a-week that, "the Jews were making progress" because instead of ten thousand, only nine thousand of them were exterminated in a subsequent week.

Those few could argue that nine thousand being exterminated is certainly "better" than ten thousand being exterminated. They could further argue that at that rate of diminishment, in time there would not be any exterminated.

We think that on the basis of the argument of those who would disavow the statement of "progress for the Jews" entirely would be that the comparison with the high point of ten thousand exterminations is a false standard with which to compare a false point of reference—that the situation of extermination SHOULD NOT HAVE EXISTED IN THE FIRST PLACE, THAT THE REFERENTIAL POINT FOR COMPARISON SHOULD BE A TIME IN THE PAST OF NON-EXTERMINATION.

Now, back to the case of African Americans in the United States, our "progress" and the choice of a REFERENTIAL POINT.

Surely, there would be many WHO WOULD AVOW WITH fervor that the REFERENTIAL POINT OF BLACK PEOPLE SHOULD BE THE CAPTIVITY PERIOD with Judge Taney's "...no rights that a white man was bound to respect...." But using that era of our chattel captivity as the referential point to measure our present state of affairs is as animalistic as the European using their point of lowest bestiality of ten thousand murders per week to measure progress. Our chattel captivity defied the "laws of nature and nature's God" and, therefore, should no more have existed than the ten thousand murders each week committed by the Europeans. That complete abrogation of natural laws would be enough in itself to explode the myth that our captivity should be a referential point with which to compare our present state of affairs.

However, this does not establish a point in time by which to measure or compare a particular and existing state of affairs, to measure whether progress has been made.

That point in time by which our present state of affairs could be measured should be the era in Western Africa just prior to the invasions of the forces of Islam and Christianity. That was the period prior to the seventeenth century in which the immediate ancestors of African-Americans enjoyed universal respect and honor as human beings. While it is not the purpose of this short paper to detail the documentation of that era, since that will be left to a later more voluminous statement, allow us to just point out that there is a great body of evidence drawn from the contemporary historians of that period sufficient in volume to convert any "doubting Thomas." We are restraining ourselves from exploring in this paper the highlights, at least of this glorious age in Africa, so that we may cling tenaciously to the subject of this treatise.

Allow us to return to the Europeans' annihilation of the Jewish people for a minute. The Jew was torn from his places of high honor, world acclaim, his homes and businesses, his respectability, and marched to the horror camps. Just merely ceasing to exterminate them could, in no way, be considered progress. He was beyond that prior to his captivity. Even returning his stolen lands and businesses, making "restitution" for his business and family losses, even that could not be termed "progress." He had already had that.

Therefore, restoration of the Jew to a state of affairs beyond that point that the Jew in Europe would have accomplished under his own momentum in Europe, HAD HE BEEN LEFT ALONE, could only be termed "progress."

Similarly, the Africans, our fathers and mothers in Songhai, in the empire of Khanem Bornu, in Benin, had world respect and recognition before the invasion of 1591. In Timbuktu, the University of Sankore had world acclaim as the mecca of scientific learning for three centuries prior to the invasion. The African was regarded not only as a member of the human race, but as one of the progenitors of progress in education and governmental administration.

Therefore, it would seem that their children, as prisoners-of-war made to labor in America under guns, COULD NOT BE TERMED AS MAKING "PROGRESS" unless restored to that state of affairs

BEYOND THE POINT THAT WOULD HAVE BEEN ACHIEVED BY THEM UNDER THEIR OWN MOMENTUM *HAD THEY BEEN LEFT ALONE.*

In short, we are saying that the REFERENTIAL POINT against which to compare our present state of affairs should not and ought not to be so-called slavery, the nadir of our existence, but the mountain-top of our illustrious history, the grandeur and honor of the Western African's state of affairs.

Today, the flouting of and resistance by white America, individually and institutionally, to all civil-rights laws, housing laws, job laws, ostensibly designed to aid the Black to obtain those rights that each and every newly arrived immigrant from Europe has a matter of course the instant he sets foot on American soil holding his citizenship papers, is based on the fact that the great masses of American whites, as well as many Blacks, compare myopically, the distance we have come by self-propulsion, grit and wit, from the zero determinant of our days of captivity when we had "no rights that a white man was bound to respect."

You validly question why all this agonizing fuss about a word "progress," this play on somewhat semantical point??? May we remind you wonderful activists about the many times that white persons have asked you as you pressed for minimal rights, "What *do you* people want?—"Look how much progress you have made." And, you have answered, "The same things you folk want." You have intuitively sensed that there was something lacking in your response, yet the words did not come. *May* we suggest to you that the answer you gave was not incorrect, but incomplete. The incompletion lies in your failure to point out that the questioner was using as a Referential Point a situation that *never* should have existed in the first place—a period of mass **brutalization** and mass murder of the millions of our ancestors. Your incompletion further failed to establish a proper Referential Point—the glorious age in Africa prior to European invasion.

The failure to establish the proper REFERENTIAL POINT dramatically influences both the proponents of equal rights for Blacks and the enemies of equal rights for Blacks.

The failure to establish the proper REFERENTIAL POINT for Blacks gags the activists in our struggle to gain the quest for uninhibited presumption of adequacy because our champions cannot psychologically overcome the argument that we have made "progress"when we use the referential point of so-called "slavery" or our state of affairs of ten or twenty years ago.

There *has* been a great deal of forward movement toward realization of our goal of PRESUMPTION OF ADEQUACY. However, in comparison with the proper REFERENTIAL POINT of the seventeenth century West Africa with world-wide acclaim of top honor and integrity of pre-invasion Songhai, where we were accorded the dignity and human rights equivalent to any human in the world, there exists even today a tremendous gap in being accorded these rights now. This dramatically *reduces* the nerve and motivation of those who would win for all, equal status in the universe of human dignity. So much for those who are "on our side."

For those who would honestly feel that we have come a "long way" toward full human dignity, the incorrect REFERENTIAL POINT of our "slavery" status serves an almost irrefutable base of comparison. In other words, "...look what we have now as compared to what we had then (slavery) (or ten or twenty years ago)."

Therefore, for our "friends" and "enemies," the incorrect REFERENTIAL POINT muffles the struggles for and reinforces the struggles against the acquisition of our full human rights.

The days of pre-European invasion are the days to remember, when the Black man was universally accorded full human dignity, when our adequacy in performance was not only a fact, but a presumption, *then* **that should be in the norm of our goals, the acquisition of that status, the** *sine qua non* **of the beginning of progress.**

While the phenomena are that we call "progress" today is a delusion and a snare, PAFO hastens to add that this delusion is not currently manufactured by some power-elitists sitting in some ivory tower. The delusion of tremendous progress is the resultant of white ignorance and Black ignorance and amnesia concerning our genesis.

However, there is another facet worth exploring of the term "progress." And that fact is whether or not it is true that as time goes on things automatically get better. And, if it is not always true, even using our captivity as our referential point, have things gotten better? If we are saying that the measure of progress is the lessening of contempt for Black genius, we say that the *contempt* has not lessened. If we're saying the measure of progress is Black ability to grapple with and control the manifestations of that contempt, in a very limited sense, there is progress when compared with our American experience.

That very limited sense is securing a greater share of the bounties of this nation in only an absolute sense. In a relative sense compared with other races, we are continuously falling behind.

For those who doubt that we are falling behind in a relative sense, let us suggest that you choose any criterion. In white collar jobs? We suggest that you will find that in the last twenty years while we have gained in an absolute sense, compared with the increase in the total of white collar jobs, we have a lower percentage of the total now than we did twenty years ago.

In percent of white median income compared with Black median income, we have lost six percentage points down to fifty-seven percent of the $13,400 white median family income.

In percent of national norms in educational tests of our youth? One only has to be semi-aware of what is happening in Black education to know that the **quality** of education for our Black youth is continuously worsening.

The same story is true in housing, in Black crime, in human relations statistics, in Equal Employment Opportunity statistics, and so on *ad nauseam*.

What is happening to delude people of good will from understanding the worsening of conditions is that they are comparing things in absolute terms instead of in relative terms. For instance, it is clear that if you are working beside a person doing the same job, and he is making the same as you today, tomorrow both of you get a raise, but his raise is ten dollars a day more and yours is five dollars a day more, PAFO is sure that you can see that you have made progress in an absolute sense (but you can only provoke havoc), over the fact that in a relative sense.you are going backwards. Everybody understands this in the rapidly escalating economy in America that though you are making more in absolute terms with inflation going on, many are worse off than they were prior to their raises.

So it is with Black people even using the incorrect referential point, conditions are worsening.

Using the correct REFERENTIAL POINT of the mountain-top of our history, the present situation of sliding backwards in a relative sense PLUS the correct Referential Point, makes the situation intolerable.

END OF SESSION XX

SESSION XXI

FROM MARCUS GARVEY TO MALCOLM X AND DR. MARTIN LUTHER KING TO JESSE JACKSON

In a way, we dislike to mention the bravery of Black soldiers in the so-called "War to Save the World for Democracy." Simply because of an extremely ungrateful America. Yes, we know that in reality the First World War was really a fight between European powers for the control of Africa and the Asiatic market. Britain and France took from Germany the part of Africa, she controlled. Also, exploitation of Asia and China continued at a greater rate as the partitioning of China reached its zenith in the post-war days that followed. Murder and mass killings were the order of the day by whites throughout the pigmented world. During the height of the war, there were thirty-eight lynchings (1917). In July of that year white workers in St. Louis turned on Blacks and killed up to two hundred of us and drove nearly six thousand of us from our homes. This was climaxed by the period known to Blacks, as the Red Summer of 1919. Twenty-six race riots ensued. Killing our people seemed to be a joy to the sadistic white mobs. The things that seemed to have set these riots off was that when returning Black veterans made the Northern white press headlines for outstanding heroism in the war and about French women having affairs with Black soldiers, their minds couldn't cope with it. Whites said, "These Niggers received medals for killing white men in Germany." Soldiers were pushed off of fast moving trains, and naturally, protests in the form of fighting back with arms followed. Black women exploded with joy and bursting

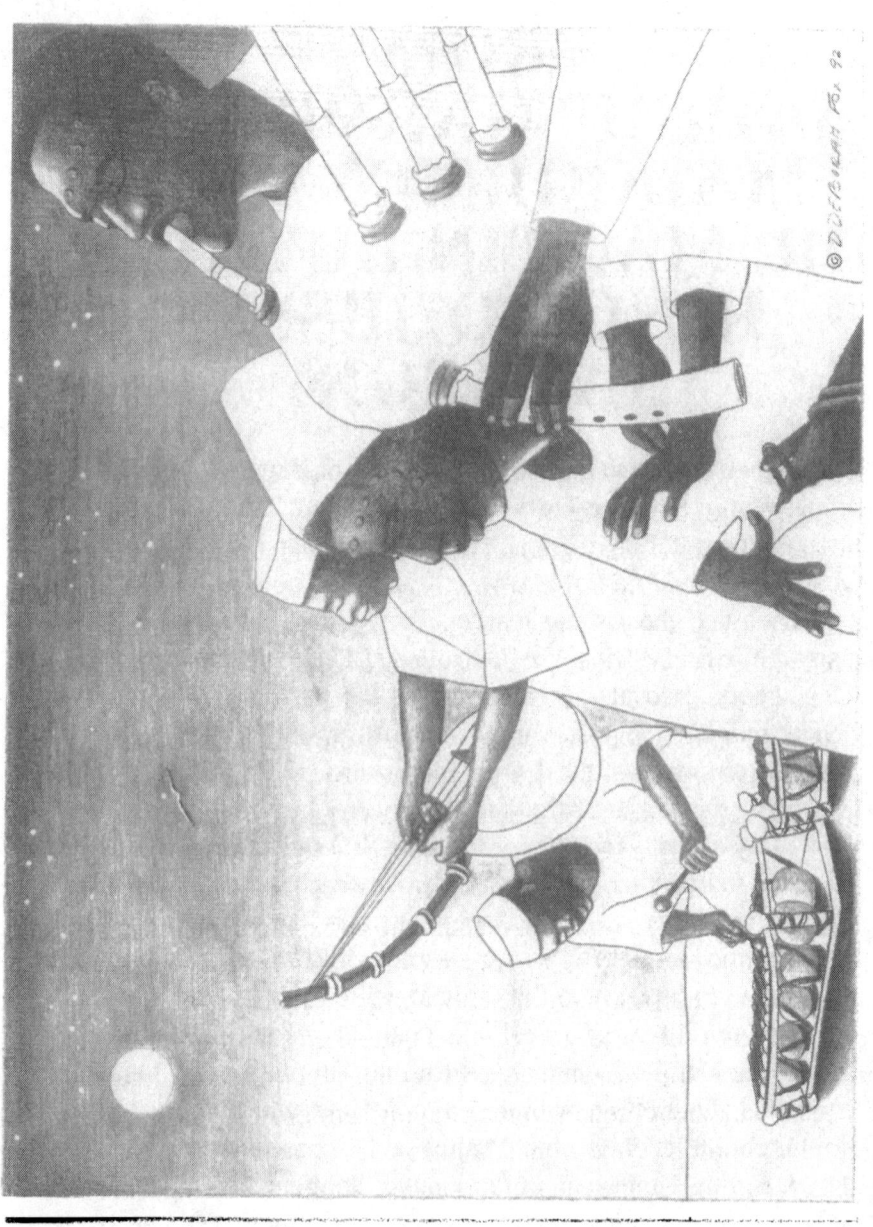

The harp guitar, an African musical instrument. One of the many instruments originating in Africa including the violin, piano, flute, trumpet, xylophone and bagpipes.

pride, crying out..."Our men, they are fighting, they are fighting, they are defending themselves and us." We did fight and we lost a lot of people. Because we were industrious, we built a financial empire in the midst of severe hostility and were punished for it.[1] In 1921, during one of the worst race riots in American history, Tulsa, Oklahoma, became the first United States' city to be bombed from the air. More than seventy-five persons—mostly Blacks—were killed.

Before the riot, Tulsa Blacks were so successful that their business district was called "The Negro Wall Street." Envy bred hatred of the Blacks, who accounted for a tenth of the segregated city's population of one hundred thousand.

Then on May 31, 1921, a white female elevator operator accused Dick Rowland, a nineteen-year-old Black who worked at a shoeshine stand, of attacking her. Though he denied the charge, Rowland was jailed. The Tulsa *Tribune* wrote a sensational account of the incident the next day, and a white lynch mob soon gathered at the jail. Armed Blacks, seeking to protect Rowland also showed up. Someone fired a gun, and the riot was on.

Whites invaded the Black district, burning, looting and killing. To break up the riot, the police commandeered private planes and dropped dynamite. Eventually, the National Guard was called in and martial law declared.

The police arrested more than four thousand Blacks and interned them in three camps. All Blacks were forced to carry green identification cards. And when Tulsa was zoned for a new railroad station, the tracks were routed through the Black business district, thus destroying it.

Two Jamaican Blacks, in 1920, viewed the American scene with horror. One, Claude McKay, a poet, said in his passionate sonnet of despair..."If Black men must die, O let us nobly die...Like men we'll face the murderous cowardly pack, pressed to the wall, dying, but fighting back."

The second Jamaican—a short Black spellbinder with a dandyish mustache and piercing magnetic eyes—scoffed at pretty words. "There is no law, he said, but *strength*. No justice but *power*." What the Black man needs is an *organization, land*, and his *own God*. Garvey reasoned that knowing the great Black past was not enough to bring the Black man out of the dilemma that he *was* and *still is* in.

---

1 Phila. Pa. Free Library — #031.02 W155S

He knew that Blacks should have reorientation in their religious concepts. He knew that more than three hundred years of negative influence about "Black," took its toll in a lot of different ways. The unending homicides committed against each other, which is the end result of self-contempt.

Garvey believed that Blacks should end their subserviency to the white man through the worship of his white God. Garvey's extreme racial nationalism *demanded* fulfillment in a truly Black religious concept. His widow explained, "it is really logical that although we all know that God is a spirit, all religions more or less visualize Him in a likeness akin to their own race..."Therefore, it was *most* important that pictures of God be in the likeness of Black people to implement the Black religion. Garvey called upon the Rev. George A. McGuire, a prominent Episcopal clergyman, who left his Boston pulpit in 1920, to become chaplain-general of the Universal Negro Improvement Association. (UNIA). From the very beginning, Bishop McGuire urged the Garveyites to forget the "white gods" erase the white gods from your hearts, he told his congregation. We must go back to our native church, to our true God.

Knowing that the Maat Concept was too big a jump to make so quickly, Garvey said "the new (Negro) Black religion would seek to be true to the principles of Christianity without the **shameful** hypocrisy of the white churches." When questioned by the white reporters as to his reputed belief, in the "Negro Ancestry of Christ," Garvey answered simply that, "Christ's ancestry included all races, so that He was divinity, reincarnated in the broadest sense of the word."

At the fourth International Convention of the Negro Peoples of the World, which met in August of 1924, Bishop McGuire advised "Negroes" to tear down and burn any pictures of the white Madonna and the white Christ that may be found in their homes. Then let us start our Black painters to work and paint our Black Gods. An aged woman had offered her African Orthodox pastor five dollars for telling her of the Black Christ, because she knew that no white man would ever die for her on the cross.

Garvey complained that the Black Man was the only one in the world that accepted the white man's characterization of the devil as being Black, and he announced that henceforth the Negro's devil would be white. With the exception of the African Orthodox Church, the regular "Negro" Clergy firmly rejected the new Black religion. Four out of five preachers strongly opposed the concept of a Black God. Shaking his head in dejection, Marcus Garvey wrote a poem that went like this: "Thou art made to be so white, that no Black Man has a claim. Couldn't this God be ever right that made it ill of fame. Thou art God in every way caring not for Black or White."

Exploiting the mood of pessimism, cynicism and despair, Marcus Mosiah Garvey built the first mass movement among American Blacks. "Up You Mighty Race," he thundered "you can accomplish what you will." He was right, but he was not acutely aware of the many methods of fight that was employed against him. When the powers saw that Black solidarity, they knew that physical confrontation would be of such magnitude, that it might not be expedient in the eyes of world opinion to so engage at that time. They used the weak of our people who were in the Garvey movement to foment trouble in the organization. This trouble came in the form of encouraging jealousies within the rank and file of the lower echelon of the organizational structure, and people being paid to sign petitions to deport the leader. Not being a so-called citizen of the United States of America, this was easily accomplished, and once the leader of a young organization is removed, disintegration begins to set in. Using the old frame-up of using the mail to defraud, Garvey was arrested in 1925 and deported in 1927. In his departing speech, in the setting of a blazing sun, where his black face shone back at the source of life in our solar system, he was hailed by the throng as one of the world's greatest orators. It has been said, that the Governor of California said to him, "Even with your great ability to persuade crowds with your eloquence, yet you or no other Black person will get out of your people's mind what we have put into it." Garvey sternly and deliberately said "I saw water fall on a rock so long, that it wore a hole in it, and people visited that place and drank of that water to cool their parched throats. That place I saw is in your Orange Mountain, New Jersey Indian Reservation. I may leave these shores, but I will be back, for there will come behind me little Marcus Garvies. To note my coming, your top soil will erode, you will have dust storms, great floods, great social unrest, economic distress with great unemployment, and when these things come to pass, you will know that Mr. Garvey is back in the land." All the governor could do was to stand there with his mouth open looking foolish.

The little Marcus Garvies followed, crying the cry of our Moses to "let my people go." Headlong into the 1930's we slid, we were sort of basking in the glow of a dying era in the late twenties. That was the era of what we thought was Black accomplishment from a whole ethnic standpoint. It was a period when local and visiting royalty were not at uncommon in Harlem. It was a time of A'Lelia Walker the "Black Heiress," the "Black Bottom of Shuffle Along," and Florence Mills. It was a period of Oscar DePriest the first Black Congressman in twenty-seven years. It was the year of a little boy born in Atlanta, Georgia, on Auburn Avenue, named Martin Luther King, Jr. It was a period of Langston Hughes, Countee Cullen, Claude McKay, Jean Toomer and James Weldon Johnson and Dr. Joseph Croom. It was the golden era of a so-called Black Renaissance. From the horror of the First World War ending in 1918, the year that the future president of the all Black Provident Home Insurance Company, was born and who is also the author of the present day famous, *Black Rhapsody*, Edward W. Robinson, Jr. Then the bubble burst on July 31, 1930. It was a long, cold winter for Black America, the depression had hit. More than ever, we were the last hired and the first fired. It took a while for the wound to bleed at first.

PART II

Unemployment was extremely high among Blacks, an average of sixty-five percent, and in Norfolk, Virginia, up to eight-one percent were on relief rolls. In some areas, men offered their services for ten cents an hour, while in other areas actual slavery returned. From the beginning of the depression to Dr. Martin Luther King's death, Black folks have been in the midst of bewilderment in many areas, but especially as to what method to use to achieve their goals. The power structure, by making survival so rigid, made people and especially Black people desperate. We wanted work, but it was not available. The white businesses made it a point to not hire us before hiring their own first. Here again Black women saved the men because they could get some work as domestics, *thus* helping to keep the family together. It was a sad time, but it was a time of much more concern for each other than now; a time before our values were entrenched in almost inflexible materialism. Black people took pride in Joe Louis, Jesse Owens, Jimmie Lunceford, Chick Webb, Ella Fitzgerald, Cab Calloway, Count Basie and Mary McLeod Bethune, as well as Duke Ellington, Louis Armstrong, Bessie Smith, W.C. Handy, Ben Webster, Billie Holliday, John Coltrane, Nat King Cole, Sugar Ray Robinson and Marian Anderson, just to name a few.

America was off to another war; this time to show Germany that she was not the superior white nation. Japan allegedly dragged America in the war by a forced attack on Pearl Harbor. Blacks, as usual, played a big role in America's victory, as she did in 1776, 1812, 1860, 1898 and 1914, in Korea, Viet Nam and the Persian Gulf, as well. This was also a period of Black assertion. The Freedom NOW rallies, the sit-ins, lay-ins, walk-ins, etc.,also a time the Supreme Court reversed itself (1954). In Montgomery, Alabama, Sister Rosa Parks was simply too tired, after having worked all day to go and sit in the back of a Montgomery bus, because a white person wanted her seat. This precipitated the Montgomery Improvement Association that grew into S.C.L.C. This movement spawned many other resistance movements and actually became the impetus for individuals to stand up and fight for their rights; there was James Meredith, Autherine Lucy, Daisy Bates and Abby Lincoln.

Black women cried and Black men gnashed their teeth when news of an assassin's bullet on February 21, 1965 cut down a brilliant self-taught prince of the genetic line of Songhai. His ability to persuade people and to put to flight groups of white learned men on the subjects of freedom for Blacks, Malcolm Little but better knows as "Malcolm X" was bent on uniting all Black groups under a single banner, and was in the process of doing that until the time of his death. Dr. King was also struck down, when his philosophy blossomed into a United Front type of program and when he saw, or maybe we should say, voiced the observance of a united Euro-American game against dark people for material wealth in Africa. (Nigerian Civil War), Black unemployment and Viet Nam. After Dr. King's death, it seems as though the green light was given to those controlling dope to dump it into the Black community in massive amounts. We know that those people who use this over and over again will eventually lose their incentives and drives for the movement. All they will want to do is become involved in feeling high and the satisfaction of a biological urge for sex. This dope use increases the crime among Blacks in the form of robberies in order to pay for the habit. The producing of super-fly pictures produced the urge in Black youth to want to emulate that kind of character. These are some of the words of Lerone Bennet, Jr., back in 1971 as he was evaluating the demonstrations of the 1960's and the so-called artistic fulfillment in the 1970's with Flip Wilson's, *"Geraldine"* and Van Peebles, *"Sweetback."* Here were two provocative and ultimately insidious reincarnations of all the Sapphires and Studs of yesteryear. Who would have believed it would come to this? Would one believe that Afros and Dashikis would lead to *Geraldine* or who would have believed the "Black is Beautiful" doctrine would lead to the *Sweetback* rhetoric that "Black is Misery?" Because of the misunderstanding of our experience, because of our misreading of the tracks of the true Black Spirit, we have a tendency to become cleft in soul and mind. This negative concept of the Black spirit makes us praise Black womanhood, and then make a cult of the Black pimps who degrade them. Black people must unite to change the image and the values by the study of themselves from the beginning of our culture. The image that we have now is the image of race deceit (like we are supposed to be that way) such as group hate, imagery of not caring, the imagery of belittlement, imagery of wanton betrayal, wanton killings, and the imagery of degrading our sacred history. We must return to the laws that made us Africans great. These laws were embodied in a concept known a Maat. It was not a wonder that Heredotus and before him Homer described the Africans as the most beautiful, the favorite of the gods, the most just of men. We were always in control of ourselves. We had developed the highest consciousness of love and unity within and with all things. We advocated the concept of the helping hand to lift our African family up as well as all mankind.

Reflecting back on this session, we have just read, one wonders if we really have a good or bright future. Are we doomed to bitter frustration without end? What if it were possible to reach back in time through that bridge of knowledge we have talked about before? Maybe, just maybe, there might be something we have overlooked. It could, perhaps be right under our very noses, but then what exactly could let us peer down the corridor of time.

Suppose that there exists somewhere a magical crystal ball in which we could look and see the future for African Americans. Let's further suppose that in that crystal ball we could see that we are at a fork in the road, with one fork leading down to bloody genocide and the other fork leading to a beautiful freedom from contempt.

If such a magical ball existed and the wise men who would read its prophesies would rush out and shout those prophesies to the assembled throng—who would accept and heed? Very few, I predict, and for a very simple reason:

The wise men would say that the crystal ball prophesied that the road to genocide lay down the road obtaining more degrees, building a bigger economic base and acquiring more political offices, as the end in itself. The wise would excitedly say that the road to full freedom lay in reprogramming America (including Black people) to know and internalize that African Americans came from a huge, highly cultured empire in West Africa and that our physical characteristics are symbols of advanced evolutionary development.

And because the wise men would say that, the masses of people would turn them off and say "Everybody knows that our full freedom lies in more degrees, building our economic base and holding political offices." The wise men would reply, "History has proven that following those ways *exclusively leads to death.*

THE COMPARISON YEARS, THE 1800'S v. 1900'S;

Let us see whether or not the wise men would be right. Let us, look into the "crystal ball." Such a prophetic "ball" does exist. It exists on a comparative analysis of history. The analysis compares the events of the 1860's, 1870's, and 1880's with the events of the 1960's, 1970's, and the 1980's. Strangely enough—*THE EVENTS ARE ALMOST IDENTICAL YEAR BY YEAR*, only one hundred years apart. Therefore, by looking at the chart of events of 1886 and onward, we probably can predict what will be coming in 1986 and onwards.

Let us start with the Sixties of both centuries.
- A. Violence erupted in the early Sixties with African Americans on center stage:
  1. The Civil War in the 1860's.
  2. The Civil Rights Movement in the 1960's.
- B. Black warriors led the fights in ridding us of our chains:
  1. The physical chains in the 1860's.
  2. The political chains in the 1960's.
- C. We "solidified" our victories with passage of civil rights acts:
  1. The Civil Rights Act of the 1860's.
  2. The Civil Rights Act of the 1960's.
- D. We elected African American political figures in significant numbers between 1868 and 1885:
  1. Eighteen to Congress with two senators.
  2. Scores to state and city governments.
- E. We elected African American political figures in significant numbers between 1968 and 1985:

---

2 Garfield was assassinated in 1881 and Arthur filled out the term.

1. Eighteen to Congress with one senators.
2. Scores to state and city governments.
F. We sought and received federal aid in education:
   1. In the 1860's and 1870's from the federally financed Freedman's Bureau.
   2. In the 1960's and 1970's from the federally financed Title I and Head Start.
G. We sought and received federal protection against discrimination in jobs.
   1. In the 1860's and 1870's from the Freedmen's Bureau.
   2. In the 1960's and 1970's from EEOC (Title 7, Equal Employment Opportunity Commission) of the 1964 Civil Rights Act.
H. Men of great charm and excellent speakers were elected presidents:
   1. In 1881—James A. Garfield.[1]
   2. In 1981—Ronald Reagan.
I. During the next four years in both centuries:
   1. Hard won civil rights were stripped away from African Americans by Chester A. Arthur and Ronald Reagan.
   2. Educational aid from the Federal government eroded into insignificance by Presidents Arthur and Reagan in both centuries.
   3. The Ku Klux Klan's membership soared under both Presidents, Arthur and Reagan.
J. African Americans sought to establish economic bases:
   1. In Baltimore and Savannah, thousands of African Americans in the 1860's and 1870's invested tens of thousands of dollars to establish businesses. All failed.
   2. In the 1860's the federal government established the Freedman's Savings and Trust Company. It failed.
   3. In the 1960's and 1970's, thousands of African Americans invested millions of dollars in businesses that failed.
   4. In the 1960's the federal government established the S.B.A. (Small Business Administration). Its losses are presently staggering.
   5. We pursued the building of an economic base in both centuries.
   6. We pursued the acquisition of degrees in both centuries.

7. We pursued the obtaining of political offices in both centuries.

Now that we have established the parallel events of the Nineteenth and Twentieth Centuries up until 1985, let us part the grey curtain of the future by looking at 1886 and onwards so that we can postulate what will happen in 1986 and onwards.

THE PROPHETIC CRYSTAL BALL

An Enigma of Compared Historical Analysis

In the above material, we have shown the amazing similarity between the events of the 1860's and the events of the 1960's; between the events of 1870's and the events of the 1970's; between the events, almost to the year, of the 1880's to 1885 and the events occurring 1980 to 1985. It seems, therefore, logical to be very thorough in our investigation of events that occurred in 1886 and thereafter because of the high probability that 1986 and thereafter will be duplicative of that era of a century ago.

From 1886 onwards, the personal and political rights of African Americans degenerated at a quickened pace. New white organizations sprang up in an unholy crusade to strip away all political rights. Some of these organizations were called Knights of the White Camelia, the White Brotherhood, the Constitutional Union Guards, Knights of the Ku Klux Klan and the Rifle Clubs of South Carolina.

Meanwhile, from 1886 and onwards, there was a national movement to return every aspect of government from the federal to local rule (Reagan has already started this, so we're a year early this century).

The North had grown weary of the crusade for justice for African American citizens. The South devised ingenious ways, including murder, to prevent Blacks from voting.

A popular movement in 1881 drew poor whites and Blacks together *briefly* in many states. The coalition was based on Black and white families uniting (Foreshadow of Rev. Jesse Jackson's Rainbow Coalition).

However, the movement failed when white anger mounted as Blacks were again elected to high offices. The white backlash was bloody and devastating. A foreshadowing of events on their way, is not only the shooting of four Black youths by subway gunman Goetz, but the fact that he is lionized as an American hero.

Another vicious attack on civil rights occurred when American apartheid (absolute separation of the races) began to harden into place by 1892 and became legalized with the supreme court decision entitled Plessy vs. Ferguson in 1896.

By 1898, the pattern for constitutional disfranchisement had been completely drawn in the South.

The pace of lynchings accelerated each year after 1892. In 1900 and 1901, there were 214 documented lynchings. The bloody murders increased in numbers and savagery during the following eighteen years.

This, therefore describes descent of the African American from halls of Congress and complete voting rights to complete segregation, no elected offices and no voting rights at all—all in the space of sixteen years—from 1886 to 1902.

During all the years from early 1860's to 1885, we had succeeded in blasting off both our physical chains and our political chains. We thought we had it made forever. We followed blindly and exclusively a path that led to complete erosion of all of the rights. That formula is labeled the *exclusive political, educational and economic path.*

In spite of the obvious lesson from history outlined above, no book we've read yet has ever questioned whether or not that there may be yet another element missing from that formula for freedom.

The way the crystal ball is reading is that **IF WE FOLLOW THE PATHS OF BUILDING THE ECONOMIC BASE, OBTAINING MORE DEGREES AND WINNING MORE POLITICAL OFFICES AND DOING THOSE THINGS EXCLUSIVELY WITHOUT ADDING THE MISSING ELEMENT, THEN OUR "GAINS" WILL BE WIPED OUT AS THEY WERE A CENTURY AGO.** *Here's how it probably will go in a century-old pattern*: 1986-2000:

Personal and political rights of African Americans will degenerate at a quickened pace. There will be an increasing movement from federal to state rule. Physical attacks on African Americans will increase. The Ku Klux Klan will begin a wave of terror.

The white liberals, in most cases, will find more and more excuses to abandon support of African Americans. Black colleges, the nurturing womb of Black leadership will be under attack by the government.
1990-2000:

States will probably seek to withdraw voting rights' laws that will have been returned to the state for local decision. Black colleges will have accreditation and financial aid withdrawn, in many cases.

Bloody lynchings of Blacks will become commonplace. The Supreme Court will "legalize" the reversal of the 1964 Civil Rights Act.

Black economic beachheads will be wiped out by federal, local and violent backlash action.

Black males will be hardest hit by the fall in educational achievement.

Black fratricide rate will rise enormously.

Black divorce rate will rise to four times the national rate.

2000 AND PLUS:

The impact of the weakening of Voting Rights Act and the sweep of terror will decelerate the elections of Blacks to political offices.

The wave of terror of the white hate groups will accelerate.

We are saying here plainly, that unless we include in that formula for freedom the element we call *the reprogramming of America,* we African Americans are doomed to repeat our bloody history of a century ago.

By "reprogramming America," we mean reaching tens of millions of minds through motion pictures, novels, articles and television series that tell exciting stories. And woven artfully in those stories is the redemptive truth of who African Americans really are. It would not be well to bludgeon because emotionally-based mind-sets are not dislodged by heavy-handed methods. But what must be skillfully told on video and screen is the story of the sophistication and grandeur of a civilization from which our fathers and mothers were driven just a few centuries ago. We must tell of the large cities in the Western Sudan, with its storied homes of polished stone on tree-lined avenues. We must tell of the university systems, of the medical schools that taught surgery for removal of cataracts from the eyes and procedures of vaccinations against smallpox, etc.

We must, somehow, speak the unspeakable, that the very physical characteristics we have been programmed to believe are badges of degradation are really symbols of advanced evolution.

The stories must be told in a way that will not cause the sense of group guilt of whites to increase. For we will dwell upon the beauty of West African life and culture before the **Voyages of Tears and the Era of the Fat Sharks,** that is before the voyages of the so-called slave ships (really prisoners-of-war ships), and before the 250 years when our fathers and mothers jumped overboard to the waiting sharks rather than remain captive.

The year 1986 is already past. The fork in the road is looming ahead. If we choose to ignore the lessons of a century ago and say it is just a mere coincidence, then, how unfortunate.

Yet, how wise and redemptive if we choose to obey the lessons of a century ago and add the ingredient of reprogramming America.

It is wise because there just might be a chance that America's minds can be reprogrammed to have respect for the intrinsic value of all people. If it doesn't work—well—what harm will have been done.

It is redemptive because TRUTH will at last be vindicated.

We sing with the poet,
TRUTH, forever on the scaffold,
WRONG, forever on the throne,
Yet that scaffold sways the future,
And behind the DIM UNKNOWN,
Stands GOD, amidst the shadows,
Keeping watch o'er HIS own.

END OF SESSION XXI

SESSION XXII
THE ECONOMIC EFFECTS OF RACISM RE: PEOPLE OF COLOR

In the previous session, we ask rhetorically what will the future be? We say, it will stay the same unless there is a major deprogramming of the entire society. And it won't change unless we Blacks initiate programs to unbrainwash all people. Two reasons why whites are not interested in deprogramming themselves is: (1) They don't feel victimized and the second reason is that there are economic benefits. Back in Session II, we spoke how evolution, anthropology and white racism affected people of color.

We pointed out how mankind evolved, how and why Africans received the rich endowments of a better heart, veins, human hair, melanin, etc. These richer endowments came about because Africans evolved in an area that the glaciers never reached, thus, the Africans' evolutionary process never slowed down.

Having ingested this historical and anthropological information, up to Session VIII, you've enriched yourself in the knowledge of the great and beautiful things that Africans at home and abroad have so heavily contributed to the progress of civilizations.

African Americans very rarely received neither the historical recognition nor the financial benefits from their inventions and scientific breakthroughs. This was a continuation of the betrayals and treachery of white society. Yet, in the face of this blatant and systematic racist policy, many Blacks are blinded by those Seven Veils of Illusion described heretofore. (See Chapter III — "Social Darwinism...")

One of the manifestations of THE PROBLEM is that Blacks are programmed to begin castigating other Blacks who mount an attack on

THE PROBLEM. Because of the programmed mentality, there is projected a defense of white society that makes the victim feel responsible for his own victimization.

Simply stated, Black people's reaction to white racism is just that—a reaction and not the usual given reason that this reaction is "racist." Etymologically speaking, racism is the negative exertion of the group in power upon a different powerless race. Since African-Americans are not the race in power, and whites are not the powerless group, it is impossible for African Americans to commit acts of racism. Blacks do not control the mass of jobs, money, the media of communications, the army or navy. Therefore, because African Americans do not control the major manifestations of power, it is impossible for them to be racists. This does not say that some Blacks do not strike back in fury against the practice of contempt against them. But this is not racism, but an entirely normal reaction to emotional and sometimes physical pain.

RACISM—IS IT PROFITABLE TODAY?

Back in Session X, we noted that a smart "slaver" could manipulate in a way to make up to five thousand percent above cost in working our fathers and mothers. In addition to that, they set up stud breeding farms, thus producing more laborers without having to purchase incoming fresh captives from Africa. We worked from sunup to sundown for ten generations without a payday. Their instruments of torture that they used against us to force us to do their bidding, produced jobs for white people for centuries in New England and Britain.

Even though so-called chattel bondage is over, yet its poison lingers on. Let us look at where the poison still lingers.

Right after the Civil War, industries refused to hire Blacks, or if they did hire them, kept them in menial positions.

What about today? We would like to quote a portion of a book called *Institutional Racism in America* by Knowles and Prewitt, who incidentally are white:

"The analysis of the delivery of benefits discloses that those benefits invariably are slotted overwhelmingly in favor of whites. On the other side of the coin, the pangs and penalties are heavily delivered against pigmented people. These rewards and punishments are delivered by the institutions of education, justice, economics, politics, health, delivery and housing."

This is what makes this a white racist society.

Let us analyze this last paragraph, and equate it with the present dilemma of Africans and Africans living in America. As was pointed out in the book, *Jesse Jackson and the Politics of Race*, by Landess and Quinn, that so many of the American industries have used various kinds of tactics to keep African Americans out of jobs. They use such methods as destroying the job application or saying that Blacks are over or under-qualified.

In the motion picture industry the script almost always calls for white actors. Protestations result in no improvement. What is required is script writing by African Americans. The *Color Purple* was a play written by a person of color, one Alice Walker. When Blacks are included in the script, they are usually portrayed in a manner demeaning to the dignity of the race. A case in point is the 1987 motion picture *Platoon*. Former Director of the now defunct Crisis Intervention Network of Philadelphia, Pennsylvania, Bennie Swans, Jr., a Black Vietnam War veteran who was awarded the Purple Heart, three Silver Stars, three Bronze Stars and the Air Medal for Heroism, denounced the motion picture. He pointed out that Blacks were portrayed as being on drugs, as cowardly, running away from danger, and sleeping on duty, thus causing an entire unit to be wiped out.

It is precisely these kinds of portrayals that reinforce THE PROBLEM of contempt of our African genesis.

Vietnam saw the African American involved as he has been in all of America's wars—that is, in a major way. Indeed, there were so many Blacks in combat duty in the NAM on the front lines that it was called "SOULVILLE." African Americans made up twenty percent of the elite military branches and forty-five percent of the Rifle Platoon, suffered twenty-three percent of the war casualties (7,261) while remaining only eleven percent of the United States population. The Army awarded ten Medals of Honor to Black soldiers, and five Medals of Honor to Black marines. Yet with this magnificent record in the Vietnam War, *Platoon*, with its brainwash is the only thing that is etched on America's consciousness, because it is told in drama.

We have explained, in this session, as well as other parts of this book how much African Americans have contributed to the world. Yet, with all of this empirical evidence of African Americans' intellectuality, in all fields of endeavor, not excluding the battlefield, we are still told to prove ourselves. As we have aforementioned, the subconscious mind has been so subliminally programmed, that only the lies told against us permeate the consciousness of white America. Here is another scenario for your brain to wrestle.

Recently, a study showed that over two-thirds of African Americans were above the poverty level, did not live in broken down ghettoes, whose educational levels were above the national average and eighty-five percent of the total were working, seventy-five percent were not in the toils of the justice system (in jail, on parole). The reason for the significance of these figures is that the news media gives the idea, to all Americans, that the majority of African Americans live in ghettoes, are poor, are uneducated, are present or past criminals, are on welfare, are not working and live in poor homes. It gives the impression that the ones who are not thus poorly situated are the exception to the rule. In a recent survey (for a month), ninety percent of the news reports portrayed African Americans as poor, uneducated, criminals, etc.

On the other hand, the majority of people, in America, who are on welfare are white, the typical and majority of dope addicts are white. There are more impoverished white families than Black families. The ones who keep the drug trade flourishing are white persons. The most heinous crimes committed, including cannibalism, are committed by whites. Yet, the news media, in reporting all-white news fails to play these facts up—they mention, but don't play them up with the lurid pictures and constant repetition.

This contradicts the arguments that white news media experts use to defend showing Black crime, Black degradation, that the news is fair, even-handed and that only negative things sell in the news market.

The vast majority of African Americans are not living in a degraded, impoverished, uneducated, poorly housed, condition. There are more than seven million Blacks who make more income than ninety million whites. We have to understand these facts in order to move ahead from moaning about our status. They are the majority, not the exceptions.

So the question arises, since so many have "made it." Then, what are you are fussing about?

PAFO's definition of "making it" boils down to two words—"presumptively adequate." Presumptively adequate means that when you are seen, or when you make application for a job, you are looked upon the same as a white person is seen, or when a white person makes application for a job. When you move into a new neighborhood, you are considered okay, as a neighbor, until you prove by your behavior something different. When you make application to medical school, or engineering schools, you are considered in the same light as a white person.

"Making it" also means that when you open a store, in a Black neighborhood, Black people treat you the same as they would a white merchant with the same amount of goods on the shelf. Or when you, as a contractor, apply to build a church for a Black congregation, it will accept your credentials the same as they would a white contractor with the same experience.

It's obvious to PAFO that we, in America, are not considered "presumptively adequate." Therefore, the question remains "why not" and then "what to do about it."

While writing the above, another statistic came to our attention. In the year 1991, in America, over four million major crimes were committed. Of these total crimes, sixteen percent were committed by Blacks and Latinos. Therefore, over eighty percent were committed by whites. This, according to the "The Uniform Gun Reports" published by the F.B.I. and the U.S. Bureau of the Census, is about the same percentage the population bears to the total. With respect to crimes involving sexual deviant behavior, grossly heinous crimes such as keeping people prisoners, performing all kinds of deviant behavior on them—use of bodily excrement, kidnapping and cannibalism—everyone knows the Black percentage of these kinds of criminals is extremely low. White deviant criminals practically have the whole field to themselves.

The reason African Americans are not looked upon as just as trustworthy, just as skilled, just as able to catch on quickly, just as good a bank risk, and just as good a contractor is not because we aren't trustworthy, not because we aren't as skilled, or able to catch on, or as good to pay back the bank, or as good a contractor, or as moral, or more than anyone else. The reason that we are at first sight—or before sight—considered a bad contractor, etc., is traced back to Americans' childhood when they saw all kinds of motion pictures showing us as stupid, lazy, immoral, child-like, comic, violent, impulsive, non-serious, unable to make independent decisions, such as in the shows where a Black person is the side-kick, who never solves the problem—just carries out orders. Seeing the same inadequacy over and over and over, does something to our brain—it's called brainwash. The final answer is not laws against redlining; not laws, because Americans would find a way around the laws. But, laws won't hurt. The final answer is not demonstrations—because demonstrations will result in band-aids which will erode in a few years like the civil rights laws. But, PAFO says go on and demonstrate—they won't hurt.

No, the final answer is psychological—it's mental changes. It's deprogramming of America through huge numbers of dramatic motion pictures and other kinds of film. The lack of the truth about African Americans, of their intellectual prowess and their ability to survive, in spite of, is what really makes white America—and Blacks too—believe all the wrong about us. And, that is what forms the opinions and sets the tone for the substandard treatment that African Americans receive in America.

CONTINUING MANIFESTATIONS OF RACISM AND BLACKS COUNTERING IT

It is almost unbelievable that in 1992 there is still the practice of two pay standards, one for whites and one for Blacks. This practice usually exists where there is no labor union, although even in some unionized work facilities, it still happens.

The various strong Black politicians like State Representative P. Richardson, Jr. (Democrat) of Pennsylvania have been struggling to force some of these firms to equalize their pay scales.

Then there were various organizations such as the Black Clergy, the Southern Christian Leadership Conference, Operation Bread Basket and later on People United to Save Humanity (PUSH) which confronted major corporations and forced many of them to alter their hiring and other discriminatory practices.

The lever of Black patronage was used to pry the corporations into line. The lever was applied with the same Black genius that guided our survival here in America for more than three centuries. The overall results, according to the Reverend Leon Sullivan[3], were that here in the Delaware Valley, the efforts of individuals and organizations, five thousand new jobs and fifteen millions of dollars in new income for the Black community were achieved.

Jesse Jackson[4] achieved similar results in the Chicago area and later on a national level.

Of course, there is much more in organizational effort and high drama in pushing for economic parity, but we just wanted to touch on

---

3 Reverend Leon Sullivan. Founder of the Opportunities Industrialization Center (O.I.C.) in Philadelphia, and pastor of one of the largest Black Churches in Philadelphia. He was very instrumental in the south African apartheid struggle before it became fashionable.

this to partially reveal how *profitable* racism is for the *dominant* race.

The definition of racism is applicable in the context of negative domination of one race over another by force whether that force is **physical or psychological**. The question within Session 19 "Is Racism Profitable Today?" is answered, and the answer is loud and clear.— Yes!

END OF SESSION XXII

4 Rev. Jesse Jackson. Founder and president of People United to Save Humanity (PUSH). Close associate and organizer with the late Dr. Martin Luther King, Jr. Also, Rev. Jackson became the political figure for the African-American community in his bid to be President of the United States in 1984 and for 1988.

SESSION XXIII

THE SPIRIT OF NATIONALISM

EVALUATION ANALYSIS AND SURVIVAL OVERVIEW

An African proverb says, "Not to know is bad, not to wish to know is worse." The Sages of past ages agree that knowledge and its application is power, but to be truly the master, get wisdom and understanding for it will be the stability of thy soul.

We, the descendants of the Songhai Empire, living in the Western Hemisphere cloaked under the name of "Negro," lost our history and cultural background. The lack of knowledge particularly today has caused us to be a *race in name*, rather than in fact; a condition, rather than a full consciousness, in terms of sentiment, rather than a joyful experience and all we've had from a total point of view, *were problems in common.*[5]

We believe that for people and nations to achieve, there must be an underlying driving purpose, the setting up of goals and objective along the road to the purpose. We believe that the purposes of nations should be continually unfolding year in and year out; like in the unending quest to end sometimes needless wars, disease, poverty, ignorance and hunger. To probe the mysteries of the stars, the seas and the materials in the earth, but not for individual gain or personal aggrandizements. Review in your mind, the past pages of this Digest and you will recall that our Songhai Empire was well on the way to that kind of purpose, at the time of the sneak attack on our territory. This precisely is what our father Abderrahman Es-Sa'Di saw during that awful time when he said, "I saw the ruin of learning and its utter collapse in Songhai."[6] As a result

---

5 Arthur D. Williams, Afro American News, 1958.
6 *Tarikh es-Sudan*

of our captivity, we had thrust on us—culture and history of others that gave us no drive and purpose relevant to Black needs. The most thorough brainwashing began to slowly form as we began to identify subconsciously with the white society. This is manifested in many ways; such as dress, language, honoring their heroes and disliking those whom the white man said to dislike including each other. In other words, out of the dust of confusion that the Black Man was thrust into, the power elitist through their power structure, **created the "Negro."** *Before captivity became institutionalized, there were no Negroes. They were a variety of different African nationalities.* The lack of knowledge that does away with real ethnic pride generally, made us accept any name that the captor might give us. We answer to Negro, nigger, shine, coon, colored, darky, boot, tan yan, American and a few other unmentionables. How can we even attempt to bind ourselves together for identification with so many names to answer to? A family of people, including nations, are bound together by common surnames, and as a family they have problems in common, they fought those problems and then shared a joyous experience in overcoming them. Their closeness was reinforced by discussing them at the supper table. Now the white people have these same experiences, which also solidifies his individual family unit, but he also has *his* ethnic name that binds him still further to his people or country. This group unit is reinforced more when studying their history whether from the text book or watching movies and television stories. But we Blacks only experiencing negative conditions since our captivity, rather than joyful experiences together, become numb or anesthetized to our sister's or brother's pain. Sometimes when a brother or sister has been cruelly wronged by the white society, and it happens to get the right amount of publicity in the press, radio and television; for a while, we will press for justice en masse. Then because of long drawn out litigations, or numbness to the plight of our kind will resurface and we tend to forget him or her. By not enjoying a life in common, our "Problems" in common such as being dogged around by this racist system, tends to make us disrespect each other even more. This is exemplified when would-be true Black leaders offer suggestions to get out of the condition, many times they are told by the more brainwashed, "If you're so smart how come you ain't rich, or you can't do anything without the white man." This is another reason why we say that most television shows are detrimental to Blacks in varying ways. A great many shows always portray white people solving Black people's problems, like the

White Shadow for example. We are not offering excuses for a lot of our people's actions, but we are trying to be like a doctor when he attempts to heal his patient; first, he must diagnose the symptoms and then prescribe a cure. Since we are not enjoying that life in common, we *will not* be like those nationalities that relate to their past, enjoying that nostalgic feeling or commemorating *their* independence day or some other traditional holiday.

METHODS TO ACHIEVE SOLIDARITY

However, we of PAFO believe beyond the shadow of a doubt, that the spirit of our fathers and mothers have shown us how we can cope with and neutralize the forces that are keeping us from getting together. We believe that most grass root organizations are sincere and want to see Black people work together. What makes PAFO unique along with the Universal Negro Improvement Association (UNIA) is that we seem to recognize the fact that it takes a particular METHOD TO ACHIEVE SOLIDARITY of which we are trying to implement. We won't say in this Digest everything we need, but one thing sure is that we need a visible symbol in order to link the past (the time in which we were in our glory) with the present, using the *sacred* family symbol of the Black man, woman and child. This is part of the great purpose that *we must establish once again* the true meaning of African family tradition and the *understanding* of the extended family concept.

Some of our people meaning well in trying to bring the African family to its former status may in reality be hurting that cause without realizing it. Naturally, it would be easy to perhaps get off the track since the historians tried to fuse Arabic history and traditions into the African realm. One must stop and consider, that everything in Africa even then was not the original or indigenous. The enemy historians as you already know, disavowed the truth about us and changed **our** history into "**his** story" and that goes for a great many Arab writers as well.

Looking back in Session IV with the inception of the African Democracy that grew out of the African constitution was where the basic social structures had its foundation. One of the main subjects that people are trying to find justification is plural marriages. Indigenous mainstream African Societies believed in basic monogamy. Egypt's great pharaoh Akhenaton espoused the one God Concept and one wife. However, among the notables there was evidence of some plural marriages but not among the ordinary people. It did not become common practice even when it was forced upon us by the Arabs. Polygamy and concubinage came as a result of the incursions starting back to about five thousand years ago. The beauty of the mainstream indigenous Africans' social structure and extended family concept was so powerful that it stood in the way of the conquest of Africa, so they had to try to break it up.

SETTING PERSONAL EXAMPLES

People best follow by personal example, therefore we must not exploit our people, especially our women. All those who do and yet talk otherwise are merely playing games. This is why PAFO must exemplify what becoming one means since indications by the score are that the probability of our survival in this country are diminishing, and to become united as one is not a choice but a dire necessity.

It is not the purpose of this chapter to detail those indications and prove by the preponderance of the evidence that such is the case. But rather, it is to assume the swift descent of probabilities of survival to zero. In the event that the assumption is incorrect, then whatever actions that are taken pursuant to this writing will not be wasted—based on the premise of "rather safe than sorry."

However, to hasten to a proposed plan of action would be improper without a historical foundation of causation of the problem that will, based on the above assumption, precipitate Black genocide.

The truth of the matter is that we are the most despised, the most scorned of all people, by all people, including us.

Our foreparents, generations ago, composed a folksong (a "spiritual") based on their sensing the rejection of our (their) personhood—their humanness.

The song—*I've Been (re) 'Buked and I've Been Scorned* has come down to us as a clear statement. A later verse is prophetic, "There will be trouble all over this land...."

A symptomatic moment of this loathing of us, is the fact that we are the only people on the planet that are viewed as "contaminating" another race by an admixture of only a "drop" of our blood. The "contaminating" element is translated into legal and sociological sanctions by classifying that Caucasian, Indian, or Asian who is known to have any admixture of Black blood is Black, Negro, Afro-American, Bilalian or whatever other name they describe those of us who are recognizably and preponderantly African.

To be even more descriptive of the problem, we should suggest that the problem is "the programmed loathing by the total American society of our geneses (i.e.—cultural and evolutionary)."

To put it in perhaps less pedantic terms—"the problem is that the total society has been historically programmed to loathe our Pre-Colonial African culture and to loathe the genetic pool from which we were produced." This scorn is evidenced by the overabundance of attacks by the mass media against African Americans when there has been any type of unruly activity by United States Blacks. The television and radio (white) and yes, even some of the members of the Black press have attacked our youth. Talk show after talk show carry these thinly veiled anti-African American propaganda. News articles of great length pour out from the mass media. Congressmen chide the whole Black Community. Psychologists are probing the recesses of Black minds and Black family structures and various Black elected officials are assailed. The fundamental question remains: Why all the negative fanfare? Why wasn't the same concentrated venom leveled at white youths and white family structures? Why weren't there psychologists probing? 1) When white college students rampaged overturning cars and terrorizing people after their basketball victories. 2) When white youths desecrated three to five hundred tombstones. 3) When for years during each college Spring break, thousands of white youths descend on Fort Lauderdale, Florida and wreak havoc on the whole town. For them, they were just overexuberant youths. For Blacks, we were animals going berserk. For them, just a brief news article. For us, questions by Congressmen, psychologists and sociologists. Why the difference? The reason for the differential treatment is rooted in the problem that we have explained in the above material.

TRULY UNDERSTANDING BRAINWASH

PAFO is about the task of reprogramming the whole society, because of the negative brainwash which makes the society believe that Black people have contributed nothing of value. Therefore, inordinate attention to any incident that supports the myths, is given full media coverage. We must do our homework by making comparative studies of treatments.

Brainwash is a strange thing. Anything that supports the brainwash is *maximized*. And in reverse, anything that is *contrary* to the brainwash is overlooked, played down, or an excuse is given (Like "Oh, he's different"). We must do our homework by making comparative studies of treatment accorded other races who engage in negative behavior. A

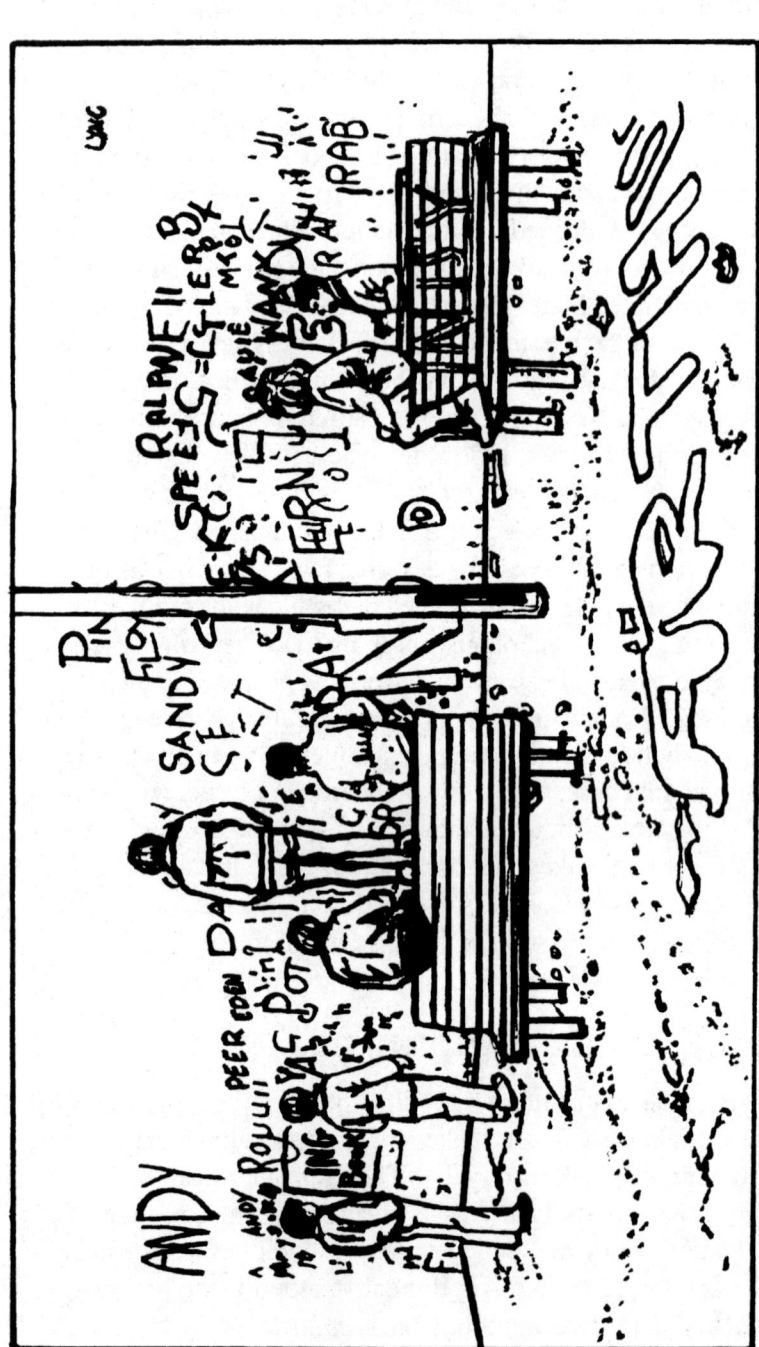

A generation on hold, youths in Glasgow's East End, where unemployment runs as high as 60%, mark time on a tenement wall, waiting for opportunity to knock. Without technical skills for today's jobs, alarming numbers of Glasgow teenagers are graduating from the classroom to the public dole, venting their frustrations in drugs and crime. for many, emigration may be the only answer, as their city undergoes a painful transition from a smokestack to a diversified economy. Built to replace teeming Victorian slums, abandoned high rises (above) in the Gorbals district stand as testaments to hasty planning, poor construction, and vandalism. (From National Geographic Magazine – 1984)

case in point appeared in *National Geographic Magazine* (1984), which cited white children in Glasgow, Scotland, writing on their vandalized buildings due to (60%) unemployment. Therefore, Graffiti is not just a Black problem, but a human problem, created only by conditions.

This loathing is translated into daily, yes, evenly hourly action by both Blacks and non-Blacks here in America. To name just two Black translations of the loathing:

A fratricide rate of eighteen hundred percent higher than white fratricide. An automatic reflex of ours to blame any ill that is inflicted on us as we being the causation of the infliction or ill.

To name just a few translations of white loathing of Blacks:

An unjust dispensation of American injustice.

Tacit approval of police and societal murder and maiming of Blacks.

Blatant discrimination in every category of our lives such as disproportionate unemployment.

De-personalization by communications media.

PAFO mentioned the word "programmed" which explicitly connotes deliberateness. We suggested, above, that the problem is the *programmed loathing* by the *total* American society of our cultural and evolutionary geneses." Let us examine this in its historical setting.

In his celebrated documentary *The Peculiar Institution*, Dr. Kenneth Stampp, distinguished history department head of the University of California pointed out in Chapter Four, that our mothers and fathers were a "troublesome property." He goes on to say that over generations of trial and error, the captors obtained some relief by the use of five conditionings. One of these conditionings of the African captives was to make him believe from early childhood that "Africa tainted him and his features and color were badges of degradation."

What troubles were visited on the captors? There were two major ones. One was the increasing frequency and intensity of armed revolts staged by our fathers. The other was the rising clamor of the Abolitionists.

Events reached a climax in Virginian Gabriel Prosser's nearly successful massive revolt in 1801.

The Bourbon (the South's wealthy, robber barons) intensified a national campaign to *neutralize* both problems, revolutionism and abolitionism, at the same time. Their control of Congress with their Northern industrial colleagues and their control of the media of communication, succeeded in reducing the number of revolts and proved to have a chilling effect on the abolitionist's fiery oratory. They bombarded the public with lurid headlines of the *subhumanness* of the African.

They painted pictures by the tens of thousands of the "Negro" being the missing link between ape and man. Their best orators orated from coast to coast about, "One drop of the accursed blood darkens the skin, kinks the hair and dulls the intellect." "The Negro," they screamed from every newspaper, every magazine, *every pulpit*, every forum, "was a beast, created to work in the fields, to be a drawer of water and a hewer of wood."

This went on after 1801, week after week, year after year, decade after decade.

In order to reinforce this malicious tirade of Black bestiality, the Bourbon South and the industrialized North, had to remove everything from books and magazines contradictory to our "so-called bestiality." After all, animals cannot build university cities like Timbuktu. The fact that this fabulous city with its world famous university was *pre-Colonial* African, grand and sophisticated, had to be removed from American *consciousness*. So did the knowledge of the beauty and grandeur of the other great cities of the mighty, larger-than-Europe Songhai Empire from whence came these African people.

By 1857 the deed was done—was in place—this conditioned reflex about African subhumanness—the picture evoked in the mind by then about Black, or African, or Negro, was primitiveness, stupidity, a jungle escapee. Judge Taney handed down his decision gathering up in the Dred Scott decision the now programmed loathing of the African in "...the Negro has no rights, the white man is bound to respect...."

We must remember that the brainwashing was being done on everybody in the society—Black as well as white. Let's look at Hollywood. "Hollywood," the film industry and its most comparatively younger brother, television. Also anything we say about Hollywood may be said of Madison Avenue in spades. Hollywood just happens to where it is, Madison Avenue determines what it is. Hollywood is faketown, the great city of make believe. Here are the culture-makers of our society, many of whom are the most uncultured of men. Here are the true head-shrinkers and the brainwashers of America. Hollywood is a Southern-oriented city, as is all of Greater Los Angeles. This statement should not surprise anyone, since Hollywood, more than any other institution has been responsible for the glorification of the South, past and present, and for creating the image of so-called Black inferiority. It created the lying, stealing, childish, eyeball rolling,—feet-shuffling, sex-obsessed, teeth-showing, dice-shooting, Black male, and told the world this was the real Black man in the United States of America. It invented the Black "mammy" whose breasts were always large enough to suckle an entire nation, and who always loved old massa's "chilluns" more than she loved her own. The men of Fake-town have brainwashed America and the entire world with the brush of white supremacy. We accuse Hollywood of being the most anti-Black influence in this nation. In the twentieth century, with *Birth of A Nation*, Hollywood fired its first big gun in its war against the Black American, and the gunfire has continued unabated ever since. Hollywood has ever glorified the Confederates' and slavery's cause, with such magnificent monstrosities as *Gone With the Wind, The Virginian, Kentucky* and many more. By employing the writers of magazines, newspapers and books, many sociologists, psychologists, and others are shaping the minds of the whole society as we, the Blacks, become the prey for open seasons of killing us any time of the day or night.

Hence, the problem today. The solution to the problem, of course, is to de-brainwash the entire society—to de-program everybody concerning our evolutionary and pre-Colonial African negation.

Meanwhile, there are pressing situations that must be addressed while the ultimate cure is being launched.

Let us suggest what we must do to survive in short form, then we'll amplify.

In short, we have to keep the wolves at bay, and at the same time dispense wolf-neutralizing rays.

Let's explain by means of an illustration:

A party of air-travelers were wandering in wolf country after their plane crashed in Siberia. To keep the large wolf-pack from closing in on them and dispatching them forthwith, the men waved flares at the wolves. The men formed a circle around the women and children and several scientists who were working on a ray that they calculated would neutralize the wolves' hatred of humans.

The analogy is pretty good because it explains why, that after it looks as though we've made monumental gains, after some years of doing nothing, we find ourselves right back where we were ten to fifteen years before. We've never neutralized the white man's programmed loathing of our evolutionary and pre-Colonial African Culture because we never identified that as the problem. What we have been doing is (and we're suggesting) that we have been working on discrimination, and injustice, which are not the problems but the symptoms or manifestations of the problem.

We have been dashing at the white wolves that have been attacking us and during the sixties, we rushed at them with the fires of our oratory, the heat of our marches. And after we tired, we extinguished our flares, and the wolves are rushing at us again and wiping out all of our previous territorial gains.

The white wolves have the same blood-thirstiness as they did before, because *our* attack was not directed at nor even contemplated to the problem of this loathing of our geneses.

The white wolves are getting bolder as our flares are extinguished. The *Syracuse Sentinal* is maintaining a Klan watch around the country. The Klan is preparing itself for the final solution to what they term the "race problem." Chapters of the Klan are spreading north and west. They engage in war training *daily* across the country and in northern states.

In Southwest-Philadelphia, Pennsylvania, a national hate-Black organization is distributing leaflets by the thousands calling upon whites to rise up.

Where are your flares of action?

The solution has to be to face the wolves boldly—physically and legally—with organizations and fires of oratory and publicity. But, this is merely to keep the wolves at bay.

More and more of us must write stories, screen plays, novels and text books. We must push forward to get on the radio, television, the stage, the motion pictures—thousands of exciting emotion-evoking stories, articles—telling in a thousand ways to reach ever-widening audiences.

We must take old "error" and turn him inside out, upside down— route him from the text books, the history books.

It can't be left to just a few of us to correct these one hundred and eighty years of distortions.

OUR TOTAL FOCUS

1. *What should be our total focus?*
    A. To re-program the entire society (us, whites and Asians)
    B. To respect and honor Songhai

2. *How?*
   Through a huge number of dramatic videos, motion pictures, stage plays and operas.
3. *Aren't there other things in which we, PAFO, should be involved in, such as politics, South Africa, discrimination, etc.?*
   No! We leave that facet to other dedicated groups who are already doing a great job.
4. *Why this total concentration or re-education?*
   Because we are totally chained, INNER and OUTER. Anyone or any group totally chained should have as their first priority to become unchained.
5. *What is meant by "totally chained inner and outer"?*
   A. Inner:
   1. Our programmed race contempt depresses and absorbs reasoning energy from our pre-frontal cortex.
   2. Our programmed race contempt destroys cultural glue hampering our sticking together.
   3. Our programmed race contempt results in physical and emotional fratricide.
   B. Outer:
   1. The programmed race contempt felt toward us by others results in unreasoning physical violence against us.
   2. The programmed race contempt felt toward us by others also results in psychic trauma suffered by us destroying creativity.
   3. The programmed race contempt felt toward us by others also results in the manifestations of discrimination, red-lining, and other denials.
6. *But, won't spreading our efforts in other directions hasten the re-programming by winning friends and influencing people?*
   No! The arrow penetrates deeper than the sledge hammer. The knife cuts deeper when it's sharp. The concentration of cutting edges hastens the end result.
7. *But will the de-programming concerning only Songhai do the job? Why not dramas on African-American successes such as Jackie Robinson, Marion Anderson, etc.?*

Because Songhai is the womb. If the womb is thought of as corrupted, poisoned, inferior and subhuman, the offspring from that womb is likewise thought of as corrupted, poisoned, inferior and subhuman.

Such thought permeates the psyche of all Americans, placed there and continuing to be placed there in a thousand subtle ways through all media of communications. Such thought requires each Songhainian to individually and personally overcome his or her presumption of human inadequacy to merely ascend to becoming functionally acceptable. Songhaians can never become presumptively adequate until Songhai becomes uncorrupted and unpoisoned.

8. *How can we win the masses to accept this philosophy of re-conversion so that enough videos, motion pictures, etc. can be produced to do the job?*

It doesn't require "masses" to do the job—just a thousand or so script writers, producers, directors and authors. It didn't require masses to program America—just a few thousands in Hollywood and in the television networks. Then, there are thousands who have not been totally corrupted by the media programming against Songhai (Africa). Just like there are biological mutants, there are also psychological mutants, relatively unaffected.

9. *Why should whites who are against the glorification of Songhai (Africa) sanction such glorification in their theaters?*

Based on the marketing of *The Songhai Princess* video, whites generally are **not** against the glorification of Songhai (Africa). People who say, "White folk won't permit this or that" are engaging in negative thinking. Such negative thinking could never have allowed the Underground Railroad to flourish, nor allowed our fathers to win the Civil War, nor allowed us in to and to dominate major league sports. Following the paralyzing mind-set of too many "Negroes" we would have still been laboring on the plantations from "kin to kant." *Too much can't-do analysis leads to suicidal paralysis.* It was "never" they would "allow" as far as our fathers and mothers were concerned. They just couldn't stop what undergirded this whole movement where conditions were created. The conditions are and were the major factors in all of these things in which we Africans were so outstanding. Our presence and our prowess created conditions that really forced the white man to cave in. As a result, we moved nearer to center stage.

The untwisting of who our world-famous West African fathers and mothers were is a monumental task. These are the rays of truth that will neutralize the white wolves' blood-thirstiness. This is our survival weapon. If it's not too late. We will never know unless we aspire, oh children of the Songhai Empire.

10. *All right, where and when do we start?*
Right here and now. Sign up for the PAFO classes to learn the historic truths about Songhai so that you can write dramas about our glorious ancestors.

END OF SESSION XXIII

SESSION XXIV

LET THE HEALING BEGIN

PAFO posed a question back in Session II, "Is there no balm in Gilead, is there no physician there? Why has not the health of my people recovered?" A little background on this Biblical question, asked by Jeremiah in Jeremiah 8:22, we feel is appropriate for clarity.

Gilead was a place in Palestine east of Jordan in a mountainous area. A land whose people were greatly troubled socially and greatly troubled spiritually. The prophet Jeremiah, in essence, was saying there seems to be nothing that was tried that was addressing the healing of the people. The word balm is defined as any salve, lotion or oil that soothes and heals. Another healing dimension is that of dealing with the mind. Balm can be psychological therapy, as well as nurturing collective consciousness.

Four hundred or more years of a negative teaching against our African genesis plus the hostile American environment require a special type of treatment if a cure is going to be procured. Therefore, there must be a strong healing balm to offset this extensive damage that is being done to our psyche. Proportionately speaking, no other nation of people as a whole has suffered such a physical and near total destruction of their people as we Africans and African Americans. Perhaps the so-called American Indian may be the only exception to this scenario. As though our physical decimation was not enough, our enemies pursued a more insidious and dangerous course of action and that was to destroy our very souls. The death and destruction set the stage for the psychological onslaught that continues even until now as we mentioned back in Session XVI. Making our fathers totally dependent upon them for mere existence was part of that psychological war. The constant rape of our illustrious mothers, wives and sisters along with other dehumanizing tactics against the male induced an uncanny degree of acquiescence.

We related in Session XVI what really forced Black people down from their position of high world respect for ourselves. Looking at it as objectively as possible, we cannot say that it was only because of the gun, but rather the philosophical follow-through of the "white is right concept." **Then they introduced the doctrine of respect, love, obedience and honor to white people which was and is relentlessly taught in every facet of African life at home and abroad.** There were published pamphlets in every conquered African country where schools were set up to teach this doctrine. They forced African people to rename their children from African names to their so-called Christian names. To really put the nails in the coffin, they teamed up with the Arabs and projected the white God Concept, giving the African the Bible and the Koran, further indoctrinating us into false concepts against Africa's traditional religious concept of Maat (NTU).

PAFO wants to make it clear that truly we are not against other peoples beliefs, because they are being obedient to their ancient parents' beliefs. Neither are we against African peoples, although, through no fault of their own have left the belief of our ancient parents' concepts. Our only hope is that they return back from whence we came and fall back in love with ourselves. Yes, it's hard for us to go back because we, as a people, don't know what or where the path is and we do not know that we are being disobedient to our foreparents. We are not talking about the fathers and mothers who were the first captives during the war started in 1591. Once they got to America, the religious brainwashing started in earnest. We would like to advance "an analogy" that may reveal to you the *real* danger of not following our ancient culture of our foreparents. Most everyone is aware that receiving the wrong blood can result in death and or becoming violently ill. Yet, the right blood going into our veins can save our lives. PAFO says that the wrong religious concepts, like the wrong blood also will kill. We are talking not on an individual basis, but rather on a whole race basis. Empirical evidence from various historical journals and history books show that as Africans absorbed other religious concepts that their power began to plummet. The other nations followed their ancient cultural concepts and they are all prospering as a people. Africans are the most powerless people next to the American Indian, who among other things, lost some of his ancient beliefs and now he is practically an outcast in his own land.

This anti-African indoctrination influenced us to give Arabic names to our children. All of the foregoing information is caught up and reinforced in today's mass media, against Africans, at home and those living in other parts of the world. Today's so-called Black films, with the exception of one or two, consistently portray us as buffoons and using curse words. This behavior is so out of character to our indigenous African personality, that one would be hard to convince that we gave the world civilization. An alien from outer space by watching television would think that only African Americans committed crime.

This type of illness necessitates a special healing balm as we aforementioned.

Back in Sessions II and XXII, we noted that Hollywood created the lying, stealing, childish, eyeball rolling, feet shuffling, sex obsessed, teeth showing, dice shooting Black male and told the world that this was the real Black man in the United States of America. The world bought it. This included African Americans, our brothers and sisters in the Caribbean, Africans in Africa, in an emotional bias against ourselves. All of this negative portrayal has its roots based in the myth about our African past. The myth of a jungle existence being depicted as subhuman; therefore, we could not have contributed anything to civilization and that one drop of our blood contaminated a person. PAFO says, that is the problem. PAFO thinks that we can begin to undo this with a start in animated films with positive settings in our West African fifteenth century glorious empire. This to be followed by motion pictures in drama showing that Fifteenth Century sophistication of our great universities, two and three story homes on tree-lined avenues with streets paved with polished stones. This is the "BALM" to start the healing. Now, the prefrontal cortex will soon not to have to spend all of its energy creating defense mechanisms to soothe a violated ego in a continuing negative environment. As the BALM is applied, Caribbean Africans will not vent haughtiness and venom on African-Americans because the African-Americans freed themselves several decades *after* Carribbean Africans were freed. Africans in America, won't have to think about retaliation with the "We African Americans created more inventions in our captivity than any other African group during the Industrial Revolution and that possibly includes white America." You see the BALM will heal and restore love that was wrenched from our cerebral sockets that had altered our ethnic behavior patterns. The BALM will cause the Black male to protect his wife and family. The BALM will cause us to effectively deal with a welfare system that, in fact, punishes the Black family for having the presence of a Black male in the home. The BALM will make us see the need to give back to the ARAB and the white man their names and their brand of religion. The BALM will teach us that obedience to our fathers and mothers is better than any sacrifice. This is the commandment given by our ancient fathers and mothers, and we honor them only through obedience. The BALM will cause Africans to evolve into a new state of mind that will unite us to work together. The BALM also will cause a greater respect to be paid to Africans, in general, by all people. Also, as we mentioned in Session X, we were well-disciplined, spiritual, and loving with each other before Christianity or Islam was forced on us. In other words, as Herodotus, the father of Western history, along with Homer and others said that surely the very gods must have made their homes among the Africans because they are so just, wise, intelligent and beautiful".

MOURNING FOR THE 100 MILLION MURDERED

It is estimated that over one hundred millions of Africans were murdered during the four hundred years of Africa's invasions. One day, there has to be an international mourning period throughout the diaspora so that the healing of our psyche will begin. The mourning will be for those murdered *during* those invasions of the beautiful cities and provinces of the homeland by the Europeans and Arabs. The mourning will be for those killed during the brutal, forced marches from the inland areas to the Atlantic shores. For those murdered, raped, sodomized and killed in the confinement rooms and in the chambers of no-return in the holding dungeons of Africa's west coastline. For those tortured and murdered on the thousand ships of death on their way to the American lands of degradation, whose bones, bleached white with time lie like sea shells on the bottom of the Atlantic Ocean. For those bludgeoned to death, worked to death, lashed to death on the plantations of America. For our tens of thousands of our beautiful mothers, raped, sodomized then killed in the thousands of Euro-American sex orgies. For those who gave their last full measure of devotion to freedom to this country as volunteers in every war of the United States which rejected and still reject their intrinsic value. Then after a half million of our fathers and mothers won America's Civil War, we mourn for those tens of thousands tortured and disemboweled or burned alive in lynchings by Euro-American bloodthirsty illegal mobs and the thousands lynched by bloodthirsty *legal* mobs—the police. We honor and pour libations to the memory of our 100 million fathers and mothers who died that we may live.

END OF SESSION XXIV

EPILOGUE
TRYING TO ACHIEVE THE ESPIRIT DE CORPS

We like to think of Epilogue as we would a lawyer or a prosecuting attorney summing up his case before the jury. This is after all the known facts and evidence have been presented and each side makes a pitch to convince the jury to side with him.

A good lawyer would say:

"Ladies and gentlemen of the jury, I would like to make a recapitulation of this case in my endeavor to make my summation.

First, I want to establish that the defendant was a victim of kidnapping by the plaintiff, after the vicious destruction of his house with the aid of another foreigner who said 'Believe in my religion or die.' These two, together, were like the beast that had two horns like a ram and he spoke as a dragon.

Secondly, the unwanton murders of millions of his household over a long period of time.

Thirdly, that the defendant, against his will, was forced illegally to serve and work for the plaintiff for two hundred forty-six years without a pay day.

Fourthly, the plaintiff did willfully and deliberately make it a crime for the defendant to talk about his beautiful homeland and was forced to change his name to that of the plaintiff's.

Fifthly, that the plaintiff continued to lynch thousands, yes, tens of thousands of the defendant's relatives because they protested the brutality; and that he, the Plaintiff, did kill because they were in position to do so with impunity.

Your Honor, I could go on and on with this empirical evidence as it soars to the moon.

I feel that my case may be in jeopardy because of the following circumstances."

In this instance, however, PAFO faces powers and principalities that never stop conjuring up the myths about African people and their ancestral home. The jury in this case never gets the chance to objectively study the presented arguments. The jury would be the entire society. PAFO would be the lawyer for the defense, differentiated into whom we know as the Africans at home and in America. The programmed elements of this society who loathe Black people as a group are constantly painting the wrong picture, because they see us through distorted lenses. Many times elements of the defense pick up the wrong glasses and do not realize they are looking through glasses of distortion. They see negativity most of the time no matter what Africans say, do, or how they act.

In this history digest that you've just read, hopefully, we were able to part the veil of misconception and plain old error. Another thing we hope we did was to not only point out the short-comings of others but to point out ours too. We believe that truth, no matter how badly it may hurt, will lift you up in the end. The truth is, that we in ancient times, as well as the modern or times present, we have always trusted other nationalities too much. Also, our brainwash separates us to the point of disassociation and the recognition of each other in the true light of respect and brotherly and sisterly love. We are not just talking about those in our immediate household or communities, but especially as a *group* because *that's* where our real hurt lies. It is pitiful but yet predictably understandable that this brainwashing is manifested in a readiness to quickly forgive everyone for all of the wrong they are doing and have done to us. This includes the desire to never refer to the nearly one hundred million that we Africans lost from 1591 to 1858. That was our physical holocaust, and as a result of that, we are still suffering a psychological holocaust. Our brainwash says to us let bygones be bygones. PAFO says, when others forget Pearl Harbor, and others forget the Nazi death camps, *then* we think it is time for us to forget, but *not* until.

THE IMPORTANCE OF KINSHIP TIES

We strongly believe that along with our quest to deprogram the entire society as a solution to the problem that we must project the truth and the benefits of **Black people's kinship ties**. We believe that the "Lunda" people were totally correct. We made mention of the Africans of Lundaland back in Session IV.

Let us take a look at African Americans and other Africans of the Western Hemisphere in general. Various authorities of history agree that upward to one hundred million were taken out of Africa as prisoners-of-war, mainly between 1591 and 1858. Some of these authorities included John W. Vandercook, who wrote a book called, *Tom Toms*. There was Basil Davidson's, *African Past*; a book called, *The African*, by G.K. Osei, who is from Africa. Also, most of the authorities that we use in this book are listed in the back of this volume.

Our fathers and mothers who were brought here like cattle, are the present day African American men and women. About ninety-three or so percent came from the Western Sudan, which included Ghana, Mali and Songhai. Out of the one hundred or so million or more rooted up from our homeland, only about two million made it to these American shores. There were scores of different societies within the Songhai Empire. We spoke many different languages. As we arrived here, the extreme harsh treatment soon taught our fathers and mothers that whatever language differences or whatever else, that we could not survive unless we stuck together. We naturally had children and over the years that two million grew and grew into the twenty-six to thirty million that we are now. This also includes so-called West Indians and Caribbean family.

Therefore, in a direct sense we are tied together by **blood and physical suffering and humiliation**. The mothers and fathers of 1591 were more together than the fathers and mothers of today. However, like Jesse Jackson says about breaking the cycle of pain and hate, we must very soon break the cycle of the brainwash. That cycle of hate, distrust, back-biting, disloyalty to each other must be replaced with the cycle of love, respect, caring and concern. This was a command given to our fathers and mothers. Even the Good Book says, "Honor Your Mother and Father that thy days may be long upon the land that the Lord thy God giveth thee." When we disrespect our parents and disrespect their commands, continuation of bad things are the order. They told us to walk together children don't you get weary. Let those that have degrees walk with those that don't. Let those that have love and understanding be a little more patient with those that might be lacking a little. With this kind of attitude prevailing, our continuing journey will be a happier one than it has been in the past. If we search in this book, we will begin to find the threads of our African *values*. Let us use them. If we do this, then perhaps TIME will exonerate us. With this, the defense rests its case.

SELECTED BIBLIOGRAPHY

Allen, James. *As a Man Thinketh.*
Aptheker, Herbert. *American Negro Slave Revolts.* New York: International Publishers, 1939.
Aptheker, Herbert. *Black Revolt.*
Aptheker, Herbert. *Documentary History of the Negro People in the United States.*
Ardrey, Robert. *African Genesis.*
Ardrey, Robert. *Social Contract.*
Arkel, A.J. *A History of the Sudan.* London, 1955.
Bakri, Abdallah Ibn Abd el Aziz el. *Description de L'Afrique Septrionale.* Translated by J. de Slane. Paris, 1859.
Batuta, Muhammad Ibn Addallah Ibn. *Travels in Asia and Africa (1325-1354).* Translated by H.A.R. Gibb. London, 1929.
Bennett, Lerone. *Before the Mayflower.*
Bennett, Lerone. *Confrontation: Black & White.*
Black Learning Centers of Philadelphia, Pennsylvania - 1973.
Bohannon, Paul. *Africa and the Africans.* Garden City, New York: Natural History Press, 1964.
Boule, M. and H. Vallois. *Fossil Men.* Second Edition. New York: The Dryden Press, 1957.
Bovill, E.W. *Caravans of the Old Sahara.* London, 1933.
Bovill, E.W. *Golden Trade of the Moors.* London, 1958.
Bovill, E.W. "The Niger and the Songhai Empire." *Journal of the African Society.* Volume XXV. London, 1925.
Bradley, Michael. *The Iceman's Inheritance.*
Cardot, Vera. *Belle Pages de L'Histoire Africaine.* Paris: Presence Africaine, 1961.

Chu, Daniel and Elliott Skinner. *A Glorious Age in Africa.*
Civilization Beginnings in Africa.
Clarke, J.D. *Atlas of Prehistory.* New York, 1967.
Clarke, J.D. *Third Pan-African Congress of Prehistory.* London: Chatto & Windus, 1957.
Cole, Sonia. *The Prehistory of East Africa.* Baltimore: Pelican Books (revised edition), 1963.
Conton, W.F. "West Africa in History". *Volume II: Sovereignty Lost and Regained.*
Davidson, Basil. *The African Past.*
Davidson, Basil. *The Lost Cities of Africa.* Boston: Little Brown and Company, 1959.
Diop, Cheikh Anta. *The Cultural Unity of Black Africa: The Domains of Matriarchy and of Patriarchy in Classical Antiquity.* Karnak House, 1989.
Diop, Cheikh Anta. *The Origin of Civilization: Myth or Reality.* Lawrence Hill & Company, 1974.
Doresse, Jean. *Le Royaume de La Reine de Saba.* Paris, 1957.
DuBois, W.E.B. *Black Reconstruction.*
DuBois, W.E.B. *The Souls of Black Folk.* New York: The Avon Library, 1965.
DuBois, W.E.B. *The World and Africa.*
Emerson, Rupert and Martin Kilson (Eds.) *The Political Awakening of Africa.*
Encyclopedia Britannica - 1979.
Excerpts from The Schomberg Collection
Fox, W.S. *Greek and Roman Mythology.*
Franklin, John Hope. *From Slavery to Freedom.*
Franklin, John Hope. *The Emancipation Proclamation.* New York: Doubleday, 1963.
Gabel, Creighton. "Prehistoric Populations of Africa." *Boston University Papers on Africa,* Volume II. J. Butler, Editor. Boston: Boston University Press, 1966.
Gallack, Georgia. *Sons of Africa.* (See especially Chapter 5: "Tshaka the Zulu—A Black Napoleon," pp. 64-76).
Grier and Cobb. *Black Rage.*
Hailey, Lord. *African Survey* (Revised Edition), 1956.

Hodgkin, Thomas. *Nationalism in Colonial Africa*. London: Frederick Muller Ltd., 1956.

Hughes, Langston. *Pictorial History of the Negro in America*.

Jackson, John. *Introduction to African Civilization*.

Journal of African Civilizations.

Kati, Mahmud. *Tarikh El Fettash* (Chronicle of the Researcher).

Kardiner and Ovessey. *Mark of Oppression*.

Ladner, Joyce A. *Death of a White Sociologist*.

Leo, Africanus (Es Zayati). *History and Description of Africa*. Translated by S. Pory. London: Hakluyt Society, 1896.

Lewis, William H. (Ed.) *New Forces in Africa*. Washington, DC: Public Affairs Press, 1962.

Lloyd, P.C. *Africa in Social Change*. Baltimore: Penguin African Library, 1967.

Louis Leakey's Findings

Lystad, Robert A. (Ed.) *The African World: A Survey of Social Rsearch*. New York: Frederick A. Praeger Press, 1965.

MacGaffey, Wyatt. "The History of Negro Migrations in the Northern Sudan." *Southwestern Journal of Anthropology*, Volume 17, No. 2, Summer 1961.

"Melanin." *Ebony Magazine*. 1979.

Murdock, George P. Africa: *Its Peoples and Their Cultural History*. New York: McGraw-Hill, 1959.

Montague, Ashley. *Man: His First Million Years*. Revised Edition. New York: Mentor Books, 1962.

Oliver, Roland A. *Sir Harry Johnston and the Scramble for Africa*. London, 1957.

Oliver, Roland and J.D. Fage. *A Short History of Africa*. Baltimore: Penguin Books, 1968.

Padmore, George. *Africa: Britain's Third Empire. 1948*. (See especially Chapters 2-3, pp. 40-80.)

Padmore, George. *How Britain Rules Africa*. 1936.

Padmore, George. *Pan-Africanism: The Coming Struggle for Africa*. 1955.

Pankhurst, Sylvia. *Ethiopia: A Cultural History*. Essex, 1955.

Quarles, Benjamin. *The Negro in the Making of America*. New York: Collier, 1964.

Ritter, E.A. *Shaka Zulu*. 1955.

Rogers, J.A. *From Superman to Man*.

Rogers, J.A. *World's Great Men of Color*. 1947. (See especially pp. 151-253).

Rouch, Jean. *Les Songhay*. Paris: Presses Universitaire de France/International African Institute, 1954.

Sadi, Abderraman es. *Tarikh es Sudan* (Chronicle of the Sudan).

Stampp, Kenneth M. *The Peculiar Institution*. New York: Vintage Books, 1956.

"Superior Blood." *Jet Magazine*. 1967.

Tabios, P.V. *Olduvai Gorge*. Volume 2. Cambridge (England): University Press, 1967.

Tax, S. (Ed.) "The Origin of Man," *Current Anthropology*. Volume 6, No. 4, 1965.

The American Society of African Culture (Ed.). *Africa Seen by American Negro Scholars*. 1963. (Distributed by the Society).

The American Society of African Culture (Ed.). *Pan-African Reconsidered*. Berkeley and Los Angeles: University of California Press. 1962.

Van Sertima, Ivan. *They Came Before Columbus*.

Wallerstein, Immanuel. Africa: *The Politics of Independence*. 1961.

Washington, Booker T. *The Future of the American Negro*. Boston: Small, Maynard and Company, 1899.

Weatherwax, John M. *Ancient Africa*.

Williams, Chancellor. *Destruction of Black Civilization*.

Woodson, Carter G. *African Heroes and Heroines*. 1939. (See especially Chapter 2: "In West African States," pp. 25-36.)

Woodson, Carter G. *The Negro in Our History*. Washington, D.C.: Associated Publishers, 1962.

World Book Encyclopedia. 1972.

BIBLIOGRAPHY BY SESSION

SESSION I
Allen, James, *As A Man Thinketh*

SESSION II
L. Kardiner, A. Ovesey, *Mark of Oppression*
Grier and Cobbs, *Black Rage*
Pan African Federation Organization, *Cultural Genesis* (1975)
Stampp, Kenneth, *The Peculiar Institution*
Fox, W.S., *Greek and Roman Mythology*
Herskovits, Melville, *The Myth of the Negro Past*
Torday, Emil, *The Journal of the Royal Anthropological Institute* (Volume 54)

SESSION III
Cann, Rebecca L., *In Search of Eve*
Ardrey, Robert, *African Genesis*
Stampp, Kenneth, *The Peculiar Institution*
Knowles, Prewitt, *Institutional Racism in America*
Kerner, *The Kerner Report*
Wattenberg and Scanmon, *Commentary Magazine*
Research Task Force of the Black Learning Centers, Historical Review of November 1973
Time-Life Books, *Barbaric Europe*
Welsing, Francis Cress, *The Cress Theory of Color Confrontation*
The Judeo-Christian Bible
Field Enterprises Educational Corporation, *The World Book Encyclopedia,* "S" book under "skin".
Johnson Enterprises, *Jet Magazine* (1958)(1957)

SESSION IV
Jackson, John, *Introduction to African History*
Pan African Federation Organization, *Cultural Genesis,* (1975)
L.H. Stanton Publications, Inc., Earl Grant, *National Science Magazine,* (African Women and the Development of Mathematics and Astronomy).

SESSION V
Chu, Daniel and Skinner, Elliott, *A Glorious Age In Africa*
Niane, D.T., *General History of Africa*

SESSION VI
Hyman, M., *Blacks Before America,* Vols. I,II, & III
Sertima, Ivan Van, *They Came Before Columbus*

SESSION VII
United Nations Educational, Scientific and Cultural Organization and Heinemann Educational Books Ltd., *General History of Africa—IV*

SESSION VIII
Chu, Daniel and Skinner, Elliott, *A Glorious Age in Africa*

SESSION IX
Quarles, B., *The Negro In Our History*
Katz, W., *Eyewitness*
Bennett, L., *Before the Mayflower*
Franklin, John H., *From Slavery to Freedom*
Davidson, Basil, *African Past*
P.A.F.O., *Cultural Genesis*
Weatherwax, J., *Ancient Africa*
Africanus, Leo, *History of Africa*
Osler, William, *Aequantimitas*

SESSION X
Jackson, John, *Introduction to African Civilization*
Jochannan, Yosef Ben, *Black Man of the Nile*
Sertima, Ivan Van, *African Presence in Early America,* 1987 ed.
Chu, Daniel and Skinner, Elliott, *A Glorious Age in Africa*
Hoffman, Eleanor, *Realm of the Evening Star. History of Morocco*
Davidson, Basil, *African Past*
Dietz, Betty Warner and Olatunji, Michael Babatunde, *Musical Instruments of Africa*
African Music Society, Tracey, M.A., *African Music*

SESSION XI
Williams, Chancellor, *Destruction of Black Civilization*
Jackson, John, *Introduction to African Civilization*
Allen, James, *As a Man Thinketh*

SESSION XII
Blake, J., *History of Slavery*
Ritter, E.A., *Shaka Zulu*
Weatherwax, John M. *Ancient Africa*

SESSION XIII
Aptheker, Herbert, *Documentary History of the Negro People in the United States of America*
Aptheker, Herbert, *American Negro Slave Revolts*
Mannix, Daniel, *Black Cargoes*
Rogers, J.A., *From Superman to Man*
Cann, Rebecca L., *In Search of Eve*

SESSION XV
Blockson, Chas., *The Underground Railroad*

SESSION XVI
Sertima, Ivan Van, *Journal of African History*
Temple, Robert K.G., *The Sirius Mystery*
Brecher, Kenneth, *Sirius Enigmas*
Haley, Alex, *Roots*

SESSION XVII
McPherson, James, *The Negro's Civil War*
Foner, J., *History of the Labor Movement in the United States*
Dunbar, Paul L., *The Complete Poems*
Sommers, P., *Richmond Redeemed*
Bennett, L., *Before the Mayflower*
Higginson, Thomas Wentworth, *Army Life In a Black Regiment*
Felder, Jack, *The Black American*

SESSION XVIII
Ballard, Allan, *One More Day's Journey*
Dubois, W.E.B., *Black Reconstruction*

SESSION XIX
Disch and Schwartz, *White Racism*

SESSION XX
Giddings, Paula, *Where and When I Enter*
The Negro Almanac

SESSION XXI
Landess, T. and Quinn, R., *Jesse Jackson and the Politics of Race*

SESSION XXII
Knowles and Prewitt, *Institutional Racism in America*
Landess, T. and Quinn, R., *Jesse Jackson and the Politics of Race*

SESSION XXIII
Stampp, Kenneth, *The Peculiar Institution*

EPILOGUE
Davidson, Basil, *African Past*
Vandercook, John W. *Tom Toms*
Osei, G.K., *The African*

SOMETHING TO PONDER

The following information we believe will be a big help in understanding why negative attitudes develop against Blacks and other minorities. Even Black people are brainwashed into believing that African People in general are responsible for Acquired Immune Deficiency Syndrome (AIDS).

MATERIAL FROM A WORKSHOP AT RUTGERS UNIVERSITY JULY 1987

Another unsettling report (*The Times* of London, May 11): AIDS may have been triggered by the mass vaccination campaign of the World Health Organization that eradicated smallpox throughout the world.

Science editor Pearce Wright said a consultant to WHO disclosed the problem. "I thought it was just a coincidence," the consultant told Wright, "until we studied the latest findings about the reactions that can be caused by [the vaccine]. Now I believe the smallpox vaccine theory is the explanation...."

Surprisingly, the *Times* report was not picked up by the Associated Press, United Press International or Rutgers. An Associated Press spokesman in the United States said the wire service had not run the story because an inquiry by its London bureau met with denial from WHO's public relations representative on AIDS.

The speculation was further fueled by the report in the *New England Journal of Medicine* by Walter Reed Army Medical Center team. Noting that a nineteen-year-old recruit died of AIDS-like symptoms soon after his vaccination, they urged that modified versions of the vaccine should be used in developing countries.

The incidence of AIDS matches the relative numbers of vaccinations in Zaire, Zambia, Tanzania, Uganda, Rwanda, Malawi and Burundi.

"Brazil, the only South American country covered in the eradication campaign, has the highest incidence of AIDS in that region," Wright said.

About 14,000 Haitians were vaccinated while in Central Africa as part of a United Nations program "and began to return home at a time when Haiti became a popular playground for San Francisco homosexuals."

Robert Gallo of the National Cancer Institute, a leading AIDS researcher said, "I have been saying for some years that the use of live vaccines...can activate a dormant infection such as [AIDS]."

QUESTIONS ASKED BY DR. FRANCES CRESS WELSING:

Dr. Frances Cress Welsing, a Washington D.C. based physician, author and lecturer, says she wants to see proof that AIDS is not a man-made disease, based on information she recently uncovered which strongly suggests otherwise.

According to Dr. Welsing, the book, *A Survey of Chemical and biological Warfare*, by John Cookson and Judith Nottingham, published by Monthly Review Press of London, England in 1969, describes what we now call the AIDS virus. The text was derived from a three year study conducted by a British biochemist and geneticist and a British political scientist and offers a comprehensive view on the subject of chemical and biological warfare.

Dr. Welsing, who first made her findings public during a lecture in Chicago, Illinois earlier this year, reaffirmed them during the Third Annual National Black Holistic Retreat at Mt. Tone, Pennsylvania recently.

"I wrote letters to different people saying, explain to me, how a virus we say we didn't know where it came from, and started among Africans and Haitians, was written about in 1969," she commented during her Chicago talk.

Among those who she said she wrote, was Senator Edward Kennedy, the U.S. Surgeon General, the heads of the American Medical Association and the National Medical Association, the United Nations and Dr. Lerone Bennett.

The letter, dated February 25, 1987 read in part:

"...a number of aware African-Americans have systematically raised the question as to whether or not this new virus was 'man-made' and possibly manufactured at a facility such as the center at Fort Detric, Maryland or other such centers in the western world that are involved in the research on and the production of chemical and biological warfare weapons.

"From the very beginning it has been clear that most of the statements about the origin of the AIDS virus were instances of deceit and outright lying or what is not referred to euphemistically, as disinformation.

"However, aware African-American people were knowledgeable about the longstanding Tuskegee syphilis experiments which where conducted for a period of forty year (1932-1972) on unsuspecting African-American men and their families causing these African American people to become sick and die through venereal disease spread. The Tuskegee experiments were conducted by the United States Government, namely, the United States Public Health Service, and the Center for Disease Control in Atlanta, Georgia. It was even then verbalized that allowing the spread of syphilis could be a method used to destroy the African American population.

"Thus aware, African American people do not find it at all inconceivable that persons with the same mind-set and psychological orientation would not go further, and develop a deadly disease that could be spread via the general route and then introduce this disease into African American and other "undesirable" population groups such as the white homosexual population and the African American and other non-white drug abusing population, again for the purpose of a systematic depopulation agenda."

In the letter, Dr. Welsing also quoted a section of the text that talked about the AIDS virus:

"It is stated on page 322, 'The question of whether new diseases could be used is of considerable interest. Vervet monkey disease may well be an example of a whole new class of disease causing organisms. Handling of blood and tissue without precaution causes infection. It is unaffected by any antibiotic substance for far tried and is unrelated to any other organism. It causes fatality in some cases and can be venereally transmitted in man....It has possible potential as an infectious disease of man. It presumably is also of biological warfare interest. New virus diseases are continually appearing. In addition to these there are the possibilities of virus and bacteria being genetically manipulated to produce 'new' organisms.'"

The vervet monkey, she noted, is "non other than the green monkey, the African green monkey that the public is now being told is in the chain of causation eventuating in the present AIDS epidemic. The same monkey that was mentioned in a 1969 book discussing a fatal blood tissue and venereally transmitted virus that is of biological warfare interest: this discussion being in a book surveying chemical and biological warfare."

"The question is," she continued, "what government officials and the learned scientists involved with the AIDS virus and its spread, explain these facts?"

According to Dr. Welsing, she only received one response to her letter, from historian Lerone Bennett who acknowledged receipt of the letter, thanked her for the material and promised to "keep our eye on it."

"Every African-American needs to monitor every African American who says they're a leader...needs to begin to raise the question about AIDS and begin to ask how could it be in a book published in 1969 under chemical and biological warfare? The question has to be raised and it has to be raised out loud," she implored.

Dr. Welsing said that the public education directed at minorities was key. In addition, she even suggested abstinence until the epidemic was brought under control, hinting that there was no such thing as "safe sex." The AIDS virus, she said, was smaller than a sperm.

FRIGHTENING STATISTICS

Of the fifty million people worldwide believed to be infected by the deadly AIDS virus, ninety-seven percent are of African descent. Thirty million live in tropical sub-Saharan Africa.

In this country, there are an estimated two million carriers of the virus. African Americans and Hispanics comprise forty percent of the victims who have AIDS, although they represent just twenty percent of the population. The Surgeon General, in his latest findings, reported that fifty-five percent of all infants with AIDS are African Americans.

By 1991, writes UCLA Assistant Professor of Psychology Vicki Mays, at least 49,000 African Americans will have AIDS.[1]

---

1 This information may be procured at the Philadelphia, Pennsylvania Logan Square Library of Philadelphia.

Appendixes 285

THE AFRICAN CONTINENT

A. SIZE, SHAPE AND GEOLOGICAL COMPOSITION OF THE CONTINENT.
   1. Africa is over three times the size of the continental United States. It's the world's second largest continent.

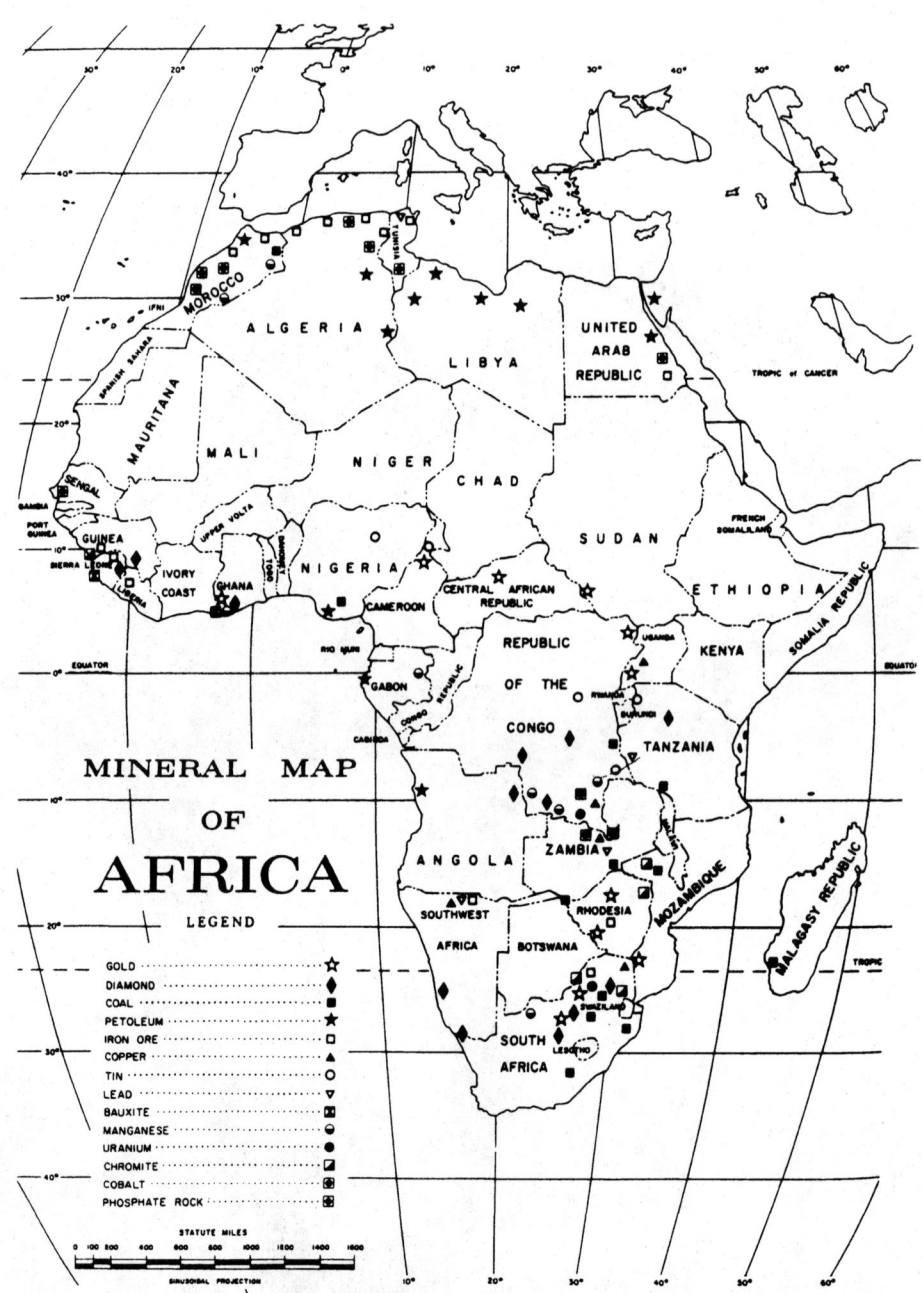

A. The African Continent is 5,200 miles in length from Tangier to Capetown.
B. The continent is 4,600 miles in width from Dakar to Cape Guardafui.
2. The African continent is a vast *plateau* of ancient hard rock.
A. Only ten percent of its land area lies at less than five hundred feet above sea level.
B. Large mountain buildup has occurred only in the extreme north and south.
C. Geologically, the whole of the Arabian peninsula is considered part of the African continent.
D. Rivers and basins are more prominent in African geography than is the case in any other continent.
(1) Niger River
(2) Nile River
(3) Volta River
(4) Zambezi River
(5) Congo River

B. CLIMATES AND VEGETATION
1. AFRICA CAN BE DIVIDED INTO FIVE MAJOR PHYSICAL AND VEGETATIONAL ZONES.
A. MEDITERRANEAN AND MEDITERRANEAN-TYPE CLIMATES AND VEGETATION AT EACH END OF CONTINENT.
B. VAST DESERTS AND ARID PLAINS ARE NEXT COMING INLAND.
(1) SAHARA IN THE NORTH
(2) KALAHARI IN THE SOUTH
C. FURTHER INLAND ARE WIDE SAVANNA REGIONS.
(1) GRASSY PLAINS
(2) WIDELY-SPACED TREES
D. HUMID AND FORESTED LANDS LIE ON EACH SIDE OF THE EQUATOR. (THESE LANDS VARY FROM TROPICAL RAIN FORESTS TO OPEN WOODED AREAS.)
E. HIGHLAND AREAS THROUGHOUT THE CONTINENT RESULTING FROM NATURAL FORCES THAT OVERRIDE CLIMATIC EFFECTS OF RAINFALL AND LATITUDE.
C. RESOURCES
1. AVAILABILITY OF VARIOUS MINERAL RESOURCES.
A. GOLD IS MINED IN MANY PARTS OF AFRICA.

(1) Ghana
(2) Congo
(3) Southern Rhodesia
(4) Rand Area of South Africa
(5) Mali
B. Copper—found in Katanga and Northern Rhodesia.
C. Iron Ore—found in Liberia and Guinea.
D. Diamonds—one of Africa's most important mineral assets.
E. Other Minerals:
(1) Mica
(2) Quartz
(3) Bauxite
(4) Zinc
(5) Uranium
(6) Columbite
(7) Cobalt

D. DISEASES
1. Malaria—mosquito carried.
2. Yellow Fever—mosquito carried.
3. Sleeping Sickness—tsetse fly carried.

The Honorable Marcus Mosiah Garvey. Father of the modern day freedom fight movement within Africa diaspora.

BRIEF HISTORY

Of The Universal Negro Improvement Association and African Communities League

The Universal Negro Improvement Association and the African Communities League was organized in Jamaica, British West Indies, August 1, 1914, by Marcus Garvey. After organizing the Association, Garvey traveled extensively studying the Negro and world conditions as they affected him. His travels brought him to the United States March of 1916.

His first public meeting in the United States was held at St. Mark's Roman Catholic Church in the heart of Harlem.

In 1917 he set up the New York Division of the Universal Negro Improvement Association with thirteen members. Within three months this little organization of thirteen, grew to three thousand five hundred. In the short space of seven and one-half years, the Association had established branches in every area of the world where Negroes lived and boasted a membership of more six million.

In January, 1918, a weekly newspaper "The Negro World" was established. Within a few months, this paper became one of the outstanding weekly newspapers in America. This paper grew by leaps and bounds. It claimed a circulation of five hundred thousand. It was printed in French, Spanish, and English. This paper was published continuously from 1918 to 1933.

In 1919, the Universal Negro Improvement Association purchased its first Liberty Hall at 114 West 138th Street, New York City. This structure had a seating capacity of 6,000. It was dedicated July 27, 1919.

This same year, 1919, saw the organization of the Association's first steamship company, which was incorporated as the Black Star Line Steamship Company. This company was capitalized at ten million dollars. It sold shares of stock to its members at $5.00 per share.

The first ship purchased by the Black Star Line was the S.S. Yarmouth. The second purchase of the Black Star Line was an excursion boat, the S.S. Shadyside.

The Shadyside was used by the Association for summer outings and excursions. It was also available for chartering by other organizations.

The third boat purchased by the Black Star Line was the Kanawha.

This was a small boat to be used for inter-island transportation in the West Indies. This boat was rechristened the S.S. Antonio Maceo, after the great Negro patriot who led the struggle of Cuba in her fight for independence from Spain.

The year 1919 also saw the birth of the Negro Factories Corporation. This organization was a business corporation capitalized at one million dollars. This corporation set up a chain of grocery stores and restaurants, a steam laundry, tailor shop, dress making shop, millinery store, publishing house and doll factory. From the year 1918 through 1924, the organization thrived and expanded. Branches of the organization purchased meeting halls, known as Liberty Halls, farms, etc. and opened local businesses.

Commissions and delegations were sent to Africa, Central America and Europe on business for the organization. Enemies of the movement began harassing and fighting the Organization almost from its very beginning and finally succeeded in getting Mr. Garvey deported from the United States of America.

This, however, did not stop the onward march of the Garvey movement. Mr. Garvey set up international headquarters in Kingston, Jamaica and continued to direct the activities of the organization.

After a few years in Jamaica, Mr. Garvey moved the International Headquarters to London, England, from which point he directed the Organization until his death on June 10, 1940.

After the death of Mr. Garvey, the organization was split into factions by ambitious U.N.I.A. leaders seeking control of the movement. These factional fights continued until August of 1951 when an International Convention convened and elected the Honorable Thomas W. Harvey, of Philadelphia, as President General.

Under Mr. Harvey's wise and sincere leadership, the organization was again united in its fight for African Redemption. In August 1953, Mr. Harvey called his first International Convention. At this convention, a complete staff of officers were elected with the Honorable William L. Sherrill as President General.

Mr. Sherrill was formerly acting President General of the Association during the imprisonment of its founder and leader, Marcus Garvey.

Under his leadership, the movement became a force and power in the affairs of the world. Today, the Universal Negro Improvement Association has thirty-six branches in America, Canada, the West Indies and Africa. Many of these divisions own valuable property upon which is erected Liberty Halls.

The Association publishes a monthly newspaper know as *Garvey's Voice*. One of the main projects is that of shipping tools, books and clothing to the Gold Coast Africa. Several shipments have been made this year.

We have by no stretch of the imagination covered the history of this great organization. We have given only a thumb-nail sketch, to enable those who are strangers to our cause, to become better acquainted with us.

WHAT IS THE U.N.I.A.?

The Universal Negro Improvement Association and African Communities League is a friendly, humanitarian, charitable, educational and expansive society, founded by persons desiring to the utmost to work for the general uplift of the Negro peoples of the world.

Our Organization seeks:

1. The abolition of colonialism in Continental Africa and full fledged Autonomy for all Colonies, either in the form of territories, dominion status, commonwealth or complete independence.

2. The establishment of a strong Negro Nation on the West Coast of Africa that may serve as an asylum for scattered and oppressed Negroes throughout the World, later after an apprenticeship under territorial and commonwealth form to be declared independent.

3. The binding of Negroes throughout the world in a bond of fraternal Unity for the purpose of securing their cooperation with the program of the Organization.

4. To establish Commissions in the principal countries and cities of the world for the representation and protection of all Africans.

5. To promote a conscientious spiritual worship among the nations of Africa.

6. To establish schools, academies, colleges and Universities for the racial education and the promotion of a higher level of culture for the Negro peoples as a whole.

7. The fostering of a West Indian Federation, either under dominion status or as an independent country.

8. To conduct world wide commercial and industrial enterprises for the economic advancement of Negro Peoples.

9. To secure full civil and political rights for all Negroes under Civil and Political disadvantages in any part of the world and especially in

the United States.

10. To stand against all forms of dictatorship, subversive organizations and individuals who teach the overthrow, or seek by any means to undermine or destroy the United States Government or its fundamental principles.

We do not make any exaggerated promises for the U.N.I.A. We do not promise the Negro anything more phenomenal than his own willingness to intelligently work and cooperate in the solving of his problems. We offer no imaginary or mysterious hope of racial salvation from sources outside of the race. We look only to that salvation that will come as a result of well organized and determined effort on the part of the Negro himself.

The Universal Negro Improvement Association offers the Negro peoples of the world a program of practical hope. Unlike the early days of the organization, there is no flag waving, no beating of drums, no flare of trumpets. These methods have served their purpose. The time is too serious and our experiences are too rich in knowledge to resort to this method of bringing our people together.

Today the UNIA seeks to work out a program by calm, sober, calculating action.

There is no excuse for shirking your duty and responsibility to your race. The world judges you not only as an individual but as a part of a race. If your race is condemned, you too are condemned. If your race is held down, you too are held down. So the work of racial salvation is the work of all of us, rich or poor, learned or unlearned. This is the day, this is the hour, now is the time for every Negro to live up to the program offered by the Universal Negro Improvement Association.

A Message From The President Of PAFO

As the current President of PAFO, I wish to thank all past members of PAFO for their part in helping to make PAFO the kind of organization it is growing into. Without you, we could not have been.

A special sense of gratitude I feel towards all of the Presidents that I have served under and also the vice-presidents and other officers.

Sure there were mistakes that were made, but mistakes are only made by people that are trying to do something.

I will now give you the names of the Presidents and their Vice Presidents:

William Mikell	VP - C. Theodore Simpson 1971-1974
C. Theodore Simpson	VP - Reginald Maddox 1975-1979
Reginald Maddox	VP - Marvin Weldon 1980-1985
Calvin R. Robinson	VP - Redman Battle 1986-

Under my administration, we instituted the office of Second Vice President, and Reginald Maddox is that person. He happens to be President of Division No. 121 of the UNIA, the organization created by the Honorable Marcus Garvey. He was PAFO's first history student and he graduated with top honors. He was also President-General of the UNIA until August 1992.

Current Active Members
(* PAFO Teacher)

Sheila Bennett
Robert Cabbagestalk
Rose Cabbagestalk*
Dorothy Carter
Jacqueline Casen
Nathaniel Cook*
Michael Cooper*
Louis Cox
Roberta Devine
Linda (Jaha) Drummond
Marcus Ellis*

Bonnie Emerson*
Dr. Jerome Fox
Gail Freeman
Ronald George*
Emily Green*
Juanita Haddad
Marvin Weldon
Maureen Connelly*
Wilson Long
Bruce Ross*
Cecil Hankins*
Bradley Harley
Brian Harris
Terry Hayes*
Consuella Hunter
Josephine Johnson
Pamela R. Johnson
Patricia Johnson
Marcella Jones*
Hattie Mayo*
Bertha Mikell
William Mikell
Edward V. Moses*
Carmen Myers
Jacqueline Patterson
Beatrice Perkins
Dorothy Perrine*
Ida Weldon
John Connelly
Eugene Frazier*
Dr. Cheryl D. Jackson*
Walter Prescott
Kay Sellers Pride*
Lamott Rothwell*
Helen Rutherford
Judith Sanders*
Lloyd Shrivers
Ruby Shrivers*
Charles Singleton*

Esther Solomon
Anthony Turner
Rose Turner
Richard Whitaker
Richard White*
Venessa (Fumi) White*
Lula Williams, Jr.
Lula Williams, Sr.
Mary J. Williams
Joyce Willis*
Estella Logan*
Linda Hampton
Elaine A. Richardson*
Edward W. Robinson, Jr.*

Reginald Bethea*
Louis Cox
Jonathan Daniels*
Perry Davis*
Terrince Ellis
Elvira Gibson*
Franklin Gibson*
Dolores Gordon
Joseph Graham*
Kenneth Graham*
Doris Johnson*
Osei A. Omowale*
Landis Rowe*

My most ardent dream and fervent wish is to establish a PAFO chapter in every State and major City in the United States of America. Concurrently I would have a program in place to reprogram America concerning the glorious African genesis of African Americans. This would solve the problem of contempt that the total society has regarding our people. In the spirit of our Fathers,

    Calvin Russell Robinson
    President

PAN AFRICAN FEDERATION ORGANIZATION RECOMMENDS THE FOLLOWING BOOKS:

Paula Giddings	*Where And When I Enter*
Rudolph Windsor	*From Babylon To Timbuktu*
Tony Martin	*Race First*
Jawanza Kunjufu	*Countering The Conspiracy To Destroy Black Boys*
	Lessons From History
Dr. Edward Robinson	
Harriette Robinson	*'Twas The Night Before Kwanzaa*
Drucella Houston	*The Wonderful Ethiopians Of The Ancient Cushite*
Dr. Yosef Ben-Jochonnan	*Black Man Of The Nile*
Cheikh Anta Diop	*Great African Thinkers, Vol. I*
Elijah Muhammad	*Message To The Black Man In America*
Marcus M. Garvey	*The Tragedy Of White Injustice*
James G. Spady	*Marcus Garvey Africa and The UNIA*
J.A. Rogers	*From Superman To Man*
Mark Hyman	*Blacks That Died For Jesus*
	Blacks Before America, Vols. I, II & III
	Survival Of Kwame
	The People Who Killed King (A Two Act Play)
Mark Mathabane	*Kaffir Boy*
Leon A. Higginbotham, Jr.	*In The Matter of Color*
George Wells Parker	*Children Of The Sun*
Eloise Prescott	*Aisha's Crowning Glory*

PAFO Has Available For Sale

This Week In African American History

Video Tapes

The Richard Allen Story; The Mother Africa Story, Parts I & II
Mother Africa, Parts I & II; How African American Soldiers Won the Civil War Part I
Creative works of Dr. Edward W. Robinson, Jr. and Carvel Watson
Produced by: Studio II Productions, Inc.
The Songhai Princess
Available in video and book stores nationwide.
The Adventures of the Star People
(The second in a series of 12 videos)
Will soon be available in video and book stores.
by Dr. Edward W. Robinson, Jr. and Harriette C. Robinson
Produced by: New Dawn, Inc.
The Magic Crown
A home video produced by Bob Law of New York of
National radio fame
Check your local video and book stores for availability

Albums

Black Rhapsody

Black History in Song, sung by Baritone, Dr. Edward Robinson, Jr.

PAFO urges all those intested in solving the African's problem to produce positive videos in drama, as we are attempting to do.

ADDENDUM

FOR YOUR INFORMATION
CHRONOLOGY OF THE PUSH FOR RIGHTS OF AFRICAN AMERICANS
* DIRECTLY INVOLVING MILITARY

February 18, 1767: Mason-Dixon Line established.

May 28, 1851: First Women's Rights convention held with Sojourner Truth presiding.

January 1, 1863: Emancipation Proclamation issued by President Lincoln.

*July 18, 1866: Black regiments became part of the United States Army.

June 17, 1871: James Weldon Johnson born. Wrote the poem *Lift Every Voice and Sing* which was set to music and adopted by Blacks as their national anthem during the 1930's. Johnson also served as secretary to the NAACP.

February 12, 1909: NAACP founded following race riot in Springfield, Illinois. Scores of Blacks killed and wounded and thousands forced from the city.

1941: James Farmer, race relations secretary with pacifist group Fellowship of Reconciliation (FOR), gathers friends and fellow admirers of Mahatma Ghandi to form congress of Racial Equality (CORE) in Chicago.

1946: Supreme Court rules segregation on interstate buses unconstitutional.

December 5, 1946: President Harry S. Truman appoints President's Committee on Civil Rights.

1947: Truman urges Congress to enact Fair Employment Practices Committee law, to outlaw poll taxes and lynching and to eliminate segregation in interstate transportation, none of which is passed by Congress.

*July 26, 1948: Truman signs Executive Order integrating the Armed Force.

*September 30, 1949: Army issues a new racial equality plan, opening new training opportunities for Negroes, but retaining segregated units.

*July 20, 1950: First United States' victory in Korea won by Black troops of the 24th Infantry Regiment.

1950: Ralph Bunche, undersecretary-general of United Nations, receives Nobel Peace prize for mediating end of 1948 Arab-Israeli War. First Black to be awarded the prize.

April 1951: Ruby Hurley comes from New York to Birmingham, Alabama to open first permanent NAACP office in Deep South, becoming only professional civil rights worker in South.

December 25, 1951: Florida NAACP leader, Harry T. Moore and wife Harriet, die after a bomb explodes under their bed in their Mims Home. Moore, an educator, had campaigned heavily to register Black voters and equalize teacher salaries in Florida.

1953: Attorney Thurgood Marshall argues for NAACP before United States Supreme Court against racial segregation in schools.

May 17, 1954: Supreme court in Brown vs. Board of Education, rules school segregation unconstitutional.

June 1955: The brutal mutilation and lynching of fourteen-year-old Emment Till served as a rallying cause that launched the Civil Rights drive. Till was accused of whistling at a white woman.

September 1, 1955: Rosa Parks arrested for violating bus segregation ordinance in Montgomery, Alabama.

*October 25, 1955: Benjamin O. Davis, Sr., became the first Black United States Army General.

December 5, 1955: Montgomery Bus Boycott begins. Rev. Martin Luther King, Jr., twenty-seven, elected president of boycott sponsor, the Montgomery Improvement Association.

February 3, 1956: Supreme Court orders University of Alabama in Tuscaloosa to admit first Black student, Autherine Lucy.

February 7, 1956: University of Alabama suspends Lucy for her "safety."

February 29, 1956: Ordered reinstated by a federal court judge, Lucy expelled from University of Alabama. She makes no further attempt to re-enter. University remained segregated until 1963.

Summer 1956: Boycott of Tallahassee bus system begins, lasts several months. Boycotters win both integration of buses and a promise Black drivers will be hired for some routes.

June 1, 1956: Alabama attorney general obtains injunction stopping NAACP activity in state as a "foreign" corporation that hadn't registered with the secretary of state.

November 13, 1956: Supreme Court upholds federal court decision that bus segregation violates Fifteenth Amendment.

December 21, 1956: Montgomery buses integrated. Montgomery Improvement Association calls off boycott after 381 days.

January 10-12, 1957: Southern Christian Leadership Conference (SCLC) founded with Dr. King as president.

May 17, 1957: Prayer Pilgrimage to Washington, DC. On steps of Lincoln Memorial, Dr. King delivers first major address, calling for Black voting rights.

*September 1957: Black student, Elizabeth Eckford, was turned away by mob and guards when she tried to enter all-white Little Rock Central High School in Arkansas. President Dwight D. Eisenhower federalized Arkansas National Guard and sent in one thousand paratroopers to restore order and escort nine Black students to high school. When Supreme Court refused to delay integration, Little Rock schools closed for 1958-59 school year, reopened on desegregation basis.

September 9, 1957: President Eisenhower signs Civil Rights Act of 1957, establishing Commission on Civil Rights to investigate voter discrimination and authorizing Justice Department to bring federal court suits against voter discrimination.

1958: Supreme Court rules segregated facilities at interstate bus terminals illegal, even when bus company doesn't own terminal.

February 1, 1960: Four Black students sit in a Woolworth's lunch counter in Greensboro, North Carolina, starting a wave of student protests all over the Deep South. Within two weeks, sit-ins spread to fifteen cities in five Southern states.

1960: President Eisenhower signs Civil Rights Act of 1960, permitting Justice Department to bring voter discrimination suits against states.

April 15, 1960: Student Nonviolent Coordinating Committee (SNCC) founded at Shaw University, Raleigh, North Carolina.

October 19-27, 1960: Dr. King is jailed during sit-in at Rich's Department Store in Atlanta, then transferred to maximum security prison. Democratic presidential nominee John F. Kennedy phones Mrs. King to express concern, an action believed by many to have won him enough Black votes to decide election.

1961: Sylvester Weaver of Cocoa, Florida, along with NAACP and other parties, files suit in federal court asking Brevard school system be forced to integrate under 1954 Supreme Court ruling.

January 10, 1961: First desegregation in public education in Georgia is peaceful, as Black students Charlayne Hunter and Hamilton Holmes enroll at University of Georgia in Athens.

May 4, 1961: Freedom Riders, led by James Farmer of Congress of Racial Equality (CORE), leave Washington, DC, (by bus) to test rights of interstate travelers.

May 14, 1961: White mob burns a Freedom Rider bus outside Anniston, Alabama. Riders aboard a second bus are beaten by Ku Klux Klan in Birmingham, Alabama.

May 20, 1961: Freedom Riders are beaten at Montgomery, Alabama, terminal. Among those injured is John Seibenthaler, administrative assistant to Attorney General Robert Kennedy. Whites riot outside church where Dr. King, Farmer and Riders are meeting.

*May 21, 1961: Freedom Riders leave Montgomery under National Guard protection and are jailed upon arriving in Jackson, Mississippi.

Summer 1962: Several civil rights groups combine in Albany, Georgia to force desegregation of all public facilities, but fail. Division occurs among civil rights leaders. Dr. King arrested for parading without a permit, released after anonymous donor pays fine.

*October 1, 1962: James Meredith becomes first Black to attend University of Mississippi in Oxford, sparking rioting in which two are killed. Meredith blocked in school doorway by Governor Ross Barnett. President Kennedy federalizes National Guard, sends in Army troops.

April 3, 1963: SCLC launches Project "C" (for confrontation) to protest segregation of lunch counters and restrooms in downtown Birmingham, Alabama.

April 12, 1963: Dr. King arrested in Birmingham, Alabama for defying a state court's injunction against protest marches.

May 10, 1963: Dr. King and Rev. Fred L. Shuttlesworth announce Birmingham's white leaders have agreed on desegregation plan. That night King's motel is bombed and Blacks riot until dawn.

June 11, 1963: Alabama Governor George Wallace states "Stand in the Schoolhouse Door" in unsuccessful effort to block enrollment of Black students Vivian Malone and James Hood at University of Alabama. Federal officials led by Deputy Attorney General Nicholas Katzenbach give him proclamation from President Kennedy. Wallace withdraws.

June 12, 1963: NAACP State Chairman Medgar Evers was shot to death at his home in Jackson, Mississippi. Medgar Evers, NAACP field secretary in Mississippi, was shot to death as a result of his involvement in civil rights activity.

*June 14, 1963: Maryland governor calls in National Guard after weeks of racial demonstrations and riots in Cambridge. Attorney General Robert Kennedy calls both sides to his office for negotiations, and July 23 announces agreement on desegregation, low-rent housing and biracial committee.

August 28, 1963: Dr. King leads 250,000 in march on Washington, DC, urging support for civil rights legislation sent to Congress by President Kennedy and delivers *I Have A Dream* speech at Lincoln Memorial.

September 15, 1963: Four Black children die in bombing of 16th Street Baptist Church in Birmingham.

November 22, 1963: President Kennedy shot to death in Dallas.

June 1, 1964: Supreme Court rules NAACP can operate in Alabama free of harassment.

June 1964: Freedom Summer begins as hundreds of volunteers arrive in Mississippi to work in Mississippi Summer Project organized by SNCC, CORE, SCLC and NAACP.

July 2, 1964: President Lyndon B. Johnson signs the 1964 Civil Rights Act outlawing segregation in public accommodations, ordering school desegregation and fair employment practices, and denying federal funding to programs in which racial discrimination occurs.

July 18-23, 1964: Rioting in New York City follows shooting of Black fifteen-year-old James Powell by off-duty police officer.

*July 24-26, 1964: Riots in Rochester, New York. Governor Nelson Rockefellow mobilizes National Guard. One white man killed, three hundred persons injured, including twenty-two police officers.

August 2-4, 1964: Riots in Jersey City, New Jersey, leave fifty-six injured, including twenty-two police officers.

*August 4, 1964: After six-week search involving more than four hundred servicemen, bodies of three missing Summer Project workers—Michael Schwerner, Andrew and James Chaney—found buried under earthen dam near Philadelphia, Mississippi.

August 7, 1964: Federal Judge George Young acts on Sylvester Weaver vs. Board of Public Instruction of Brevard County, signing plan for complete integration of county schools within three years. "Freedom of Choice" plan later ruled inadequate by appeals court. Further studies, lawsuit and court-granted delays result in full integration more than ten years after original 1961 lawsuit.

August 11-28, 1964: Riots in Paterson and Elizabeth, New Jersey; Dixmoor, suburb of Chicago, Illinois; and, Philadelphia, Pennsylvania.

December 4, 1964: FBI arrests twenty-one white men, including the sheriff and deputy sheriff of Neshoba County, Mississippi on federal charges of conspiracy to violate Civil Rights Code in connection with the three rights workers' deaths. At preliminary hearing,

December 10, charges dismissed based on "hearsay."

December 10, 1964: Dr. King receives Nobel Peace Prize.

January - February 1965: Dr. King leads Selma, Alabama voting drive. During demonstrations, February 1-4, more than 3,000 arrested, including King.

February 4, 1965: Federal court bans literacy test and other technicalities used against Black voter applicants.

February 21, 1965: Malcolm X, outspoken leader in the Nation of Islam, was assassinated in New York City.

March 7, 1965: "Bloody Sunday." Alabama troopers and Dallas County deputies beat and gas voting rights marchers in Selma.

March 11, 1965: Rev. James Reeb dies after he and two other white Unitarian ministers beaten by white men while assisting Selma voter drive March 9. (Three white men indicted for Reeb's murder April 13; acquitted by Selma jury December 10).

March 15, 1965: In *We Shall Overcome* speech, President Johnson responds to events in Selma by condemning "crippling legacy of bigotry and injustice," and announcing he is submitting Voting Rights Bill to Congress.

March 21-21, 1965: Dr. King and Ralph Bunche lead marchers from Selma to Montgomery. After march, Mrs. Viola Liuzzo, a marcher from Detroit, is shot to death by nightriders.

May 3, 1965: Klansman Collie Leroy Wilkins tried for murder of Liuzzo. Trial ends in hung jury. (In October 22 trial, jury acquits Wilkins. December 3, Wilkins and two others, Eugene Thomas and William Eaton, convicted of conspiracy charges and sentenced to ten years).

July 13, 1965: Thurgood Marshall named solicitor general, first Black to hold the office.

August 6, 1965: President Johnson signs Voting Rights Act.

August 11-16, 1965: Thirty-four killed, 1,032 injured in several days of rioting in Watts area of Los Angeles, California, sparked by arrest of Black man for drunken driving.

March 25, 1966: Supreme Court bars poll tax for all elections.

May 4, 1966: More than eighty percent of Alabama's registered Blacks vote in Democratic primary. Sheriffs James Clark (Selma) and Al Lingo (Birmingham) fail to get renominated.

June 6, 1966: James Meredith leads "Walk Against Fear" from Memphis, Tennessee to Jackson, Mississippi. Meredith wounded by roadside sniper soon after start. During march, about four thousand Blacks registered to vote.

June 6-16, 1966: "Black Power" first enunciated by Stokely Carmichael during Meredith march. Concept endorsed by CORE at July 1-4 national convention, but condemned by Dr. King, NAACP leader Roy Wilkins, and other moderates.

July 12-15, 1966: Three nights of riots in Chicago's West Side Black district leave two Blacks killed, scores of police and civilians injured, more than 350 arrested. Dr. King meets with Major Richard Daley, announces four-point agreement to ease tensions in city.

July 18-23, 1966: Four killed, fifty injured as shooting, firebombing and looting sweep Black area of Hough in Cleveland.

July 30, 1966: Constance Baker Motley became the nation's first Black woman Federal judge.

August 5, 1966: Dr. King stoned as he leads march through angry White crowds in Gage Park section of Chicago. Near-riot ensues as whites battle police.

November 8, 1966: Edward Brooke (R-Massachusetts) was the first Black in eighty-five years to be elected to the United States Senate.

March 25, 1967: Dr. King leads march of five thousand white and Black anti-war demonstrators in Chicago.

April 4, 1967: At New York City press conference, Dr. King calls on young whites and Blacks to boycott Vietnam War by declaring themselves conscientious objectors. King's position assailed by NAACP and others.

May 10-11, 1967: One Black killed, two wounded in rioting at all Black Jackson State College in Mississippi.

May 12, 1967: H. Rap Brown succeeds Stokely Carmichael as SNCC chairman.

May 13, 1967: Thurgood Marshall appointed to U.S. Supreme Court by President Johnson.

June 2-5, 1967: More than sixty injured, nearly one hundred arrested in rioting in Boston's Roxbury area.

*June 11-13, 1967: Rioting in Tampa after police kill Black robbery suspect. At NAACP suggestion, youth patrol replaces National Guard in Black section and order is maintained.

June 12-15, 1967: More than sixty injured, 404 arrested in Cincinnati riots.

June 16-17, 1967: Black students riot at Texas State University; one policeman killed, two wounded; one student wounded, 488 arrested.

June 17, 1967: Stokely Carmichael provokes Atlanta police, is arrested.

July 6, 1967: Justice department reports more than fifty percent of eligible Black voters are registered in Mississippi, Georgia, Alabama, Louisiana, South Carolina.

July 12-17, 1967: Arrest and rumored death of Black cab driver John Smith in Newark, NJ, triggers six days of rioting, looting, burning, twenty-three die, 725 injured, more than 1,000 arrested.

July 20-23, 1967: Black Power conference held in Newark. Largest and most diverse group of American Black leaders ever assembled. Militant and separatist mood dominates. Press is barred.

*July 23-30, 1967: Massive riots in Detroit leave forty-three dead, 324 injured, five thousand homeless after houses burned. More than fifteen thousand troops, National Guardsman and police on duty.

July 25, 1967: Nearly twenty Cambridge, Maryland buildings destroyed, mostly in Black business section. Outbreak follows speech by H. Rap Brown in which he tells young Blacks to "burn this town down." Brown arrested next day for inciting to riot.

July 26, 1967: In joint statement, moderate Black leaders Dr. King, A. Philip Randolph, Roy Wilkins and Whitney Young appeal for end to riots.

July 27, 1967: President Johnson appoints National Advisory Committee on Civil Disorders to "investigate origins of recent disorders" and recommend ways to prevent them.

July 30, 1967: Four killed in Milwaukee riots.

July 1967: Other riots: Lansing, Kalamazoo, Saginaw and Grand Rapids, Michigan; San Francisco, San Bernardino, Long Beach, Fresno and Marin City, California; Rochester, Mount Vernon, Poughkeepsi, Peekskill and Nyack, New York; Hartford, Connecticut; Englewood, Paterson, Elizabeth, New Brunswick, Jersey City, Palmyra and Passaic, New Jersey; Philadelphia, Pennsylvania; Providence, Rhode Island; Phoenix, Arizona; Portland, Oregon; Wichita, Kansas; South Bend, Indiana; Memphis, Tennessee; Wilmington, Delaware.

October 2, 1967: Thurgood Marshall sworn in as United States Supreme Court Justice, the first Black to be seated on high court.

October 20, 1967: Federal court jury in Meridian, Mississippi, convicts seven men of conspiracy to murder in 1964 killings of three civil rights workers. Chief deputy sheriff of Neshoba County, Cecil Price, sentenced to maximum ten years in prison. Klan Imperial Wizard Sam Bowers sentenced to six years, others three to ten years.

November 7, 1967: Carl Stokes elected mayor of Cleveland; first Black elected mayor of major United States' city.

February 29, 1968: President's National Advisory Commission on Civil Disorders issues report warning nation "is moving toward two societies, one Black, one white — separate and unequal."

March 28, 1968: Dr. King leads six thousand strong protest marches through downtown Memphis in support of sanitation workers' strike. Disorders break out, Black youths loot stores, one killed, fifty injured.

April 4, 1968: Dr. King shot to death in Memphis, Tennessee.

April 5-8, 1968: Violence, looting and arson flare in Washington, Chicago, Pittsburgh, Baltimore.

April 7, 1968: National day of mourning for Dr. King.

April 8, 1968: Coretta Scott King takes husband's place leading massive, silent, orderly march through streets of Memphis. Tells estimated twenty to forty thousand marchers from all over nation: "We must carry on."

*April 11, 1968: Figures released: Rioting in aftermath of Dr. King's death recorded in 125 cities in twenty-eight states. Total of forty-six dead, 2,600 injured, 21,270 arrested, $45 million property damage, 55,000 troops involved.

April 11, 1968: Congress passes 1968 Civil Rights Act, prohibiting racial discrimination in sale or rental of housing.

May 11, 1968: Poor People's Campaign, headed by Ralph Abernathy, president of SCLC, gets under way in Washington, DC. Month-long campaign intends to pressure for anti-poverty legislation. Resurrection City USA, plywood and canvas encampment near Lincoln Memorial, houses three thousand participants.

June 5, 1968: Robert Kennedy shot in Lost Angeles after winning California Democratic nomination for president. Dies the next day.

June 19, 1968: Solidarity Day march climaxes Poor People's Campaign. More than fifty thousand march mile from Washington Monument to Lincoln Memorial. Half of participants are white and include Vice President Hubert Humphrey.

August 6, 1968: Poor People's Campaign moves to Miami Beach, to demonstrate to Republican National Convention aims of campaign against poverty.

*August 1968: Five days of violence, looting, burning in Miami's Liberty City area during GOP convention leave three dead, 30 hurt. National Guard restores order. Federal report says violence "originated spontaneously almost entirely out of the accumulated deprivations, discriminations and frustrations of the Black community in Liberty City."

*November 5, 1968: Shirley Chisholm, Democrat-New York, is first Black woman elected to Congress.

November 13, 1968: Representative Joe Lang Kershaw, Democrat-Miami, sworn in as Florida's first Black state legislator since Reconstruction.

June 1, 1969: Supreme Court rules privately operated public accommodations cannot practice racial discrimination by calling themselves clubs and admitting only whites on payment of nominal fee. Ruling applies to recreation areas and other facilities, but not exclusive social and country clubs.

July 17, 1969: Rev. Ralph Abernathy leads Poor People's Campaign on visit to Cape Kennedy area, not to protest space program but to use publicity surrounding Apollo 11 launch to draw attention to plight of the poor.

October 30, 1969: Supreme Court hands down unanimous decision ordering segregation in schools must end "at once" — replacing previous wording of "all deliberate speed."

March 8, 1970: H. Rap Brown disappears day before scheduled trial in Bel Air, Maryland, for 1967 indictment for inciting riot in Cambridge, Maryland.

March 24, 1970: President Nixon makes statement on school desegregation. While applying all government resources toward eliminating de jure segregation, he cannot require elimination of de facto segregation (resulting from housing patterns) until the courts provide further guidance.

April 11, 1970: Commission on Civil Rights, independent six-member federal agency, criticizes President Nixon's March 24 statement, calling it inadequate, overcautious and possibly signaling major retreat on issue of school desegregation.

May 11, 1970: Six Black men killed in Atlanta when rioting flares during demonstration by Black community protesting murder of sixteen-year-old boy in prison.

May 15, 1970: Jackson State College student and a high school senior, both Black killed in barrage of gunfire that riddles Jackson, Mississippi college dormitory. Incident reportedly starts with bottles and stones thrown at cars driven by whites. Police say they shot in response to sniper fire.

May 20, 1970: SCLC Vice President Hosea Williams organizes one hundred-mile march from Perry, Georgia to Atlanta to protest "growing repressions of Blacks and students in the state and the nation."

May 26-27, 1970: Two days of racial disturbance in Melbourne, Florida bring rock-throwing and firebombing.

July 9, 1970: Justice department brings school desegregation suits against state of Mississippi and school districts in Arkansas, Florida and South Carolina which have failed to produce acceptable desegregation plans.

August 1970: Chicago Black Coalition reportedly breaking up, due in part to disappointment in jobs program, which has provided only seventy-five instead of promised four thousand openings, according to Washing Post. Gang violence resumes. Rev. Jesse Jackson forms group called Black Men Moving to protect Black community from gangs.

August 19, 1970: Black Panther minister of education Eldridge Cleaver arrives in Hanoi with Panther delegation for "Solidarity Day" between North Vietnam and American Blacks.

October 15, 1970: Mistaken report of Black cheerleader at Rockledge High School, Rockledge, Florida being dismissed from squad triggers racial outbreak that closes school for the day.

December 30, 1970: Governor Reubin Askew appoints Athalia Range secretary of community services, making her the first Black to head a Florida state agency since Reconstruction. In 1967, Range had been appointed to Miami City Commission, the first Black to hold that office; she was elected to the commission a year later.

January 31, 1971: Barbara Jordon (Democrat-Texas) was the first Black from the south to be elected to the United States Congress since Reconstruction. She served in the House of Representatives from 1972 - 1978.

January - May 1971: Racial disturbances at junior high and high schools in Melbourne and Cocoa result in more than one hundred suspensions and several arrests.

February 1971: Disturbances at recently integrated Fort Pierce Central High School spill over into city. Emergency curfew called after second day of firebombings and vandalism. Curfew extended to all St. Lucie County. Three young Blacks injured by gunfire. Justice Department says it will probe after Blacks complain of civil rights violations in arrest of thirty-four students.

*March 15, 1971: Defense Secretary Melvin Laird announces program to improve race relations in military. Program calls for mandatory race relations classes as part of each recruit's training, *establishes Defense Department Race Relations Institute* to train instructors for race relations classes.

*March 19, 1971: Army announces formation of housing referral office to mediate between landlords and military tenants after Black soldiers overseas experience months of housing discrimination.

April 21, 1971: Supreme Court unanimously upholds constitu-tionality of busing to "dismantle the dual school systems" in south. Does not affect segregation in North based on housing patterns.

*June 24, 1971: Black and white servicemen battle for twenty-four hours at Travis Air Force Base, California. Trouble begins when two hundred Black airmen march on stockade holding three Blacks after fight over discriminatory treatment.

July 4, 1971: Eight hurt, $3,500 property damage done in two days of rioting in Titusville, Florida.

*July 19, 1971: Racial melee breaks out in Army mess hall in Darmstadt, West Germany. Said to be result of "pattern of discrimination and a failure of the military to suppress white racism."

*July 24, 1971: Pentagon announces a dozen high ranking officers reprimanded and transferred for failure to comply with racial equality guidelines.

October 15, 1971: H. Rap Brown, fugitive from justice since May 1970, shot in holdup attempt at westside New York City bar.

December 18, 1971: After continuing disagreement with SCLC President Ralph Abernathy, Rev. Jesse Jackson resigns as national direction of Operation Breadbasket, economic arm of the Group. Jackson organizes People United to Save Humanity (PUSH) in Chicago.

December 29, 1971: Arrest of Black Titusville resident Frederick Dublin on armed robbery charge touches off two nights of firebombings. City Human Relations Commission charges police "roughed up" Dublin somewhere else during robbery. Dublin found not guilty February 9, 1972.

January 1, 1972: United States Representative Shirley Chisholm, Democrat-New York, announces candidacy for Democratic presidential nomination, becoming first Black to run for President.

February 15, 1972: Senate reverses itself in 45-39 vote denying Equal Employment Opportunity Commission enforcement powers of its own. Seen as victory for Nixon administration, setback for civil rights groups, labor and women's rights organizations.

*February 24, 1972: United States Civil Rights Commission orders probe into complaints by Black servicemen of housing discrimination. Probe is to begin in Tampa with complaints by Blacks stationed at MacDill Air Force Base.

February-March 1972: Racial disturbances at junior and high schools in Titusville, Key West, Jacksonville, Gainesville, Mariana, Winter Garden and Tallahassee, Florida range from boycotts to rioting.

April 20, 1972: Graduate student Sam Taylor, a Gainesville native and political science major, is first Black student body president at University of Florida.

*October 12-13, 1972: More than one hundred men aboard Navy ship Kitty Hawk—among crew of 5,000—involved in two-day skirmish over racial issues.

*November 4, 1972: One hundred eleven Black and about twelve white crewmen on carrier Constellation protect "discrimination in assignments, ratings and discharges" with sit-down strike.

*November 10, 1972: Senator William Proximire, Chairman of Senate Banking and Currency Committee, releases six-city survey showing that even when income and credit characteristics are the same, minority applicants for mortgage loans are turned down almost twice as often as white applicants.

February-March 1976: Racial disturbances cancel classes and bring arrests at schools in Pensacola and St. Petersburg, Florida.

December 16, 1976: President Jimmy Carter announces intention to appoint Representative Andrew Young, Democrat-Georgia, United States Ambassador to United Nations. Young becomes highest ranking Black in United States government.

February 11, 1977: Clifford Alexander, Jr., confirmed as the first Black Secretary of the Army.

August 1, 1978: Commission on Civil Rights reports women and minority males still lag behind white males in education, employment, earnings and housing.

February 13, 1979: Commission on Civil Rights reports nearly half the minority children in the nation still attend segregated schools, with the percentage highest outside the South.

*May 17, 1980: All-white jury in Tampa, Florida, finds four Miami ex-policemen innocent in beating death of Black insurance executive. Within four hours, rioting breaks out in Miami's Black community. Two days later, 18 are dead, 370 injured and 740 arrested. Mayor invites Black leaders Andrew Young, Jesse Jackson and Benjamin Hooks to come help establish calm. Some 3,500 National Guardsmen ordered to area, including Cocoa-based 705th Military Police Unite. Property damage estimated at $100 million.

May 24, 1980: *Newsweek* survey shows fifty-four percent of 525 Black adults interviewed nationwide feel riots ultimately hurt the cause of Black rights. Barely half feel the lot of Blacks has improved in the past five years and half don't think conditions will improve in the next five years.

July 28, 1980: Allegations of Police brutality during barroom arrest ignite three nights of disturbance in Black area in Orlando, Florida. Police later cleared of brutality charges.

January 24, 1981: The United States Senate confirmed the nomination of Samuel R. Pierce, Jr., to be the Director of Housing and Urban Development. At the time, Mr. Pierce was the only Black member of President Reagan's cabinet.

September 1981: Roy Wilkins, leader of the NAACP from 1931 to 1977, died in New York City at the age of eighty.

February 13, 1983: United States Office for Civil Rights says Florida has made little progress since the 1970's toward racial desegregation of public colleges and universities.

May 1983: Civil rights groups outraged by President Ronald Reagan's plan to replace three members of United States Commission on Civil

Rights who have been critical of his administration's Policies. Commission due to expire November 29 if not reinstituted by Congress and President.

October 1, 1983: Jesse Jackson granted leave as president of PUSH to seek Democratic presidential nomination.

October 19, 1983: By a 78 to 22 margin, the Senate approves to mark Martin Luther King's birthday as a national holiday. The measure was approved by the house in August 1983, and now goes to the President for signature.

November 1983: Dr. Martin L. King's birthday declared a national holiday. The first observance will be January 20, 1986.

November 30, 1983: President Reagan signs compromise legislation reconstituting United States Commission on Civil Rights. Bill enlarges panel from six members to eight and divides authority to appoint them between president and Congress.

March 6, 1984: Racial fighting between Blacks and whites broke out at Charlottesville High School in Virginia.

March 7, 1984: Anti-Semitic incidents occurred at the University of Massachusetts.

April 24, 1984: United States Supreme Court rules race must never be a factor in determining that parents in a divorce should have custody of a child.

June 1984: By a vote of 6 to 3, the Supreme Court opinion in "Stotts vs. Memphis Firefighters" found that last hired, first fired seniority systems cannot be over-turned in affirmative action plans that give preference to women and minorities.

August 10, 1984: Whites and Hispanics clashed in Lawrence, Massachusetts as they battled each other with rocks, bottles and fire-bombs.

August 20, 1984: Thirty people were arrested in Waynesboro, Georgia following a night of firebombings and clashes between Blacks and whites.

October 2, 1984: Civil Rights Act of 1984, previously approved by the House of Representatives, was tabled by the Senate.

October 31, 1984: Franklin, Tennessee, a suburb of Nashville, was the scene of violence between Blacks and whites as shootings and beatings lasted three and one-half hours on Halloween night.

November 1984: Jesse Jackson runs for president garnering a very significant number of votes.

January 31, 1985: Reuben V. Anderson — first Black appointed to Mississippi supreme court.

January 31, 1985: The Civil Rights Commission issues a statement hailing a recent Supreme Court decision that limited the use of race and sex-based hiring quotas. The Commission said that the insistence of civil rights leaders for the use of such remedies was "devisive, unpopular, and immoral."

*February 28, 1985: The United States Army announced that six Blacks were promoted from colonel to Brigadier General—the highest number at any given time by any Service.

March 3, 1985: Two thousand people celebrated the twentieth anniversary of the voting rights march, from Selma to Montgomery, by retracing the steps of that march to "resurrect the spirit" of the civil rights struggle.

*March 27, 1985: Public Law 98-245, 98th Congress—Congress acknowledges Blacks and slave participation in the American Revolution and recommends appropriate activities during Black History Month 1985 to honor Black involvement and heroism in the battles of the American Revolution.

April 7, 1985: Comparable worth - The theory of comparable worth received a set-back in Tallahassee, Florida when a senate committee chose to study an existing law which already mandates equal pay for equal work.

April 15, 1985: The Supreme Court ruled that states cannot insist there be a time limit when filing civil rights violations against states.

May 1985: The Civil Rights Commission held hearings to debate the pros and cons of Affirmative Action. The hearings were boycotted by certain Civil Rights groups including the National Urban League, National Organization for Women, the Mexican American Legal Defense and Educational Fund, and the NAACP Legal Defense and Educational Fund. Representative Parren Mitchell (D-Maryland), submitted written testimony for the record, and then walked out of the session after saying he viewed the hearings "As being part of a public relations campaign to destroy Affirmative Action."

June 1985: Two of the nation's leading Black mayors clashed on Capitol Hill over whether the administration's subminimum wage program would reduce the tragic forty-two percent Black youth unemployment level.

June 1985: The first of the nation's 7,200 federal buildings named in honor of a Black hero was dedicated in Jackson, Mississippi. The honoree was the late Dr. A.H. McCoy, a Jackson dentist who headed the state NAACP and led the drive to desegregate Mississippi's public schools.

June 1985: A Michigan NAACP chapter is dissatisfied with a letter of reprimand punishment given to a white high school administrator who allegedly told four high school students to dress as Ku Klux Klan members as a prank on a Black teacher.

June 1985: Civil rights groups fear United States Commission on Civil Rights may become too conservative. State advisory committees are being led by an overwhelming majority of white men. The committees monitor and report on civil rights developments in their states. Of the current membership of the new committee heads, thirty-six are white, nine are Black, three are Hispanic and two are Native-Americans.

June 1985: The United States Commission on Civil Rights recommended that Federal Civil Rights enforcement agencies and Congress reject the doctrine of comparable worth. The definition of "comparable worth" refers to "the general formulation that employees in jobs held predominantly by females should be paid the same as jobs of comparable worth to the employer held predominantly by males." The Commission recommended to rely instead on the principle of equal pay for equal work.

July 1985: Inter-Church Federal Credit Union, the first Black church banking system, was established in Houston, Texas.

August 1985: An all-white federal jury recently found an Alexandria, Virginia restaurateur guilty of discrimination for refusing to serve a Black woman and her two daughters. The restaurant owner, who has a history of discriminating against Blacks, was ordered by the court in 1967 to serve people of all races but has refused several times since that date. He has admitted in court that he didn't serve Blacks. This most recent incident netted him a fine of three thousand dollars.

August 1985: Rev. Jesse Jackson, founding President of PUSH (People United to Save Humanity), brought to national attention the plight of two hundred Black residents of Tunica, Mississippi. The shanty homes of this town have caused it to be nicknamed "America's Ethiopia."

September 1985: Black, Hispanic and women representatives met with Secretary of Labor William Brock to protest the consideration of the Reagan Administration to eliminate the Affirmative Action programs put into place twenty years previously by President Lyndon B. Johnson.

October 1985: L. Douglas Wilder, Lieutenant Governor of the State of Virginia, was elected to that position, becoming the first Black to win a state-wide election in Virginia. He also became the highest ranking Black elected state official in the country.

October 1985: Open acts of harassment and vandalism were perpetrated against a Black family and an interracial couple who had moved into a predominantly white neighborhood in Philadelphia, Pennsylvania.

*October 1985: Black pilot, Lieutenant Commander Donnie Cochran, nine-year veteran with more than two thousand hours flight time and 469 carrier landings, was chosen to become a member of the Navy's Blue Angels elite flight demonstration team.

October 1985: The United States Commission on Civil Rights approved a study to determine the extent and depth of discrimination towards Blacks in the United States Criminal Justice System.

*November 1985: Brigadier General Sherian Cadoria was promoted to the present rank, making her the highest ranking Black woman in the Army and the first woman to be promoted from the combat support area. She is currently the Director of Manpower and Personnel in the Organization of the Joint Chiefs of Staff.

January 28, 1986: Black astronaut, Dr. Ronald E. McNair, was killed along with six other astronauts in the Space Shuttle Challenger tragedy.

April 1986: John H. Bunzel, member of the United States Commission on Civil Rights, since 183, asked Clarence Pendleton, Jr., to resign his post as chairman of the Commission because his "inflammatory rhetoric" has undermined the panel's credibility.

April 1986: Interracial dating ignited harassment of Black high school students by the Ku Klux Klan in Madison County, Georgia. Members of the Invisible Knights of the Ku Klux Klan have recruited white students at the thirty percent Black Madison County High School and passed out literature condemning interracial dating.

November 1988: Jesse Jackson runs for a second time for president of the United States, again garnering a very significant number of votes.

March 1991: Rodney King, an African American, was beaten unmercifully by nine white Los Angeles police, the beating videotape, shown around the world and yet the police absolved by a jury.

April 1992: Los Angeles insurrection ensued following the "not guilty" verdict of the jury regarding the police who had beaten Rodney King.

PAFO feels privileged in paying homage to a giant of a pioneer in the field of anthropology and African civilization.

We mentioned Professor William Leo Hansberry in the third session of The Journey of The Songhai People. *We believe that every one especially African American should know something about this great man. Therefore, we humbly and proudly submit* The William Leo Hansberry Notebook *for your perusal.*

THE WILLIAM LEO HANSBERRY NOTEBOOK

> Along with W.E.B. DuBois and Carter G. Woodson, Hansberry probably did more than another scholar in these early days to advance the study of the culture and civilization of Africa.
>
> William H. Lofton — *Howard University*

> You (Hansberry) initiated me into the sanctuaries of anthropology and ancient African history.
>
> *Letter from Nnamdi Azikiwe First President of Nigeria*

> Mr. Hansberry, a professor at Howard University, is the one modern scholar who has tried to study the Negro in Egypt and Ethiopia.
>
> Foreword, *The World and Africa* W.E.B. DuBois

Williston Lofton, one of Hansberry's students, was later a colleague and office mate at Howard University; Nnamdi Azikiwe was also Hansberry's student and a friend, William E.B. DuBois was Hansberry's mentor (wise, trusted advisor-counselor). His scholarship inspired Hansberry as early as 1916. These three have captured the central theme of Hansberry's professional career; he was a pioneer whose influence spread from the *diaspora* to Africa and impressed both Blacks and whites.[1]

This great achievement had its beginning in Gloster, Mississippi, where Hansberry was born. At the death of his father, a professor at Alcorn A & M College in Mississippi, the family inherited "a reasonable well-stocked library" with many books on ancient history. This, no doubt, influenced young Hansberry and became his first guidepost along the way to his future career. In the son's own words: "I acquired, while still quite young, a deep interest in the stirring epic of human strivings in the distant and romantic ages...and by the end of my freshman year, in college, at old Atlanta University I had become, largely through independent reading...something of an authority on the 'glory that was Greece' and the 'grandeur that was Rome.'" But he was unable in his search to add to his "exceedingly limited knowledge of Black

Africa's story in olden days." Although he did not then comprehend the fact of, and reasons for, the distortion and suppression of African and African-American history, he was "tempted" to question the general theory that prior to European discovery in the fifteenth century "Black Africa was altogether devoid of any history worthy of serious academic concern."

During the summer of 1916, *a second* guidepost appeared when Hansberry read W.E.B. DuBois' book, *The Negro*, which included chapters on kingdoms and empires in tropical Africa during ancient and medieval times. These revelations took Hansberry by surprise. For the first time he read about the various societies and kingdoms in ancient and medieval Africa. Hansberry was thus inspired to pursue the subject further by reading several of the books cited in DuBois' *Suggestions for Further Reading*. Unable to obtain the books he wanted at Atlanta University, Hansberry transferred to Harvard College where he pursued courses relating to Africa in anthropology and archaeology. He received his B.A. degree in 1921 and the M.A. degree in 1932, both at Harvard.

The Harvard experience better prepared Hansberry to pursue his mission in African studies. He became deeply concerned over the lack of efforts by Black schools and colleges to make use of recent discoveries and studies that confirmed that Africans and their descendants have an honorable, and indeed glorious past. The time had arrived, in his view, for blacks to affirm their identity by displaying a self-confidence that only a true knowledge of their past could assure. Thus, in 1921, after receiving his B.A. degree, Hansberry issued the following printed statement: *Announcing an Effort to Promote the Study and Facilitate the Teaching of the Fundamentals of Negro Life and History.*[2] This announcement explained that Hansberry would visit several schools and colleges that summer (1921) "in an attempt to bring to the attention of teachers and students the significance of African civilization." His immediate objectives were to stimulate formal studies of Africa, to secure funds to publish source books for school use, and to establish a bureau to promote popular interest in Black studies through magazines, lecture, visual aids, and other sources. His longer-range objective was twofold; to prepare Black leaders to become knowledgeable about their past and world affairs; and to build Black pride and confidence.

This interest led Hansberry to develop a "plan for expanding a pioneer project in collegiate education." In 1922, Howard University, in response to correspondence from Hansberry, authorized the establishment of a series of courses on *Negro Civilizations of Ancient Africa*; and Hansberry, after having taught a year at Straight College in New Orleans, joined Howard University to inaugurate these courses as part of an African Civilization Section of the History Department. Within two years he had established the following three courses in which more than eight hundred students had enrolled:[3]

1. *Negro Peoples in The Cultures and Civilizations of Pre-Historic and Proto-Historic Times*. This was a survey course based on the latest archaeological and anthropological findings concerning the Paleolithic and Neolithic cultures of Africa, the pre-dynastic civilization of Ancient Egypt, and relations to the proto-historic and early historic civilizations of the eastern Mediterranean, and western and southern Asia.

2. *The Ancient Civilizations of Ethiopia*. This course was a survey from about 4000 B.C., covering the general areas encompassed by the present-day countries of Sudan and Ethiopia. Hansberry relied on Egyptian, Hebrew and Greek sources as well as archaeological and anthropological data from several expeditions, including the Harvard-Boston Expedition at Kerma, Napata, and Meroe.

3. *The Civilizations of West Africa in Medieval and Early Modern Times*. This course surveyed the political and cultural developments of Ghana, Mali, Songhai, and Yorubaland as portrayed in Arab chronicles, and the archaeological and anthropological evidence of English, French, and German investigations.

To teach these courses, today, would require tremendous preparation, source materials, and energy; in the 1920's the task was even more monumental. But Hansberry had begun to identify and acquire the necessary materials while at Harvard, and was able to launch his program with source materials that several universities lack even today. His bibliography included the principal Arabic works, in English or French translation, as well as those originally written in Western languages. In addition, Professor Hansberry, with the cooperation of the Geology Department, produced hundreds of slides (more than two hundred by 1925) to illustrate various aspects of his courses. Extensive use was made of maps and charts. Within two years, Hansberry had equipped an office and workshop sufficient for his classes. But to do so had required the generous cooperation also of the Library of Congress, the Anthropological, and Archaeological sections of the Smithsonian

Institution and the libraries at Harvard. In all of these efforts, including the use of various translators, he was forced to rely heavily on his personal funds.

In June 1925, Hansberry's African Civilization Section of the History Department sponsored a symposium on *The Cultures and Civilizations of Negro Peoples in Africa*.[4] This pioneer effort presented twenty-eight scholarly papers by his students, including some from Panama, British Guiana (now Guyana), and Colombia. On view at the symposium (friendly discussions, broadcast talks by various authors on one subject) were fossil finds and various archaeological objects. Indeed, Howard University and Professor Hansberry would seem to have been well on the way to carving out a very special niche in African studies.

However, the 1920's also witnessed some deep disappointments. Shortly after he inaugurated the program, Professor Hansberry had to withstand attempts, by some of his colleagues, to discredit him personally and professionally. Two of Howard's most distinguished professors reported to J. Stanley Durkee, Howard University's last white president (1918-1926), that Hansberry "was endangering the standards and reputation of the University by teaching matters for which there is no foundation in fact."[5] They also questioned Hansberry's ability to coordinate the African studies program. Based on this report, President Durkee and the board of trustees voted to discontinue Hansberry's program; but subsequent appeals, from where it is still not clear, persuaded the president and board to rescind their earlier decision. However, during the remainder of Durkee's administration, financial and moral support were no longer given. In spite of this, Hansberry expressed no antagonism against his adversaries; instead, he simply explained that it was their ignorance of the African heritage that caused them to make their baseless charges.[6]

Neither the doubts of some colleagues nor the lack of strong support by the University deterred Hansberry. He continued to develop a program that required financial support greater than the administration at Howard provided. In June 1927, for example, Professor Hansberry, in a report to the administration expressed the belief "that no other department has achieved so much in proportion to University funds expended for the past five years—fifty dollars."[7] He appealed to the administration to support his efforts so that Howard could achieve a "unique and superior distinction in the academic world in the immediate future." As late as 1935, Hansberry wrote the dean that "I no longer can personally finance the cost for materials." He then requested funds to purchase a book on "the remarkable 'finds' by (L.S.B.) Leakey."[8] In September 1935, Hansberry told the Howard President, Mordecai Johnson, that "I feel very strongly that my efforts and the cause of Negro History as I have tried to promote it at Howard University deserve better from the University."[9]

Those early years were indeed difficult financially and psychologically; but they were also the gestation period of African studies at Howard University; and Professor Hansberry was young, ambitious, and determined. He was particularly encouraged in his endeavors by the response of his students, not only because of their enthusiastic enrollment in his elective courses, but also because of the expense many of them undertook to purchase various illustrative materials. The public response was also gratifying. Hansberry received letters of commendation from persons across the country: from Canada, Portugal, the Harvard Anthropology Department, and the editor of the Scientific American. In addition, favorable comments were reported in *The Nation of New York, The Southwestern Christian Advocate* of New Orleans, and *The Tribune* of Georgetown, British Guiana.

Encouragement, such as this, was buttressed (supported) Professor Hansberry's high aspirations for his program and the University. Indeed, he began to formulate *"a plan for expanding a pioneer project in collegiate education."* He called it, *Varia Africana Plan for Howard University.*[10] This was a proposal, in which, Hansberry explained, "there is no dearth (scarcity) of published information about Africa; the published literature is most abundant. But the general public knows very little of those publications and their content. This is also true of many specialists who are required to formulate and express opinions about the achievements of Negro people."

Hansberry cited four key reasons for this state of affairs:

1. The information "has never been made accessible to the public."

2. It was technical in character and was written for specialists.

3. Most of the historical data were collected and described incidentally, or were indirectly concerned with African history, and to extract from these required a working knowledge of the basic principals and techniques of the specialists and their nomenclature.

4. The many national origins of the authors meant that much of the data appeared in a variety of languages, including Amharic, Arabic, Ethiopic, Coptic and Syriac.

However, Hansberry did not regard the problems as being insurmountable. He stressed the need to assemble, correlate, simplify and make the material readable and accessible to the public. He listed some of the great repositories that would have to be visited; Widener Library, Harvard; Bodlein and Ashmolean at Oxford; British Museum; F.L. Griffith Library at Boars Hill, England; Bibliotheque Nationale, Paris; Koniglische Bibliothek, Berlin; the Oriental Institute, University of Chicago; and the Library of Congress. During his lifetime, he visited all but one of these libraries.

Hansberry believed that his *Varia Africana*[11] would make Howard University capable of revolutionizing the old and deeply ingrained misconception about Africa, Africans, and Black people generally. He noted: "No institution is more obligated and no Negro school is in a better position to develop such a program as Howard. No institution has access to specialized libraries—the Moorland Collection (at Howard), and city repositories; no where else are the thought and planning put forth; no better courses exist anywhere else; there are no better trained students anywhere, by virtue of racial background. This is the area in which Howard has the most promising and immediate opportunity to distinguish itself as a leader in the general cause of public enlightenment."[12]

Thus, long before the era of Black studies and academic Black power demands for community control of education and the development of curricula to meet the needs of African Americans, Professor Hansberry perceived of Howard University as the vanguard (leading division) of Black education. To help realize that goal, he submitted several proposals to foundations to finance his projects. His first major proposal was submitted to The Spellman Fund, July 11, 1929. Extracts from that proposal not only reveal Hansberry's keen perspectives and goals in the area of African studies, but also reveal the revolutionary character of his plan for education at Howard University. He proposed to show that:

1. "Africa, rather than Asia, was in all probability the *birthplace of the human race*," and "it was they (Africans), it appears, who first learned and then taught the rest of mankind how to make and use tools, to develop a religion, to practice art, to domesticate animals and to melt metals, particularly iron, and to create and maintain a deliberately constructed and tradition-bound...state;"[13]

2. that *desiccation of the Sahara and Libyan* deserts caused "the *autochthonous Negroids and Negroes*...to emigrate to Europe and Asia;[14]

3. that "many of the peoples and cultures of Ancient Egypt originated in equatorial Africa;"

4. that "the peoples of Ethiopia...vied (compete, struggle for superiority) with the mighty Assyrian Empire for the position of first place among the great organized world powers of that age;"

5. that "Ghana, Melle, Songhai and Nupe were larger in size, more effectively organized, and higher in culture than most of the contemporary states of the Anglo-Saxon, the Germanic, and the Slavic regions of Europe," and that "increased desiccation (drying, dry-up) of the Sahara, the introduction of the Mohammedan religion and the Islamic systems of polity, and the establishment of the Arab, Berber, and European systems of slave trading brought on the disintegration of these Negro states and their civilizations."

Hansberry concluded his proposal by expressing the hope that his efforts at Howard would arouse "Negro peoples in particular to make a specific effort to revive and develop to the full these creative and *spiritual powers* which...*are Nature's pre-eminent gifts to the African*."[15]

Professor Hansberry's stated objectives were clearly "at odds with prevailing notions about Africa's past," to use his own assessment; not all of these are universally accepted even today. In any case, he eventually received a modest fellowship from the General Education Board, which enabled him to continue limited research at Harvard University (1929-30) while on *sabbatical* (a period of rest, recurs in regular cycles) leave from Howard.

Although he failed to secure additional funds from Howard or elsewhere, to supplement the small fellowship, Hansberry was reassured in his work by sources he examined at Harvard and the patient support of his advisor, Professor Earnest A. Hooton, chairman of Harvard's Anthropology Department. After completing his sabbatical, at Harvard, Hansberry returned to Howard where he strengthened his courses on Africa, enlarged the library holdings, and rededicated himself in efforts to secure sufficient funds for developing his program and publishing the much needed source books.

Although, in 1923, he had corresponded with Professor F.L. Griffith, a distinguished Egyptologist, who complimented his work and expressed hope of seeing him if he visited England, it was during the early 1930's that Hansberry entered into extensive correspondence with several well-known European scholars about his courses at Howard and the research he wanted to continue in preparation for source books.

E.A. Wallis Budge, of the British Museum and early authority on Egypt, Ethiopia, and the eastern Sudan, encouraged Hansberry to pursue his work in England and offered his assistance; A. H. Sayce, a philologist at Oxford, offered his counsel and recommended others Hansberry could contact; E.L. Collie, *curator* (custodian at a museum) at the Logan Museum, encouraged Hansberry to pursue his stated aims; Sir W.M. Flinders Petrie, another renowned Egyptologist, offered his help; C.G. Seligmann, the Oxford anthropologist, offered his counsel; and L.P. Kirwan, an archaeologist at Oxford, agreed to serve as his advisor if he went to Oxford.[16]

Hansberry began seeking opportunities for field work in Africa. In 1932, he learned that Professor Griffith was planning to lead an expedition to the Sudan. The young Hansberry, therefore, diplomatically sought the counsel of two trusted advisors, Dows Dunham at the Museum of Fine Arts (Boston), and Professor Hooton, on whether or not his being Black might disqualify his joining the expedition. I have been unable to find a response from Hooton on this subject, but Dunham said in part:

> "To be perfectly frank with you, if I were in charge of such an expedition, I should hesitate long before taking an American Negro on my staff...I should fear that the mere fact of your being a member of the staff would seriously affect the prestige of the other members and the respect which the native employees would have for them...I feel sure that you know me well enough to realize that I do not say this out of any feeling of race prejudice."[17]

Hansberry did not accompany the expedition; and I have nothing to suggest that he was discouraged by Dunham's reply (which he probably anticipated), or that he ever used the incident to rationalize his limited success during those early years. He continued to seek funds for his program at Howard and for his own research. Finally, the General Education Board awarded him a fellowship to study at Oxford. Hansberry prepared for that opportunity by pursuing independent research in African history and archaeology at the University of Chicago in 1936.

At Oxford (1937-38) Hansberry worked with L.P. Kirwan, who was director of the Oxford Expedition to Nubia. It appeared that at last Professor Hansberry had received his golden opportunity of working under an expert archaeologist, and in Sudan! For in their previous exchange of letters, Kirwan was impressed by Hansberry's proposal for study in England, Egypt, and Sudan, though he did express some concern about the petitioner's "limited training" in archaeology. As it turned out, however, Kirwan attempted to steer Hansberry away from his initial proposal. In fact, he later suggested a project that Hansberry might conduct out of Boston! But Hansberry was determined. With no prospect of joining Kirwan's expedition to Sudan, Hansberry pursued what research he could at Oxford, and consulted with several other authorities, including long discussions with A.J. Arkell, who was on leave at Oxford from his post as Director of Antiquities for the Sudan.[18]

Hansberry's project proposed a historical reinterpretation of archaeological work in Ethiopia and Nubia between the eighth century B.C. and the sixth century A.D. He especially wanted to study more recent evidence and apply modern techniques in the re-examination of the conclusions reached by Herman Junker, whose article, *The First Appearance of the Negroes in History* (Journal of Egyptian Archaeology, 1921, VII), maintains that Egyptians and neighboring people of the Sudan are not Negroid but *Hamites* (Caucasians)....The answer as to whether or not Kirwan's attempts to dissuade Hansberry from pursuing the project were personal or professional must await additional research. Hansberry's report to the General Education Board was that his project closely paralleled one under consideration by Kirwan himself. In any case, the Howard professor remained steadfast, and completed his year's study at Oxford.

In 1938, he returned from his Oxford studies and continued to expand his program at Howard. At this time, he was promoted to assistant professor (sixteen years after his initial appointment). Although his Oxford experience had not been as rewarding s he had hoped, he was more convinced than ever that his research efforts had to be continued. Consequently, he revised and expanded his research proposal, received the counsel of Hooton at Harvard and W.F. Albright, an anthropologist at the Johns Hopkins University, and in 1947 submitted his project to the Rosenwald and Carnegie Foundations. It was in this connection that Hooton wrote his much quoted letter in Hansberry's behalf:

> "I am quite confident that no present-day scholar has anything like the knowledge of this field (prehistory of Africa) that Hansberry has developed. He has been unable to take the Ph.D. degree...because there is no university or institution...that has manifested a really profound interest in this subject.[19]

Albright had written President Mordecai Johnson earlier, "What was my pleasure...to find that Mr. Hansberry had covered the ground with extraordinary thoroughness and competence."[20]

In spite of this support, the intercession of some Howard University officials, and an extensively detailed project with evidence that several stages of the study were nearing completion. Hansberry was denied financial support by both foundations. This latest setback, coming twenty-five years after he had inaugurated the African studies program at Howard with great personal and financial sacrifices, was no doubt one of Hansberry's greatest disappointments.

However, this pioneering Africanist was relentless. As African studies became more popular during the post World War II era, Hansberry began to receive some of the recognition due him. In 1953, he became a Fulbright Research Scholar in Egypt and for the next year, he engaged in field work there, in the Republic of Sudan, and in Ethiopia. He also gave lectures to academic and general audiences in several African countries during that year.

Ironically, it was during Hansberry's leave as Fulbright Scholar that Howard University received a Ford Foundation grant to develop a program of African studies. Hansberry was neither included in any of the decisions related to those developments no was he informed that such discussions were underway. His feelings about this are best described by him:

> "While in Liberia, the last country visited during my extensive African travels in 1954, I learned from one of my former students—for the first time and to my great surprise—that the University was establishing a program of African Studies under the direction of the Head of the Department of Sociology. Since I had been engaged in a program of African Studies at the University for more than thirty years, it was difficult for me to understand why I had received—during my year aborad—no official word concerning this unusual development. On my return, to the University, I learned that the program had been made possible by a substantial grant in funds by the Ford Foundation under arrangements which excluded my courses in African Studies from the program and therefore from any of the benefits accruing from the grant. In view of my years of service which I had given—at much personal sacrifice—to the effort to establish a broadly based program of African Studies at Howard and taking into account the wide recognition which I had received for these endeavors from agencies outside the University, it is needless to say that the University's attitude in this matter was not a particularly enheartening experience."[21]

To attempt an unraveling of the complex developments that lead to the situation described above is a precarious (uncertain) endeavor. It is clear that Professor Hansberry was excluded from the initial consultations and planning for the new African Studies Program although his ideas served as a guide for it; it is less clear, however, what his role was in the program during subsequent years. Rayford W. Logan, former chairman of the Department of History at Howard University, has written that the program was administered by an Interdepartmental Committee including, among others, himself, Hansberry, and E. Franklin Frazier, who served for several years as chairman.[22] One would assume that this meant the endorsement of Hansberry's courses by the committee at some point, if not at the outset. But whatever the case, Hansberry did not play a major role in the programs although he had already more than thirty years to academic and experiential preparation in the field, a credential few American scholars could claim. One also should note that while Howard was withholding this recognition from Hansberry, several persons and organizations outside the University not only recognized his achievements, but sought his counsel on Africa; his distinctions were crowned by the African Research Award from the *Haile Selassie I Prize* Trust in 1964. Very likely, then, Hansberry's peripheral (outside) role in the new program resulted from politics within the University, which have not yet been evaluated.

By the 1950's Hansberry's contribution to the study of Africa at Howard included five courses: *People's and Cultures of Africa in Stone Age Times; Culture and Political History of Nilotic Lands in Historical Antiquity; Culture and Political History of Kushite or Ethiopian Lands in the Middle Ages; Cultural and Political History of the Kingdoms and Empires of the Western Sudan;* and *Archaeological Methods and Materials*. Not only does an examination of the available syllabi, notes, and lectures convince one of the incredible number of diverse sources Professor Hansberry used, or the tremendous scope of his courses; but one is equally impressed by the fact that he concentrated his efforts in ancient and medieval times. In 1957, in addition to teaching at Howard, Professor Hansberry became a lecturer on early African civilizations at the New School for Social Research in New York.

Professor Hansberry retired from Howard in 1959. He ended his teaching career among the peoples and lands of Africa. The University of Nigeria, which awarded him the doctorate of letters in 1961, established in his name the Hansberry Institute of African Studies. In

September 1963, the former Howard Professor became a Distinguished Visiting Professor at the University of Nigeria where he gave the inaugural address for the Hansberry Institute. Symbolically, only a few hundred miles away in Africa (Ghana) and just a few weeks previously, Hansberry's great mentor, W.E. B. DuBois, had died (in August, 1963) while still actively engaged in African studies.

One of the most important aspects of Professor Hansberry's academic career was the enthusiastic response and support of his students. Perhaps his first great joy in this regard came when he entered his class to the cheers of his students, after the Howard University president and board of trustees reversed their decision to discontinue his courses in the 1920's. He gave untiringly of his time to all of his students; but he assumed a particular interest in the African students. Hansberry realized that the African students not only had to contend with life in this racist country, but that they also had the obligation to return to their countries with both the skills acquired at Howard, and an Afro-centric perspective of their heritage. It was in this latter connection, through his coursed and personal contacts, that Hansberry made his great contribution to African students, dispelling the derogatory myths and stereotypes about their culture and affirming their dignity, pride, and sense of achievement among the peoples of the world.

In 1946, Professor Hansberry was appointed Faculty Advisor to African students, and in 1950 he was appointed to Howard's Emergency Aid to the African Students Committee. The latter assignment concerned African scholarships and related financial matters. Both positions seemed to merge with Hansberry's personal concern for the general welfare of African students, who continually brought a multitude of private and university matters for him to resolve. Hansberry accepted those responsibilities without extra compensation or additional clerical assistance. But his correspondence increased two or three-fold. Letters were written in response to queries from Africa about admissions and financial aid for students; replies were sent to African parents inquiring about a student's academic and social problems; petitions were submitted to foundations for student aid; recommendations were written for students to enter graduate or professional school; and in at least one case, extensive and detailed correspondence was undertaken in connection with an African student's death. Much of the cost of all this was paid for by Professor Hansberry.

In another instance, Hansberry wrote President W.V.S. Tubman of

Liberia to reinstate a student's scholarship (a student who later became a highly placed public official in Liberia). There is correspondence relating to several thousand dollars that Emperor Haile Selassie of Ethiopia contributed to the Committee on Aid to African Students.[23] In 1958, Professor Hansberry recorded that more $24,000 had been made available to African students from sources outside Howard University.

Up to the 1960's, Howard University still had the largest African student enrollment in the country, and most of those students received scholarship assistance. While some countries made contributions, Ethiopia and Liberia, for example, most of the aid during the 1950's came from the Scholarship Committee of the African American Institute (AAI). In 1951, for instance, African students received AAI grants at thirty-seven American institutions: fourteen were at Howard University; five were at Harvard; and three each at Cornell and Ohio Wesleyan. Between October 1957 and January 1959, Hansberry's records show that $8,099 were contributed as grants to African students at Howard. Most of this resulted from the initiative and efforts of Professor Hansberry, who was appointed to the AAI Scholarship Committee in 1959.

With the increased interest of the United States government in Africa and Africans during the 1950's, Hansberry's role with students became even more important as a fund raiser, counselor (many referred to him as father), and teacher. He was instrumental in the organization of the African Students Association of the United States and Canada, and in 1951, 1959, and 1963 he received that organization's Award of Honor. Recognition and thanks also came over the years in many letters from former students and their parents. One former student wrote in 1958 that he had started a "Hansberry Club" at the Queen's Royal College in the West Indies.[24] A study of the high esteem Hansberry's students had for him would indeed constitute an important and moving chapter of one of America's most dedicated Africanist.

Although the number and identity of everyone who benefited from Professor Hansberry's counsel and assistance will never be known, it is certain, however, that such beneficiaries were not limited to former students. His papers are full of references to materials sent or lent to colleagues, friends, and others who requested them. In addition, friends and relatives recall how Hansberry spent hours discussing various aspects of African history with persons who subsequently established themselves in print in fields relating to Africa. Hansberry sent references to W.E.B. DuBois in 1933 and also provided materials to help DuBois prepare a course on ancient Africa at Atlanta University in 1936. This DuBois greatly appreciated, and he, unlike many lesser scholars, readily acknowledged the value of Hansberry's work and encouraged him to continue it. In the forward of his book, *The World and Africa*, DuBois noted that: "...of greatest help to me has been Leo Hansberry." Professor Hansberry also counseled and sent syllabi, bibliographies, visual aids, and other materials to Edwin Smith, who, in 1943, was organizing African studies at Fisk University.

Hansberry also corresponded and had personal contacts with many African political leaders, including A.J. Luthuli, the black South African who won the Nobel Peace Award for 1960, and J. Boakye Danquah, the Ghanaian lawyer who headed the United Gold Coast Convention Party. In 1955, Danquah wrote to Hansberry requesting information on ancient Ghana.[25] He had read DuBois's, *The World and Africa* and had seen where the latter has relied on Hansberry for data regarding Ethiopia and Egypt. He also requested a copy of Delafosse's, *The Negroes of Africa* and any publication by Hansberry himself, which he evidently received, since in a letter dated May 28, 1956, Danquah expressed thanks for Hansberry's "Africa and the Western World," *The Midwest Journal*, 1955, Vol. VII.

Despite his difficulties and his tremendous teaching and counseling duties, Professor Hansberry found the time and energy to publish. In addition to book reviews and review articles that appeared in the *Journal of Negro Education, Africa Special Report, Panorama,* and the *Washington Post* newspaper, Professor Hansberry wrote many articles that were unusual for their time because few people were writing seriously in this field. Most of those who wrote focused on a more recent period. They were also unusual because they revealed Hansberry's wide familiarity with diverse sources in various languages. Some of these were as follows:

"Sources for the Study of Ethiopian History." *Howard University Studies in History*, 1930, Vol. II.

"A Negro in Anthropology." *Opportunity*, 1933, Vol. XI.

"African Studies." *Phylon*, 1944, Vol. V.

"Imperial Ethiopia in Ancient Times." *The Ethiopian Review* (Addis Ababa, Ethiopia: August, 1944), Vol. I.

"Ethiopia in the Middle Ages." *The Ethiopian Review* (September and November, 1944). Vol. I.

"The Historical Background of African Art." *Howard University Gallery of Art,* 1953.

"Africa and the Western World." *The Midwest Journal,* 1955, Vol. VII.

"Indigenous African Religions." *Africa Seen by American Negro Scholars.* (Presence Africaine, 1958).

"Ancient Kush, Old Ethiopia and the Balad es Sudan." *Journal of Human Relations,* 1960, Vol. VIII.

"Africa: The World's Richest Continent." *Freedomways,* 1963, Vol. III.

Africana at Nsukka. (Viking Press, 1964).

"Ethiopian Ambassadors to Latin Courts and Latin Emissaries to Prester John." *Ethiopia Observer* (Ethiopia and Britain, 1965), Vol. IX, No. 2.

"W.E.B. DuBois's Influence on African History." *Freedomways,* 1965, Vol. V. No. 1.

Although seldom mentioned in connection with political activities, Hansberry's involvement in African issues did indeed extend into various political arenas. In fact, one may argue that the fulfillment of his commitment to the unpopular effort "to bring to the attention of teachers and students the significance of ancient African civilization" required political activities. Professor Hansberry believed that all persons of African descent needed to know the richness of their past and appreciate the great potential for this present and future. He regarded African studies as a necessary means to develop or maintain Black pride and confidence in a world dominated politically, economically and culturally by whites. However, he was by no stretch of the imagination a racist; he believed in racial harmony; but he also believed that a prerequisite for that harmony was a fuller appreciation of the Black heritage. This resulted in his plans for a "pioneer project in collegiate education," and his efforts to educate the public in general. His attempts to reorient America's racial perspectives by destroying the old myths and stereotypes had to assume political implications; his difficulties at Howard confirm this at the university level.

But Hansberry also took very deliberate political courses of action at the national and international levels. As early as the Fourth Pan-African Conference (New York, 1927) the young Hansberry began to make his knowledge available for the mobilization of African peoples. At that conference, he discussed the archaeological history of Africa and its significance for Blacks. In 1934, Hansberry and others organized the Ethiopian Research Council, of which he became director, and William M. Steen, secretary. The objectives of the council were to stimulate American interest in Ethiopia's efforts to resist the Italian invasion, and to disseminate (spread about, scatter) information on Ethiopian history, ancient and modern. Correspondents were located in London, Paris, Rome, and Addis Ababa; affiliates were listed in Ethiopia, France and Panama, in addition to Chicago, New York, and Philadelphia. Associates included African Americans, a Ugandan, a Nigerian, and some Ethiopians. Ralph Bunche served as Advisor on International Law.[26]

Although it is difficult at this stage of research to determine the extent of the council's success, it is noteworthy that in 1936, Count Ciano, the Italian Minister of Foreign Affairs, informed the United States State Department of Italy's displeasure and concern over a plan for Emperor Haile Selassie to visit the United States. The Count's communication identified Hansberry as director of the group sponsoring the visit "for propaganda purposes."[27] It is also worthy of note that during the 1940's, after the emperor regained his throne, Hansberry assisted the Ethiopian ambassador in recruiting teachers and technicians.[28] These activities merit additional research.

In the 1950's, the United States took an increasingly serious interest in Africa, and among persons invited to testify before the Senate Foreign Relations Committee to discuss the Point Four program (foreign aid) was Professor Hansberry. He stressed the need for the following: provisions to help African organizations, corporations, and businessmen make direct application for financial and technical aid; educational provisions to train Africans; and provisions for funds to non-self-governing Africans' territories. He also referred to Howard University's success in training Africans. While there is no way to assess the impact of his testimony, it is important that his expertise was sought by the government and that his suggestions showed that he perceived Africa's pressing needs.

In 1952, a group that included William Steen, James Grant, Robert W. Williams, Jr., Henrietta Van Noy, and Hansberry organized the Institute of African American Relations to further understanding of Africa and to improve relations with Africans. The institute published *The African American Bulletin.* Shortly after founding the institute, Hansberry and other members entered into discussions with several groups interested in Africa. The result was the organization of the African American Institute (AAI) where Hansberry served as a trustee. As one of its activities, the AAI sponsored Africa House (Washington, D.C.) as a home base for African students in the United States. Given that concern, there was hardly any person better suited to administer Africa House than Professor Hansberry, who became chairman of its governing council. The All-African Student Union of the lively concerns and diverse programs of Africa House.

Professor Hansberry's long and dedicated experience with African studies and students won him tremendous respect, among Africans in particular. His many contacts helped him to maintain at Africa House a program that was both substantive and timely. There were lectures, seminars, movies, slides, exhibits, field trips, dances, and receptions. Among the guests who were honored at Africa House were Prime Minister Sylvanus Olympio of Togo; Chief Justice Kobina Arku-Korsah of Ghana; President Sekou Toure of Guinea; and Alioune Diop, Director of the Society of African Culture (Paris). Indeed, for the 1950's and early 1960's Hansberry developed an impressive program for Africa House.[29] As noted earlier, Hansberry also served on AAI's Scholarship Committee. Future research on Hansberry's influence in AAI would no doubt prove very revealing.

The profile, of Professor Hansberry would be remiss without some mention of his readiness to speak for social groups and counsel the layman about Africa. His private correspondence is *replete* (filled) with references to these kinds of activities. He was often an underpaid (or unpaid) but welcome speaker for church groups, school organizations, community clubs, lodges, and student groups. Many times after giving a talk, Hansberry would be asked for a copy of his speech, a list of books, or a syllabus; and he usually complied with such requests. Although justice cannot be done in evaluating this aspect of Hansberry's activities until further research is undertaken, it is already clear that he was, in a very real sense, a peoples' professor. Indeed, the fact that Hansberry often delayed his research and writing to make himself available for a discussion of Africa with anyone so interested, is a basic justification for publishing his *Notebook* for the general reader. Such a publication of his works for this audience probably honors him at least as much as any of the several awards he received in life.

Professor Hansberry's honors include three Awards of Honor from the African Student Association of the United States and Canada (1951,

1959, 1963); a bronze citation for "Forty Years of Service in the Cause of African Freedom," from the United Friends of Africa (1961); an Achievement Award from The Omega Psi Phi Fraternity (1961); the first African Research Award from the Haile Selassie I Prize Trust (1964); the LL.D. degree by Virginia State College and the Litt.D. degree by the University of Nigeria (both in 1960); and the LL.D. by Morgan State College (1965).

A few comments should be made about Professor Hansberry's views on African historiography. He spent most of his professional career attempting to rescue African history from the denigrated (Blacker, a reputation) status Europeans had established for it. He observed that the custom had developed to associate Ethiopia and Europe in much the same way as the expressions "Negro" and "Nordic," the former being considered inferior to the latter. Hansberry thus dedicated himself to the task of showing that this popular conception was historically ill-founded, a central theme of much of his writings.

Professor Hansberry was fascinated by the obsession of early European writers with Ethiopia. The designation itself was "distinctly a European product, for no Africans referred to themselves as Ethiopians or their country as Ethiopia until after Europeans coined the label;"[30] and neither ancient Egyptians nor Hebrews referred to Africans by those terms. Hansberry noted that the first writer to employ the terms seems to have been Homer, in his ninth-century B.C. work, *The Iliad*. In time, the designations Ethiopia and Ethiopians became perhaps more widespread and commonly known than those of any other land and people of ancient times. Hansberry wrote:

> It is a curious fact that centuries before the geographical and historical terms Babylon, Assyria, Persia, Carthage, and Etruria, or for that matter Greece and Rome themselves, had made their first appearance in the writings of classical authors, Ethiopia was already an old and familiar expression; and long after the names Babylon, Assyria, Carthage, and Etruria had become scarcely more than vague memories, preserved only in the morgue of history, the hoary designation "Ethiopia" continued in use.[31]

As a student and teacher of Greek history also, he observed that Europe's earliest poetry, geography, and history memorialized Ethiopia and Ethiopians; the great classical writers—Homer, Hesiod, Herodotus, Aeschylus, Sophocles, Euripides, Diodorus, Pliny the Elder, and others—contributed to the internationalization of those designations and helped to establish them as among the "oldest living terms" in European literature.

The reasons for this long, continuous European preoccupation with Ethiopia have puzzled many historians for centuries. Undoubtedly, however, the meaning of the terms itself—land of the sunburned of Black-faced men—is an important key. It referred to and indeed reflected a sensitivity to people of Black complexion. Professor Snowden has emphasized this point:

> Color was obviously uppermost in the minds of the Greeks and Romans, whether they were describing Ethiopians in the land of their origin or their expatriated congeners in Egypt, Greece, or Italy. The distinguishing mark of an Ethiopian was the color of his skin.[32]

However, the more crucial questions are what that sensitivity meant in ancient times, and to what extent it influenced the personal attitudes of subsequent eras.

Some historians see in much of the classical literature the genesis of denigratory racial and color attitudes and concepts. In defense of that conclusion, they cite such classical descriptions of Ethiopians as "Mysterious, with tightly curled or wooly hair, broad and flattened noses, thick and puffy lips." Herodotus characterized their speech as resembling "the shrieking of a bat rather than the language of men." Pliny the Elder described them as having "by report...no heads but mouth and eyes in their breast." The proverbial expression, "to wash an Ethiopian white," falls into the same stereotypic pattern. Black is associated with dirt that cannot be washed white (clean). The label, "man-eating Aeothiopians," further stereotyped Black people. Whatever the intent and whether conscious or not, these critics point to the classical writers a purveyors of racist germs.

On the other hands, there are critics, including Professor Hansberry, who have emphasized that stream of ancient description that characterized the Ethiopians as "pious and just." While snowden's book cites much of the information included in the above paragraph, he concludes: "Classical texts have often been misinterpreted because scholars have mistakenly attributed to antiquity racial attitudes and concepts that derive from certain modern views regarding the Negro." Hansberry shared that point of view (and many have discussed it with his long-time friend and colleague) and believed that an acquaintance with the "real position of ancient Ethiopians in early European tradition would provide correctives to the opprobrious and mistaken connotations" related to Africans "connotations that certain historical and social developments have caused to become almost universally accepted as the genuine and original characterizations." In short, Professor Hansberry sought to rehabilitate "that attitude of mind which prevailed in the lands and among the people who originated the terms Ethiopia and Ethiopians as designations of a culture and people who they knew at first hand."[33]

It should be emphasized that Professor Hansberry wrote at a time when the academic and political vogue was "to prove" the Black man's equality by presenting evidence of his culture and noting his contributions to world civilization. Hansberry not only has demonstrated such a contribution, he has revealed the very close contact and interrelationships that existed between ancient and medieval Africans, in this case, Ethiopians and Europeans. Based on his evaluation of those interactions, Hansberry concluded that the early Greeks and Romans regarded Ethiopians as full human beings. Such a conclusion meant that the explanation for the evolution of the concept of Black inferiority had to be traced to some other source. And until recently, the source was traced to the slave trade and slavery, a position Hansberry accepted. On the other hand, and somewhat ironically, Hansberry's research also can be used to suggest conscious or unconscious Black derogation (discredit, degrading, derogatory) in ancient times. Indeed, changing times demand reinterpretation not only in terms of new data but also in terms of new perspectives and no reputable historian would deny that; certainly Hansberry would not. In fact, for his generation, Hansberry pioneered a reinterpretation of the African heritage.

PAFO thanks Gail Hansberry and Kay Hansberry, daughters of Professor William Leo Hansberry for using their father's notes, supra.

The following books by Professor Hansberry are recommended for your stimulation and enlightenment, Pillars in Ethiopian History, Notebook, Volume 1m *edited by Dr. Joseph Harris, Howard University Press, 1974 and* Africa and Africans, Notebook Volume II, *Howard University Press.*

PAFO wishes to thank Sister Ruby Shivers and Sister Rose Cabbagestalk of the Plainfield, New Jersey branch of PAFO for gathering this vital information.

FOOTNOTES

1 Symbolic of Professor Hansberry within the context of the Pan African tradition is the following: When Hansberry died, Edward W. Blyden III was Director of the Hansberry Institute of African Studies located in the Russwurm Building at the University of Nigeria in Nsukka which was established largely because of the efforts of Nnamdi Azikiwe. For those who wish a fuller understanding of the importance of this, consult: Hollis Lynch, Edward Wilmot Blyden (London, 1967); the several works by Blyden himself; Robert W. July, *The Origins of Modern African Thought* (New York, 1967); Jean H. Kopytoff, *A Preface to Modern Nigeria* (Madison, Wise, 1965); and Joseph E. Harris, *The Unveiling of a Pioneer, A Tribute to the Memory of Professor William Leo Hansberry* (Department of History, Howard, 1972).

2 A pamphlet in Hansberry's private papers (HPP).

3 Hansberry's scrapbook, referred to as HS.

4 Program in HPP.

5 From a report also in HPP.

6 HPP

7 HS

8 Letter to Dean E.P. Davis, May 7, 1935.

9 Letter to Mordecai Johnson, September 17, 1935.

10 HPP.

11 a plan for expanding a pioneer project on collegiate education.

12 HPP.

13 This is now a generally accepted point of view.

14 See also Chester Chand, *Implication of Early Human Migrations from Africa to Europe*, Man, August 1963. Vol 63, No. 153, p. 124.

15 A Proposal for Funds, July 11, 1929, p. 11.

16 a letter file, HPP: Budge to Hansberry, January 29, 1932; Griffith to Hansberry, February 6, 1923; Sayce to Hansberry, February 11, 1932; Collie to Hansberry, November 8, 1928; Petrie to Hansberry, February 10, 1932; Selegman to Hansberry, September 30, 1936; and noted in the scrapbook, p. 12.

17 Letter file Hpp, Dunham to Hansberry, February 2, 1932.

18 HS.

19 Hooton to W.W. Alexander (Rosenwald Fund) September 17, 1948.

20 Albright to Mordecai Johnson, January 6, 1947. Found in HPP.

21 This appears on a page in hansberry's scrapbook. There is no evidence that it was sent to anyone and is undated.

22 Rayford W. Logan, Howard University: *The First Hundred Years* (New York: New York University Press, 1969), pp. 436, 540.

23 Letters on these and many other matters abound in the Hansberry private papers.

24 Letter file, HPP, Neville Clark to Hansberry, March 15, 1958.

25 Lituli (sic) to Hansberry, 1961; Danquah to Hansberry, may, 18, 1956.

26 HS; also a letter written on Ethiopian Research Council stationery dated June, 1936, listing officers, advisors and affiliates, found in HPP.

27 "Foreign Relations of the United States." *The Near East and Africa,* 1936, Vol. 3, p. 218.
28 HS.
29 HS.
30 The Greeks and Romans applied the term Ethiopian to the several dark or Black ethnic groups in Africa; the description, therefore, bore n necessary relationship to the present country of that name.
31 Undated manuscript in HPP.
32 The most recent and thorough evaluative synthesis in this area is Frank Snowden, *Blacks in Antiquity; Ethiopians in the Greco-Roman Experience* (Cambridge, Massachusetts; Harvard University Press, 1970). Snowden and Hansberry were colleagues and friends at Howard University for many years. Another valuable book is Grace H. Beardsley, *The Negro in Greek and Roman Civilization: A Study of the Ethiopian Type* (Baltimore and London, 1929).
33 Hansberry lecture notes, undated, HPP.
34 For more information on the Seminoles, consult author Jan Carew, D.S., Northwestern University.
35 Garlic and onion was part of the diet of the workers.

THE ICING

BLACK PEOPLES' CONTRIBUTIONS TO UNGRATEFUL AMERICA
THE SPIRIT OF 1776

When the thirteen original colonies finally broke the bonds that bound them to their Mother England, the Black man though bound in chains himself, figured very prominently in *that* struggle for the freedom of the Colonies. By hiding the truth from the people about the part that the Black Man played in the development of this country, the white leaders (power elite) were able to empower the ordinary white people to feel justified in their inhumane treatment of us by lying to them that they we were not really human.

Consider this paradox of the American Revolution; a colony with a half a million of prisoners-of-war (POW's) being forced into servitude, decides to go to war against their mother country supporting a theory that all men are created equal and endowed by their Creator with certain unalienable rights that among these are "Life, liberty and the pursuit of happiness."

Leading up to this Revolution, many events took place. The main event was the "Boston Massacre" in which several Blacks in a group, fought British soldiers on the night of March 5, 1770. The leader of this group of people that fought the British, which incidentally, was a mixed group, happened to be a Black man named Crispus Attucks; he was the first to be shot and the first to die for their cause. Crispus Attucks only had a stick when he advanced towards the contingent of British soldiers.

Being a man of great persuasion, he encouraged the whites to stand up for their rights and told the soldiers to shoot and be damned. Along with Crispus Attucks, a Black man named Samuel Gray was also shot. This act of bravery and determination seemed to spark the whites towards their self-determination that grew to fever pitch by the end of 1775. Incidentally, the first blood shed in the Civil War was that of a black man. He was Nicholas Biddle (of Pottsville) wounded in Baltimore, on April 18, 1861. He was not killed, but severely hurt by a brick, thrown by an irate white man, angry at seeing a Black man in uniform. There were patriots of color also at Bunker Hill, such as Peter Salem and Salem Poor. These battles preceded the take over by George Washington of the Minutemen and other patriotic groups. When George

Washington took command, he issued an order forbidding enlistments of Blacks.

Now the irony of it all as Harriet Beecher Stowe said about Blacks fighting at Concord, Lexington and Bunker Hill and also dying on King Street (in Boston) is that, "It was not for their own land that they fought, not even for a land that adopted them but for a land that forced involuntary servitude upon them and whose laws even in supposed freedom often oppressed them than protected them. Bravery under such circumstances has a peculiar beauty and merit. The truth is, that behind the Revolutionary rhetoric, the dying and the bleeding, the Black man toiled and fought for white liberty and, that in fact and deed, "HE WAS THE SPIRIT OF 1776." We believe that the Spirit of freedom and compassion burned so deeply in the minds of our people, that in our minds we created a hope of freedom for ourselves. We believed that we would have been nurtured out of the milk of human kindness and gratitude when our cry for freedom would ring out.

The British offered freedom for us if we fought on their side. Thousands of us did cross the lines because our thirst for freedom had to be quenched. This prompted George Washington and the Continental Congress to reverse itself, and Black freedom joined back into the Revolutionary Army. The five thousand of us that fought against the British Empire was a great factor in helping to turn the tide of battle in favor of the Colonies.

Besides being just soldiers in the Revolutionary War, Blacks served as spies. One, James Armstead is credited with having helped save Marquis de Lafayette, colonists, from defeat by Cornwallis. In the Continental Navy, many Blacks served as sailors on gunboats. Captain Mark Starlin, a Black Man of the Virginia Navy was commander of the Patriot. However, at the end of the war, in spite of a brilliant battle record, he was forced back into servitude by his old captor.

Deborah Sampson Gannett disguised as a man, enrolled in the service for the revolution and was commended by Massachusetts (her home state) for extraordinary instance of female heroism. Some of us did receive freedom for fighting in the Revolutionary War, but most of our fathers who fought did not become free; even those who fought with the British were later transported to the British West Indies and forced to serve on the sugar plantations.

IMPLICATIONS OF THE WAR

There were six main reasons of the "Why" the Revolutionary War came about. They are:

(1) The economic failure of involuntary servitude in the middle and eastern colonies,

(2) The new philosophy of "freedom" and the rights of man (this made the cornerstone of the revolt) showing that the revolution, the trade in African prisoners-of-war and the struggle for liberty were not consistent.

(3) The old fear of African insurrections which had long played so prominent a part in legislation now gained a new power from the imminence of war and from the well-founded fear that the British might incite servile uprisings.

(4) That nearly all the American slave markets in 1774-1775 were over—stocked with us—POWs, and, consequently many of the strongest partisans of the system were "bulls" on the market an desired to raise the value of their property by at least a temporary stoppage of the trade.

(5) That since the vested interest of the p.o.w. trading merchants were liable to be swept away by the opening of hostilities and since the price of p.o.w.s were low, there was from this quarter, little active opposition to a cessation of the trade for a season.

(6) This was the long favorite belief of the supporters of the Revolution that an English exploitation of colonial resources had caused the quarrel and the best weapon to bring England to terms was the economic expedient of stopping all commercial intercourse with her.

THE WAR OF 1812 AND HOW THE BLACK MAN FIGURES IN ITS EXECUTION

After the close of the Revolutionary War, and also during that period, the establishment of the BLACK CHURCH had begun. By 1776, in Virginia and Georgia, the Black Baptists still remained under the jurisdiction of the whites, until legal separation with full control over property was achieved by the African Methodist Episcopal Church at Philadelphia, Pennsylvania, starting with Bethel (Mother). The Black Church quickly became the most effective, organized Black institution in the United States. It was the minister indeed, who provided the first real communal leadership, while the church itself gave the Black community a social cohesion and resilience providing a subsidy for its poorer members, establishing and running schools and encouraging insurance companies. In 1787, the Philadelphia, Pennsylvania "Free African Society" was founded to provide for its members without regard to religious tenets—support in sickness and assistance to widows and fatherless children. This was initiated by Richard Allen and Absalom Jones.

Many of the present Black-owned insurance companies were founded by men whose roots go back to the founding fathers of the "Black Church." It was there that the inspiration and the love of racial identity and initiative were germinated. The spirit of Richard Allen and other great Blacks came down to us to provide the impetus to succeed against all odds. In the first African Methodist Church, "Mother Bethel," at Sixth and Lombard Streets in Philadelphia, Pennsylvania, a Black man named (Captain) James Edwards, born in British West Indies was a member of that congregation. Undoubtedly, he studied the life of Richard Allen and became so inspired, that he too wanted to make a contribution. He thought of the Free African Society that was organized by Absalom Jones and Richard Allen. Along with some other interested people, they secured a charter, thus starting the Provident Home Beneficial Society, which later under such men and women as William Hester, Lucinda Mackrey, Jenkins, Hooper, Edward Robinson, Jr., and Joseph Faison who built it into a multi-million dollar company starting from less than two hundred dollars.

We can readily see that by studying the life of these great men, it would be hard not to want to try to measure up to their greatness. This is especially true when you realize how they achieved under such difficulties, being surrounded by such hostility. The Black minister before his own congregation in those days could freely denounce the injustices of white America, even if no more than for a few hours once a week to escape the constant reminder of the white majority authority. The Black church restored some lost pride and dignity and nourished Black art, a new spiritual music and poetry (Edward W. Robinson, Jr.'s *Black Rhapsody*) pertaining to the songs our fathers and mothers used after the white man outlawed the talking drum—that was part of that spiritual music.

Also in 1787, the first Black Masonic Lodge was founded here in this servile predicament by Prince Hall, the first master of masonry in this country, but we know that masonry belonged to the Black Man from the beginning.

Prince Hall also petitioned the state of Massachusetts for equal educational facilities for all free Black citizens and their children, but the petition was rejected and Prince Hall started a school for Black children at his home in 1798. With this kind of Black projected atmosphere imposing itself on the white American psyche right after their war for freedom from England, slavery in the physical form practically died in the North. It seemed for a time that slavery would die in the South too, had it not been for the invention of the cotton gin. This invention breathed new life into the institution of involuntary servitude, by the fact that the cotton gin was able to separate the seed and stem from out of the cotton extremely fast. Therefore, the growth of cotton was doubled and redoubled by the clearing away of new land that demanded an ever-increasing number of laborers.

REASONS FOR THE 1812 WAR

The War of 1812 between the United States and England was a strange war. The United States declared war to protect its sailors and shipping. Yet, in the United States, the West that had neither sailors nor shipping was for the war, while New England that had both, was against it. Even more strange was the fact that the greatest victory took place after the war had officially ended.

From 1800 to 1815, the Napoleonic Wars were fought between France and most other European nations. France and England both *thought* they had the right to capture United States' ships to either stop the trade with England or to search for British sailors who had deserted to the United States. In about June of 1807, the British War ship *Leopard* had ordered the *Chesapeake*, United States frigate to stop and be searched for deserters. The captain refused, and the British warship fired on the United States ship killing and wounding a number of men.

As people moved westward, difficulties grew between the whites and the Indians. Under the leadership of Tecumseh, the Indians began to unite. They hoped to keep the whites from taking more and more of their land. The Westerners believed that the British gave the Indians guns and gun powder, and for this reason the West wanted the war.

When Washington was captured and burned, among the leading freedmen citizens of Philadelphia who requested to help defend Philadelphia from a similar fate were Bishop Richard Allen and Rev. Absalom Jones. These fathers of ours recruited more than two thousand Black men who worked continuously for forty-eight hours, building fortifications at Grays Ferry. Later, a battalion of Philadelphia Blacks was formed for military service. A number of Blacks served in the Navy on the Great Lakes, and for the Battle of Lake Erie. It was reported that seventy percent of the flag ship of Perry was made up of Black men. Nathaniel Shaler, the commander of the "Tompkins" said "When America has such *stars* as J. Johnson, who was killed in a naval battle, she has little to fear from such tyrants of the ocean." New York State passed a bill providing for the formation of two regiments of Blacks for the army. General Andrew Jackson in preparing for the battle of New Orleans, called for all free Blacks to come to the ranks and stated, "Through a mistaken policy you have heretofore been deprived of participation in the glorious struggle for national rights in which our country is engaged. This no longer shall exist." Blacks fought with such valor, that it brought great praise beyond what he ever dreamed. After the smoke of battle had cleared, the Black soldier was soon forgotten and most were forced back into servitude like in the American Revolutionary War.

OUR INDIAN BROTHER

Leaving the War of 1812 with the bulk of Black people still being held in involuntary servitude, Black people began to take many courses of action.

Looking at the Indian and the African during this period of time when whites were begging Blacks as well as Indian men to help them gain their freedom, the implications were astounding. There were very many indications and proof that the Black and Red Man, particularly on an individual level helped each other against a common enemy. True, a couple of the Indian Nations did hold Blacks in involuntary servitude, but this was not anywhere near the general trend. A Black, even though having been held in servitude, could become a councillor or even a chieftain. Such a case in point involved an offshoot of the Creek Nation, known as the Seminoles.

The relations between the Seminoles and the Africans living in America led to the largest and most expensive of all Indian wars, a fact that opens a fascinating load of speculation. By and large, Africans and Indians dealt with each other on an individual basis. The Seminoles were constantly being harassed by white slave holders seeking those of our people escaping forced servitude. The pace of events was greatly accelerated during the War of 1812. At the end of the war, the British abandoned a fort on the eastern side of the Appalechicola River. A group of Choctaw Indians and a group of Blacks took the fort under the leadership of a Black named *Garcon*. Things came to a head in July 1816 when Garcon ambushed a United States gun boat, killed one, captured all of the crew except one sailor. Now the Creek Nation aided the United States forces and laid siege to the fort. Artillery fire hitting the forts magazine killed most of the freedom fighters. This defeat enraged the Seminoles who had become physically very Africanized, and it also enraged the pure Blacks. Faced with determined and organized force, the United States authorities tried to divide the two groups into selling the pure Blacks down the river, but it didn't work. After a seven year war, and forty-two million dollars, under Andrew Jackson's command, he captured the Seminole stronghold on the Swanee River. The Seminoles and the Blacks withdrew in an orderly fashion into the swamps and the United States decided not to pursue them. Jackson called it the "savage" and "Negro" War.

One factor of the war was the opposition of Seminole Blacks to the Indian Removal Act (removing Indians to barren reservations, after the United States acquired Florida from Spain). The approximate or immediate cause of the war was the determination of southern whites to humiliate Seminole Blacks. As it happened, the fabled Indian Chief was married to a Black woman with the entrancing name of "Che-Cho-Ter" which translated means, "Morning Dew." While visiting an Indian agency, Morning Dew, the mother of Osceola's four children , was captured by whites and carried into slavery in Georgia. Osceola immediately threw down the gage to battle, telling whites "you have guns, powder and lead, and so doe we." This was clear enough and ominous enough; that's when Osceola punctuated his words by cutting down a United States Army patrol, killing one hundred soldiers. At the time, Osceola had a force of about two thousand warriors, including three hundred Blacks. One of the leading Blacks was John Caesar, who successfully raided plantations for Black recruits. Inos, the commander of the Black forces on the Withlacoochee, the chief councillor among the Blacks, and the most important character and Abraham, the principal Black Chief had been called one of the outstanding Black men produced in America was about forty years of age at the beginning of the war. As a child, he had fled slavery in Pensacola and settled among the Seminoles. For a spell, he served as a captive of Micanopy, the principal Seminole chief. He received his freedom after serving as an interpreter for Micanopy on his trip to Washington. He later married the widow of the former chief of the nation.

Abraham was the undisputed leader of the Seminole Blacks and he had as much influence in the nation as any leader. A large man, generally pictured in the traditional Seminole turban. Abraham was described as plausible, pliable, a sensible and shrewd man; the United States authorities considered him most cunning and intelligent, a cruel and malignant enemy.

An officer said, "Ten resolute Blacks with the knowledge of the country are sufficient to desolate the frontier from one extent to the other." The United States' commanding officer also said, "This, you may be assured, is mostly a Black war more so than an Indian war and if it is not speedily put down, the South will feel the effects of it on their servile population before the end of the next season."

Slaveholders feared that the Seminole-African War would trigger a South-wide alliance between the Indians and the Blacks who were still in servitude. The war came to an inconclusive end in 1842 after the treacherous capture of Osceola and other Indian chiefs who were lured to a peace conference under a flag of truce and then surrounded by United States warriors. They were unconquerable on the battlefield, showing that the white United States of America had not been successful in field fighting with those endowed with pigmentation. A treaty was concluded which gave the Indians and the Africans the status of prisoner-of-war. Most of the Seminole Indians and Africans migrated to Mexico where they became guardians of the border, and the Mexican government awarded them with grants of land.

Just to mention a few Blacks who became chiefs of other Indian nations or held great influence; one was James Beckworth, a leader of the Crow nation. There was Jean Point Baptiste DuSable, the founder of Chicago. He married an Indian woman and had enormous influence on the Indians of Lake Michigan territory.

NATIVE AMERICANS AND BLACKS: A PROUD LEGACY

Before we leave this tiny portion of the Indians, PAFO would like to inform you of the following information:

Looking at the *lie* that America was discovered, even though it was inhabited by an educated and civilized people, we are appalled at the gall of such indignities projected on and imposed against such a wonderful people.

The first thing, of course, that the Europeans did was to change their historical names from Choctaw, Creek, Crow and all of the other scores of indigenous nations living here for thousands of years. Secondly, the European changed the name of the land mass to America. It already had a name before the advent of the Europeans. In what is now North America, the indigenous people called it "Eria." In the Great Lakes' area, it was called, "Akela." In the Southeast, it was called "Tamarac." For those that are familiar with Egyptian history, you will remember that the people of Egypt also called their land "Tamara." In South Central America, they called it "Nazca." One more brief point: If Robert Hieronimus, Ph.D., who wrote a book called, *America's Secret Destiny* and Cadwallader Colden, who wrote a book called, *The History of the Five Indian Nations* are correct in their exhaustive research; then the great constitution of these United States are almost an exact duplication of the Mohawk/Iroquois federation of nations now called Indians. Not only were they civilized and governing themselves with great sophistication, but their constitution was well documented. It was learned that Benjamin Franklin was commissioned to write and detail these documents so that the colonies would have something to adopt.

First Black Renaissance in America

Another course that our people took during the post-war period of 1812 was that of becoming seamen. By 1859, half of the seamen in the United States were free Blacks. Work was so scarce for free Blacks in the North because whites opposed Blacks in competing for work. Only a few Blacks were able to accumulate some wealth, from ten thousand dollars up to a half a million dollars. Some of these, to name a few are: a Black doctor who worked for his freedom, his name was Dr. James Derham; there was Paul Cuffee; Thomy Lafon; and a dentist named Dr. Roderick Badger.

Blacks also began to set up schools of learning for themselves as some had done before, like Prince Hall (1798). It was also a time when Blacks, who were free, began holding conventions in various cities throughout the North.

Almost all free Blacks were outspoken against involuntary servitude. Some became outstanding abolitionists, speakers and organizers of meetings and conventions. As early as 1817, at Bethel A.M.E. Church in Philadelphia, Pennsylvania, under the leadership of James Forten, Richard Allen and Absalom Jones, a large group of free Blacks came together in opposition to the American Colonization Society. The idea or purpose of the American Colonization Society was to repatriate free Blacks on the grounds that they were incapable of leading useful lives in the United States and would by their removal, make the institution of captivity more secure. The American Colonization Society was organized in December, 1816 by whites among which were several prominent captors of human beings who represented the first organized effort at substantial emigration. Black groups were quick to oppose the Society and its objectives, at a meeting in Philadelphia, Pennsylvania. In January 1817, registering its strong protest at the description of free Blacks as a dangerous and useless part of the community, it was resolved: "THAT WE WILL NEVER SEPARATE OURSELVES VOLUNTARILY FROM THOSE HELD IN INVOLUNTARY SERVITUDE IN THIS COUNTRY: THEY ARE OUR BRETHREN BY THE TIES OF CONSANGUINITY (Blood), OF SUFFERING, AND OF WRONG, AND WE FEEL THAT THERE IS MORE VIRTUE IN SUFFERING PRIVATIONS WITH THEM THAN FANCIED ADVANTAGES FOR A SEASON." The Philadelphia meeting had fittingly been convened at Bethel Church. Through the Black Church, Blacks became organized to a far better degree for their mutual interest as well as for religious purpose.

From that time on, large groups of Blacks continued to hold conventions and other meetings in various Northern cities to protest against involuntary servitude and to petition the state legislatures and congress for freedom of their brothers and sisters in bondage. Among the outstanding organizers and speakers in the convention movements were: William Wells Brown, Samuel Cornish, John B. Voshon, Robert Purvis and a Presbyterian minister, Henry H. Garnet. At the Buffalo convention of Black citizens in 1843, Garnet urged Blacks to rise and make a strike for your lives and liberty. Some whites, like Benjamin Lundy, Arthur Tappan and William Lloyd Garrison made their entire country aware of our sentiments, which did much to disprove the charge of Black docility. Though methods differed as to how their goals should be achieved (just like today), there was a great unity among Blacks for citizenship and freedom.

To fully appreciate the struggle of yesteryear, we mut not leave out the Black Abolitionists. They began to speak about freedom, write about freedom and to meet among themselves—and with white abolitionists, who were dedicated to their own cause. Pulpit, platform and press were turned over to their use and the demand grew for political action. Petitions enraged and embarrassed state legislatures. Life, the free Black had, but real liberty was precarious and the pursuit of happiness was still a far-off goal. David Walker, a free born, was the son of one held in involuntary servitude. He hated captivity so badly, that he moved from North Carolina to Massachusetts where he became a leader in the "Boston Colored Association" and an agent for the first Black newspaper, *Freedom's Journal*. Within a year, it went into three printings, greatly stirring up Blacks who could read and infuriating those still in bondage. Other abolitionists were Prince Saunders who was an ardent orator; Lunsford Lane of Raleigh, North Carolina; Jermain Loguen, an escapee from Tennessee; Charles L. Remond; and, Samuel Ringold Ward, Pastor of a New York Presbyterian church. So much went into the setting of the stage for the final removal of the physical shackles that made us bondsmen and bondswomen. All happenings abroad, and here in America, molded the future for the destiny that is ours. It was a time of the Blacks coming to the rescue of whites wanting their freedom, a time of the Indian Brother and the Black Brothers, a time of Gabriel Prosser, Denmark Vessey, Nat Turner, Gideon Jackson and so many like these four just mentioned who were responsible for the development of the great captivity debates because they refused to just be still and do nothing about a situation.

We will mention, here, that many whites in the South were tarred and feathered, half drowned, beaten, killed and many other things had happened to them for being an abolitionist. We must not hide the truth about whites, good or bad. Yes, there were some who did help us, but pitifully, a relative few.

However, there are records of white people doing things for Blacks whose bloodline was questionable so far as being so-called pure white is concerned. When we used the word, few whites helping us, it was really a relative terminology. Miscegenation was a big factor in the dilution of our evolutionary advantages, but the ties of blood helped to change the attitude of whites in the North and South. So many mixed bloods were passing into the white world, that laws against it were passed into the legislature. Many a so-called white abolitionist was passing for white and using this vantage point to help the more unfortunate. Also, some passing mixed bloods being afraid of recognition were actually more cruel than some of the unmixed whites.

They felt that this extreme cruel action would blind all people to their identity when they had risen to higher realms of power in the white world (See J.A. Rogers, *Sex and Race*, Vol. II).

BLACK RENAISSANCE—PHASE II

In another series of history, as taught by PAFO, you would learn that long ago, in Mother Africa, of the Western Sudan area where the majority of the Black people in America come from, we had invented many of the tools and other things that go into making civilizations. Ancient and early modern Africa did much to raise mankind out of the stone age and into the age of metal and the refining of carpentry. These ancient Africans that did these marvelous wonders spread out from Kush-Egypt into the area of the Western Sudan. They became known as Ghanaians, Malians, and Songhaians. The Black men in America who are the direct descendants of the last great empire in the Western Sudan known as the Songhai Empire, carries in his genes the creativity, resourcefulness and genius of our ancestors.

After the final fall of the Songhai Empire and of Kanem Bornu, the prisoners-of-war were forced on waiting ships and brought into America. We, their sons and daughters became known as hewers of wood and drawers of water, in this land of the free and the home of the brave. During this period of servitude, harsh laws were imposed on us, restricting us from an opportunity to learn to read and write.

As a matter of fact, cruel penalties were inflected not only on us Blacks for attempting to learn if caught, but also on those who tried to teach us. Yet, it was during this period that we, Blacks contributed more then sixty percent of the inventions in this country by the projection of their genius at that time.

There were many an invention created by our fathers in pre-Civil War years. They were never accorded the white historical recognition for reasons that we are already aware of. To name just a few of these inventors and medical geniuses, like Blair who invented the cotton planter in 1836, and the corn planter in 1934. There was J. Hawkins, in 1845, who invented the grid iron. Around 1790, a Black man, held by force in servitude, by Eli Whitney created the pattern for the cotton gin; also a servant of Robert Fulton invented the steam boat. (For more information, consult Roi Otley, *Brown Geniuses of America*)

Before and after the Civil War, from 1834 to 1900, our fathers created more than six hundred patented inventions. (Mentioning the type of inventions only) Our fathers invented the combined truss and bandage, folding bed, ladder scaffold support, street sweeper, ironing board by Sarah Boone. The train alarm, car coupling device, railway switch, electric lamp, drip cut, lubricating lawn sprinkler, air ship, magnetic car balancing device, propeller for vessels, inhalator and gas mask also were invented by Black people. We will now give you the story of a few of our fathers' creations. There was Jan Matzeliger, 1852-1889, who was born in Guinea. He immigrated to the United States, first to Philadelphia, Pennsylvania, then to Lynn, Massachusetts.

After some preliminary work in a shoe factory, he learned the trade. By that time, the Industrial Revolution was in progress and had resulted in a number of machines to cut, sew, and tack shoes, but none had been perfected to last a shoe. Over the years, Matzeliger refined it to such a point that it was able to adjust a shoe, arrange the leather over the sole, drive in the nails and deliver the finished product all in one minute's time.

Elijah McCoy's (1844-1928) inventions were primarily connected with the automatic lubrication of moving machinery. Perhaps, the most valuable design was that of the drip cup; a tiny container filled with oil, whose flow to essential parts that move of heavy-duty machinery, which was regulated by a stop-cock. The "drip cup" was a key device for perfecting the overall lubrication system used in industry today. In the early days of his creativity, many white crooks tried to steal his patents and devices. He managed to keep the main secret of his invention obscure from others. Some people were fooled and bought an imitation of McCoy's invention, but it didn't work. What evolved out of this was a phrase by future purchasers of his many inventions, "Is this the real McCoy?"

When one thinks of the electric light, if he is uninformed, he automatically thinks of Thomas Edison. By turning on the search light of inquiry, you will find that Louis Latimer (1848-1928) as the true inventory. Latimer was employed by Alexander Graham Bell to make the patent drawings for the first telephone, and later went on to become chief draftsman for both the General Electric and Westinghouse Companies. Born in Chelsea, Massachusetts, on September, Latimer enlisted in the Union Navy at the age of fifteen, and began to study of drafting after completion of military service. In 1881, he invented and patented the first incandescent electric light bulb with a carbon filament. Even though Edison got the historical credit for the electric light bulb invention, Latimer told him "you have my invention, but let me see you light up the world." Latimer wrote the first text book on lighting systems, and was called by England to light up London, then Paris, New York, Montreal and Philadelphia. An apparatus for cooling and disinfecting is also credited to his genius.

To many, Alexander Bell's name stands out as the inventor of the telephone. Yet in reality, a man with a major percent of African blood coursing through his veins was the true inventor. His name was Granville T. Woods (1856-1910). Born in Columbus, Ohio on December 2, 1856, he obtained a patent #308,8176 for the telephone transmitter, and on October 11, 1887, he obtained another patent #371,241 for the telephone system and apparatus. Here again, white historians never bothered to reveal the truth of what Africans in America contributed to world technical advancement. During his lifetime, Granville T. Woods secured some fifty patents including one for an incubator which was the forerunner of present machines capable of hatching fifty thousand eggs at one time. Another famous invention of his was the synchronous Multiplex Railway Telegraph, also the electric railway conduit, system of electrical distribution, overhead conducting system for electric railway conduit, system of electrical distribution, overhead conducting system for electric railway, electric magnetic brakes apparatus, polarized relay and relay instrument and many more.

In this Industrial Revolutionary time period, Black people produced the great Doctor Daniel Hale Williams (1856-1831), who performed the first successful open heart surgery. There was Dr. Charles Drew (1904-1950) developer of blood plasma, evolving from the process of separating and preserving blood, he set up the first blood bank in England.

This was the time of Ernest Just (1883-1941), a famed biologist and renowned in the field of egg fertilization, relating to the structure of the living cell. He wrote sixty dissertations relating to this field receiving also the "Magna Cum Laude" and the Phi Beta Kappa honors. There was Theodore Lawless (1892-L) who achieved fame for valuable contributions to scientific treatment of syphilis and leprosy. The winner of many awards, he continues practicing in Chicago's Provident Hospital of Dr. Daniel Hale Williams' fame. There was Dr. William Hinton (1883-1959); he was a medical scientist leading world authorities on venereal disease. He developed the Hinton Test and later collaborated with Dr. Davies and now the test bears both names. Dr. George Washington Carver (1864-1943) developed various products from the peanut and soybean (three hundred by-products). He also laid the foundation for the whole plastic industry. This was a time in which Percy Julian, chemist (1898-L) was born and created derivative drugs for sufferers of arthritis. In 1935, Dr. Julian successfully synthesized the drug physotigimine, which is used today in the treatment of glaucoma. There was Benjamin Banneker (1731-1806). He was an inventor of the first striking clock in America (1761). He was a mathematician and astrologer; he could predict solar eclipses. He published an almanac in scientific form, and also helped to lay out the blueprint for the city of Washington, DC. There are hundreds of others.

THE BUFFALO SOLDIERS

After the Civil War, in the reorganization for peacetime duty, the authorized strength of the U. S. Army was reduced to 54,641 men and officers. By an act of Congress on July 28, 1866, provisions were made to accommodate a number of Black soldiers who served in the force. As a result, the Ninth and Tenth Calvary Regiments and the Twenty-fourth and Twenty-fifth Infantry Regiment were created.

The calvary regiments, later called the "Buffalo Soldiers," were assigned to patrol the vast expanse of the Southwest frontier, and the infantry regiments were posted to guard duty at various locations in the same area. The Southwest frontier comprised the Great Plains—the eastern part of Montana, Wyoming, Colorado and New Mexico, the western parts of the Dakotas, Nebraska, Kansas, Oklahoma and Texas. Much of the area consisted of brush jungle, rough and broken terrain, waterless desert and temperatures ranging from 100 degrees in the summer to below freezing in the winter.

Peopling the area, for the most part, were warring Indians, Mexican revolutionaries, bandits, murderous gunmen, cattle thieves, bootleggers, petty and scheming politicians and land-hungry homesteaders. Besides campaigning against the Indians, the Black soldiers often had to intervene when the scope of the civil broils grew beyond control of local and state authorities. Many frontier officials and pioneers owed their lives and well-being to the undaunted support of these soldiers.

Typical of the violent civil strifes were the occurrences in El Paso, Texas, where a group of politicians had been able to gain a monopoly of salt deposits and levy mining taxes; and, in Lincoln Nebraska, where two factions of businessmen fought to control the town and its resources. Also confronting the Black soldiers was the extensive job of clearing Oklahoma, New Mexico, Nevada and Arkansas of invading and unauthorized homesteaders, who were often belligerent.

Ten years of the Buffalo soldiers span of duty were required to subdue the wild-riding nomads of the Arapahos, Comanches, Kiowas, Kiowa-Apaches and Southern Cheyennes and to contain them secured in their reservations. It took another five years to calm the Kickapoos and Lipans, the Mexican bandits and outlaws. Five years more were required before the Apaches, in their mountain abodes were conquered. There were also the Utes and the Sioux, who could be quieted only by force.

In protecting life and property, the Black cavalrymen demonstrated the toughness and tenacity of the buffalo, an animal sacred to the Indian. A further resemblance to the buffalo was found in their short, tightly curled hair. Respect for these similarities led the Indians to dub them "Buffalo Soldiers." The title was proudly accepted by the regiments, and the buffalo was made the most prominent feature of their regimental crest.

Some of the victories won by the Buffalo Soldiers against revengeful elements of Indians were harder to win than others: the Red River War in West Texas, from the spring of 1874 to the spring of 1875; the various campaigns against the Apaches, particularly against Victorio from August 1879 to October 1880, and against Geronimo, from May 1885 to September 1886. Each of these warriors had escaped captivity with a number of his followers and each was able to elude recapture on American soil, even though losing battle after battle to the Buffalo Soldiers. Victorio and Geronimo were finally driven into Mexico, where the calvarymen could not go.

Victorio had been forced into Mexico twice before, and had the Mexican troops cooperated to an extent, the struggle would have ended. However, it was not until Victorio was driven into Mexico the third time, beaten badly and lacking the will to fight, that he was killed by Mexican troops in a quick battle on October 14, 1880.

At the close of the campaign, General John Pope made the following remarks with reference to the Ninth Cavalry; "Everything that men could do, they did, and it is little to say that their services in the field were marked by unusual hardships and difficulties." Their duties were performed with zeal and intelligence and they are worthy of all consideration." Also, General E.O.C. Ord made the following remarks with reference to the Tenth Calvary; "I trust that the services of the troops engaged will meet with that recognition that such earnest and zealous efforts in the line of duty deserves. They are entitled to more than commendation."

After Geronimo escaped from capture on March 29, 1886, he killed and butchered indiscriminately, while being relentlessly trailed. After he crossed the border into Mexico, troops and scouts of the Fourth Calvary tried, for months, to apprehend him without success. Geronimo was seemingly invincible, but found it impossible to find a safe retreat. Accordingly, he let it be known that terms of surrender would be considered. A special emissary contacted him, and on September 6, 1886, he formally surrendered and was given over to the Buffalo Soldiers, who escorted him to Fort Sill in Oklahoma.

PAFO thinks it's not prudent to laud these soldiers who were aiding the United States in ousting our Indian brother from his own land. It reminds us of when Europeans and Arabs were invading Africa. Yet, in other aspects of their greatness, the Buffalo Soldier did a herculean job. There were many tests one had to pass to become a Buffalo Soldier; one being that you had to shoot at a target fifty feet away, hitting the bull's-eye while riding backward on a horse at full speed. If you didn't make this shot, you couldn't be a Buffalo Soldier.

DO YOU KNOW THESE BLACK MEN AND THEIR INVENTIONS?

From the beginning of the captivity of Africans in the United States, they were denied rudimentary education. Laws were passed early making it a crime to teach Africans to read and write or to learn to read and write. In 1870, more than 80% of African Americans were illiterate, and even in 1910, more than one-third over 10 years of age had still never been to school. It is against this background of systematic, brutally enforced educational deprivation that the achievements of the African American inventor stand out as a brilliant testament to the African's innate creativity.

In addition to educational deprivation, the African American inventor was confronted with numerous legal and social obstacles. In the pre-Civil War era inventions of the African captive (so-called slave) were expropriated by their captors (so-called master), so there is no way of determining the actual number of African captives' inventions. In the following pages only five Africans who were free were permitted to have patents issued in their own names: Henry Blair, inventor of the corn planter and the cotton planter; James Forten, inventor of a device for controlling ships' sails; Norbert Rillieux, inventor of the sugar refiner which revolutionized the whole sugar industry; Lewis Temple, inventor of the toggle harpoon and James Hawkins, the gridiron. It was evidently thought that allowing such dignity to be accorded to Africans could upset the mind control practiced against all Africans in America. In the post-Civil War era, inventions of African Americans faced social obstacles. The inventor of the electric, automatic traffic signal, Garret A. Morgan, also invented the inhalator, later known as the gas mask. Orders for it poured in from all over America until his racial identity became known. The orders were summarily canceled. And this was in 1915. It was necessary for Morgan to employ the services of a white man to demonstrate his invention. His gas mask was utilized to save lives of Allied armed forces in World War I.

There have been thousands of inventions of African Americans utilized by people all over the world which have not been identified as their having been the inventors. But even if one considers only the verifiable ones, the total still runs into the thousands. They range from simple household conveniences to more complex mechanical devices such as the electric railway system invented by Granville T. Woods.

Some are as familiar as the potato chip of Hyram S. Thomas, a Saratoga chef; the ice cream of Augustus Jackson, a Philadelphia confectioner known as "the man who invented ice cream" (1832) and the player pianos of J. H. and S. L. Dickinson. The engines of Elijah McCoy brought into the language the expression "the real Mcoy". Nor should one forget that most of these achievements were often made in the face of overwhelming odds, and frequently greeted with hostility and derision.

The following pages have just a few of these inventions and their patent numbers, concentrated in the period up to 1902. We thank the editors of Afro USA, Bellwether Publishing Co., Inc. Edward Robinson, Pauline Pitts and Harriette C. Robinson.

INVENTOR	INVENTION	DATE	PATENT
Abrams, W. B.	Hame Attachment	Apr. 14, 1891	450,550
Allen, C.W.	Self-Leveling Table	Nov. 1, 1898	613,436
Allen, J.B.	Clothes Line Support	Dec. 10, 1895	551,105
Ashbourne, A.P.	Process for Preparing Coconut for Domestic Use	June 1, 1875	163,962
Ashbourne, A.P.	Biscuit Cutter	Nov. 30, 1875	170,460
Ashbourne, A.P.	Process of Treating Coconut	Aug. 21, 1877	194,287
Bailes, Wm.	Ladder Scaffold-Support	Aug. 5, 1879	218,154
Bailey, L.C.	Combined Truss and Bandage	Sep. 25, 1883	285,545
Bailey, L.C.	Folding Bed	July 18, 1899	629,286
Bailiff, C. O.	Shampoo Headrest	Oct. 11, 1898	612,008
Ballow, W.J.	Combined Hatrack and Table	Mar. 29, 1898	601,422
Barnes, G.A.E.	Design for Sign	Aug. 19, 1898	29,183
Beard, A. J.	Car Coupler	Nov. 23, 1897	594,059
Beard, A. J.	Rotary Engine	July 5, 1892	478,271
Becket, G.E.	Letter Box	Oct. 4, 1892	483,525
Bell, L.	Locomotive Smoke Stack	May 23, 1871	115.153
Bell, L.	Dough Kneader	Dec. 10, 1872	133,823
Benjamin, L.W.	Broom Moisteners and Bridles	May 16, 1893	497,747
Benjamin, M.E.	Gong and Signal Chairs for Hotels	July 17, 1888	386,286
Binga, M.W.	Street Sprinkling Apparatus	July 22, 1879	217,843
Blackburn, A. B.	Railway Signal	Jan. 10, 1888	376,362
Blackburn, A. B.	Spring Seat for Chairs	Apr. 3, 1888	380,420
Blackburn, A. B.	Cash Carrier	Oct. 23, 1888	391,577
Blair, Henry	Corn Planter	Oct. 14, 1834	—
Blair, Henry	Cotton Planter	Aug. 31, 1836	—
Blue, L.	Hand Corn Shelling Device	May 20, 1884	298,937
Booker, L. F.	Design Rubber Scraping Knife	Mar. 28, 1899	30,404
Boone, Sarah	Ironing Board	Apr. 26, 1892	473,653

Bowman, H. A.	Making Flags	Feb. 23, 1892	469,395
Brooks, C. B.	Punch	Oct. 31, 1893	507,672
Brooks, C. B.	Street Sweepers	Mar. 17, 1896	556,711
Brooks, C. B.	Street Sweepers	May 12, 1896	560,154
Brooks, Hallstead and Page	Street Sweepers	Apr. 21, 1896	558,719
Brown, Henry	Receptacle for Storing and Preserving Papers	Nov. 2, 1886	352,036
Brown, L. F.	Bridle Bit	Oct. 25, 1892	484,994
Brown, O. E.	Horseshoe	Aug. 23, 1892	481,271
Brown & Latimer	Water Closets for Railway Cars	Feb. 10, 1874	147,363
Burr, J. A.	Lawn Mower	May 9, 1899	624,749
Burr, W. F.	Switching Device for Railways	Oct. 31, 1899	636,197
Burwell, W.	Boot or Shoe	Nov. 28, 1899	638,143
Butler, R. A.	Train Alarm	June 15, 1897	584,540
Butts, J. W.	Luggage Carrier	Oct. 10, 1899	634,611
Byrd, T. J.	Improvement in Holders for Reins for Horses	Feb. 6, 1872	123,328
Byrd, T. J.	Apparatus for Detaching Horses from Carriages	Mar. 19, 1872	124,790
Byrd, T. J.	Improvement in Neck Yokes for Wagons	Apr. 30, 1872	126,181
Byrd, T. J.	Improvement in Car Couplings	Dec. 1, 1874	157,370
Campbell, W. S.	Self-Setting Animal Trap	Aug. 30, 1881	246,369
Cargill, B.F.	Invalid Cot	July 25, 1899	629,658
Carrington, T. A.	Range	July 25, 1876	180,323
Carter, W. C.	Umbrella Stand	Aug. 4, 1885	323,397
Certain, J. M.	Parcel Carrier for Bicycles	Dec. 26, 1899	639,708
Cherry, M. A.	Velocipede	May 8, 1888	382,351
Cherry, M. A.	Street Car Fender	Jan. 1, 1895	531,908
Church, T. S.	Carpet Beating Machne	July 29, 1884	302,237
Clare, O. B.	Trestle	Oct. 9, 1888	390,753
Coates, R.	Overboot for Horses	Apr. 19, 1892	473,295
Cook, G.	Automatic Fishing Device	May 30, 1899	625,829
Coolidge, J. S.	Harness Attachment	Nov. 13, 1888	392,908
Cooper, A. R.	Shoemaker's Jack	Aug. 22, 1899	631,519
Cooper, J.	Shutter and Fastening	May 1, 1883	276,563
Cooper, J.	Elevator Device	Apr. 2, 1895	536,605
Cooper, J.	Elevator Device	Sep. 21, 1897	590,157
Cornwell, P. W.	Draft Regulator	Oct. 2, 1888	390,284
Cornwell, P. W.	Draft Regulator	Feb. 7, 1893	491,082
Cralle, A. L.	Ice-Cream Mold	Feb. 2, 1897	576,395
Creamer, H.	Steam Feed Water Trap	Mar. 17, 1895	313,854
Creamer, H.	Steam Trap Feeder	Dec. 11, 1888	394,463

(Creamer also patented five steam traps between 1887 and 1893)

Cosgrove, W. F.	Automatic Stop Plug for Gas Oil Pipes	Mar. 17, 1885	313,993
Darkins, J. T.	Ventilation Aid	Feb. 19, 1895	534,322
Davis, I. D.	Tonic	Nov. 2, 1886	351,829
Davis, W. D.	Riding Saddles	Oct. 6, 1896	568,9
Davis, W. R., Jr.	Library Table	Sep. 24, 1878	208,378
Deitz, W. A.	Shoe	Apr. 30, 1867	64,205

Name	Invention	Date	Patent No.
Dickinson, J. H.	Pianola	(Detroit, Mich.) 1899	
Dorsey, O.	Door-Holding Device	Dec. 10, 1878	210,764
Dorticus, C. J.	Device for Applying Coloring Liquids to Sides of Soles of Heels of Shoes	Mar. 19, 1895	535,820
Dorticus, C. J.	Machine for Embossing Photo	Apr. 16, 1895	537,442
Dorticus, C. J.	Photographic Print Wash	Apr. 23, 1895	537,968
Dorticus, C. J.	Hose Leak Stop	July 18, 1899	629,315
Downing, P. B.	Electric Switch ofr Railroad	June 17, 1890	430,118
Downing, P. B.	Letter Box	Oct. 27, 1891	462,093
Downing, P. B.	Street Letter Box	Oct. 27, 1891	462,096
Dunnington, J. H.	Horse Detachers	Mar. 16, 1897	578,979
Edmonds, T. H.	Separating Screens	July 20, 1897	586,724
Elkins, T.	Dining, Ironing Table and Quilting Frame Combined	Feb. 22, 1870	100,020
Elkins, T.	Chamber Commode	Jan. 9, 1872	122,518
Elkins, T.	Refrigerating Apparatus	Nov. 4, 1879	221,222
Evans, J. H.	Convertible Settees	Oct. 5, 1897	591,095
Faulkner, H.	Ventilated Shoe	Apr. 29, 1890	426,495
Ferrell, F. J.	Steam Trap	Feb. 11, 1890	420,993
Ferrell, F. J.	Apparatus for Melting Snow	May 27, 1890	428,670
(Ferrell also patented eight valves between 1890 and 1893)			
Fisher, D. A.	Joiners' Clamp	Apr. 20, 1875	162,281
Fisher, D. A.	Furniture Castor	Mar. 14, 1876	174,794
Fleming, R. F., Jr.	Guitar	Mar. 3, 1886	338,727
Forten, J.	Sail Control (b. 1766-abolitionist) Mass. Newspaper 1850		
Goode. Sarah E.	Folding Cabinet Bed	July 14, 1885	322,177
Grant, G. F.	Golf Tee	Dec. 12, 1899	638,920
Grant, W. S.	Curtain Rod Support	Aug. 4, 1896	565,075
Gray, R. H.	Baling Press	Aug. 28, 1894	525,203
Gray, R. H.	Cistern Cleaners	Apr. 9, 1895	537,151
Gregory, J.	Motor	Apr. 26, 1887	361,937
Grenon, H.	Razor Stropping Device	Feb. 18, 1896	554,867
Griffin, F. W.	Pool table Attachment	June 13, 1899	626,902
Gunn, S. W.	Boot or Shoe	Jan. 16, 1900	641,642
Haines, J. H.	Portable Basin	Sep. 28, 1897	590,833
Hammonds, J. F.	Apparatus for Holding Yarn Skeins	Dec. 15, 1896	572,985
Harding, F. H.	Extension Banquet Table	Nov. 22, 1898	614,468
Hawkins, J.	Gridiron	Mar. 26, 1845	3
Hawkins, R.	Harness Attachment	Oct. 4, 1887	370,943
Headen, M.	Foot power Hammer	Oct. 5, 1886	350,363
Hearness, R.	Sealing Attachment for Bottles	Feb. 15, 1898	598,929
Hearness, R.	Detachable Car Fender	July 4, 1899	628,003
Hilyer, A. F.	Water Evaporator Attachment for Hot Air Registers	Aug. 26, 1890	435,095
Hilyer, A. F.	Registers	Oct. 14, 1890	438,159
Holmes, E. H.	Gage	Nov. 12, 1895	549.513
Hunter, J. H.	Portable Weighing Scales	Nov. 3, 1896	570,553
Hyde, R. N.	Composition for Cleaning and Preserving Carpets	Nov. 6, 1888	392,205
Jackson, B. F.	Heating Apparatus	Mar. 1, 1898	599,985

Jackson, B. F.	Matrix Drying Apparatus	May 10, 1898	603,879
Jackson, B. F.	Gas Burner	Apr. 4, 1899	622,482
Jackson, H. A.	Kitchen Table	Oct. 6, 1896	569,135
Jackson, W. H.	Railway Switch	Mar. 9, 1897	578,641
Jackson, W. H.	Railway Switch	Mar. 16, 1897	593,665
Jackson, W. H.	Automatic Locking Switch	Aug. 23, 1898	609,436
Johnson, D.	Rotary Dining Table	Jan. 15, 1888	396,089
Johnson, D.	Lawn Mower Attachment	Sep. 10, 1889	410,836
Johnson, D.	Grass Receivers for Lawn Mowers	June 10, 1890	429,629
Johnson, I. R.	Bicycle Frame	Oct. 10, 1899	634,823
Johnson, P.	Swinging Chairs	Nov. 15, 1881	249,530
Johnson, P.	Eye Protector	Nov. 2, 1880	234,039
Johnson, W.	Velocipede	June 20, 1899	627,335
Johnson, W. A.	Paint Vehicle	Dec. 4, 1888	393,763
Johnson, W. H.	Overcoming Dead Centers	Feb. 4, 1896	554,223
Johnson, W. H.	Overcoming Dead Centers	Oct. 11, 1898	612,345
Johnson, W.	Egg Beater	Feb. 5, 1884	292,821
Jones, F. M.	Ticket Dispensing Machine	June 27, 1939	2,163,754
Jones, F. M.	Air Conditioning Unit	July 12, 1949	2,475,841
Jones, F. M.	Method for Air Conditioning	Dec. 7, 1954	2,696,086
Jones, F. M.	Method for Preserving Perishables	Feb. 12, 1957	2,780,923
Jones, F. M.	Two-Cycle Gasoline Engine	Nov. 28, 1950	2,523,273
Jones, F. M.	Two-cycle Gas Engine	May 29, 1945	2,376,968
Jones, F. M.	Starter Generator	July 12, 1949	2,475,842
Jones, F. M.	Starter Generator for Cooling Gas Engines	July 12, 1949	2,475,843
Jones, F. M.	Two-Cycle Gas Engine		
Jones, F. M.	Means for Thermostatically Operating Gas Engines	July 26, 1949	2,477,377
Jones, F. M.	Rotary Compressor	Apr. 18, 1950	2,504,841
Jones, F. M.	System for Controlling Operation of Refrigeration Units	May 23, 1950	2,509,099
Jones, F. M.	Apparatus for Heating or Cooling Atmosphere Within an Enclosure	Oct. 24, 1950	2,526,874
Jones, F. M.	Prefabricated Refrigerator Construction	Dec. 26, 1950	2,535,682
Jones, F. M.	Refrigeration Control Device	Jan. 8, 1952	2,581,956
Jones, F. M.	Methods and Means of Defrosting a Cold Diffuser	Jan. 19 1954	2,666,298
Jones, F. M.	Control Device for Internal Combustion Engine	Sep. 2, 1958	2,850,001
Jones, F. M.	Thermostat and Termperature Control System	Feb. 23, 1960	2,926,005
Jones, F. M.	Removable Cooling Units for Compartments		2,336,735
Jones, F. M.	Means for Automatically Stopping & Starting Gas Engines ("J. A. Numero et al")	Dec. 21, 1943	2,337,164
Jones, F. M.	Design for Air Conditioning Unit	July 4, 1950	2,159,209
Jones, F. M.	Design for Air Conditioning Unit	Apr. 28, 1942	2,132,182

Name	Invention	Date	Patent No.
Jones & Long	Caps for Bottles	Sep. 13, 1898	610,715
Joyce, J. A.	Ore Bucket	Apr. 26, 1898	603,143
Latimer and Brown	Water Closets for Railway Cars	Feb. 10, 1874	147,363
Latimer, L. H.	Manufacturing Carbons	June 17, 1882	252,386
Latimer, L. H.	Apparatus for Cooling and Disinfecting	Jan. 12, 1886	334,078
Latimer, L. H.	Locking Racks for Coats, Hats, and Umbrellas	Mar. 24, 1896	557,076
Latimer & Nichols	Electric Lamp	Sep. 13, 1881	247,097
Latimer & Tregoning	Globe Support for Electric Lamps	Mar. 21, 1882	255,212
Lavelette, W. A.	Printing Press	Sep. 17, 1878	208,208
Lee, H.	Animal Trap	Feb. 12, 1867	61,941
Lee, J.	Kneading Machine	Aug. 7, 1894	524,042
Lee, J.	Bread Crumbing Machine	June 4, 1895	540,553
Leslie, F. W.	Envelope Seal	Sep. 21, 1897	590,325
Lewis, A. L.	Window Cleaner	Sep. 27, 1892	483,359
Lewis, E. R.	Spring Gun	May 3, 1887	362,096
Linden, H.	Piano Truck	Sep. 8, 1891	459,365
Little, E.	Bridle-Bit	Mar. 7, 1882	254,666
Loudin, F. J.	Sash Fastener	Dec. 12, 1892	510,432
Loudin, F. J.	Key Fastener	Jan. 9, 1894	512,308
Love, J. L.	Plassterers' Hawk	July 9, 1895	542,419
Love, J. L.	Pencil Sharpener	Nov. 23, 1897	594,114
Marshall, T. J.	Fire Extinguisher	May 26, 1872	125,063
Marshall, W.	Grain Binder	May 11, 1886	341,599
Martin, W. A.	Lock	July 23, 1889	407,738
Martin, W. A.	Lock	Dec. 30, 1890	443,945
Matzeliger, J. E.	Mechanism for Distributing Tacks	Nov. 26, 1899	414,726
Matzeliger, J. E.	Nailing Machine	Feb. 25, 1896	421,954
Matzeliger, J. E.	Tack Separating Mechanism	Mar. 25, 1890	423,937
Matzeliger, J. E.	Lasting Machine	Sep. 22, 1891	429,899
McCoy, E. J.	Lubricator	May 27, 1873	139,407
McCoy, E. J.	Lubricator	Mar. 28, 1882	255,443
McCoy, E. J.	Lubricator	July 18, 1882	261,166
McCoy, E. J.	Lubricator	June 16, 1885	320,379
McCoy, E. J.	Lubricator	Feb. 8, 1887	357,491
McCoy, E. J.	Lubricator	May 29, 1888	383,745
McCoy, E. J.	Lubricator	May 29, 1888	383,746
McCoy, E. J.	Lubricator	Dec. 24, 1889	418,139
McCoy, E. J.	Lubricator	Dec. 29, 1891	465,875
McCoy, E. J.	Lubricator	Apr. 5, 1892	472,066
McCoy, E. J.	Lubricator	Sep. 13, 1898	610,634
McCoy, E. J.	Lubricator	Oct. 4, 1898	611,759
McCoy, E. J.	Oil Cup	Nov. 15, 1898	614,307
McCoy, E. J.	Lubricator	June 27, 1899	627,623
McCoy, E. J.	Lubricator for Steam Engines	July 2, 1872	129,843
McCoy, E. J.	Lubricator for Steam Engines	Aug. 6, 1872	130,305
McCoy, E. J.	Steam Lubricator	Jan. 20, 1874	146,697
McCoy, E. J.	Ironing Table	May 12, 1874	150,876
McCoy, E. J.	Steam Cylinder Lubricator	Feb. 1, 1876	173,032

Name	Invention	Date	Patent No.
McCoy, E. J.	Steam Cylinder Lubricator	July 4, 1876	179,585
McCoy, E. J.	Lawn Sprinkler Design	Sep. 26, 1899	631,549
McCoy, E. J.	Steam Dome	June 16, 1885	320,354
McCoy, E. J.	Lubricator Attachment	Apr. 19, 1887	361,435
McCoy, E. J.	Lubricator for Safety Valves	May 24, 1887	363,529
McCoy, E. J.	Drip Cup	Sep. 29, 1891	460,215
McCoy & Hodges	Lubricator	Dec. 24, 1889	418,139
McCree, D.	Portable Fire Escape	Nov. 11, 1890	440,322
Mendenhall, A.	Holder for Driving Reins	Nov. 28, 1899	637,811
Miles, A.	Elevator	Oct. 11, 1887	371,207
Mitchell, C. L.	Phoneterisin	Jan. 1, 1884	291,071
Mitchell, J. M.	Cheek Row Corn Planter	Jan. 16, 1900	641,462
Moody, W. U.	Game Board Design	May 11, 1897	27,046
Morehead, K.	Reel Carrier	Oct. 6, 1896	568,916
Murray, G. W.	Combined Furrow Opener and Stalk Knocker	Apr. 10, 1894	517,906
Murray, G. W.	Cultivator and Marker	April 10, 1894	517,961
Murray, G. W.	Planter	June 5, 1894	520,887
Murray, G. W.	Cotton Chopper	June 5, 1894	520,888
Murray, G. W.	Fertilizer Distributor	June 5, 1894	520,889
Murray, G. W.	Planter	June 5, 1894	520,890
Murray, G. W.	Combined Cotton Seed	June 5, 1894	520,891
Murray, G. W.	Planter and Fertilizer Distributor Reaper	June 5, 1894	520,892
Murray, W.	Attachment for bicycles	Jan. 27, 2892	445,452
Nance, L.	Game Apparatus	Dec. 1, 1891	464,035
Nash, H. H.	Life Preserving Stool	Oct. 5, 1875	168,519
Newman, L. D.	Brush	Nov. 15, 1898	614,335
Newson, S.	Oil Heater or Cooker	May 22, 1894	520,188
Nichols & Latimer	Electric Lamp	Sep. 13, 1881	247,097
Nickerson, W. J.	Mandolin and Guitar Attachment for Pianos	June 27, 1899	627,7
O'Connor & Turner	Alarm for Boilers	Aug. 25, 1896	566,612
O'Connor & Turner	Steam Gage	Aug. 25, 1896	566,613
O'Connor & Turner	Alarm for Coasts Containing Vessels	Feb. 8, 1898	598,572
Outlaw, J. W.	Horseshoes	Nov. 15, 1898	614,273
Perryman, F. R.	Caterers' Tray Table	Feb. 2, 1892	468,038
Peterson, H.	Attachment for Lawn Mowers	Apr. 30, 1889	402,189
Phelps, W. H.	Apparatus for Washing Vehicles	Mar. 23, 1897	579,242
Pickering, J. F.	Air Ship	Feb. 20, 1900	643,975
Pickett, H.	Scaffold	June 30, 1874	152,511
Pinn, T. B.	File Holder	Aug. 17, 1880	231,355
Polk, A. J.	Bicycle Support	Apr. 14, 1896	558,103
Pugsley, A.	Blind Stop	July 29, 1890	433,306
Purdy & Peters	Design for Spoons	Apr. 23, 1895	24,228
Purdy & Sadgwar	Folding Chair	June 11, 1889	405,117
Purdy, W.	Device for Sharpening Edged Tools	Oct. 27, 1896	570,337
Purdy, W.	Device for Sharpening Edged Tools	Aug. 16, 1898	609,367

Name	Invention	Date	Patent No.
Purdy, W.	Device for Sharpening Edged Tools	Aug. 1, 1899	630,106
Purvis, W. B.	Bag Fastener	Apr. 25, 1882	256,856
Purvis, W. B.	Hand Stamp	Feb. 27, 1883	273,149
Purvis, W. B.	Fountain Pen	Jan. 7, 1890	419,065
Purvis, W. B.	Electric Railway	May 1, 1894	519,291
Purvis, W. B.	Magnetic Car Balancing Device	May 21, 1895	539,542
Purvis, W. B.	Electric Railway Switch	Aug. 17, 1897	588,176

(Purvis also patented ten paper bag machines between 1884 and 1894)

Name	Invention	Date	Patent No.
Queen, W.	Guard for Companion Ways and Hatches	Aug. 18, 1891	458,131
Ray, E. P.	Chair Supporting Device	Feb. 21, 1899	620,078
Ray, L. P.	Dust Pan	Aug. 3, 1897	587,607
Reed, J. W.	Dough Kneader and Roller	Sep. 23, 1884	305,474
Reynolds, H. H.	Window Ventilator for Railroad Cars	Apr. 3, 1883	275,271
Reynolds, H. H.	Safety Gate for Bridges	Oct. 7, 1890	437,937
Reynolds, R. R.	Non-Refillable Bottle	May 2, 1899	624,092
Rhodes, J. B.	Water Closets	Dec. 19, 1899	639,290
Richardson, A. C.	Hame Fastener	Mar. 14, 1882	255,022
Richardson, A. C.	Churn	Feb. 17, 1891	446,470
Richardson, A. C.	Casket Lowering Device	Nov. 13, 1894	529,311
Richardson, A. C.	Insect Destroyer	Feb. 28, 1899	620,362
Richardson, A. C.	Bottle	Dec. 12, 1899	638,811
Richardson, W. H.	Cotton Chopper	June 1, 1886	343,140
Richardson, W. H.	Child's Carriage	June 18, 1889	405,599
Richardson, W. H.	Child's Carriage	June 18, 1889	405,600
Richey, C. V.	Car Coupling	June 15, 1897	584,650
Richey, C. V.	Railroad Switch	Aug. 3, 1897	587,657
Richey, C. V.	Railroad Switch	Oct. 26, 1897	592,448
Richey, C. V.	Fire Escape Bracket	Dec. 28, 1897	596,427
Richey, C. V.	Combined Hammock and Stretcher	Dec. 13, 1898	615,907
Rickman, A. L.	Overshoe	Feb. 8, 1898	598,816
Ricks, J.	Horseshoe	Mar. 30, 1886	338,781
Ricks, J.	Overshoe for Horses	June 6, 1899	626,245
Rillieux, N.	Sugar Refiner (Evaporating Pan)	Dec. 10, 1846	4,879
Robinson, E. R.	Casting Composite	Nov. 23, 1897	594,286
Robinson, E. R.	Electric Railway Trolley	Sep. 19, 1893	505,370
Robinson, J. H.	Life Saving Guards for Locomotives	Mar. 14, 1899	621,143
Robinson, J. H.	Life Saving Guards for Street Cars	Apr. 25, 1899	623,929
Robinson, J.	Dinner Pail	Feb. 1, 1887	356,852
Romaine, A.	Passenger Register	Apr. 23, 1889	402,035
Ross, A. L.	Runner for Stops	Aug. 4, 1896	565,301
Ross, A. L.	Bag Closure	June 7, 1898	605,343
Ross, A. L.	Trousers Support	Nov. 28, 1899	638,068
Ross, J.	Bailing Press	Sep. 5, 1899	632,539
Roster, D. N.	Feather Curler	Mar. 10, 1896	555,166
Ruffin, S.	Vessels for Liquids and Manner of Sealing	Nov. 20, 1899	737,603

Russell, L. A.	Guard Attachment for Beds	Aug. 13, 1895	544,381
Sampson, G. T.	Sled Propeller	Feb. 17, 1885	312,388
Sampson, G. T.	Clothes Drier	June 7, 1892	476,416
Scottron, S. R.	Adjustable Window Cornice	Feb. 17, 1880	224,732
Scottron, S. R.	Pole Tip	Sep. 31, 1886	349,525
Scottron, S. R.	Curtain Rod	Aug. 30, 1892	481,720
Scottron, S. R.	Supporting Bracket	Sep. 12, 1893	505,008
Shanks, S. C.	Sleeping Car Berth Register	July 21, 1897	587,165
Shewcraft, F.	Letter Box	Detroit, Michigan	
Shorter, D. W.	Feed Rack	May 17, 1887	363,089
Smith, J. W.	Improvement in Games	Apr. 17, 1900	647,887
Smith, J. W.	Lawn Sprinkler	May 4, 1897	581,785
Smith, J. W.	Lawn Sprinkler	Mar. 22, 1898	601,065
Smith, P. D.	Potato Digger	Jan. 21, 1891	445,206
Smith, P. D.	Grain Binder	Feb. 23, 1892	469,279
Snow & Johns	Linament	Oct. 7, 1890	437,728
Spears, H.	Portable Shield for Infantry	Dec. 27, 1870	110,599
Spikes, R. B.	Combination Milk Bottle Opener and Bottle Cover	June 29, 1926	1,590,557
Spikes, R. B.	Method and Apparatus for Obtaining Average Samples and Temperature of Tank Liquids	Oct. 27, 1931	1,828,753
Spikes, R. B.	Automatic Gear Shift	Dec. 6, 1932	1,888,814
Spikes, R. B.	Transmission and Shifting Thereof	Nov. 28, 1933	1,936,996
Spikes, R. B.	Self-Locking Rack for Billiard Cues	around 1910	not found
Spkes, R. B.	Automatic Shoe Shine Chair	around 1939	not found
Spikes, R. B.	Multiple Barrel Machine Gun	around 1940	not found

(Some patents are not included here because of current litigation; or because they were so basic in nature that redesigning and refiling procedures are now in process)

Standard, J.	Oil Stove	Oct. 29, 1889	413,689
Standard, J.	Refrigerator	July 14, 1891	455,891
Steward & Johnson	Metal Bending Machine	Dec. 27, 1887	375,512
Stewart, E. W.	Punching Machine	May 3, 1887	362,190
Steward, E. W.	Machine for Forming Vehicle Seat Bars	Mar. 22, 1887	373,698
Stewart, T. W.	Mop	June 13, 1893	499,402
Stewart, T. W.	Station Indicator	June 29, 1893	499,895
Sutton, E. H.	Cotton Cultivator	Apr. 7, 1874	149,543
Sweeting, J. A.	Device for Rolling Cigarettes	Nov. 30, 1897	594,501
Sweeting, J. A.	Combined Knife and Scoop	June 7, 1898	605,209
Taylor, B. H.	Rotary Engine	Apr. 23, 1878	202,888
Taylor, B. H.	Slide Valve	July 6, 1897	585,798
Temple, L.	Toggle Harpoon		

Prior to Civil War—See Katz,"Eyewitness to Black History"

Thomas, S. E.	Waste Trap	Oct. 16, 1883	286,746
Thomas, S. E.	Waste Trap for Basins, Closets, Etc.	Oct. 4, 1887	371,107
Thomas, S. E.	Casting	July 31, 1888	386,941
Thomas, S. E.	Pipe Connection	Oct. 9, 1888	390,821

Toliver, G.	Propeller for Vessels	Apr. 28, 1891	451,086
Tregoning & Latimer	Globe Supporter for Electric Lamps	Mar. 21, 1882	255,212
Walker, P.	Machine for Cleaning Seed Cotton	Feb. 16, 1897	577,153
Walker, P.	Bait Holder	Mar. 8, 1898	600,241
Waller, J. N.	Shoemaker's Cabinet or Bench	Feb. 3, 1880	
Washington, W.	Corn Husking Machine	Aug. 14, 1883	283,173
Watkins, Isaac	Scrubbing Frame	Oct. 7, 1890	437,849
Watts, J. R.	Bracket for Miners' Lamp	Mar. 7, 1893	493,137
West, E. H.	Weather Shield	Sep. 5, 1899	632,385
West, J. W.	Wagon	Oct. 18, 1870	108.419
White, D. L.	Extension Steps for Cars	Jan. 12, 1897	574,969
White, J. T.	Lemon Squeezer	Dec. 8, 1896	572,849
Williams, C.	Canopy Frame	Feb. 2, 1892	468,280
Williams, J. P.	Pillow Sham Holder	Oct. 10, 1899	634,784
Winn, Frank	Direct Acting Steam Engine	Dec. 4, 1888	394,047
Winters, J. R.	Fire Escape Ladder	May 7, 1878	203,517
Winters, J. R.	Fire Escape Ladder	Apr. 8, 1879	214,224
Woods, G. T.	Steam Boiler Furnace	June 3, 1884	299,894
Woods, G. T.	Telephone Transmitter	Dec. 2, 1884	308,876
Woods, G. T.	Apparatus for Transmission of Messages by Electricity	Apr. 7, 1885	315,368
Woods, G. T.	Relay Instrument	June 7, 1887	364,619
Woods, G. T.	Polarized Relay	July 5, 1887	366,192
Woods, G. T.	Electro Mechanical Brake	Aug. 16, 1887	368,265
Woods, G. T.	Telephone System and Apparatus	Oct. 11, 1887	371,241
Woods, G. T.	Electro Magnetic Brake Apparatus	Oct. 18, 1887	371,655
Woods, G. T.	Railway Telegraphy	Nov. 15, 1887	373,383
Woods, G. T.	Induction Telegraph System	Nov. 29, 1887	373,915
Woods, G. T.	Overhead Conducting System for Electric Railway	May 29, 1888	383,844
Woods, G. T.	Electro-Motive Railway System	June 26, 1888	385,034
Woods, G. T.	Runnel Contruction for Electric Railway	July 17, 1888	386,282
Woods, G. T.	Galvanic Battery	Aug. 14, 1888	387,839
Woods, G. T.	Railway Telegraphy	Aug. 28, 1888	388,803
Woods, G. T.	Automatic Safety Cut-out for Electric Circuits	Jan. 1, 1889	395,533
Woods, G. T.	Electric Railway System	Nov. 10, 1891	463,020
Woods, G. T.	Electric Railway Conduit	Nov. 21, 1893	509,065
Woods, G. T.	System of Electrical Distribution	Oct. 13, 1896	569,443
Woods, G. T.	Amusement Apparatus	Dec. 19, 1899	639,692
Woods, G. T.	Electric Railway	Jan. 29, 1901	667,110
Woods, G. T.	Electric Railway System	July 9, 1901	678,086
Woods, G. T.	Regulating and Controlling Electrical Translating Devices	Sep. 3, 1901	681,768
Woods, G. T.	Electric Railway	Nov. 19, 1901	687,098
G. T. Woods	Automatic Air Brake	June 10, 1902	701,981
G. T. Woods	Electric Railway System	Jan. 13, 1903	718,183

G. T. Woods	Electric Railway	May 26, 1903	729,481
Wormley, J.	Life Saving Apparatus	May 24, 1881	242,091

LIST OF A FEW SIGNIFICANT INVENTIONS

Air Conditioner—F. M. Jones
Automatic Air Brakes—G. T. Woods
Automatic Gear Shift for Cars—R. B. Spikes
Electric Railway System—G.T. Woods
Electric Railway—W. B. Purvis
Electric Railway Trolley—E. R. Robinson
Engines—E. J. McCoy; E. J. Murray; F. M. Jones; F. M. Jones
Fountain Pen—W. B.Purvis
Railway Inventions—W. H. Jackson; P.B. Downing; L. Bell; A. B. Blackburn; Brown & Latimer; T. J. Byrd; Latimer and Brown; G. T. Woods; W. B. Purvis; C.V. Richey; H. H. Reynolds.
Refrigeration Within an Enclosure to Preserve Perishables (Trains, Trucks)—F. M. Jones
Sugar Refiner (Evaporating Pan)—Norbert Rillieux
Telephone inventions—G. T. Woods

WHAT MANNER OF PEOPLE ARE AFRICAN AMERICANS?

What manner of people are African Americans? Despised, lynched, beaten in body and spirit for nearly four centuries yet gave to the world only creations which enhanced man's quality of life. Look at the list of 382 inventions above—just a few of the thousands. Look at J. H. Robinson's life saving guards for locomotives, at J. Wormley's life saving apparatus, at Nash's life preserving stool, and at J. H. Robinson's life saving guards for street cars, at J. B. Winters' fire escape ladder— of Dr. Charles Drew's marvelous creation of separating out the blood plasma to save millions of lives all over the world—all for the purpose of enhancing life—not its destruction. The field of psychology has proven that man's creativity springs from nurturing but is crushed by hatred. Suppose African Americans had been allowed to learn to read and write for the two centuries that we were stopped by law—had been accorded a small measure of human rights, had been loved instead of lynched. I have no doubt we would have found the cure for cancer and the answer to aids.

The character of our creations reflect the nobility of our nature. The above inventions speak loudly of the correctness of the thesis that melanin is the innate key to the beauty of spirit—Alkebulan—the land of the spirit people.

In the spirit of our illustrious fathers and mothers,

Calvin Robinson, Redman Battle, Harriette Robinson, Elaine Richardson and Edward Robinson

BIBLIOGRAPHY
American Council of Learned Societies. *A Guide to Documents in the National Archives for Negro Studies.* D.C.'47
Begeman, Myron L. *Manufacturing Processes.* New York: Wiley, 1952
Bennett, Jr., Lerone. *Before the Mayflower.* Johnson, 1962
Cross, Theodore L. *Black Capitalism.* New York: Atheneum, 1969
Herkimer, Herbert. *The Engineer's Illustrated Thesaurus.* New York: Chem.Pub.Co. 1952
Ploski and Brown. *The Negro Almanac.* New York: Bellwether, 1967
The United States Patent Office

This limited list of inventions reflects the pure genius of our fathers, in spite of the laws of this period punishing any one who would teach them to read or write.

Compiled in the spirit of our fathers, duplicated for the kidnapped cultural giants of the Songhai Empire...The Black men and women of the Americas. African intellectuality not only laid the foundation for what became known as civilization, but was responsible for civilization's continuing journey.

We have given you only a small accounting of the great contributions Africans made. So many of our contributions were stolen by the greediness of others and there was no recognition afforded us Africans.

The medical genius of Africans, at home and in the United States, certainly put America on center stage in the field of not only medical science, but also in modern technology in almost all fields. Ivan Van Sertima, in his *Blacks in Science*, details to a great extent these modern achievements by Africans. To mention a few, there is Frederick D. Gregory, who redesigned the cockpit of the space shuttle; Isaac Gillam IV, who was responsible for integrating the efforts of a thousand space personnel to help get the space shuttle off the ground; Patricia Carving, whose job is to prepare the astronaut to cope with psychophysiological and "biological problems," Robert Shurney; Dr. Lloyd Quarterman, a nuclear scientist; Elmer Imes, a physicist; Jesse E. Russell, Sr.; Robert

Shurney; and, Courtland Robinson.

African Americans and Africans have been and still are greatly involved in world of technical advancement. Let us remind you that Black geniuses, even though greatly held back by racism, still have figured most prominently in scientific development in the United States of America and the world.

ARCHIE ALEXANDER, 1888-1958

Archie Alexander, a design and construction engineer, left his stamp on the landscape of America by building bridges, freeways, airfields, railroad trestles and powerplants.

Born in Iowa, Alexander attended the State University and received an engineering degree in 1912. After several years as a design engineer, he and a former classmate established their own engineering firm and constructed major projects across the Nation. Starting at home, they built the heating plant and powerhouse at the University of Iowa, a sewage treatment plant in Grand Rapids, Michigan, an airfield in Tuskegee, Alabama, and the Tidal Basin bridge and seawall and the Whitehurst Freeway in Washington, D.C.

Alexander received many awards during the course of his career. At the centennial celebration of the University of Iowa in 1947, he was named one of its outstanding alumni. In 1954, President Eisenhower honored him with the appointment as Territorial Governor of the Virgin Islands.

OTIS BOYKIN, 1920-

Otis Boykin, who began his career as a laboratory assistant testing automatic controls for airplanes, has invented a wide range of electronic devices. One of his first achievements was a type of resistor now used in many computers, radios, television sets, and other electronically controlled devices. In addition, Boykin has developed a control unit for artificial heart stimulators, a variable resistor used in guided missiles, small components such as thick film resistors for computers, a burglar-proof cash register, and chemical air filter.

His innovations have had both military and commercial application. Some have reduced the cost of producing electronic controls for radio and television. At present, more than three dozen products with Boykin components are used throughout the world.

ERNEST COLEMAN, 1942-

Ernest Coleman has directed high energy physics at three Federal agencies—the Atomic Energy Commission, the Energy Research and Development Administration, and the Department of Energy.

Coleman, a Phi Beta Kappa student at the University of Michigan, received his B.S., M.S., and Ph.D. degrees there. After graduation he was awarded a year's fellowship in high energy physics by the German Government and studied in Hamburg. Upon his return to the United States, Coleman taught at the University of Minnesota, first as Assistant Professor of Physics and then as Associate Professor.

During a year as visiting Professor at Stanford University he became director of the summer science program for gifted disadvantaged college students. He has continued to head this program and has brought highly motivated and able students into the field of physics.

For his contributions to physics education, particularly for disadvantaged students, and for his contributions to physics research and its applications in education, Coleman received the Distinguished Service Award of the American Association of Physics Teachers.

DONALD COTTON, 1939-

Donald Cotton, the technical lead for nuclear chemistry research and development at the Department of Energy, plans, manages, and evaluates research and development on reactor materials and chemistry carried out in DOE national laboratories. He identifies the breeder reactor needs of less-developed nations an assignment which has taken him to several European states.

Dr. Cotton first worked as a physical chemist at the Naval Propellant Plant at Indian Head, Maryland. From there he moved to the Marine Engineering Laboratory in Annapolis where he worked on the combustion of hydrocarbon fuels and invented a microwave absorption technique for measuring solid propellant burning rates. Later he researched liquid state chemistry and liquid gas propellants.

His career extended beyond the laboratory. For two years Cotton was science editor for Libratterian Books, presenting scientific and technical subjects to lay readers.

Cotton's degrees in physical chemistry include an M.S. from Yale University and a Ph.D. from Howard. He has lectured at universities in Africa and South America, has patents to his credit, and has written many scientific papers.

DAVID CROSTHWAIT, 1891-1976

For his outstanding contributions to engineering technology, David Crosthwait was awarded an honorary doctoral degree in 1975 from Purdue University, the same school that had awarded him a B.S. in mechanical engineering sixty-two years earlier. In the years between, he had received thirty-four U.S. patents and eighty foreign patents relating to the design, installation, testing, and servicing of power plants and heating and ventilating systems.

Crosthwait worked for the Dunham Company of Chicago during much of his career and headed its research laboratory in Marshalltown, Iowa. Later he served as technical advisor to the company.

An authority on heat transfer, ventilation, and air conditioning, Crosthwait invented several new systems. He developed the control systems and the variable vacuum system of heating for major buildings including Rockefeller Center in New York City. His writings included a manual on heating and cooling with water and guides, standards and codes dealing with heating ventilation, refrigeration, and air conditioning.

After retiring from industry in 1969, Crosthwait continued to share his knowledge by teaching a course on steam heating theory and controls at Purdue.

ANNIE EASLEY, 1932-

Annie Easley is among the growing group of women who are making major contributions to energy research and management. Working at the National Aeronautics and Space Administration's Lewis Research Center in Cleveland, Ohio, Easley develops and implements computer codes used in solar, wind, and other energy projects. Her energy assignments have included studies to determine the life of storage batteries (such as those used in electronic vehicles) and to identify energy conversion systems that offer the greatest improvement over commercially available technology.

A native of Birmingham, Alabama, Easley has worked for NASA and its predecessor agency since 1955. She continued her education while working and, in 1977, obtained a degree in mathematics from Cleveland State University. Over the years she attended many courses in her specialization offered by NASA.

CLARENCE L. ELDER, 1935-

Head of his own research and development firm in Baltimore, Clarence Elder was awarded a patent in 1976 for a monitoring and control energy conservation system. His "Occustat" is designed to reduce energy waste in temporarily vacant homes and other buildings, and may be especially valuable for motels and hotels. The system consists of connecting each energy unit to an electronic beam attached to the building entrance to monitor incoming and outgoing occupants. When the house or apartment is empty of people, the beam sets the Occustat system into motion, reducing energy demand and achieving energy savings up to thirty percent.

Elder and his associates also have developed other systems and devices for which they have received twelve United States and foreign patents, trademarks and copyrights.

Born in Georgia, and graduated from Morgan State College, Elder was awarded a plaque at the New York International Patent Exposition in 1969 for "Outstanding Achievement in the Field of Electronics."

MEREDITH GOURDINE, 1929-

Meredith Gourdine is best known for his pioneering work in electro-gasdynamics, a way of producing high-voltage electricity from natural gas. His research has the potential to improve refrigeration for preserving foods, supply power for heat and light in homes, burn coal more efficiently, and desalt sea water.

Head of his own research and development company in New Jersey, Gourdine and is associates have developed a variety of devices: an exhaust-purifying system for cars; equipment for reducing incinerator smoke pollution from older apartment houses; a technique for dispersing fog from airport runways; and a system for production-line coating of metal products, which reduces production costs and the amount of pollutants released to the atmosphere.

Formerly chief scientist with the Curtiss-Wright Corporation, Gourdine served on the Presidential Advisory Panel on Energy in 1964. A man of many talents, he also won a silver medal in track in the 1952 Olympics.

JAMES HARRIS, 1932-

Nuclear chemist James Harris was a member of the scientific team at Lawrence Berkeley Laboratory that discovered two new elements just a few years ago. Harris joined the laboratory, which is operated for the Department of Energy by the University of California, in 1960, after years of research at Tracerlab, Inc. At Berkeley he sought to complete the periodic table of chemical elements.

In the course of several years the laboratory produced a number of new elements by bombarding special targets in an accelerator. The research team purified and purified and prepared the target material and, after hundreds of hours of bombarding the target with carbon, detected element 104 for a few seconds in 1969. Element 105 was produced in 1970 when the same target was bombarded with nitrogen. Element 104 was named Rutherfordium, and 105, Hahnium, in honor of two atomic pioneers.

Unlike most of his colleagues, Harris did not have a Ph.D. degree. The Texas native had a B.S. from Houston-Tillotson College in Austin and had taken graduate courses in chemistry and physics. However, his alma mater conferred him an honorary doctorate upon him in 1973, largely because of his work as a co-discoverer of elements 104 and 105.

KATHERINE JOHNSON, 1918-

Katherine Johnson is an Aerospace Technologist at the National Aeronautics and Space Administration's Langley Research Center, Hampton, Virginia. Trained as a mathematician and physicist in colleges of her native West Virginia, she has worked on absorbing problems of interplanetary trajectories, space navigation, and the orbits of spacecraft. These spacecraft included the Earth Resources Satellite which has helped locate underground minerals and other essential earth resources.

Johnson analyzed data gathered by tracking stations around the world during the lunar orbital missions—the moon shots. Later, she studied new navigation procedures to determine more practical ways to track manned and unmanned space missions. For her pioneer work this field, she was a recipient of the Group Achievement Award presented to NASA's Lunar Spacecraft and Operations team.

FREDERICK M. JONES, 1892-1961

Frederick M. Jones held more than sixty patents in a variety of fields, but refrigeration was his specialization. In 1935, he invented the first automatic refrigeration system for long-haul trucks. Later, the system was adapted to a variety of other carriers, including ships and railway cars. His invention eliminated the problem of food spoilage and changed America's eating habits. In addition, Jones developed an air-conditioning unit for military field hospitals, a portable x-ray machine, and a refrigerator for military field kitchens.

Born in Ohio, Jones served in France during World War I. After the war, he worked as a garage mechanic and, from the knowledge gained in this early experience, developed a self—starting gasoline motor. In the late 1920's, Jones designed a series of devices for the growing movie industry, adapting silent movie projectors to accommodate talking films, and developing the box-office equipment that delivers tickets and spills out change.

CALDWELL McCOY, 1933

As a program manager for the National Magnetic Fusion Energy Computer Network, Caldwell McCoy directs the Nation's largest network devoted to a single scientific problem—that of achieving usable energy from magnetic fusion. The Department of Energy network serves over eight hundred users of experimental data across the country.

A native of Hartford, McCoy earned an electrical engineering degree at the University of Connecticut and then received both Master and Doctor of Science degrees, the latter in telecommunications, from George Washington University.

From 1959 to 1976, McCoy designed, tested, and evaluated systems for detecting and tracking submarines. For his achievements in developing long-range anti-submarine systems at the Naval Research Laboratory in Washington, D.C., he was awarded the Laboratory's Thomas Edison Fellowship in 1968. Since 1976 he has been part of the magnetic fusion energy program, first with the Energy Research and Development Adminstration and then its successor agency, the Department of Energy.

GARRETT A. MORGAN, 1877-1963

Kentucky-born Garrett Morgan received wide recognition for his outstanding contributions to public safety. Firemen in many cities in the early 1900's wore the safety helmet and gas mask that he invented, and for which he was awarded a gold medal at the Second International Exposition of Safety and Sanitation in New York in 1914. Two years later, he himself used the mask to rescue men trapped by a gas explosion in a tunnel being constructed under Lake Erie. Following the disaster which took twenty-one lives, the City of Cleveland honored him with a gold medal for his heroic efforts.

In 1923, Morgan received a patent for his new concept—a traffic signal to regulate vehicle movement in city areas. "Stop" and "Go" signs were systematically raised and lowered at intersections to bring order out of chaos and improve traffic safety. Some years later, after he had sold his design to the General Electric Company, Morgan's device was replaced with the light signal in use today.

CORDELL REED, 1938-

Cordell Reed, Assistant Vice President of the Commonwealth Edison Company of Chicago, is in charge of nuclear licensing and environmental activities.

Reed has been with the company since 1960, starting as an engineer assigned to the design, construction and operation of coal-fired generating stations. In 1967, he transferred to the nuclear division, with the task of developing more efficient and productive powerplants. In 1975, Reed was appointed manager of the nuclear engineering department, where he headed a group of seventy-five engineers who were responsible for the engineering design of all nuclear projects. In this period, Commonwealth became the Nation's leading nuclear utility; currently the company has seven nuclear powerplants in operation capable of producing more than 5,400,000 kilowatts of electricity, and is constructing additional units with a capacity of 6,600,000 kilowatts.

A native of Chicago, Reed holds a masters degree in engineering from the University of Illinois.

NORBERT RILLIEUX, 1806-1894

Norbert Rillieux revolutionized the sugar industry by inventing a refining process that reduced the time, cost, and safety risk involved in producing good sugar from cane and beets.

The son of a French planter/engineer and a slave mother, Rillieux was born in New Orleans and educated in France, where he majored in engineering and also served as an instructor.

Returning to New Orleans, he noted that methods for refining sugar from beets were crude, backbreaking and dangerous, requiring slaves to ladle boiling cane juice from one kettle to another to produce a dark sugar. Rillieux designed an evaporating pan which enclosed a series of condensing coils in vacuum chambers. His system took much of the hand labor out of refining, saved fuel because the juice boiled at lower temperatures, and produced a superior product.

Rillieux's device was patented in 1846, and was in great demand on plantations in Louisiana, Mexico and the West Indies, where it increased sugar production and reduced operating costs.

LOUIS W. ROBERTS, 1913-

Louis W. Roberts, a physicist, mathematician and electronics specialist, is Director of Energy and Environment at the Transportation System Center in Cambridge, Mass. The center, part of the United States Department of Transportation, develops energy conservation practices for the transportation industry. Currently, the industry uses about half of this country's total petroleum demand, but is required by the Energy Conservation Policy Act to reduce fuel use in all vehicles.

Roberts' productive career has included an assignment as chief of the Optics and Microwave Laboratory in the Electronics Research Center of the National Aeronautics and Space Administration. Earlier, he founded, and was president of, his own microwave concern. In addition to his industrial and government research experience, Roberts has served as a professor of physics at Howard University and professor of math and physics at St. Augustine's College.

Educated at Fisk University and the University of Michigan, Roberts holds eleven patents, all in electronic devices, and has written many papers on electromagnetism, optics and microwaves.

RUFUS STOKES, 1924-

Rufus Stokes' concern for cleaner air for all Americans caused him to focus his research on developing air filtration equipment. Born in Alabama, Stokes later moved to Illinois where he worked as a machinist for an incinerator company. In 1968, he was granted a patent on an air-purification device to reduce to a safe level the gases and ash from furnace and powerplant smoke; the filtered smoke also became nearly invisible.

Stokes has tested and demonstrated several models of his "clean air machine" in Chicago and elsewhere to show that it may be used in many ways. His system is intended, not only to help people with respiratory problems, but to benefit plants and animals as well; a side effect of the filtered air the improvement in the appearance and durability of objects such as cars and buildings that are usually exposed to outdoor pollution for lengthy periods.

VIRGIL G. TRICE, JR., 1926-

Virgil Trice has spent almost thirty years in developing nuclear energy and now is primarily concerned with managing the radioactive waste that results from nuclear power generation.

He has been working in the waste management field since 1971 when he joined the Atomic Energy Commission. In 1975 the AEC was abolished and he transferred to the Energy Research and Development Administration and then to the Department of Energy when it was established in 1977. He is responsible for radioactive waste management planning, reporting, and program control—an area important to the future of nuclear power.

From 1949 to 1971 Trice worked at the Argonne National Laboratory on research and development, economic evaluation, and program planning of concepts for nuclear fuel reprocessing and power reactors.

Born in Indianapolis, Trice attended Purdue University where he received B.S. and M.S. degrees in chemical engineering. He also received an M.S. in industrial engineering from the Illinois Institute of Technology. His career includes teaching part time as Associate Professor of Chemical Engineering at Howard University.

LAWNIE TAYLOR

Physicist Lawnie Taylor, chief of market development and training in the Department of Energy's solar offices, plans and directs programs to accelerate the commercialization of newly developed solar technologies.

Before joining the Energy Research and Development Administration in 1975, Taylor operated his own building-system engineering firm in Los Angeles. Previously he held scientific research and management positions in Columbia University's Nuclear Laboratory, the Aerojet-General Corporation's nuclear rocket project, and the Xerox Corporation's space program. Taylor received a NASA award for his development of an Apollo experiment.

Taylor received his B.S. and M.A. degrees in physics from Columbia University and has completed academic requirements for the Ph.D. in physics at the University of Southern California.

Among his many civic activities Taylor has been a newspaper publisher and the founder of several recognized organizations concerned with housing, education, and economic development in the low-income community. Taylor has also authored many publications on science and technology, education, and equal opportunity.

J. ERNEST WILKINS, JR., 1923-

Mathematician, physicist and engineer, J. Ernest Wilkins, Jr., has contributed his talents mainly to the research and development of nuclear power.

As a teenager, Wilkins attracted nationwide attention when he received his college degree at age seventeen and his doctorate from the University of Chicago at nineteen. He taught mathematics and did research at the University's Metallurgical Laboratory which has working on the atomic bomb. Later, he became part owner of a company which designed and developed nuclear reactors for power generation.

His primary achievement has been the development of shields against gamma rays from the sun and nuclear sources. He developed mathematical models by which the amount of gamma rays absorbed by a given material may be calculated; this technique is in wide use among researchers in space and nuclear projects.

Wilkins served for several years as Distinguished Professor of Applied Mathematical Physics at Howard University. A member of the National Academy of Engineering, he was formerly president of the American Nuclear Society.

O.S. (OZZIE) WILLIAMS, 1921-

O.S. (Ozzie) Williams was the first Black aeronautical engineer to be hire by Republic Aviation, Inc., during World War II. Subsequently, he joined Greer Hydraulics, Inc., where he became a group project engineer and helped develop the first airborne radar beacon for locating crashed aircraft. A specialist in small rocket engine design, Williams also was associated with the Reaction Motors Division of Thiokol Chemical Corporation.

In 1961, he joined Grumman International, where he was in charge of developing and producing the control rocket systems that guided lunar modules during moon landings. This responsibility included administering nearly forty million dollars in subcontracts. Williams now is vice president of the firm, in charge of trade and industrial relations with emerging African nations; here his work includes the application of solar and wind energy to African needs.

INFORMATION ON BLACKS IN SCIENCE

(AFRICAN BLACKS)
IMHOTEP

He was an unmixed African Egyptian. He lived during the third dynasty of the Pharoah Zoser. He was a scientist, architect and medical genius. Imhotep means "he who cometh in peace."

EUCLID

He too, was an unmixed African and was born in Egypt. He was known for his thirteen books and sixty-five propositions of geometry. Thus, his teaching dominated the field of mathematics for two thousand years. It became known as "Euclid's Elements." The Greeks tried to claim him for their own.

SURGEONS AND MEDICAL DOCTORS

Surgery, such as for the removal of cataracts of the eyes, also the transplanting of limbs was of common practice in the Songhai Empire of Western Africa.

Leo Africanus, a noted historyian of the Emperor, wrote that in 1573, there were stories of doctors involved in the art of healing. This knowledge of medicine made Africa the healing center of the world. It was in Africa where immunization against bacterial diseases began.

AN OVERVIEW OF ACCOMPLISHMENTS BY SOME AFRICAN AMERICAN SCIENTISTS

Dr. Charles Drew, 1904-1950

He was the developer of blood plasma. A method evolved from the process of separating and preserving blood. He set up the first blood bank in England.

Dr. Christine Darden

Christine Darden is an Aerospace Engineer in the high speed Aerodynamics division of NASA's Langley Research Center at Hampton, Virginia. Before coming to Langley, in 1967, she was a mathematics instructor at Virginia State College (which is a "Black University") and did aerosol physics research. She received her Masters of Science degree in mathematics at the same University, and is now doing her doctorate in the Department of Mechanical Engineering in the School of Engineering and Applied Sciences at George Washington University. A capsulized rendition of what she is working on is as follows:

She is the leading NASA researcher in supersonic and hypersonic aircraft with expertise in the area of reducing sonic boom and to eventually alleviate that factor.

Dr. George Carruthers

Born in Cincinatti, Ohio (October 1, 1939), he demonstrated great discipline at an early age. HIs knowledge of physics andmathematics did not come easy. Added to his insatiable desire to learn more about the physical structure of other planets, was Carruthers interest in the physical construction of mechanism to be used in outer space. One of his most important inventions in the NASA program is a camera used on the various space missions to send pictures of other planets back to earth. A forerunner of this marvelous camera was an image converter for detecting electromatic Radiation especially in Short Wave Lengths. He was just twenty-three years of age then.

A MESSAGE TO THE BLACK JEWS OF AMERICA

PAFO says to our brothers of the Black Hebrews, also known as Israelites/Jews... 'We Love You."

We love you not just because some of us in PAFO were on that same road many years ago, but because you are good people.

Back in the 1930's, the Honorable Elijah Muhammad and our Dr. J.S. Croom, along with Prophet F.S. Cherry were with the great honorable Marcus M. Garvey. They were known as Garveyites, then. Only F.S. Cherry and Dr. Croom stayed on the main stem of the Garvey movement. They established, through the Bible, a so-called nationality of the Blacks, or as we were called then, the "Negro." That national identity was called the Black Jews by those two men. We, in PAFO, came under the teaching of Dr. Croom. He lectured on the street corners of Philadelphia, Pennsylvania; Baltimore, Maryland; New York, New York; Newark, New Jersey; Detroit, Michigan; Chicago, Illinois; and other cities. Brothers Calvin Robinson and Redman Battle had wanted to promulgate the Songhai history, but we had too much opposition from all quarters at that time. Since our main goal was unity of all Black people, we went along with the "Israelite Doctrine." Our main doctrine was Black race first and that is why we got along with all other Black religious groups—Moslems, all denominations of Christians and of course, Black Jews.

After Brothers Robinson and Battle finally decided to introduce the Songhai history, we were told that the Songhai Empire people were responsible for the Black Jews being sold into "bondage" in Africa.

From a sentimental point of view, having once considered ourselves Black Jews, we were quick to check that story out. Prior to 1960, we had never seen anything in our study of the three main empires in West Africa. For the last thirty years, our search had intensified, and we have not found even the slightest evidence that the indigenous Africans, of any of those empires had sold Black Hebrews or any other group.

We believe that there probably were some errors in the historical assessments of West African history. Those who think that the Songhai people pointed the Black Jews out to the slave traders are in error. Arabs engaged in the so-called slave trade. Whites viewed Arabs as

Black and spread the lie we sold each other into captivity.

In Songhai, there was a great protection for those of any religious belief under the African constitutional democratic system. Check back in the text of The Journey of the Songhai People, Session IV, "Origin of African Democracy." Also, in Session V, that same system gave redress in court systems; higher and supreme court; and freedom of the press and assembly. After all, from where do you think Europeans got the whole idea of this high form of civilization?

When the invasion of Songhai came in 1591, the following information must be taken into consideration.

Constant incursions by the Arabs, Israelis, and Persians produced children; so-called nationalities, who looked like indigenous Africans, but their loyalty was with the rapist father. T.A. Osae, S.M. Nwabara and Ato Oduwsi, in their book, Short History of West Africa, state that it was fanatical Arabs and other Moslems that really did the selling to the Europeans.

They joined in the destruction and slaughter of Songhai, including so-called African Israelites and marched us all to the waiting ships. Ship records show that on those ships were the Songhai People, Ghanaians, Yoruba, Ibo, Nupe, Benine, Borgu, Jukun, Kanem, Borni, and many, many more. They all came to North America and South America. Those in the United States who adopted the so-called Judean religion, that heard us on the street, are of that stock of Songhai people who were kidnapped and brought here. Question: Of what African nation are you?

In PAFO's research, on Black Jews in Africa, besides the Falesha Jeudi, is this: It was in Egypt where the doctrine of not eating pork, rites of passage for children, the belief in a circumcision, the hereafter, etc., was initiated. As a matter of fact, there is much similarity between various aspects of the Egyptian so-called mystery system and Judaism; just remember Akhenaton. As Africa continued to be invaded, the invaders proselyted among the Africans and that's how some Africans became Jews or Hebrews (Haribu). This is the same way Africans began to finally accept Islam and Christianity. Before these incursions had such a drastic effect on us, various African nations (tribes) such as the Ashantes, Ghanaian, Dahou and Mandingo practiced the indigenous traditional African religions.

In summation, PAFO urges that we, as a total Black race should study the history of the indigenous Black people of Africa (Alkebu-lan). Africa is where Black people originated, no other place. Research has shown that melanin in abundance (over the whole body) excluding soles of the feet and palms of the hands is and was only produced in Africa.

MATTHEW ALEXANDER HENSON
Co-discoverer of the North Pole with
Admiral Robert Edwin Perry—April 6, 1909
Born: August 8, 1866 Died March 9, 1955
Son of Maryland • An inspiration to young people
The first man to reach the top of the world

Matthew A. Henson was born August 8, 1866 on a former slave farm in Nanjemoy, Charles County, Maryland.

At eleven years of age, he walked away from home one night, to Washington, D. C.

He worked during the day in a cheap cook shop, and slept at nights in the kitchen on the floor behind a stove.

After two years, Mr. Henson walked to Baltimore, where he secured a job as cabin boy on a ship sailing for China. He was taught to read and write. He was also taught mathematics and principles of navigation by the skipper, Captain Childs.

He returned to Washington where he secured a job in a hat store. He later met Lieutenant Robert E. Perry, who hired Mr. Henson as his valet on an expedition to Nicaragua.

Later, Perry hired Henson to accompany him on his expeditions in search of the North Pole. Mr. Henson proved, writes Perry, to be the best hunter, sled builder, cook, companion and only member to learn the Eskimo language. Also, he saved Perry's life twice.

Mr. Henson was selected by Perry to lead the last dash to the North Pole, arriving forty-five minutes ahead of Perry (April 6, 1909).

Initiated and sponsored by Dr. Herbert M. Frisby, himself an Arctic explorer, Henson received the following recognitions:

Citation by United States Department of Defense —
April 6, 1949.

Commendation from President Eisenhower at White House —
April 6, 1954.

Erection of Henson Memorial Tablet by State of Maryland in State House, Annapolis, Maryland — November 18, 1961.

Naming of Matthew A. Henson elementary School, Baltimore, Maryland — April 6, 1962.

Memorial flight to North Pole, August 12, 1956 by Dr. Herbert Frisby at which he dropped a memorial tablet honoring Henson.

The Herbert M. Frisby Historical Society is working to have Mr. Henson's remains transferred from an unmarked grave in New York City to the United States National Cemetery, Arlington, interred as close as possible to those of Perry's.

DR. HERBERT M. FRISBY
Arctic Explorer, Researcher, Lecturer
Sponsor—Matthew A. Henson Memorial Projects
Alaska, Canada, Labrador, Greenland, Spitsbergen (European), Siberia (Russian) Arctic Expeditions
Second African American to go to the North Pole
(August 12, 1956)

Dr. Herbert M. Frisby was born and reared in a slum section of Baltimore, Maryland.

He worked his way through high school by selling peanuts in alleys and on streets, after school hours.

Dr. Frisby worked his way through Howard, Columbia, New York Universities and other graduate schools, playing in jazz orchestras on weekends and during summer vacations.

"I'm going to be the second Negro to go to the North Pole," Frisby cried out loudly one day in classroom when a white teacher told his disorderly class of the discovery of the North Pole, and that Matthew Henson, an African-American, was a member of the Perry party. For this intrusion, he was detained after school and made to write five hundred times as punishment—"I must not say foolish things in class."

Some forty years later, after many attempts, he was flown on a special mission in a United States of America Air Force plane to drop a memorial on the North Pole in honor of Matthew Henson (August 12, 1956), thereby realizing his boyhood dream and becoming the second Negro to go to the North Pole.

Dr. Frisby completed twenty-four missions throughout the world's Arctic and Polar regions, including Alaska, Canada, Labrador, Greenland, Spitsbergen and Siberia. His life reads like a novel.

As chairman of the Matthew A. Henson Memorial Projects, he initiated and sponsored numerous projects focusing attention upon and honoring Henson.

During World War II, he volunteered and served as the United States

War Correspondent in the Arctic and Polar theaters of operation.

He taught high school biology for many years.

Dr. Frisby maintained in his home (The Igloo), an unusual display of Eskimo artifacts—pelts, slides, sculptures, carvings, recordings, pictures, etc.

Dr. Frisby was born March 16, 1886. He died July 26, 1983.

(Written with the permission of Russell Frisby and family.)

PONDERING THE CREATION STORY

The Bible states in Genesis, that before the earth there was nothing but void. Bible scholars and so-called authorities say that six thousand years ago the heavens and the earth were created. Let's take a close look at it.

Biblical Scripture Chronology	Historical Secular Documentation
4500 BC and beyond there was supposed to be nothing but void.	4,500 BC and beyond the Sphinx was already standing. About 11,000 BC Meroe arose. In 37,000 BC communities developed on the Jos Plateau (in West Africa).
Six thousand years ago, the earth and the heavens and man were created, says the Bible.	6,200 years ago, Egyptian civilization developed and began the first 365 day solar calendar.
3,900 BC, Biblical account. The story of Cain who killed his brother Abel was sentenced to the land of Nod where he knew his wife.	Before 3,900 BC agricultural communities first appeared in Jericho and near the delta of the Nile River. There were plenty of people living before 3,900 BC.
2,000 BC, Biblical Account of the flood. "All flesh perished," says the Bible.	Yet, Egyptian history records that in 2,000 BC, the Pharaoh Amenemhet III was establishing merchant colonies in Phoenicia.
2,100 BC, the building of the Tower of Babel. Allegedly, only one language was on the earth after the flood.	2,100 BC. There were over a thousand different languages in Alkebu-lan alone. Not counting India, Asia and Europe. Most of these languages existed before 2,100 BC and still do today.

MA'AT THE PERSONIFICATION OF THE ANCIENT AFRICAN MIND

As what is generally conceived about the various religions, Maat doesn't fall in any of those categories. Maat is not only a conglomeration of mysteries (in part) that goes back before Egypt; but its principles are based on the balance of unchanging laws that governs the universe.

We have also been asked about other religions as being the African religion. In our book, we try to avoid religious dogmas because it's too personal; especially if one does not have an open mind. Our reason for mentioning Maat is because it truly belongs to the Africans. It is truly an African-Centered (Afro-Centric) concept.

Even in this treatise, we are not going to argue about who or what is right or wrong. It's an individual thing. All we are going to do is point out what our early African forebearers promulgated what became known as Maat.

Dr. C. Tsehloane Keto, in his book, The Africa Centered Perspective of History, on page 27 states the following, "Ma'at is the essence of a social justice as practiced by the Ancient Africans of the Nile."

A few of the mysteries as taught in the so-called mystery system, spawned the concept of the soul or spirit of man. In essence, it said that the soul if liberated from the body could transform from its lower self to its higher self, and become godlike. As Dr. Keto said that ancient Africans had set up a code of ethics that even Pharaohs had to obey. Maat was in every facet of mainstream African life.

It was symbolized in the make-believe story of Isis, Osiris and Horus. Osiris was killed and was cut up and his parts were scattered about. Isis searched for the pieces and sewed him back together, because she had so much love for him. However, one part was not found. This part was later found and became the sixth vowel in the much later Hebrew language. This Kemitic mythological story became the basis for a certain religion today.

In the ancient African social strata, all Africans were more or less considered lawyers. The African law was not just rules and regulations for social and political intercourse, but knowledge of the immutable laws of the universe. It included the doctrine of the knowledge of the human body and its dependence for quality of life when these laws were adhered to. This also includes the observance of laws of nature and of nature's God to protect the earth, the waterways, the air and the ozone. Life, as we know it, could be erased if we insist on continuing to upset this delicate balance. Now let us take a quick look at another side of the myths that were created by non-African writers of history.

When the Western (European) writers of history rewrote African history, they conjured up a diabolical plan to erase us from the annals of the history of mankind. The plan was as follows:

CLASSIFICATION AND TERMINOLOGY

In the place where there were towns, they placed elephants, and in the place where the indigenous Africans were and are, they, by terminology placed Semitic, Hamites, Caucasians, Bantus, Negroes, Hottentots, Bushmen and a host of their other creations to satisfy their religious bigotry and racist hypothesis. This is part of the reflection as shown in PAFO's Session I of The Journey of The Songhai People that was about the great switch in 382 A.D.

The undergirding factor to replace the Black God Concept with the white God Concept had a two-pronged main purpose. First, to not only get Blacks to begin the worship of white, but to forever demean the real religious beliefs of Black people.

The lack of knowledge about the ancient Egyptian beliefs, involving the seemingly worship of animals, as well as the Cosmic Gods, cause Europeans to be confused, thus interpreting the wrong meaning of our religion. In fact, it is so deep in its meaning, but yet in reality so simple, that for those who are caught up in today's religious dogmas, believe it to be paganism; but in reality, it is not.

Coming down from ancient Egypt over the eons of time, varying degrees of the Egyptian religious concepts filtered throughout Africa. It manifested itself in most African societies, and it became their religious philosophy. Almost all Africans have a deep reverence for the Wind, the Earth, for Water, for Fire and some type of animal. Africans are very good conservationist. They do not kill animals for fun, nor do they abuse the earth. Also, today, they would be called ecologists.

Judaism also got its "One God Concept" from Akhenaton, the great Pharaoh of Egypt. The abstention from eating pork and other scavengers also came from Egypt. The Egyptian scientists found that creatures like the pig, crab, duck, etc. would do your body harm. This too was part of that Maat Concept. We will now make some observations from the days of the "Ancients" for a comparative study.

Much earlier, Africans that included Africa's female goddesses, along with Imhotep and other great Africans, were the first to promulgate the concept of the "Ancient African Life Forces Philosophy, Of All Peoples Oneness, And Their Unity With the Forces of the Natural World." Down into our time, which is about four thousand years later, a polygraph expert discovered that plants demonstrate an emotional response similar to that in humans. A polygraph or a lie detector, measures the change in people's breathing, blood pressure, pulse activity, and perspiration caused by emotional stimuli. The change in perspiration is known as galvanic skin response or psychogalvanic reflex (PGR). The results are revealed on the polygraph's strip chart by a pen that makes lines on paper according to the electrical activity of the subject. Baxter, the polygraph expert, attached the electrodes to the plants. A thought came into his mind to burn a leaf of one of the plants. The instant he conceived the thought, there was a dramatic change in the PGR tracing. He was several feet away, and had not even lighted the match, and yet the pen was dancing all over the strip chart. Believing that if he killed shrimps by having them dumped into scalding hot water on an automated random basis, that there would not be any response on the PGR chart. To make doubly sure, the killing of the shrimps would be in another room altogether. He found, that the instant the shrimps died, the PGR chart showed great agitation and movement. Out of this, evolved a hypothesis of an unsuspected life signal that might possibly connect all creation. There is a belief, that all life forms are connected through consciousness at the cellular level. This is a much higher level than any other forms of telepathy now known. Distance and steel rooms or vaults do not seem to be a barrier.

In the late 1900's, two European doctors reported that human's physical and emotional states change rhythmically. In 1920, another European doctor concluded that human intellectuality also undergoes rhythmic changes. These three cycles are said to have specific time limits. The physical cycle lasts twenty-three days, the emotional twenty-eight days, and the intellectual thirty-three days. All cycles begin at the same moment—your birth—and continue throughout life.

Appendixes
CHRONOBIOLOGY

Circannual. A yearly cycle, believed to be connected with animals and humans alike, growing extra hair for each winter.

Circamensual. The twenty-eight to thirty period associated with women.

Circadian. The cycle that functions on a twenty-four basis, relating to sleep, wakefulness, sickness. blood pressure and body temperature.

Ultradian. The cycle that lasts about ninety minutes, and recurs all day long whether you are asleep or awake. During each cycle, there are highs and lows—periods of daydreaming, good concentration, hunger and so on.

Ancient Africans had also concluded that all things are made of energy, not solid matter. This was centuries before white scientists had discovered finally, that a piece of steel was really nothing but tiny spinning bits of energy with spaces in between.

As we search back, we find that Man was not a creation by an artificer, but he is a growth by "Law." The wisdom of our Fathers and Mothers is coming down to us as we are beginning to understand some of these laws. For instance, a law of cause and effect says "he that seeketh findeth, he that knocketh, it shall be opened, for only by ceaseless importunity, does a person dare to enter the door of the temple of knowledge."

Our foreparents knew that the God Concept was not based on the principle of Being, but on the principle of principles. They summed it up with this narrative:

"ONENESS"

Maat is the oneness, that spans the fathomless deep of space, and the measureless eons of time, binding them together in act as we do in thought. Maat is the sameness, in the elemental substance of stars and planets of this our earthly abode and all that it holds. Maat is the rhythm of all things, the uniformity of all that moves, and the nature of their interaction. Maat is the mystery of life enkindling inert matter, with inner drive and purpose, 'til it turns to the radiant glow of feeling, and the blue* fire of thought. Maat is the faith, by which we overcome the fear of loneliness of helplessness, of failure and of death. Maat is the hope that like a shaft of light, cleaves the white abyss of sin, suffering and despair. Maat is the love which creates, protects and forgives. Maat is the spirit that broods upon the chaos men have wrought disturbing its static wrongs. Maat is the pain of growth, the seed of sorrow, the lure

*Blue represents the sacred color of the source of life. "Amen or or Ammon" also the "Ram."

of thought, and in all "laws" of fulfillment, *that bind men and stars together*.

The ancient Africans expressed their religious beliefs by defining the concept of Maat as a divine order established at the time of creation. This order is manifested in the normalcy of phenomena. In the African societies, it manifests itself as *justice,* and in an individual's life as *truth.* Maat is this order, the essence of existence, the concept of *harmony* with the divine order of the universe.

MAN'S DESTINY

As Perceval said in his book, *Thinking Destiny,* PAFO regards that as a truism since we have already stated, in *The Journey of the Songhai People,* that as a man is taught so are his thoughts and as a man thinketh, so he is. Therefore, man's thoughts create his destiny.

It is not too poetic to imagine that hidden somewhat in its history, its mathematical perfection its purpose for being, are men's long-sought answers to his own destiny. Surely, then, the Great Pyramid would be the philosopher's guide.

While the Great Pyramid was confounding experimentation and tantalizing its investigators to construct better technologies, it charitably offered up one of its many secrets - its shape alone conjured up known and unknown forms of energy affecting both animate and inanimate objects. No sooner had the discovery been made by M. Bovis that structures built to the exact ratio of the Great Pyramid and placed in the same manner on the north-south magnetic axis would mummify meat, preserve food, sharpen razor blades, etc., than a whole new set of questions was launched concerning the nature of unexplained energy fields - to say nothing of the fresh wonderment about the pyramid itself.

The effects on persons sitting, sleeping, meditating in pyramid structures have some implication to the fields of physiology, psychology, and metaphysics. Shortened healing time, relief from headaches, better relaxation, weight loss for overweight people, rejuvenation, etc., should say something to the medical profession. Results from meditating within the pyramid and heightened psychic sensitivity should interest the metaphysician and those interested in transcendental states. The effects on plant growth and seed germination should arouse the interest of the horticulturist. And food and water purification and preservation should claim the attention of every concerned person.

Life indeed, does move in mysterious circles, and experiences have a way of remembering itself. It may be that the historians have been right all along; that knowing the past is imperative to understanding the present and projecting the future. Perhaps the pyramid is a window to both the past and the future.

THE PYRAMID

PAFO thinks that it is befitting to afford its readers the classic account of the architectural wonderment of the building of the pyramid as related by Herodotus who was dubbed the father of Western history.

The Pyramid itself was twenty years in the building. It is a square, eight hundred feet each way,...built in utmost care. The stones of which it is composed are none of them less than thirty feet in length...after laying the stones for the base, they raised the remaining stones to their places by means of machines formed of short wooden plans...There is an inscription in Egyptian characters on the pyramid which records the quantity of radishes36, and I perfectly well remember that the interpreter who read the writing to me said that the money expended in this was about 1,600 talents of silver. So the modern equivalent of 1,600 talents would be the value of 89,000 pounds of silver.) If this then is a true record, what a vast sum must have been spent on the iron tools used in the work, and on the feeding and clothing of the laborers, considering the length of time the work lasted, which has already been stated, and the additional time - no small space, I imagine - which must have been occupied by the quarrying of the stones, their conveyance, and the formation of the underground apartments (The History of Herodotus, p. 125).

The French astronomer, Abbe Thomas Moreaux, Director of the observatory of Bourges, wrote a book entitled *The Mysterious Science of the Pharaohs*. In this work the Abbe argues that the Great Pyramid was used as a vault for the preservation of scientific instruments, and of standard weights and measures, rather than as a tomb. In place of a sarcophagus there is a granite slab, which evidently served as a standard of measure. The length of this slab is one ten millionth of the distance from the North Pole to the equator. This length is also called a meter (39.37 inches). This invariable distance, only recently determined by modern scientists, is the basis of the metric system. The distance from each of the poles to the center of earth is 3,949.79 miles. From this measurement we are enabled to calculate the circumference of the earth which is 24,859.82 miles through the poles. Abbe Moreaux is convinced that this fact was known to the Egyptian astronomers six thousand years ago. The Chaldeans were able students of astronomy, but their best estimate of the circumference of earth was twenty-four thousand miles.

It seems that the knowledge of mathematics and astronomy among the ancient Egyptians was considerably more extensive and exact than we had hitherto been led to suspect. The height of the Great Pyramid is one-billionth of the distance from Earth to the sun, a unit of measure not accurately established in modern times until 1874. Abbe Moreaux notes that this pyramid is oriented within one-twelfth of a degree, a remarkably accurate precision; and that the paralleled of longitude passing through the pyramid traverses the most land and the least sea of any in the world—a fact which also applies to the parallel of latitude passing through the structure. In the north side of the Great Pyramid is the entrance to an underground tunnel, which is bored through 350 feet of solid rock, at an angle of twenty-six degrees seventeen minutes to the horizon. Alpha Draconis, or Thuban, was the pole-star about 3440 B.C., and for several hundred years before and after that date. At its lower culmination, three degrees forty-two minutes from the pole, this star shone down the underground tunnel of the pyramid at the base-line level, and leads into the grand gallery. Both the ascending passage and the grand gallery are inclined to the horizon at an angle of twenty-six degrees seventeen minutes—the same as that of the underground tunnel, but in the opposite direction. These passages seem to have served two purposes; first, they enabled the builders to orient the base and the lower layers of the masonry up to the king's chamber in a true north and south line; and secondly, the passages were so arranged that the grand gallery could serve as the equivalent of the equatorial telescope of a modern astronomical observatory.

The English astronomer, Richard A. Proctor, in his *Problems of the Pyramids,* presents convincing evidence tending to show the Great Pyramid was used as an astronomical observatory. "The sun's annual course round the celestial sphere, says Proctor, could be determined much more exactly than by any observations made from the great gallery." The moon's monthly path and its changes could have been dealt within the same effective way. The geometric paths, and thence the true paths of the planets, could be determined very accurately. The place of any visible star along the Zodiac could be most accurately determined." (Cited by Samuel Laing, in *Human Origins,* p. 56). The triangular area of each of the four sides of the pyramid equals the square of the vertical base bear to the vertical height, a fact mentioned by Herodotus. The added lengths of the four sides of the square base bear to the vertical height the same proportion as that of the circumference of a circle to its radius. This involves the mathematical constant (3.1416), so important in modern mathematics. The length of each side of the square base is equal to 365_ sacred cubits, an equivalence of the length of the year in days. The two diagonals of the base contain 25,834 pyramid inches, a good approximation of the number of years in the processional cycle. Professor Piazzi Smyth made very careful measurements of the Great Pyramid; and his results were summarized by Dr. Alfred Russel Wallace in an address before the British Association for the Advancement of Science, at Glasgow in 1876, as follows:

1. That the pyramid is truly square, the sides become equal and the angles right angles.

2. That the four sockets on which the first four stones of the corners rested are truly on the same level.

3. That the directions of the sides are accurately to the four cardinal points.

4. That the vertical height of the pyramid bears the same proportion to its circumference at the base as the radius of a circle does to its circumference.

Now all these measures, angles, and levels are accurate, not as an ordinary surveyor or builder could make them, but to such a degree as requires the best modern instruments and all the refinements of geometrical science to discover any error at all. In addition to this, we have the wonderful perfection of the workmanship in the interior of the pyramid, the passages and chambers being lined with huge blocks of stone fitted with the utmost accuracy, while every part of the building exhibits the highest structural science.

An unusual feature connected with the orientation of the pyramid has been studied by Colonel Braghine, and we give it in his own words: A detailed study of the structure will convince any investigator that the wealth of mathematical, geometrical and astronomical data concealed within it is not accidental, but has been produced intentionally after numerous and complex calculations, made by somebody possessing an astounding amount of knowledge....Not the least interesting detail concerning the orientation of the pyramid is the following: the reflection of the sunrays from the sides of the pyramid indicates almost exactly the quinoxes and solstices and therefore, the sowing time. The northern side of the pyramid is lighted at sunrise for some moments during the period from the spring equinox till the autumn equinox. During the remainder of the year, the southern side is lighted from sunrise till sunset. This phenomenon fixes the moment of the equinoxes within twelve hours. When the stonefacing was intact, this phenomenon of the missing shadows must have been still more pronounced and was noticed by the ancients. The Latin poet Ausoniuss writes: "Quadrata cui in fastigio cono Surgit et ipsa suas consumit puranis umbras." ("The pyramid itself swallows the shadow born on its summit.") This phenomenon has now been explained by Professor Pocha, who discovered that the northern and southern sides of the pyramid are not true planes, but dihedral angles of 179 degrees 50 minutes. Thus in plain speaking, the sides in question have been hollowed out to the extent of 94 centimeters, insuring a rapid disappearance of the shadow of the sunrise at the equinoxes *(The Shadow of Atlantis,* pp. 237-38).

*The Numerology involved in the building of numerous temples, pyramids, colossal statues, dams, canals, stelae, measurements from Earth to other planets and stars, cosmology, astrology, various branches of science, medicine, philosophy, etc., along the entire length of the Blue Nile and White Nile Valleys, also the great lakes regions down to the tip of Monomotapa (Southern Alkebu-lan), formed much of the basic formulae and other calculations employed in the following data to be presented. Due mostly to the complexity of the mathematics of this ancient science created and developed by the indigenous Africans in the Lodges of The Osirica that maintained its major or prime seat of learning at Luxor (Later called Thebes). Luxor, the Holy of Holies that was originally part of Ta-Nehisi (Nubia or Zeti) before the Second Dynasty, is the same center of major learning mentioned here. It is impossible to make the calculations any clearer than they are shown in this very much condensed and simplified introduction to the Numerology of the Lunar, solar, Nile, Tropical, Siarcdis and so this calendar year system for calculating time-periods of the pre-Christian and Christian Era.

Now we enter into the mathematical calculations developed by the indigenous Africans of the Great Lakes and Nile Valleys many of which formed the basis of the works attributed to certain mythological Greeks, most of whom there are no records of their birth, life or death. The methods of integral calculus were used in estimating the volume of the pyramids. By 2200 B.C. Egypt had produced the first known mathe-

---

* See Session IV — "African Women's Contributions to Civilization."

matical treatise - the Abmose-Papyrus.

The Triangle of the Pyramid field - Man's earliest numerological and mathematical challenge began. This was the basis for Trigonometry and Mathematics long before Pythagoras and Euclid. The triangular field contains mathematical calculations that solved the area of the Tri-Leg or House of Amenta (Pyramid or House of Heaven). It was developed in the predynastic era, but the problem was solved in the fourth century B.C., during the ending of the Thirtieth Dynasty. The indigenous Africans of the Nile Valley who came from points farther South along the great lakes regions of Central Alkebu-lan, not only solved the triangle or pyramid field in such an early stage in man's beginning into the reaches of scientific intellect before the origin of Western Civilization (Greek society); they also squared the circle by using an equation of the geometrical equivalent of eight/ninths (8/9) of the lengths of the diameter and reached the constant number 3.16. It is almost the exact number adopted by the Greeks for the sixteenth letter of their alphabet pi or pe. It is a symbol that designates the ratio of the circumference of a circle to its diameter of 3.14159265. The Nile Valley Africans also solved the area of all of the objects they used in the building and development of their earliest high cultures. Their geometricians and triometricians had also begun to challenge much more complex mathematical and scientific problems. They all started from the most basic mathematical formulae of the masonfield numerology of the Osirica's Mysteries System.

These complex mathematical and scientific problems possibly were solved with fourth dimensional mathematics. This seemingly new mathematics is called Tetrahedral Dimensional Mathematics which involved electro-magnetic power. To understand man's destiny better, read page 393. These powers and energies are reputed to be the result of the particular shape of the pyramid. One point on that note is that its ground position is located exactly on the north/south magnetic axis. The Egyptian ankh is linked to that magnetism. Extensive research discloses that the Alkebu-lan/Kemitic people were the creators of that science. When finally the Europeans heard of the African science of electricity, suddenly Franklin, Hertz and Volta "discovered" some facts about electricity. The Egyptian ankh and the advent of melanin are the key elements in what is the inner sanctum of the so-called mystery system of the ankh science.

The Religious Symbols of Africa (inside the Pyramid)

1. **Swatzthika** (Swastika adopted by Adolph Hitler et al of the Nazis Party of Germany)—imposed upon the Sun-burst (Ra or Re) at the top of the Pyramid.

2. **The Ever-Seeing Eye of Horus** (adopted by the United States of America)— on the reverse side of the one-dollar bill.

3. **Tears** from the Eye of Horus.
4. **The Sephulcup** receiving Tears from the Eye of Horus (adopted by the Christians as the Chalice).

5. **The Ankh** (Key of Life, the original Cross, corrupted by the Christians of Rome).

6. **Lotus Plant**—Flower of Lower Kemit (Plant in the Book of the Dead judgement scene.

7. **Ra** (.) in His Pole Star (the Double Pyramid adopted by the Hebrews, or Jews, as the Star of David).

8. **The Cross**—symbol of death (adopted by European Christians and of North Africa for Jesus of Nazareth.)

9. **Star of Amenta** (adopted by the Muslims as the Fertile Crescent of Al'lah).

10. **Pointer of Re With Imposed Pole Star**— (adopted by the Freemasons and other "secret societies" as the Plumbbob that symbolizes mankind's "UPRIGHT POSITION").

11. **Double-Right Angle Pyramid or Square** (adopted by the above-mentioned organizations as the symbol of the "Squaring of Man's Deeds".

A. **Double-Right Angle Pyramid House of Fire,** House of the Nether World, House of Amenta, House of Heaven (adopted by every civilization of the so-called "Western World" as a symbol of strength and the "Reaching Out Into the Heavens" to the God Jehovah—an offspring of the God Ra or Re, etc.)

B. **Seven-Steps Sepulcher-Chest** (adopted by the Haribus, so-called "Jews," as the "Ark of the Covenant that Jehovah gave to Moses").

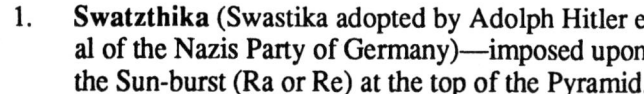
C. **Earth's Dead-Level** (adopted by Freemasonry and other secret societies as the "Dead-Level from whence man cometh into life".

Note: Numbers 2 throught 11 and letter B, are all inside the Pyramid; number 10 is inside number 11.

PAFO wishes to thank Dr. Yosef ben-Jochannan for his permission to use his cover design of The religious Symbols of Africa

KWANZAA

The Seven Principles (Nguzo Saba)
1. Umoja (Unity)
2. Kujichagulia (Self Determination)
3. Ujima (Collective Work)
4. Ujamaa (Cooperative Economics)
5. Nia (Purpose)
6. Kuumba (Creativity)
7. Imani (Faith)

Kwanzaa Symbols
The natural elegance of Kwanzaa symbolism is demonstrated through:

1. The Mkeka (straw mat) - symbolic of our Afrikan tradition and history.
2. The Kinara (seven lamp candle holder) - symbolizes the parent stalk, the first cause of our origin.
3. The Mshumaa (seven candles) - symbolizes the seven principles of our Black Value System.
4. The Muhindi (ears of corn) - represents the precious gift of our children, the most valued treasure of our race.
5. The Zawadi (gifts) - are symbolic of the rewards of right actions.
6. The Mazao (crops) - represents the fruits of our labors.
7. The Kikombe (unity cup) - symbolizes our oneness of purpose.

(For more information, consult *Twas the Night Before Kwanzaa* by Dr. Edward Robinson and Harriette Robinson)

SELF-ANALYSIS REGARDING CHILDREN

A Are You?	Yes	No	B Do You?	Yes	No	Rate Yourself A–C A	B
Supervising all activities			Know your job as a parent				
Being a good role model			Gossip with your children				
Honest in truth and deed			Allow pornography books in your home				
A loving parent			Give in to your child's demands				
Exhibiting tough love when necessary			Give children household chores				
Shirking your duties			Give them enough of your time				
Delegating your responsibilities to others			Have any spiritual family meditations				
Favoring one child over another			Have family conferences				
Condoning sex, drugs or alcohol in the home			Take your child to "Sunday School"				
Attending any religious edifice			Send your child to "Sunday School"				
Attending parent teacher meeting			Tell them you love them				
Questioning child's coming home late			Command respect from your children				
Checking out friends			Encourage family reunions — extended families				
Seeking rapport with parents of children's friends			Check their homework				
Teaching social graces			Inquire if teacher does not give them homework				
Teaching race pride			Eat one family meal daily together				
Suspicious of your child's extra money			Investigate the excessive extra money of your child				
A pal to your child or a parent			Think a child really needs you as a parent or pal				

The African norm for this "Code of Conduct" was and always will be to have the right words coming out of our mouths, shying away from the use of foul language and aspiring to show higher levels of regard and respect for one another, extending social graces and respect.

Index

Aait, 74
Abdul Ahu-Suleiman, 2
Abolitionists, 351ff
Abraham (Black leader of Seminoles), 349
Abu Bakar, 90
Abmose-Papyrus (1st mathematical treatise), 398
Abubakari II, 90,93
Aegyptus, 77
Africa 22; birthplace of human race, 325
African colonies, 1
African Communities League, 289
African contributions, 80
African democracy, 82
African Genesis, 38
African Past, The, Basil Davidson, 107
Africanus, Leo, 107, 113, 381
AIDS (Aquired Immune Deficiency Syndrome)
    smallpox vaccine infectected Africans, 281; aim
    to destroy Blacks, 284; man-made 282; Welsing
    report,283
Akhenaton (Pharaoh), 253,267,268,383
Akil, 103
Alexander, Archie, 371
Ali Kolon, xix,100,101
Ali, Noble Drew, 4
Al-Mansur, Sultan Ahmad, 125
Alkebulan, 15,22,72,121,370
Allen, Richard, 345
Almoravids, 91
A.M.E. Church, 344
Amen (temple), 80
Amnesia, (amnesiac), 24
America (original name "Eria", 350
American Colonization Society, 350ff.
American History Association, 86
Ammar, 103
Anderson, Marian, 1
Angelou, Maya, xxxi
Angola, 136, 214
Anthropological genesis, 67
Antietam, Battle of, 181
Ape/African comparisons, 36,208
Arab(s), 16,85,117,120,141,211,253,267
    268,383
Arabic numbers, 122
Ardrey, Robert, 38
Armstrong, Louis, 1

Index

"As a Man Thinketh", 5,131
Assibai, Dia, 99
Attucks, Crispus, 342
Australopithecus, 38,66,67,85
Azan kingdom, 211,214
Azikiwe, Nnandi, 320

Babo, Ahmed, 123,126,127
Balm, The healing, 265-268
Ballard, Allen B, 202
Bambara, 173
Banneker, Benjamin, 356
Barbaric Europe, 49
Barnett, Ida B. Wells, 219,221
Bartholdi, Frederic Auguste, 195-196
Battuta, Ibn, 112
Battle of Petersburg, 187
Battle, Redman, xi,2,383
Bekri, El, 90
Bennet, Lerone, 110
Ber, Sunni Ali, xxvi,103,106,113,115
Berber nomads, 99,102
Berlin Conference, 210,212
Bibliography, 272ff,275
Bibliography by session, 276-279
Biddle, Nicholas, 180,342
Birth of a Nation, 259
Blackamoor, 85,122
Black Christ, 16,77,232
Black Family Pledge, xxxi
Black Farmers' Alliance, 221
Black House, 4
Black Jews, 383
Black-on-Black crime, xxxiii,xxxv
Black Power, 17
Black Reconstruction, 199-203
Black Renaissance II, 353
Black Rhapsody, xii, 234
Blair, Henry, 353
Blood, one drop contaminates, 254; societal translation, 254
Blood types, Rh factor, 68,69
Bones, 68
Books Recommendations By PAFO, 296
Boykin, Otis, 371
Bozo, 173
Black People's Unity Movement (BPUM), 2

Index

Brainwash, xxi, 5,6,7,24,131,214,247, 255-260, 270, 271
Breaking-in African captives, 149
British, 343; offered Blacks freedom, 343
Brown, Tony, 4
Brown University (built from Black torture factory money), 148
Bruce, Blanche K. (U.S.Senator), 200,203
Budge, E.A. Wallace, 74,76,78
Buffalo Soldiers, 356ff (incorrect to laud)
Bull, John, 211
Bulletin, The Phila. Evening and Sunday, 358
Bunker Hill, 342
Butler, General Benjamin, 181,191

Calendar, first, 72
Calley, Lieutenant, 50
Cambrian Period, 37
Cameron, Secretary of War (Civil), 179
Cane Hay Massacre, 216ff
"can't-do analysis leads to suicidal paralysis", 262
Carmichael, Stokely, 17
Carruthers, Dr. George, physicist (camera sends pictures back to earth), 221
Carter, President Jimmy, 7
Cartesian Theory, xix, 81
Carver, George Washington, 1,355
Carthage, 80
Caucasians, xxxv
Cenozoic Period, 37
Cetshway, 136
Chad, 210
Chaldeans, 395
Champollion, 112
Chellean Axe Science, 38
Chem (ancient name of Africa--"black") chemistry--study of black, 121
Cherry, Prophet F.S., 383
Cheops, 72
Chiefless societies, 82
Cheyney University, xiv,202
Christ (Black), 16
Chronology of Push for Rights, 298ff
Church,Ecumenical Council, 16
Chronobiology, 392
Churchville, John, 2

Index

Christendom, 120
Cicero, Marcus Tullius, 34,35
City-wide Black Community Council, 2
Civilization—def. 31; 73ff, 79, 122, 129ff, 132-134, 143, 267, 319, 384, 397, 398.
Civil Rights Congress, 4
Civil War, 177ff; Black fighters 182; why Blacks won--N.Y. Herald Newspaper quote, 183-184; America erased Blacks winning (see Meyer) 192; praise of Blacks by Lincoln and generals, 191
Cole, Nat King, 1
Coleman, Ernest, 372
Coleman, Ronald, 2
Color Purple, 245
Commentary Magazine, 46
Comparison Years, 1800's vs. 1900's, 237ff
Constitution, U.S.-dup. of Mohawk/Iroquois Constitution, 350
Croom, Dr. J.S., 4,87,383
Crow Nation, 349
Crosthwait, David, 373
Crystal ball, The magical, 236ff
Cultural genesis, 16,72
Cultural glue, xxxiii, 27,28,29
Cudgo, 153
Cushite, 81

Darden, Dr. Christine, engineer, 382
Darien, 94
Davis, Park Ranger, John, 187
Davidson, Basil, 107,109,134
Davis, Jefferson, "execute Negro soldiers captured", 183
Dawn man, 42
Dawn man syndrome, 50
Delphi, 78
DePriest, Oscar, 234
Descartes, Rene, 81
Diop, Dr. Cheikh Anton, 132,133
D N A research, 38
Dodona, 78
Dogon, 173
Douglas, Frederick, 23,221
Douglas, Sarah Mapp, 202
Drama, Necessary for changing attitudes, 245
Drew, Dr. Charles, 23,355,381
Dryopithecus, 38
Dubois, Dr. W.E.B., 179,320
Dynasties--series, 75
Dynasty, first, 72

Egypt, 16,72,74,81,96
El Bekri, 90
Elder, Clarence L, 374
Elkins, Stanley, 170
Emancipation Proclamation, did not free anyone but to legalize Blacks bearing arms, 176; forced by Northern losses, 181; misnomer, 222
Epilogue, 269ff
Es'Sadi, Abderrahman, 128,251
Euclid, 381
Europe, history barbaric, 49
Europe, named after Black Europa, 80
European Westward, 49
Evans, Samuel, 4
Evolution, 67
Farrakhan, Minister Louis, 4
Fattah, Fallaka, 221
Fayum, Lake, 72
F.B.I., 14,17
Fencing, 110
Fifteenth Amendment, 222
Finot, 69,146
First life insurance co. (Free African Society), 345
Fitzgerald, Ella, 1
Fleetwood, Christian A., 184ff
Flutes, 110
Focus, The Total (of PAFO), 260
Fort Harrison, 190
Fort Pillow Massacre, 185
Fort Sumter, 177
Fort Wagner, 183
Forty acres and a mule, 199
Fourteenth Amendment, 222
Franklin, Dr. John Hope, 108,109
Freedom Libray, 2
Freedom, types of, xxxvi
French Anti-Slavery Society, 195
Frisby, Dr. Herbert, 63,386,387

Gannett, Deborah Sampson, 343
Gao, 94,97,99,111
Garvey, Marcus, ix,xxii,2,4,17,23,221, 231ff; Black God, 233; mass movement, 383; deportation, 233;289ff
Garvey's Voice, 291
Geronimo, 357,358
Gerontology, 61

Index

Ghana, 89,91,120
Gilead, is there a balm in?, 265
Glaciers, xvii,53
Gluteous maximus, 66
Goetz (N.Y. gunman), 239
Gonorrhea, 69,146
Gourdine, Meridity, 374
Gray, Samuel, 342
Great Pyramid, 72,79
<u>Greek and Roman Mythology</u> by Fox, 20
Guitars, 110
Guns, 125,126

Haeckel, Dr. Ernest H., 53
Hall, Katherine, 2
Hannibal, 80
Hansberry, William, 37,320
Harlem Renaissance, xxviii
Harris, Clarence, 2
Harris, James, 374
Haskins, Dr. Jim, 195
Hathor, 75
Hatshepsut, 81
Henry, Prince, 115
Henson, Matthew, 63,385
Hermes, 76
Herodotus, 58,127,396
Hinton, Dr. William, 355
Hippocrates, 80
Hitler, Adolph, 1
Hollywood, (anti-African brainwash), 258ff
Holmes, Mrs. J.E., 221
Holocaust, 170
Homer, 127
Homo Habilis, 38
Homo Sapiens, 37,50
Horus, 16,76
Houston, Drucella, 4
Howard University, 323ff
Humphrey, Mattie, 4
Hunter, General David, report of Black Civil War soldiers' excellence, 191
Hurst, Pattie, 7
Hutchins, Walter and Yvonne, 4
Huxley, Thomas, 34

Ice Age, 85

Icing, African American genius, 342ff
I.C.Y.(Institute for Colored Youths), 202
Imhotep, 80,112,381,391
Indian Removal Act, 348
Industrial Revolution, 142,143
Ink Spots, 1
In Search of Eve, Rebecca Cann, 38,146
Institutional Racism in America, Knowles and Prewitt, 45
Invasion of Songhai, 124,127,128
Inventions, xxiii,222,354,359,369; Blacks' inventions enhance quality of life, 369
Iron ore smelting (early Africa), 108
Isis, 16,75,76
Islam, xxvii,90,99,120,211,268

Jackson, Jesse, 4,239,249
Jackson, Dr. John, 4,72,122,129
Janes Memorial U.M. Church, xiv
Jeffreys, Dr. M.W., 67
Jenne, (The Beautiful City), xix, 107,110,111,113
Jericho, 72
Jet Magazine, 67
Judaism, 390
Julian, Dr. Percy, 356
Just, Dr. Ernest, 355
Jochannan, Dr. Ben, 4,124,398
Johnson, James Weldon
Johnson, Katherine, 375
Jones, Absalom, 345
Jones, Frederick M., 375
Jos Plateau, 72
Journal of the Royal Anthropological Institute, 32

Kankan Musa, 94
Kano, 110
Karnak, 80
Kati, Mohammed, 128
Kemit, 77
Kennedy, President John, 35
Kenyapithecus, 38
Kerner Commission, xxxv,45
Knowles and Prewitt, Institutional Racism in America, 45,47,52,244
Kolon, Ali, xix,100
Koumbi, 90
Ku Klux Klan, xxvii, 185,205,221; current spread of, 260; war training against Blacks, 260

Index

Kukya, 99
Kush, 81
Kwanzaa, xiv,xxv

Laboulaye, Dr. Edourd de, 195
Landerstiner, Karl, 69
Latimer, Lewis, 354
Law of July 17th, 1862, 182
Leakey, Dr. Louis, 37
Lewis brothers blood, 69
Lester, "Jim", 4
Liberia, 170f
Life Magazine, 53
Lincoln, Abraham, 177; support of African captivity, 178; admitted Black soldiers won war, 191
Lineage, 83,84
Lips, xviii,66
Livingston, Dr., 69,146
Lofton, William H., 320
Long, Wilson, 4
Louis, "Joe", 1
L'Ouverture, Toussaint, 153,155
Lumumba, Patrice, 120
Lunda Empire, 83,91,271
Lynchings, 183,216

Ma'at, xxvii,75,78,86,95,130,171,172,210,232,236,389,392
Madonna, Black, 16
Maghan, 98
Magical crystal ball, 236
"Making it", "presumptively adequate", 246
Malcolm X, 4,236
Mali Empire, 90,91,92,93,97.98,120
Mallophaga, 42
Mancandal, 155
Mandingo, 98
Manifest Destiny, 49
Man's Destiny, 393
Mansa Musa, xix,93,94,96,98,99,101
Manifestations of PROBLEM, xxxv
Map,11th C. W. Africa, 88
Map,14th C. W. Africa, 97
Map,16th C. W. Africa, 105
Marcus Garvey Shule, 3
Maroons, xxvii,154
Marshall, Thurgood, 221
Massey, Gerald, 74,76

Index

Masons, Prince Hall African Masonic Lodge, 345
Matamba, 140
Matrilineal System, 76,132
Matzeliger, Jan, 23,354 (see inventions)
McCabe, Edwin P., 221
McCoy, Caldwell (inventor), 376
McCoy, Elijah, (inventor), 354
McKay, Claude, 231
McPherson, Dr. James, 179ff,183,194
Medulla oblongata, 42
Meeks, William, 2
Melanin, 59,62,63,64,68,121
Memory Hole,- America's, 192,197
Menes, 71,79
Meroe, 72
Mesozoic Period, 37
Meyer, Howard, how America erased Blacks winning Civil War, 192
Middle Passage, 143,145ff
Mikell, William, 2
Minianka, 173
Moors, xxvii,85,121,122
Moore, Cecil B., 2,4
Morgan, Garrett A., 376
Morocco, Sultan of, 121
Myrdal, Gunnar, 199
Moslem, 16,124
Mother Bethel, 345
Muhammed, The Honorable Elijah, 383
<u>Myth of the African Past, The</u> by Melville Herskovits, 28

NAACP, 219,221
Names--Black African, 86
Napoleon, 111
Napier, James (Reconstruction leader), 200
National Afro-American Council, 221
National Association of Colored Women, 221
National Institutes of Mental Health, 50
Necromantia, 210
Nefertari, 81
Negro Soldier Law (Confederates Black enlistment attempt --end of war), 191
Nekhbit, 84
New Market Heights, 186
Nursing, 111
Numbers, Arabic, 122,124
Nzinga, 136ff, 214

Index

Ogie, 151
Ol'Duvai Gorge, 37,38
Olympics, (1968), 17
Oneness, 392
Osceola, 348
Owens, Jesse, 1
PAFO, vii,x,xi,xxix,xxxv,1-5,14,19,22,24,25,33,34,59,
    69,72,86,92,95,120,124,125,129,215,166,383
PAFO's President, Calvin Robinson's message, 293ff
Paleozoic Period, 37
Palmer, Walter, 2
Papyrus, Ebers, 112
Parks, Rosa, 235
Pasha, General Judar, 124
Peculiar Institution, The, K. Stampp, 18, 28,33,34,169,257
Perry, Admiral Robert, 63,385
Phi Delta Kkappa, xiv
P G R Psychogalvanic Reflex, 391
Philadelphia, PA, 17,64
Philip I, 139
Pinchback, Gov. P.B.S., 199-200
Piongeon, Augustus, 75
Pitts, Pauline, 2,360
Plantation mentality development, 207-210
Platoon,(motion picture), 245
Pleasant, Mammy, 221
Pleistocenic Period, 37
Plessy (Plessy vs. Ferguson), 219
Poland, 16
Political power of Old South, 175
Poor Salem, 342
Pope, John Paul, 16
Portugal, 136ff
Poussaint, Dr. Alvin, 19
Potassium Argon process, 37
Poyas, Peter, 163
Pre-frontal cortex theory, xxviii,227
Presumption of adequacy, xxviii,227
Prewitt, 45,47,52
Prisoners-of-war, 18
Prince Hall, 346
PROBLEM, THE, xxxii,xxxv,xxxvi,3,244,255,259
Pro-Consul, 38
Progress, no progress made, 222; referential point, 224;
    alleviation of white guilt, 223; proper referential
    point, 224-226; absolute vs. relative, 228
Prophetic Crystal Ball, 239ff

Prosser, Gabriel, xxvii,155ff
Prosser, Solomon, 157
Provident Home Insurance Co., xxii,3,345
Psyche, 5
Psychic trauma, xxxiii
Psychological warfare, xxviii
P U S H, 248
Ptolemy Epiphanes, 112
Pygmies, 79
Pyramid (The Great), 393; astronomical observatory, 395; contains mathematical, geometrical and astronomical data, 396; trig and calculus bases, 398

Quarles, Dr. Benjamin, 110
Queen Mother of Jenne, (Dara), 113,115

Racism, profit of, 224ff
Radio carbon process, 37
Raglan, Lord, 32
Ramapithecus, 38
Rawls, Spencer, 124
Recapitulation science, xxvi, 53
Reconstruction,xxvii, 203,205,210
Reed, Cordell, 377
Remond, Charles L., 7
Research Task Force, 48
Revolts on plantations,xxvii, 153
Revolutionary War, 342; 5000 Blacks fought, Black spies, 343; reasons for, 344; Black heroes forced back into captivity, 347
Rhodes, James, 179
Rh factor, 68,69
Richard, Captain James, "history's bravest act", 190
Richardson, David P., Jr. xv,2,552,53,248
Richardson, David P., Sr., xv
Richardson, Elaine, A., xv,2,3,62,113
Rift Valley, 72
Rillieux, Norbert, 377
Roberts, Louis, 378
Robeson, Paul, 12
Robinson, Calvin, R., x,2,3,62,383
Robinson, Dr. Edward W., xii,23,25,62,188, 234,345
Robinson, E.J., 23
Robinson, Harriette C., xiv,3,360
Robinson, Sugar Ray, 1
Rogers, J.A., 32,146
Romans, 85,86

Index

<u>Roots</u>, 174
Rosetta Stone, 111

Sable, Jean Baptiste Pointe du, founder of Chicago, leader of
      Michigan Indians, 349
Sais, 77
Sadi (Abderrahman es' (se Es)
Sakura, xxvi,93
Salem, Peter, 342
Sankore University, 103,113
Sarrounia, Queen, xxviii,211ff
Schomburg, Arthur, 33
SCLC, 17,248
Seminoles, 7,347
Senegal River, 94
Sertima, Ivan Van, 4,94,173
Settling the West, 49
Seward, Secretary of State, 181
Seven Veils of Illusion, 47,243
Shaka Zulu, 136
Shakespeare plays
Simpson, C. T., 2
Single Bone Theory, 48
Sirius, 173ff
Skin color, 55,58
Sloan, Sir Hands, 149
Smith, Dr. James, 187
Sociological Equation, 8
Social Darwinism, 47f,243
Sokoto Nation, 211
SOLUTION, THE xxxvi,221,141f(reprogramming America);
      248,259ff,271
Sommers, <u>Richmond Redeemed</u>, 188
Songhai Empire, 19,97,98,99,106,120,121,135
Songhai Invasion, 124,127,128
<u>Songhai Princess</u>, video by Robinson, 46
Soninkes, 89
Sosso, 89,91
SCLC, 14
<u>Southern Planter</u>, 44
South Africa, 67
Sphinx, 79
Spock, 13,20
Stampp, Kenneth, 18,28,33,34,169,
Spikes, R.B. automatic gear shift for cars, 369
Starlin, Mark, 343
Standard, J.J., (oil stove,refrigerator)

Stateless society, 82
Statue of Liberty, 193,196
Steam boat, invention, 353
Stevens, Thaddeus, 199
Still, William Grant, 164
Stockholm Syndrome, 7
Stokes, Rufus, 378
Stone Age, 81
Stowe, Harriet Beecher, 19,343
Strawberry Mansion High School, 2
Sullivan, Rev. Leon, 248
Sulyman Nar, xix,100,101
Sumunguru, 91
Sundiata, 91,115
Sunni Ail Ber, xxvi,103,106,113,115
Sunni dynasty, 101
Sunni Ali Ber II, 117
Supreme Life Insurance Co., 3
Synonyms, 208
Syphilis, 69,146
Syracuse Sentinel, (Klanwatcher), 260
Swans, Bennie, 245

Tagedda, 97
Taghaza, 121
Taney, Judge Roger B., 244,258
Taylor, Lawnie, 379
Tenka Menin, 90
Thedosius I, 129
They Came Before Columbus, Sertima, 94
Timbuktu, 97-99,103,106,110,111,113
Tilden-Hayes Compromise, 204
Time & Life Publishers Barbaric Europe, 49
Tolbert, Tom, 216
Tom and Pharaoh, betrayers of Prosser, 159
Torday, Emil, 32
Torture of captives, 149ff; by lions, 127
Torture instruments, 148
Toure, Askia Muhammad, 120,121
Treherne, Virginia, 2
Triangular Trade, 148
Trice, Virgil G., Jr., 379
Trigonometry, (in Black Africa before Greeks), 398
Truth, Sojourner, 221
Tuareg, 103,106,120
Tubman, Harriet, 164ff,191
Tulsa riot, 231

Index

Turner, Nat, 17,163
Twenty-Fifth Corps, Black regiment chased and made Lee surrender, 191
Two-Cradle Theory, 132
Typhonians, 78
Twa, 79

Ultimate solution (of Germans), 49
Underground Railroad, 202
Universal Negro Improvement, Association, 2,203,253,289ff
Urban League, 221
Urshu, (a star), 78
Van Peebles, Melvin, reinforcing PROBLEM by Sweetback, 235
Vassar, Cynthia, 2
Vesey, Denmar, 17,162ff
"Vibes", (from melanin), 65
Vietnam War, 51
Vitamin "I", 26
Walata, 97, 111
Wali, 93
Walker, A'lelia, 234
Walker, Alice, 245
War of 1812, 344ff; reasons for,346; defense of Phila. by Blacks, 346; heroes forced back into captivity, 347; Gen.Jackson praise of Black soldiers, 347
Waring, E.J., 221
Washington, Booker T., 219
Washington, George, 342,343
Washington, Father Paul, 2
Watson, Diadra, 2
Watson, Goldie, 4
W D A S, 3
Weatherwax, John, 124
Welsing, Frances Cress, 283
Western Africa, 23,24
White-is-right destruction, 266
White, Charles, 216
White Christ, destruction by, 16,77,232
White Oppression, xxviii
White wolves, 259,260
Wiener, Alexander, 69
Wilkins, J. Ernest, Jr., 380
Williams, Chancellor, 4,129,133
Williams, Daniel Hale, 355
Williams, Hardy, 3
Williams, O.S. (Ozzie), 380

Willie Horton Syndrome, 46
Wilson, Flip, reinforcing PROBLEM, 236,237
Women, Black, 73
Woods, Granville, T., 23,355
Woodson, Carter G., 4
Writing goddess (Neith), 75
WW I atrocities against Blacks, 229
WW II, 63,64

X, Malcolm, 4 (see Malcolm X)

Zoser, Pharaoh, 112, also spelled <u>Djoser</u>

Additions to Index

A-free-ka occupier, 121
Arlene Herbert, 206
Conyers, John, 206
Electro Magnetic Power, 398
Judaism, 116
Kahena QUEEN, 116
Kuscila (General), 116
Mourning, 268
Numida, 116
Race-first-only doctrine, 116
Reparations Study, 206
Richardson, David, 206
Tetrahedral mathematics, 398